INTEGRATED PEST MANAGEMENT FOR
STONE FRUITS

INTEGRATED PEST MANAGEMENT FOR
STONE FRUITS

UNIVERSITY OF CALIFORNIA
STATEWIDE INTEGRATED PEST MANAGEMENT PROJECT
DIVISION OF AGRICULTURE AND NATURAL RESOURCES
PUBLICATION 3389

1999

PRECAUTIONS FOR USING PESTICIDES

Pesticides are poisonous and must be used with caution. READ THE LABEL CAREFULLY BEFORE OPENING A PESTICIDE CONTAINER. Follow all label precautions and directions, including requirements for protective equipment. Use a pesticide only on crops specified on the label. Apply pesticides at the rates specified on the label or at lower rates if suggested in this publication. In California, all agricultural uses of pesticides must be reported. Contact your county agricultural commissioner for details. Laws, regulations, and information concerning pesticides change frequently, so be sure the publication you are using is up to date.

Legal Responsibility. The user is legally responsible for any damage due to misuse of pesticides. Responsibility extends to effects caused by drift, runoff, or residues.

Transportation. Do not ship or carry pesticides together with foods or feeds in a way that allows contamination of the edible items. Never transport pesticides in a closed passenger vehicle or in a closed cab.

Storage. Keep pesticides in original containers until used. Store them in a locked cabinet, building, or fenced area where they are not accessible to children, unauthorized persons, pets, or livestock. DO NOT store pesticides with foods, feeds, fertilizers, or other materials that may become contaminated by the pesticides.

Container Disposal. Dispose of empty containers carefully. Never reuse them. Make sure empty containers are not accessible to children or animals. Never dispose of containers where they may contaminate water supplies or natural waterways. Consult your county agricultural commissioner for correct procedures for handling and disposal of large quantities of empty containers.

Protection of Nonpest Animals and Plants. Many pesticides are toxic to useful or desirable animals, including honey bees, natural enemies, fish, domestic animals, and birds. Crops and other plants may also be damaged by misapplied pesticides. Take precautions to protect nonpest species from direct exposure to pesticides and from contamination due to drift, runoff, or residues. Certain rodenticides may pose a special hazard to animals that eat poisoned rodents.

Posting Treated Fields. For some materials, reentry intervals are established to protect field workers. Keep workers out of the field for the required time after application and, when required by regulations, post the treated areas with signs indicating the safe reentry date.

Harvest Intervals. Some materials or rates cannot be used in certain crops within a specific time before harvest. Follow pesticide label instructions and allow the required time between application and harvest.

Permit Requirements. Many pesticides require a permit from the county agricultural commissioner before possession or use. When such materials are recommended in this publication, they are marked with an asterisk (*).

Processed Crops. Some processors will not accept a crop treated with certain chemicals. If your crop is going to a processor, be sure to check with the processor before applying a pesticide.

Crop Injury. Certain chemicals may cause injury to crops (phytotoxicity) under certain conditions. Always consult the label for limitations. Before applying any pesticide, take into account the stage of plant development, the soil type and condition, the temperature, moisture, and wind direction. Injury may also result from the use of incompatible materials.

Personal Safety. Follow label directions carefully. Avoid splashing, spilling, leaks, spray drift, and contamination of clothing. NEVER eat, smoke, drink, or chew while using pesticides. Provide for emergency medical care IN ADVANCE as required by regulation.

ORDERING

For information about ordering this publication, contact

University of California
Division of Agriculture and Natural Resources
Communication Services—Publications
6701 San Pablo Avenue, 2nd Floor
Oakland, California 94608-1239

Telephone 1-800-994-8849
(510) 642-2431
FAX (510) 643-5470
e-mail: danrcs@ucdavis.edu

http://danrcs.ucdavis.edu

Publication 3389

Other books in this series include:
Integrated Pest Management for Walnuts, Publication 3270
Integrated Pest Management for Tomatoes, Publication 3274
Integrated Pest Management for Rice, Publication 3280
Integrated Pest Management for Citrus, Publication 3303
Integrated Pest Management for Cotton, Publication 3305
Integrated Pest Management for Cole Crops and Lettuce, Publication 3307
Integrated Pest Management for Almonds, Publication 3308
Integrated Pest Management for Alfalfa Hay, Publication 3312
Integrated Pest Management for Potatoes, Publication 3316
Pests of the Garden and Small Farm, Publication 3332
Integrated Pest Management for Small Grains, Publication 3333
Integrated Pest Management for Apples and Pears, Publication 3340
Integrated Pest Management for Strawberries, Publication 3351
Pests of Landscape Trees and Shrubs, Publication 3359
Natural Enemies Handbook, Publication 3386

ISBN 1-879906-36-8

Library of Congress Catalog Card No. 97-78043

©1999 by the Regents of the University of California
Division of Agriculture and Natural Resources

Printed in Canada.

6m-pr-4/99-WJC/NS

Contributors and Acknowledgments

Written by Larry L. Strand
Photographs by Jack Kelly Clark
Mary Louise Flint, Technical Editor

Prepared by IPM Education and Publications, an office of the University of California Statewide IPM Project at Davis.

Acknowledgments

Technical Coordinators for Pomology
> R. Scott Johnson, Department of Pomology, University of California, Davis; located at Kearney Agricultural Research Center, Parlier
> Stephen M. Southwick, Department of Pomology, University of California, Davis

Technical Coordinators for Insects and Mites
> Walter J. Bentley, UC Statewide IPM Project, Kearney Agricultural Research Center, Parlier
> Richard E. Rice, Department of Entomology, University of California, Davis; located at Kearney Agricultural Research Center, Parlier
> Frank G. Zalom, UC Statewide IPM Project, University of California, Davis

Technical Coordinators for Diseases
> James E. Adaskaveg, Department of Plant Pathology, University of California, Riverside
> Beth L. Teviotdale, Department of Plant Pathology, University of California, Davis; located at Kearney Agricultural Research Center, Parlier
> Jerry K. Uyemoto, USDA-ARS, Department of Plant Pathology, University of California, Davis

Technical Coordinator for Nematodes
> Michael V. McKenry, Department of Nematology, University of California, Riverside; located at Kearney Agricultural Research Center, Parlier

Technical Coordinator for Vegetation Management
> Clyde L. Elmore, Department of Vegetable Crops, Weed Science Program, University of California, Davis

Technical Coordinator for Vertebrates
> Rex E. Marsh, Department of Wildlife, Fish, and Conservation Biology, University of California, Davis

Contributors

Entomology: William W. Barnett, Walter J. Bentley, Kent M. Daane, Nicholas J. Mills, Eric C. Mussen, Carolyn Pickel, Alexander H. Purcell, Richard E. Rice, Robert A. VanSteenwyk, Frank G. Zalom

Pomology, Soil and Water Relations: Richard P. Buchner, William W. Coates, Kevin R. Day, Theodore M. DeJong, Thomas M. Gradziel, Joseph A. Grant, F. Scott Johnson, William H. Olson, Richard L. Snyder, Stephen M. Southwick

Nematology: Edward P. Casswell-Chen, Michael V. McKenry

Plant Pathology: James E. Adaskaveg, Greg T. Browne, W. Harley English, W. Douglas Gubler, Bruce C. Kirkpatrick, Bill T. Manji, Themis J. Michailides, Gaylord I. Mink, John M. Mircetich, Joseph M. Ogawa, George N. Oldfield, James J. Stapleton, Beth L. Teviotdale, Jerry K. Uyemoto

Vertebrate Biology: W. Paul Gorenzel, Richard A. Marovich, Rex E. Marsh, Desley Whisson

Weed Science: Clyde L. Elmore, Bill B. Fischer, Timothy S. Prather

Special Thanks

The following have generously provided information, offered suggestions, reviewed draft manuscripts, or helped obtain photographs:
H. L. Andris, P. Baca, S. Bautista, R. H. Beede, J. Caprile, R. L. Coviello, P. DaSilva, S. H. Dreistadt, L. E. Ehler, T. D. Eichlin, D. A. Golino, E. Grafton-Cardwell, R. R. Hansen, J. K. Hasey, L. C. Hendricks, B. A. Holtz, T. Jacobs, R. A. Jones, C. E. Joshel, K. Kelley, W. H. Krueger, R. Llamos, R. Mansfield, J. P. McCaa, M. S. Moratorio, C. Norton, M. V. Norton, P. J. O'Connor-Marer, B. L. Ohlendorf, I. M. Petersen, W. O. Reil, D. M. Rizzo, A. Rowhani, M. W. Stimmann, J. F. Strand, G. Walker, K. Walker, S. C. Welter, J. T. Yeager

Production

Design and Production Coordination:
Seventeenth Street Studios
Drawings; Jaqueline Lamer Lockwood
Editing: Jim Coats

Contents

Integrated Pest Management for Stone Fruits

This manual is designed to help growers and pest control professionals apply the principles of integrated pest management (IPM) to stone fruit crops in California. IPM is an ecosystem-based management strategy that achieves economical control of pest injury by coordinating pest management activities with recommended crop production practices, while minimizing hazards to crops, human health, and the natural environment. An IPM program emphasizes the anticipation and avoidance of problems whenever possible, uses established monitoring techniques and treatment guidelines as bases for pest management decisions, and employs management methods that are minimally disruptive to the environment. The term pest, as used in this manual, refers to insects, mites, pathogens, weeds, nematodes, and vertebrates that cause damage in stone fruits.

The first chapter is a brief overview of stone fruit production in California. The second chapter discusses the growth and development of stone fruits, and presents information that will help you understand how cultural practices, environmental conditions, and pests affect tree growth and fruit production. The third chapter covers orchard management methods that are important to successful crop production and pest control. More detailed information on orchard management can be found in the publications *California Sweet Cherry Production Workshop Proceedings*, *Prune Orchard Management* (UC DANR Publication 3269), and *Peaches, Plums, and Nectarines: Growing and Handling for Fresh Market* (UC DANR Publication 3331), which are listed in the references. The remaining chapters feature detailed descriptions and illustrations that will help you identify pest problems, as well as management guidelines that will help you choose the best control strategies for your situation. The References list that follows the final chapter will guide you to more information on specific subjects. The Glossary at the end of the book defines technical terms that may be unfamiliar to some readers.

Biological and cultural control methods are discussed throughout this manual. The careful management of beneficial insect and mite populations, proper orchard management, and avoidance of conditions that promote pest problems are important components of a successful IPM program. Biological and cultural management methods reduce the need for pesticide applications, but are unlikely by themselves to provide commercially acceptable levels of control for all the pest problems encountered in stone fruits. In an

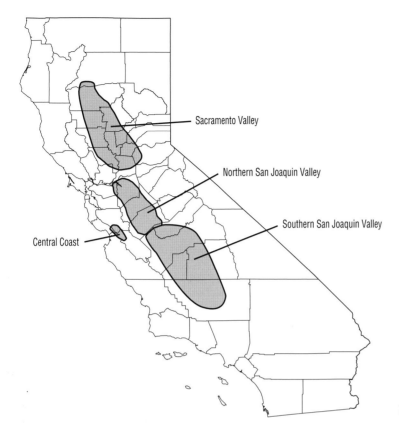

Figure 1. Major stone fruit growing areas of California.

IPM program, pesticides are used when monitoring, treatment guidelines, and local conditions indicate they are necessary. IPM emphasizes the early identification of pest problems and timely control of those problems with the most effective and least disruptive materials and methods available. Because registrations and label directions are subject to frequent change, this manual makes no specific pesticide recommendations. Publications on pesticide use and sources of pesticide recommendations are listed in the references. Check with your local UC Cooperative Extension Farm Advisor or local pest control professionals for the latest recommendations. You can obtain current information on registrations and label directions from your county Agricultural Commissioner.

Stone Fruit Production in California

Stone fruits are tree crops of the genus *Prunus*, including apricots, cherries, nectarines, peaches, plums, and prunes. They are characterized by a hard stone or pit that encloses the seed, and sweet, fleshy fruit that surrounds the stone. Technically, almonds also are stone fruits, but they are grown for the seed, which is eaten as a nut; the almond's counterpart to the edible portion of other stone fruits is the tough,

dry hull that surrounds the mature nut. For information on almond pest management and production, see *Integrated Pest Management for Almonds* (UC DANR Publication 3308) and *Almond Production Manual* (UC DANR Publication 3364).

California has four major growing areas for stone fruits (Figure 1). The most productive areas are the three that make up the Central Valley; total production is much lower from the inland coastal valleys (Table 1). California's prevailing climate of mild, wet winters, warm, relatively dry springs, and hot, dry summers favors the production of most stone fruits with few disease problems. Many stone fruits require pollinators (primarily honey bees) for good fruit set. Bee activity is critical for cherries and many plum varieties that require cross-pollination. Prolonged cold weather, rains, or windy conditions during bloom can substantially reduce fruit set.

Peach twig borer and San Jose scale are major insect pests of stone fruits in California, and several leafroller, green fruitworm, and stink bug species may cause substantial damage. European red mite and webspinning spider mites can be problems, often turning into serious pests when natural enemy populations are destroyed by broad-spectrum insecticides applied in an attempt to control other pests, or when trees are stressed by lack of water. All stone fruits can be attacked by

Table 1. California Stone Fruit Acreage (1997).[1]

	Sacramento Valley	Northern San Joaquin Valley	Southern San Joaquin Valley	Central Coast	Other	Total
apricots	625	13,834	3,612	2,395	19	20,485
nectarines	0	344	35,177	0	110	35,631
peaches						
clingstone	15,966	14,085	4,408	0	0	34,459
freestone	3.169	3,607	41,724	0	768	49,268
plums	611	255	40,505	0	28	41,399
prunes	71,030	2,134	10,333	891	0	84,388
sweet cherries	332	14,020	722	1,690	188	16,952
Total	91,733	48,279	136,481	4,976	1,113	282,582

1. From Agricultural Commissioners' data, 1997, compiled by the California Agricultural Statistics Service.

peachtree borer and wood-boring beetles, although these pests usually do not become serious in well-managed orchards.

Brown rot attacks all stone fruits, and is the most serious disease problem for apricots, nectarines, peaches, and prunes. Bacterial canker, Phytophthora root and crown rot, and crown gall are potentially serious diseases on all stone fruits. Armillaria root rot is a sporadic problem on all stone fruits, and is difficult to control if it invades orchard soils. Several viruses affect stone fruits: the most important are Prunus necrotic ringspot virus, prune dwarf virus, and tomato ringspot virus. By using certified planting stock, you can help reduce the impact of virus diseases on stone fruits.

Several nematode species attack the roots of stone fruit trees, so you should check the soils in prospective orchards for nematodes before you prepare for planting. Some rootstocks are resistant to root knot nematode.

Pocket gophers, ground squirrels, voles (meadow mice), and some bird species can become problems in all stone fruit orchards. Deer may cause damage in certain locations, especially in newly planted orchards.

Apricot, *Prunus armeniaca*. About 97% of the apricots produced in the United States are grown in California. In the northern San Joaquin Valley, where most of the acreage is concentrated, the fruit is grown primarily for canning. In the other areas, most apricots are grown for fresh market and drying. Apricots bloom earlier than most other stone fruits, and harvest takes place from May through early August.

In addition to the pests that attack all stone fruits, there are some that are more troublesome in apricots. Earwigs can cause serious problems in apricots if they invade trees to feed on ripening fruit. In coastal valleys, western tussock moth and orange tortrix occasionally become serious pests. Brown rot is the greatest disease threat in apricots. Shot hole, bacterial canker, jacket rot (green fruit rot), powdery mildew, and Eutypa dieback also are major diseases. Verticillium wilt is more likely to be a problem in apricots than in the other stone fruits. Apricots grown on plum rootstocks have fewer

problems with waterlogging and Phytophthora root rot when grown on wetter soils. Apricot rootstock is resistant to root knot nematodes.

Cherries, *Prunus avium*. Sweet cherries are grown throughout the Central Valley and in the central coast, with most of the production concentrated in the northern San Joaquin Valley. Sour cherries, *Prunus cerasus*, are not grown in significant quantities in California. Most sweet cherries are produced for fresh market, with harvest seasons running from late April to late June in the Central Valley and from early June to late June in central coast and foothill orchards.

The black cherry aphid is a potentially serious early-season pest, especially in coastal orchards. Leafhopper vectors of the X-disease pathogen constitute a major concern in Central Valley orchards. Brown rot usually is less of a problem on cherries than on apricots, nectarines, or peaches. Powdery mildew on cherry foliage can be a serious problem, but fruit infections are rare. X-disease (buckskin) is a major threat to cherry trees in the San Joaquin Valley.

Sweet cherries are grown on cherry rootstocks. These rootstocks are resistant or immune to some species of root knot nematode and differ in their susceptibility to several diseases; for example, Stockton Morello is resistant to Phytophthora root and crown rot, whereas Mahaleb is highly susceptible.

Nectarines and Peaches, *Prunus persica*. Peach varieties are classified as freestone or clingstone (cling), depending on how firmly the fruit flesh is attached to the stone at harvest. Freestone peaches are grown primarily for fresh market and cling peaches primarily for canning or other processing. Fresh market peaches are called freestone even if they are cling or semi-cling in character. Most of the peaches grown in the Sacramento Valley and northern San Joaquin Valley are clingstone types. The southern San Joaquin Valley is the main production area for freestone peaches. Nectarines are genetic variants of the peach that lack trichomes ("fuzz") on the fruit's skin. Virtually all nectarines are grown for fresh market, and almost all production is in the southern San Joaquin Valley. Growing and production characteristics for peaches and nectarines are essentially the same. Harvest begins with early-season varieties early in May and runs until late September. More than 90% of the U.S. nectarine and clingstone peach production and about 70% of the freestone peach production occur in California.

Oriental fruit moth and peach twig borer are the most serious insect pests of peaches and nectarines, although stink bugs and lygus bugs can become serious problems. Western flower thrips is a serious pest of nectarines, but usually is not a problem on peaches. Aphids may cause problems early in the season. Brown rot is the most serious disease of peaches and nectarines; nectarines are more susceptible than peaches. Other major disease problems include shot hole, jacket rot, leaf curl, and powdery mildew. Peaches and nectarines usually are grown on peach rootstock, which makes waterlogging and Phytophthora root rot more serious threats to trees grown on wetter soils. Some peach rootstocks are resistant to root knot nematode.

Plums and Prunes, *Prunus salicina* **and** *P. domestica.* Several species of plums are native to most temperate regions of the Northern Hemisphere, but most cultivated plums are varieties of the European plum, *Prunus domestica,* and the Japanese plum, *Prunus salicina.* Most of the fresh market plums grown in California are Japanese plums, with over 95% of the acreage located in the southern San Joaquin Valley. A little less than 90% of the U.S. crop comes from California. Prunes are European plum varieties that produce fruit with a very high sugar concentration when ripe, so it can be dried without fermenting around the pit. Almost all of the prunes grown in California are a selection of Prune d'Agen, a French variety of European plum known as the Improved French prune. Virtually all of the nation's dried prune production is in California.

Aphids tend to be more of a problem on plums and prunes than on other stone fruits. Codling moth attacks plums in some areas of the San Joaquin Valley and prunes in a few locations in the Sacramento Valley. This insect pest rarely attacks other stone fruits. Of all the stone fruits, Japanese plums are the least seriously affected by brown rot. Prunes, on the other hand, can be seriously harmed by brown rot if spring weather is favorable for disease development. Prunes are susceptible to rust, although usually the disease is not serious enough to affect yields. Russet scab is a disorder that develops on prunes following wet weather during bloom, but does not occur on other stone fruits. Potassium deficiency is a problem that requires regular management in prunes, especially in the northern San Joaquin Valley and the Sacramento Valley, or elsewhere when the crop load is heavy.

Growth and Development of Stone Fruits

The primary objective of any management program in stone fruits is to maximize production of top-quality fruit in the most cost-effective way while maintaining the long-term health and productivity of the orchard. Optimum fruit production depends on getting trees successfully established, maintaining their health, and using practices that favor a good balance between vegetative growth and fruit production. A knowledge of the tree's growth requirements and processes will help the grower understand how cultural practices, environmental factors, and pests affect growth and development. Developing an understanding of how cultural practices and pest management activities affect the total orchard system is an important part of implementing an IPM program. Without a basic knowledge of tree and fruit development, a grower may easily confuse symptoms of environmental stress or physiological disorders with pest damage.

Growth Requirements

Stone fruit trees use water and mineral nutrients from the soil and carbon dioxide and oxygen from the air to make the products needed for growth and fruit production. Water and air provide the elements carbon, hydrogen, and oxygen, which make up more than 90% of tree and fruit dry weight. The mineral nutrients needed in the largest quantities by fruit trees include nitrogen, phosphorus, calcium, potassium, sulfur, and magnesium. With the exception of nitrogen, most California soils contain adequate levels of all these nutrients to support growth and fruit production. Nitrogen must be added to orchard soils every season to support optimum growth and fruit yield. Prune trees use more potassium than other stone fruits, so prune orchards (especially those with fine-textured soils) need potassium supplements from time to time. Mineral nutrients that trees require only in trace quantities, often called micronutrients, include iron, manganese, boron, zinc, copper, molybdenum, and chlorine. Zinc supplements are often needed in stone fruit orchards. Natural levels of other micronutrients usually are adequate; deficiencies sometimes occur, however, and soil conditions can interfere with proper uptake of micronutrients such as iron. In some cases high levels of a micronutrient may cause phytotoxicity. The best way to determine the nutrient status of trees is to have leaf samples that are taken in June or July analyzed for nutrients. This is discussed in the section on fertilization in the next chapter.

Water and mineral nutrients are taken up from the soil by the roots and distributed throughout the tree via its vascular system (Figure 2). Most of the water taken up by the tree's roots evaporates through pores called *stomata* in leaves and green shoots. This evaporation process, called *transpiration,* occurs while stomata remain open to let the tree's foliage absorb carbon dioxide from the air. Water stress causes stomata to close, reducing absorption of carbon dioxide and slowing the rate of photosynthesis. In order to prevent reductions in growth and fruit production, the grower must make sure that irrigations replenish the transpired water.

Chlorophyll and other pigments in the leaves and green shoots capture energy from sunlight so that it can be used for *photosynthesis*—the process of synthesizing carbohydrates from carbon dioxide and water. The products of photosynthesis (*photosynthate*) are moved throughout the tree in the phloem (Figure 2) to supply the energy needs of the tree. *Respiration,* the process by which these energy-rich molecules are metabolized to provide the energy needed for cellular activities, always has first priority for the plant's photosynthetic output. What is left after respiration is available for vegetative and fruit growth. Heavy crops of fruit tend to reduce shoot growth, leaf size, and root growth. Pests can affect yield by reducing the available photosynthate. For example, foliage-feeding insects and foliar diseases reduce the amount of leaf area available for photosynthesis. Foliar diseases also increase respiration. Orchard management practices such as tree spacing, pruning, and training are used to optimize the amount of leaf area exposed to sunlight and thus to maximize photosynthetic output.

Development

The development of a stone fruit tree over its lifetime involves the growth of several plant organs: shoots, leaves, fruit, branches, and roots. The objective of a good orchard management program is to optimize the growth of these different organs such that good tree health and fruit production can be maintained for as long as possible. To achieve this goal, you need to maintain a balance among the different organs so that neither vegetative growth nor fruit growth dominates at the expense of the other. During the nonbearing years, a major part of the tree's root system is developed and the basic framework of the tree is established. Avoidance of pest damage during this time is critical to the establishment of a tree that will have a long, productive life.

Plants grow by a combination of cell division and cell expansion. In plants, cell division occurs in specific locations

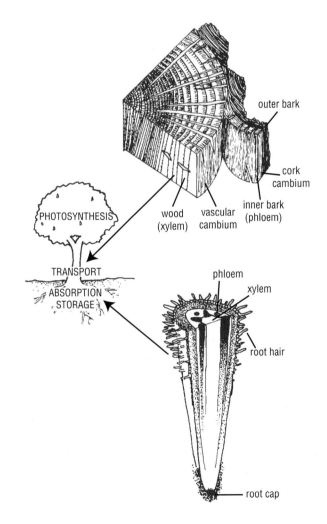

Figure 2. Basic tree structures and functions. Young roots absorb water and mineral nutrients, which are transported in the xylem to the canopy, where foliage produces sugars by the process of photosynthesis. The tree uses sugars immediately for respiration (which requires oxygen from the air) and growth, or transports them in the phloem mainly to the roots for storage.

called *meristems* or meristematic zones. During development, the cells produced in meristems differentiate into the different types of cells that make up each plant organ. Tree growth is classified as extension or primary growth when the cell divisions occur in apical meristems, which are located at shoot tips and in buds. As shoots expand and leaves develop, lateral buds form at the base of leaf petioles. Lateral buds are either vegetative buds, which develop into shoots, or flower buds, which develop into fruit. Tree growth is classified as expansion or secondary growth when the cell divisions occur in the *vascular cambium*, a cylinder of meristematic tissue that lies between the wood and the bark (Figure 2). Cell division on the inside of the vascular cambium gives rise to the *xylem*, which transports water and mineral nutrients from the roots to shoots and leaves. Cell division on the outside of the vascular cambium gives rise to the *phloem*, which carries photosynthate throughout the tree. On the outside of the phloem is a second cambium layer, the *cork cambium*, that gives rise to the outer bark.

Dormancy and Chilling Requirements

With cooler weather and shorter days in late fall and winter, stone fruit trees enter a period of rest called *dormancy*. During this time development of both flower and vegetative buds is greatly reduced, and the tree maintains a low level of carbohydrate consumption. Breakdown of stored carbohydrate in the winter increases the concentration of sugars in the cell sap throughout the tree. The elevated sugar level acts as an antifreeze, helping protect the tree from freezing injury. Trees must be provided with adequate water in the fall, either as postharvest irrigations or as rainfall, if they are to keep functioning through the dormant season.

Buds must be exposed to a certain amount of chilling to complete dormancy and achieve optimum bloom. This *chilling requirement*, measured as the accumulated number of hours between 32° and 45°F (0° and 7°C), varies widely depending on the stone fruit and variety. Ranges of chilling requirements for the flower buds of stone fruit varieties commonly grown in California are listed in Table 2.

A number of problems may develop if the chilling requirement for a given stone fruit variety is not fully met. The bloom period usually is delayed and prolonged, making flower-infecting diseases such as brown rot more difficult to control. Late-blooming varieties are affected more severely. For stone fruits that require cross-pollination, the bloom overlap period for pollenizer varieties may be reduced, resulting in poor pollination. Too little chilling may cause loss of flower buds and delays in leaf development.

Shoot Growth and Development

Vegetative buds begin growing in early spring, after they have received sufficient chilling to break their dormancy. Usually they begin to grow at the same time as or shortly after the flower buds begin to grow. Shoots leaf out quickly, and most grow for only a short time. Some vigorous shoots continue to grow throughout the season and may reach lengths of 5 to 10 feet when lack of water is not a limiting factor. On peaches, nectarines, and some plums, many of the lateral buds formed on these shoots grow into secondary shoots during the season, and some tertiary shoots may develop from lateral buds on the secondary shoots. On peaches and nectarines, next season's flower buds develop laterally on longer, current-season extension shoots. On apricots, plums, and prunes, flower buds are formed on short shoots called spurs as well as on extension shoots. Cherry flower buds form on spurs and basal buds of 1-year-old shoots. Pruning practices for a particular stone fruit variety are determined in large part by where the flower buds are formed.

Vegetative growth creates the leaves and next season's fruiting wood. A full canopy of healthy leaves that intercepts an optimal amount of sunlight provides the tree sufficient photosynthate to support vegetative growth and current-season fruit production without excessive shading of the inner canopy. Many of the crop and pest management practices outlined in the following chapters have the objective of maintaining a healthy canopy. It is important to avoid excessive shoot growth because it can shade out the interior of the tree. Too much shading causes poor fruit color and flavor quality, and can cause interior fruiting wood to die out. Inadequate shading of branches, on the other hand, can result in sunburn, which predisposes limbs to wood-boring beetles and Cytospora canker. A good pruning and training program ensures that adequate sunlight will reach the lower and interior fruiting wood, and at the same time minimizes problems with sunburn. By avoiding overfertilization with nitrogen, you can reduce excessive shoot growth, which can increase problems with pests such as peach twig borer, oriental fruit moth, and aphids that attack young shoot tips.

Fruit Growth and Development

Fruit development begins with the formation of flower buds during the previous season. Flower buds usually are formed after spurs and short shoots have stopped growing in May or June. Development continues within flower buds during

Table 2. Chilling Requirements for Stone Fruits.[1]

Stone fruit	Chilling hours
apricot	700–1,000
cherry	650–1,300
nectarine	400–1,000
peach	400–1,000
plum (Japanese)	600–1,200
prune (French)	850–1,100

1. The total number of hours between 32° and 45°F (0° and 7°C) between November 1 and February 15 needed for optimum bloom. These are ranges; actual chilling hours depend on scion variety, and some varieties have lower chilling requirements than those listed in this table. Chilling hour accumulations for a number of locations throughout California can be obtained from the UC Fruit and Nuts Information Center (http://fruitsandnuts.ucdavis.edu/).

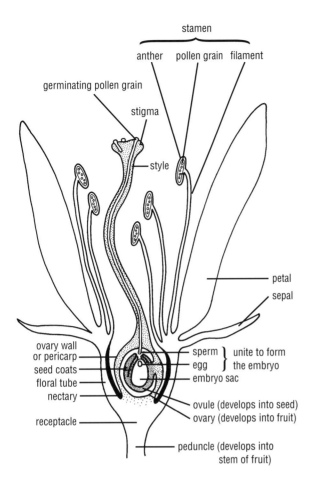

Figure 3. Structures of the stone fruit flower. The diagram above shows a flower in longitudinal section (drawing by Reid M. Brooks). In this figure a pollen tube has developed and fertilization is about to take place. Most of the structures illustrated in the diagram can be seen in the photo (*below*) of a cherry blossom with one petal and sepal removed.

summer and fall, and stress to the tree can interfere with proper flower bud development. In cherries, water stress or heat stress in midsummer will increase the incidence of fruit "doubles" the following season. Overhead sprinkler irrigation during hot weather from late June until early September can reduce the incidence of fruit doubles. Water stress in late summer increases fruit doubles in other stone fruits. Excessive shading of fruiting wood inhibits flower bud development.

Bloom and Pollination. The structure of the flower is basically the same for all stone fruits (Figure 3). Each flower has five petals, a number of *stamens* that bear the pollen-producing *anthers*, and a single *pistil* containing the ovary, which after successful fertilization develops into the fruit. For fertilization to take place, pollen grains must be transferred from anthers to the *stigma*, the uppermost surface of the pistil. This process is called *pollination*, and may involve either self-pollination, where pollen is transferred from the anthers to the stigma of the same flower, or *cross-pollination*, where pollen from other trees is carried to the stigma. Some cross-pollination is accomplished by wind movement, but most pollination relies on the activity of insects, primarily honey bees. After it contacts the stigma, the pollen grain germinates and forms a pollen tube that penetrates the length of the stigma to reach the *ovule* (Figure 3). This allows transfer of a sperm nucleus from the pollen grain to the ovule, and fertilization takes place. If the ovule is not fertilized, the entire flower structure usually drops within 6 to 8 weeks after petal fall.

Flowers of nectarines, peaches, prunes, and most apricots are *self-fruitful*, that is, the pollen of a flower can successfully fertilize the ovule of the same flower. Most cherry and Japanese plum varieties and a few apricot varieties are *self-sterile*—they require cross-pollination from a different variety, called a *pollenizer*, for successful fertilization. Bee activity during bloom is essential for fruit set in stone fruits that require pollenizers, and is also needed for good fruit set in some self-fruitful varieties. Adverse weather conditions during bloom will interfere with bee activity, resulting in poor fruit set. More information on using pollenizers and managing honey bees is given in the next chapter.

The timing of management actions for a number of stone fruit pests is based on bloom stage, so it is important that growers and pest control professionals be familiar with these stages. Bloom stages for stone fruits are illustrated in Figures 75 through 79 in Appendix I. Timing for some actions is based on an estimate of when a certain proportion of the flower buds are fully open—for example, "5% bloom" and "10% bloom" are estimates of when the first 5% or 10% of flower buds have reached the full bloom stage.

For purposes of management, the term "full bloom" refers to the point at which the majority of flowers in the orchard are at the full bloom stage; by this time some will be past full bloom, while others will be at earlier stages. The proportion of flowers that are fully open when the orchard is at full bloom can vary substantially depending on winter chilling.

In high chilling years, as many as 80% of the blossoms may reach full bloom at the same time. In low chilling years, the proportion may be below 50%.

Fruit Growth. The ovary of the stone fruit flower has two ovules. Normally one ovule will be fertilized and develop into the seed, while the other ovule will disintegrate. Surrounding the ovule is the ovary wall or *pericarp*. The pericarp is made up of three layers (Figure 4): the *exocarp*, which develops into the skin of the fruit; the *mesocarp*, which forms the fleshy, edible portion of the fruit; and the *endocarp*, which becomes the pit or stone.

After fertilization, the fruit generally goes through three stages of growth (Figure 5). The length of each stage varies depending on the variety. Stage I is a period of rapid growth, primarily from cell division, and lasts about 30 days. By the end of this stage nearly all the cells of the fruit have been formed. A significant amount of stress to the tree from heat, cold, lack of water, or nutrient deficiency will reduce the length of this growth stage and can substantially reduce final fruit size, which is directly related to the number of cells in the fruit. The endocarp (pit) begins to harden at the end of Stage I. Conditions that favor mesocarp growth and enlargement during pit hardening may increase the incidence of split pits at harvest.

Pit hardening marks the beginning of Stage II, during which fruit size increases more slowly. Growth of the pericarp slows and finally stops during this stage, while the embryo (seed) develops to its full size. Stage II is very short and may overlap with Stage III in early-maturing varieties, but lasts several weeks in late maturing varieties.

Stage III is the period of rapid exocarp and mesocarp growth that usually begins 4 to 6 weeks before harvest. Most growth during this stage involves the expansion of the exocarp and mesocarp cells that were formed during Stage I. During this period, avoidance of water stress is critical; water stress at this point will reduce final fruit size for most stone fruits. Irrigation of previously water-stressed orchards at this time can result in the sudden expansion of mesocarp cells, splitting the fruit.

Flower and Fruit Drop. Flower and fruit drop may occur at any time during the season in response to environmental or physiological conditions. A large number of flowers and fruitlets may drop shortly after bloom because their ovules were not fertilized. Sometimes a drop of young fruit, often called "June drop," occurs in April or May. This probably is often caused by competition between fruit for nutrients or growth hormones. The number of young fruit lost at this time can be large in some varieties, such as Casselman, Simka, and Santa Rosa plums. Another fruit drop can occur shortly before harvest in many mid- and late-season varieties of peach and nectarine that have heavy crops. The timing, duration, and magnitude of the different flower and fruit drops varies among varieties. Changes from year to year for a given variety result in part from changes in weather conditions and fruit load. Fruit drop usually is higher for young trees during their first few bearing seasons, especially if they are very vigorous. It is important that the grower understand that fruit drop is normal in well-managed orchards, particularly for certain varieties.

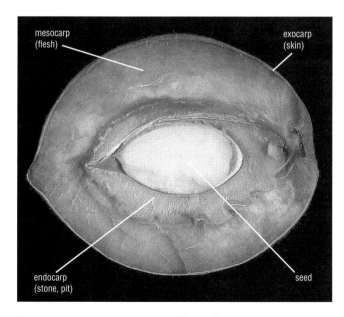

Figure 4. Structures of a stone fruit. (Photo of longitudinal section of peach fruit after pit hardening.) After the end of growth stage II, the seed is fully formed, the pit is hardened, and the mesocarp begins to expand.

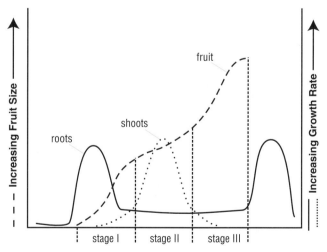

Figure 5. Relationship between growth of roots, shoots, and fruit of a late-season peach variety, showing growth stages of the fruit. During stage I all the cells of the fruit are formed. During stage II the endocarp (pit) hardens and the seed develops to full size. During stage III the cells of the mesocarp (flesh) and exocarp (skin) expand until fruit reaches full size.

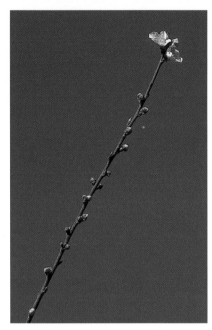

This peach shoot illustrates 10% bloom—when the first 1/10 of the blossoms are fully open.

Irrigating a water-stressed orchard can cause fruit splitting when the sudden availability of water results in rapid expansion of the fruit's mesocarp cells, bursting the exocarp (skin) of the fruit.

The yellow plum fruitlet is about to be shed. Large numbers of young fruit are shed in many varieties of plums and other stone fruits.

Root Growth and Development

The roots of stone fruit trees generally undergo two major periods of root growth each season (Figure 5). The first flush of growth occurs in February or March, before flower and vegetative buds begin to open. Root growth slows after fruit growth and shoot growth reach full swing. The second flush of root growth begins after fruit are harvested and shoot growth has slowed. Roots continue to grow slowly during the dormant season, but nutrient uptake essentially stops after leaves have fallen.

It is important to maximize the volume of soil into which the roots grow to maximize the amount of water and nutrients each tree can take up. Roots will not grow where the soil is too dry or too wet. Therefore, it is important to maintain adequate but not excessive soil moisture throughout the zone where root proliferation is desired. Deep, well-drained soils of medium texture are ideal for optimum root growth. Any problems with soil compaction or impervious soil layers should be corrected before planting. These interfere physically with root growth and impede the movement of water and oxygen, creating conditions unfavorable to root growth. Adherence to recommended management practices for control of nematodes, *Phytophthora*, and other root rot pathogens is important for optimum root growth and development. Weed management also is important, because tree roots will not proliferate where weed and grass roots are abundant. The avoidance of stress from weeds and root pathogens is most critical during the first year after planting.

Growth Interactions

Roots, shoots, and fruit have a strong influence on one another's growth. Root growth occurs primarily in early spring and in fall, when shoot and fruit growth are at a minimum. The peak in shoot growth tends to coincide with early stages of fruit development (see Figure 5). A heavy crop load reduces shoot growth. Crops usually are thinned before or shortly after the beginning of growth stage II (pit hardening).

Apical Dominance. In fruit trees and other plants, hormones produced in actively growing shoot tips (*apical meristems*) tend to suppress lateral growth lower down on the shoot. This phenomenon is known as *apical dominance*. Apical dominance that results from rapid growth of shoot tips is the primary cause of shortness in current-season lateral shoots of tree fruits. In the vigorous shoots that commonly develop on plums and cherries, apical dominance phenomena are so strong that lateral shoot buds do not grow. Apical dominance also causes the upper shoots of a given growth flush to be more upright with narrower branch angles than lower shoots. Pruning and training techniques are designed to manipulate the effects of apical dominance to shape the tree and control the production of fruiting wood. For example, heading cuts remove some of the dominance of terminal and upper buds, and produce vigorous growth of new shoots below the heading cuts.

Managing Pests in Stone Fruits

Integrated pest management regards the crop production system as an ecosystem that includes the crop, its culture, its pests, and the physical and biological components of the crop environment. In an IPM program, pest management activities are integrated with crop management operations. The goal is to achieve economical, long-lasting solutions to pest problems while minimizing impact on the environment. Emphasis is on long-term, cost-effective management of pest problems whenever possible. This includes monitoring crop development and pest occurrence for optimal timing of control actions, choosing the best control methods available, based on a knowledge of each pest's life cycle, and taking steps to preserve or enhance biological control.

The key components of an IPM program are:

- accurate pest identification
- field monitoring
- control action guidelines
- effective management methods

No single program works for all stone fruit orchards. The best management program for a given location is determined by a number of factors. These include the stone fruit variety being grown, soil characteristics, geographical location, surroundings, local climate, and field history. The general discussion of management practices that follows will help you develop programs for your own orchards.

Pest Identification

You need to know which pests are likely to be problems in your orchard before you can plan the most effective pest management program. Accurate identification is essential because different management methods may be needed even for closely related pest species or for diseases that cause similar symptoms. This requires practice. By making a habit of looking for arthropod and vertebrate pests, weeds, and disease symptoms, you will soon learn how to recognize them. Also, you need to recognize important beneficial organisms so you can assess the effectiveness of biological control.

The descriptions and photographs in this manual will help you identify pest problems and beneficial natural enemies that may occur in California stone fruit orchards. Other sources of information that will help in pest identification are listed in the references at the back of the manual. You will need assistance from experienced professionals to identify the causes of some pest problems. Do not hesitate to seek their help if you are not sure what is causing a problem. Farm advisors (listed under "University of California Cooperative Extension Service" or "Cooperative Agricultural Extension University of California" in the County Government listings of your local telephone directory), county agricultural commissioners, and pest control professionals can help, and can direct you to other specialists when necessary.

Orchard Monitoring

Regular monitoring of each orchard gives you critical information for making pest management decisions. A good monitoring program involves surveys throughout the year to keep track of orchard conditions, cultural practices, and development of pest populations. You can use the information you gather to assess the orchard's performance and predict potential problems. Check regularly for pests, natural enemies of pest species, the maturity and health of the crop, soil moisture, and weather. To save time, plan to include pest monitoring whenever you are in the orchard for routine cultural practices. The pest problems you are likely to encounter and the timing and nature of orchard manage-

ment activities depend on which stone fruits you are growing and where you are growing them. Recommended timings for monitoring and management activities for the major stone fruit growing areas of California are illustrated in Figures 6 through 13.

Keep records of your monitoring results; they will help you forecast pest outbreaks and schedule cultural practices. Tables or graphs of pest counts will help you identify populations patterns. Maps of pest damage or weed populations will help you identify localized problems and pest distribution. Records of monitoring results, such as total seasonal trap catches for each insect pest species, are invaluable for long-term planning. They tell you what to expect, which management techniques have been effective, and which have not.

Monitoring before Planting the Orchard
A number of monitoring activities undertaken before you begin to prepare the planting site will help you plan your pest management program and will keep some potential problems from developing.

- Consult field records for cropping history, cultural practices, pesticide use, and problems with pests and soil conditions.

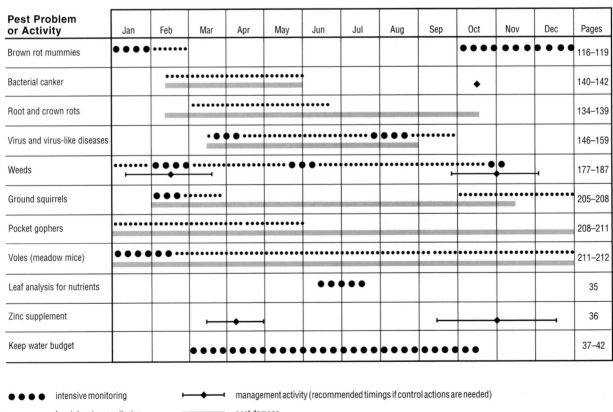

Figure 6. Schedule of stone fruit monitoring and management activities with similar timing in all growing areas.

- Survey the field for weeds, and plan appropriate management strategies. Infestations of perennials are easier to control at this time.
- Collect samples of irrigation water for analysis of nitrate and salinity.
- Collect soil samples for analysis of salinity.
- Collect soil samples for analysis of nematode populations.

- Check for soil compaction.
- Survey adjacent areas for pests that may move into the orchard, especially vertebrate pests such as deer, rabbits, and voles that can seriously damage newly planted orchards. Nearby abandoned or unmanaged orchards may be sources of pests that you will want to take precautions against, such as X-disease, codling moth, and wood borers.

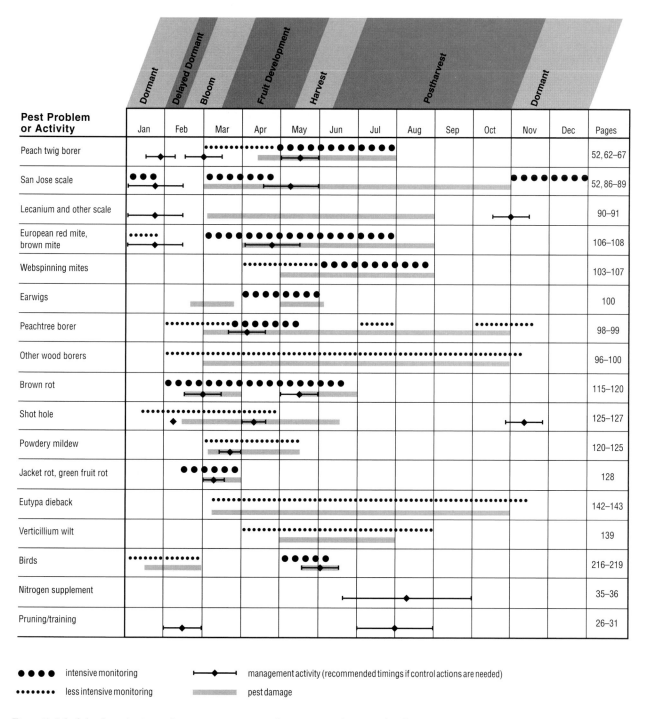

Figure 7. Schedule of monitoring and management activities for apricots in the Central Valley.

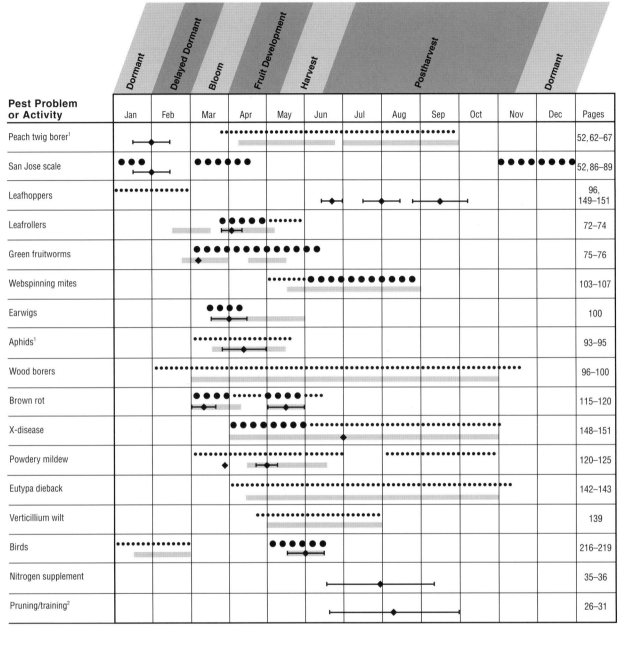

Figure 8. Schedule of monitoring and management activities for cherries in the Central Valley.

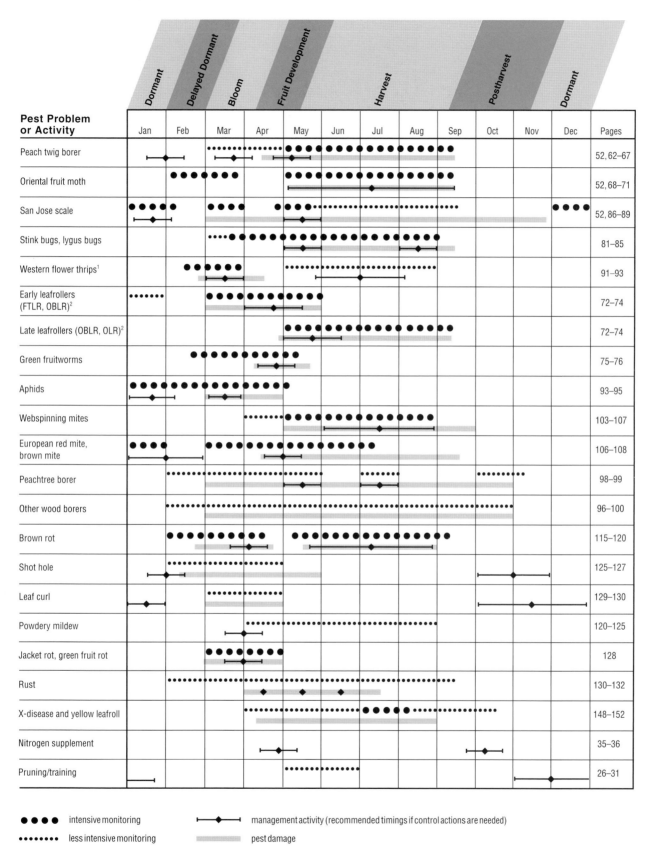

Figure 9. Schedule of monitoring and management activities for peaches and nectarines in the Central Valley.

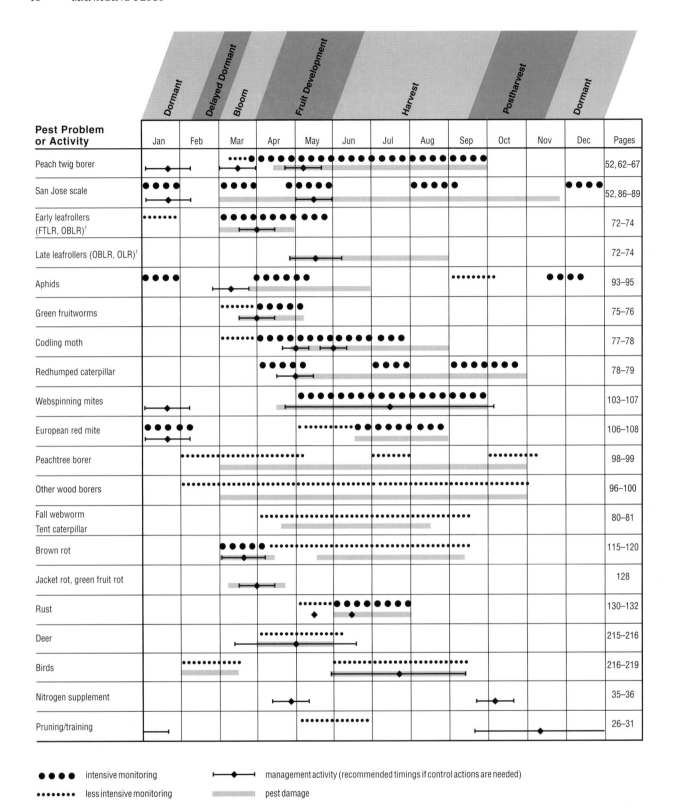

Figure 10. Schedule of monitoring and management activities for plums in the Central Valley.

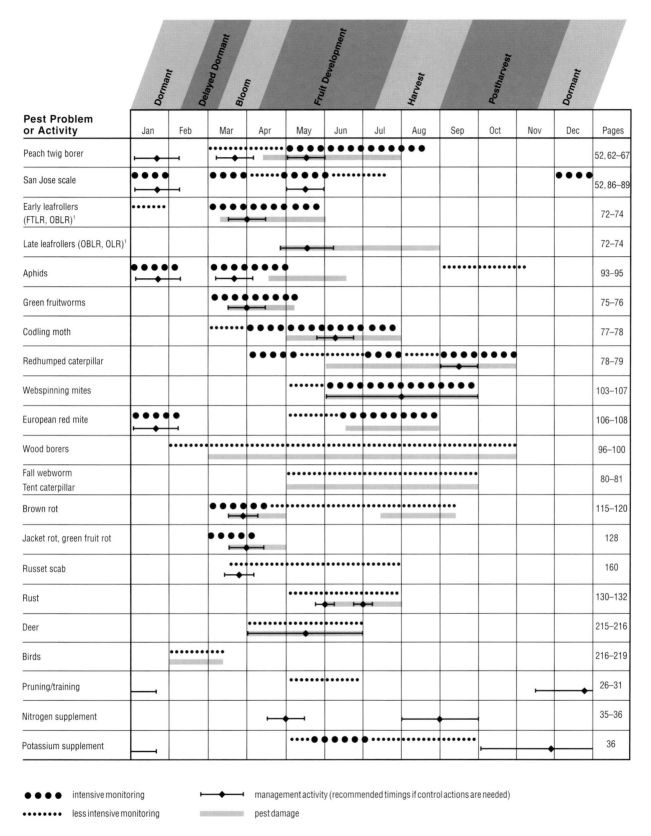

Pest Problem or Activity

Pest Problem or Activity	Jan	Feb	Mar	Apr	May	Jun	Jul	Aug	Sep	Oct	Nov	Dec	Pages
Peach twig borer													52, 62–67
San Jose scale													52, 86–89
Early leafrollers (FTLR, OBLR)[1]													72–74
Late leafrollers (OBLR, OLR)[1]													72–74
Aphids													93–95
Green fruitworms													75–76
Codling moth													77–78
Redhumped caterpillar													78–79
Webspinning mites													103–107
European red mite													106–108
Wood borers													96–100
Fall webworm Tent caterpillar													80–81
Brown rot													115–120
Jacket rot, green fruit rot													128
Russet scab													160
Rust													130–132
Deer													215–216
Birds													216–219
Pruning/training													26–31
Nitrogen supplement													35–36
Potassium supplement													36

● ● ● ● intensive monitoring   ├───◆───┤ management activity (recommended timings if control actions are needed)

••••••• less intensive monitoring   ▨▨▨▨ pest damage

1. FTLR = fruittree leafroller, OBLR = obliquebanded leafroller, OLR = omnivorous leafroller.

Figure 11. Schedule of monitoring and management activities for prunes in the Central Valley.

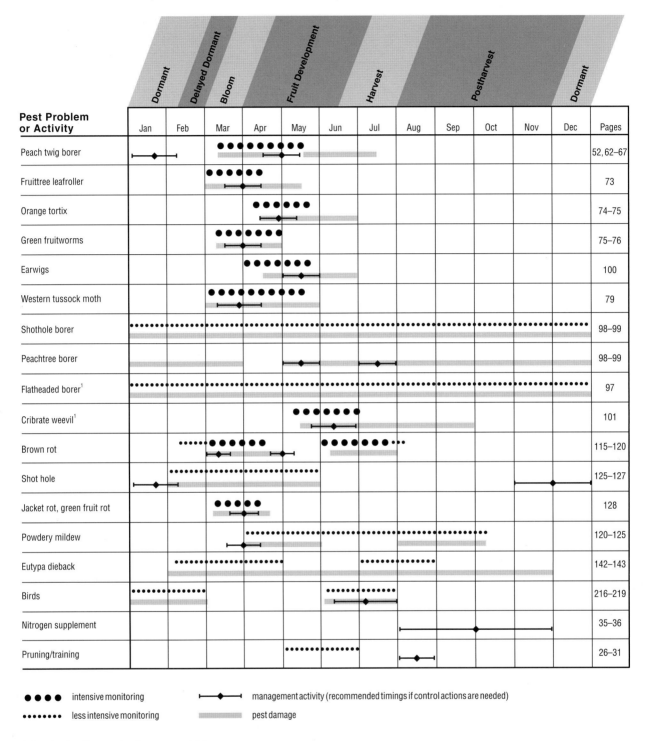

Pest Problem or Activity	Jan	Feb	Mar	Apr	May	Jun	Jul	Aug	Sep	Oct	Nov	Dec	Pages
Peach twig borer													52, 62–67
Fruittree leafroller													73
Orange tortix													74–75
Green fruitworms													75–76
Earwigs													100
Western tussock moth													79
Shothole borer													98–99
Peachtree borer													98–99
Flatheaded borer[1]													97
Cribrate weevil[1]													101
Brown rot													115–120
Shot hole													125–127
Jacket rot, green fruit rot													128
Powdery mildew													120–125
Eutypa dieback													142–143
Birds													216–219
Nitrogen supplement													35–36
Pruning/training													26–31

●●●● intensive monitoring   ├─◆─┤ management activity (recommended timings if control actions are needed)

•••••••• less intensive monitoring   ▓▓▓▓ pest damage

1. Occasional problem, most serious on young trees.

Figure 12. Schedule of monitoring and management activities for apricots in the coastal valleys.

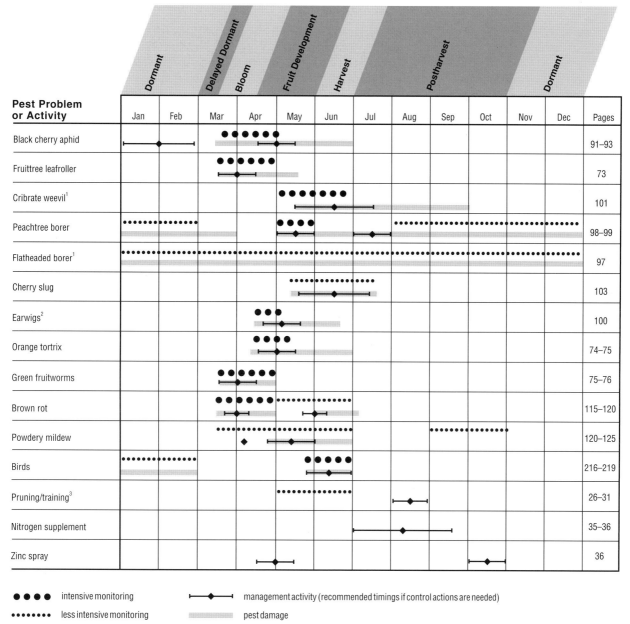

Pest Problem or Activity	Jan	Feb	Mar	Apr	May	Jun	Jul	Aug	Sep	Oct	Nov	Dec	Pages
Black cherry aphid													91–93
Fruittree leafroller													73
Cribrate weevil[1]													101
Peachtree borer													98–99
Flatheaded borer[1]													97
Cherry slug													103
Earwigs[2]													100
Orange tortrix													74–75
Green fruitworms													75–76
Brown rot													115–120
Powdery mildew													120–125
Birds													216–219
Pruning/training[3]													26–31
Nitrogen supplement													35–36
Zinc spray													36

●●●● intensive monitoring

●●●●●●● less intensive monitoring

├──◆──┤ management activity (recommended timings if control actions are needed)

 pest damage

1. Primarily a problem on young trees.
2. Fruit contamination problem at harvest.
3. Recommended timing to minimize risk of Eutypa dieback infection. Cherries can be pruned anytime during dormant season.

Figure 13. Schedule of monitoring and management activities for cherries in the coastal valleys.

Monitoring during the Season

The types of pest problems and rates at which pest problems develop change during the season. Most pests require monitoring only at certain times of the year, but you need to begin monitoring before populations begin to increase and continue until either you make a treatment decision or the chance of pest damage is past. Use the timetables in Figures 6 through 13 as guides for when to begin monitoring, and consult the sections on individual pests in the following chapters for more specific information.

As a general rule, you should sample your orchards at least once a week when insect and mite pests are likely to be present. More-frequent sampling may be necessary at critical times, such as when you are pinpointing a biofix for degree-day calculations (see below). Frequent monitoring of bloom stages is necessary in the spring to properly schedule fungicide applications for brown rot and other diseases. Look for the presence of weeds, diseases, and vertebrate pests while you monitor for arthropod pests or during routine orchard operations. Keep track of their presence and watch for any changes. It is a good idea to prepare a record for each orchard once each quarter, noting weed species, disease symptoms, vertebrate activity, and signs of any other significant stresses. Sample for nematodes before planting the orchard, after any treatments intended to reduce their numbers, and any time you suspect they are causing damage.

Weather Monitoring

Weather has a major influence on the development of stone fruits and the pests that affect them. Temperature controls the rate at which insects, mites, and diseases develop, and wetness from rainfall or fog is a primary factor favoring development of fruit and foliage diseases. Too little winter chilling will lengthen the bloom period of some stone fruit varieties, increasing the length of time over which you may need to take control actions for diseases such as brown rot. A reliable source of weather information is critical to many of your pest management decisions. You need to keep track of daily high and low temperatures if you are using degree-day accumulations to schedule monitoring and management activities for pests such as peach twig borer, oriental fruit moth, and San Jose scale, or to schedule frost protection activities. You can use evapotranspiration and rainfall data to schedule irrigations and calculate water requirements. Weather forecasts are essential for scheduling frost protection measures and protective treatments for brown rot.

Many newspapers and radio stations in agricultural areas report local weather information. The National Weather Service broadcasts local and regional weather information on NOAA Weather Radio, VHF channels 162.42, 162.50, and 162.55 MHz. Evapotranspiration information is available from the California Department of Water Resources's CIMIS program. Daily weather information for a number of locations throughout California is also available from the University of California Statewide Integrated Pest Management Project (UC IPM). (See references for ways to access CIMIS and UC IPM weather information; both of these programs are available via the World Wide Web.) Chilling hour accumulations are available from the UC Fruit and Nut Information Center, listed in the references.

Significant local variations often occur in weather conditions, especially in temperature and rainfall. For the most accurate weather data, set up your own weather station in or near your orchard (Figure 14). Weather instruments can range from simple devices such as a maximum/minimum thermometer to electronic devices that continuously monitor and record weather information for transfer to a computer. Even more sophisticated stations transmit the data to a remote computer. Set up and maintain the weather instruments according to manufacturers' instructions, and calibrate them regularly to ensure accuracy. Keep records of all your observations.

Accumulating Degree-Days

The growth rates of trees and invertebrate and microbial pests are closely related to temperature. In warmer years, pests such as peach twig borer will appear sooner and generations will develop more quickly than in colder years. For this reason, the calendar date alone cannot be used to schedule pest management activities. More accurate predictions of a pest's development can be made by measuring the amount of heat the pest is exposed to over time. Degree-day accumulations are used to measure this, and are calculated using mathematical models developed for each pest.

Each species of plant, insect, or microbe has specific lower and upper *developmental thresholds*. Degree-day models assume that no development occurs at temperatures below the lower threshold. Between the lower and upper thresholds, the development rate increases in a roughly linear fashion as temperature increases. For temperatures above the upper threshold, degree-day models may use a horizontal cutoff, which assumes that the development rate remains constant, or a vertical cutoff, which assumes that development stops above the upper threshold. These concepts are illustrated in Figure 15. The calculation of degree-days is illustrated in Figure 16. A *degree-day* (°D) is defined as the area under the temperature-time curve, between the lower and upper developmental thresholds, equal to $1° \times 1$ day (24 degree-hours). To use degree-days to keep track of crop or pest development, you need to know how many degree-days are required to complete each growth stage or generation as well as the temperature thresholds for that specific organism.

The UC IPM World Wide Web site (http://www.ipm.ucdavis.edu) has programs that accumulate degree-days using data provided directly to UC IPM from remote weather stations. At the present time, degree-day calculations can be used to forecast the development of peach twig borer, oriental fruit moth, codling moth, orange tortrix, and San Jose scale. Degree-day reference tables for these pests, which can be used to estimate degree-days, are included in Appendix II at the back of this book.

You can estimate degree-days based on daily maximum and minimum temperatures using a computer program or by hand using a reference table such as those in Appendix II. *An Easy Way to Calculate Degree-Days* (UC DANR Publication 7174), listed in the references, presents a simple method for calculating degree-days. Electronic instruments that record temperatures hourly or more frequently often include software to compute degree-days. Degree-days estimated from daily maximum and minimum temperatures can differ widely from those computed from temperature data collected at

Figure 14. A weather station placed in or near your orchard will give you the most accurate weather information for making management decisions.

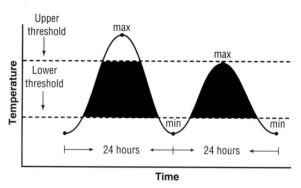

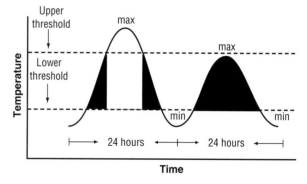

Figure 16. Degree-days can be estimated by using daily minimum and maximum temperatures to generate a temperature-time curve, then calculating the area under that curve between the upper and lower developmental thresholds for that organism. If a horizontal cutoff method is used to calculate degree-days, the organism's development rate is assumed to remain constant above the upper threshold. A vertical cutoff method assumes development stops above the upper threshold.

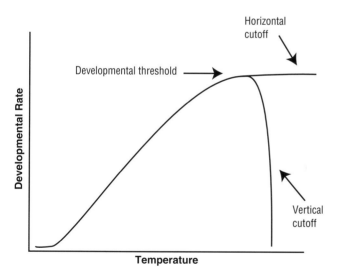

Figure 15. The growth rate curve for a specific pest can be used to develop a degree-day model, which can be used to schedule management actions. Degree-day models assume the growth rate increases at an approximately linear rate until it reaches an upper developmental threshold. Models for some pests use a horizontal cutoff, which assumes growth rate remains constant above the upper threshold. Some pest models use a vertical cutoff, which assumes growth stops above the upper threshold.

more frequent intervals. Therefore, if you are calculating degree-days to schedule management activities for a pest, it is important that you use the same technique as was used to develop the predictive model for that pest.

Control Action Guidelines

Growers and pest control professionals use control action guidelines to help them decide when management actions are necessary to prevent losses to pests or other stresses. Some guidelines take the form of numerical thresholds based on specific sampling techniques, such as leaf analysis for nutrient levels or counts of insect numbers. Most guidelines require that you consider field history, stage of crop development, presence of pests or damage, weather conditions, and other observations. Control action guidelines may change as new varieties and cultural practices are introduced and as new information on pests and management techniques becomes available.

Management Methods

An effective IPM program protects the crop from economic damage while interfering as little as possible with the long-term viability of the production system. The cheapest and most reliable way to do this is to anticipate pest problems and prevent them whenever possible or to minimize the number of treatments by beginning control actions as soon as monitoring indicates they are needed. While often not considered pest management activities, many cultural practices can play major roles in minimizing pest problems. Cultural practices that help prevent pest problems include the use of certified planting stock, rootstocks and scion varieties that have some resistance to potential pest problems, deep and well-drained planting sites with favorable soil characteristics, proper preparation of the planting site, orchard design techniques that make management activities easier, and appropriate irrigation methods, as well as adequate though not excessive levels of key nutrients and proper training and pruning of trees. Use pesticides only when your monitoring indicates they are needed to prevent economic losses or where orchard history indicates a need for preventive treatments. Use materials and application methods that have a minimum of harmful side effects, such as disruption of biological controls or environmental degradation, but are still effective and economical.

Biological Control

The activity of any organism (whether parasite, predator, pathogen, antagonist, or competitor) that keeps a pest population lower than it would otherwise be is termed *biological control*. The role of natural enemies and other beneficial organisms is one of the first things you should assess as you develop your IPM program. Biological control can be disrupted by chemical treatments intended to control orchard pests, and can thus trigger secondary pest outbreaks or pest resurgence (discussed below, under Pesticides). To keep your biological control efforts as effective as possible, choose pesticides and use rates and techniques that are least harmful to the natural enemies of orchard pests.

Natural enemies contribute to the control of most insect pests of stone fruits and usually keep mite pests from causing serious problems. A number of important natural enemy species are discussed in the next chapter. Natural enemies also play a role in regulating populations of plant pathogens, weeds, nematodes, and vertebrates, but they usually do not provide economic control. Strains of the bacterium *Agrobacterium radiobacter* are available as commercial formulations for control of crown gall in stone fruits. The roots of young trees are treated before planting, and the biological control agent acts as an antagonist to the pathogen *Agrobacterium tumefaciens*. In nontilled orchards and undisturbed areas adjacent to orchards, a stem and seed weevil may control puncturevine, but that control is disrupted by tillage.

Variety and Rootstock Selection

Consider potential pest problems when you choose rootstocks and scions. Stone fruit rootstocks vary in their resistance or tolerance to some pests, such as root knot nematodes, root diseases, and bacterial canker (Table 3).

Apricots can be grown on apricot, peach, or plum rootstocks. Peaches and nectarines are grown on peach rootstock; there may be some incompatibility between peach and nectarine scions and apricot, plum, and almond rootstocks. Plums and prunes can be grown on plum or peach rootstock. When grown on peach rootstock, plums tend to be more resistant to bacterial canker, and some plum scions are more productive. There is a tendency for young plum trees to develop zinc deficiency when grown on Nemaguard rootstock.

Certified Planting Stock

Clean planting stock is the first line of defense against nematode pests and a number of diseases and genetic disorders. X-disease and all of the virus diseases that affect stone fruits can be transmitted during budding and grafting operations. The use of Certified planting stock is the primary means of controlling these diseases. The certification program for fruit trees is administered by the California Department of Food and Agriculture (CDFA). This program provides nurseries with planting material that has been tested and shown to be apparently free of viruses, and oversees the process whereby nurseries propagate this material to produce Certified nursery stock. Because of state requirements for testing, inspections, and keeping nursery orchards free of pest problems, it is highly unlikely that the Certified planting stock you buy will be infected with viruses, carry other diseases such as crown gall or shot hole, or harbor harmful nematodes or propagules of perennial weeds.

Table 3. Rootstock Resistance to Selected Pest Problems for Rootstocks Commonly Used for California Stone Fruits.

RESISTANCE TO PEST PROBLEMS

Rootstock	Peachtree borer	Bacterial canker[1]	Phytophthora root and crown rot	Crown gall	Armillaria root rot[2]	Verticillium wilt	Root knot nematode[3]	Root lesion nematode[3]	Pocket gophers and voles
APRICOT									
Royal seedling *Prunus armeniaca*	moderately resistant	susceptible	highly susceptible	moderately resistant	susceptible	very susceptible	resistant	resistant	very susceptible
CHERRY									
Colt *P. avium* × *P. pseudocerasus*	resistant	susceptible	moderately resistant	highly susceptible	susceptible	—	—	—	moderately resistant
Mahaleb *P. mahaleb*	moderately susceptible	moderately resistant[4]	highly susceptible	moderately resistant	susceptible	susceptible	resistant	susceptible	highly susceptible
Mazzard *P. avium*	less suscepible than Mahaleb	variable resistance[5]	moderately resistant	susceptible	moderately resistant	susceptible	immune	susceptible	moderately resistant
Stockton Morello *P. cerasus*	moderately resistant	moderately resistant[4]	resistant	moderately resistant	susceptible	susceptible	immune	susceptible	moderately resistant
PEACH									
Lovell seedling *P. persica*	very susceptible	moderately resistant	susceptible	susceptible	susceptible	very susceptible	susceptible	susceptible	moderately resistant
Nemaguard *P. persicsa*	very susceptible	moderately resistant	susceptible	susceptible	susceptible	very susceptible	resistant	susceptible	moderately resistant
PLUM									
Marianna 2624 *P. cerasifera* × *P. munsoniana*	susceptible	highly susceptible	moderately resistant	moderately resistant	moderately resistant	moderately susceptible	resistant	moderately resistant	susceptible
Myrobalan 29C *P. cerasifera*	susceptible	less susceptible than 2624	resistant	slightly resistant	slightly resistant	moderately susceptible	resistant	moderately resistant	susceptible
Myrobalan seedling	susceptible	susceptible	highly resistant	slightly resistant	susceptible	moderately susceptible	susceptible	susceptible	susceptible

1. Resistance of scion grown on the rootstock listed.
2. Slower-growing rootstocks, apparently, are infected more slowly. This provides some tolerance, but not immunity to infection.
3. Immune: nematodes cannot invade roots. Resistant: nematodes can invade and feed in roots but cannot multiply. Susceptible: nematodes can invade roots, feed, and multiply. For more specific information on nematode resistance, see Table 27 in the "Nematodes" chapter.
4. Scions high-worked on a scaffold of this rootstock have some resistance to bacterial canker.
5. Scions high-worked on a scaffold of F12/1 Mazzard rootstock have some resistance to bacterial canker.
— = No information.

Nursery Propagation. The production of planting stock for use in commercial orchards or home gardens involves growing rootstocks and budding the desired scion varieties onto them. Rootstocks may be produced directly from seed (*seedling rootstocks*) or vegetatively from rooted cuttings (*clonal rootstocks*). Most apricot and peach rootstocks are seedling rootstocks. Some cherry and plum rootstocks are seedling; some are clonal. Nursery operators graft scion buds onto rootstocks to produce the desired scion-rootstock combination. Rootstock seed or rooted cuttings are usually planted in the fall and budded with scion wood the following May. These trees are dug in the fall and delivered for transplanting in commercial orchards in the winter or held in cold storage

for planting the following spring or summer. "Yearling" trees are 2-year-old trees used primarily for backyard planting. They are budded in late summer, scion growth occurs the following spring and summer, and they are harvested for sale in the fall. (Figure 17 illustrates the propagation process as well as the rootstock certification process.)

Certified Nursery Stock. The University of California Foundation Plant Material Service (FPMS) makes available Foundation stock seed and budding material to nurseries for production of Registered and Certified planting stock. All Foundation trees are tested yearly for the pollen-borne viruses prunus necrotic ringspot virus and prune dwarf virus. They

FOUNDATION STOCK
(for nursery plantings)

Every tree is tested yearly for
prunus necrotic ringspot
virus and prune dwarf virus.

REGISTERED STOCK
(for nursery plantings, may
be sold for orchard
plantings)

Every Registered tree is tested
yearly for prunus necrotic
ringspot virus and prune dwarf
virus. Trees and orchard blocks
are visually inspected for
diseases and other pests.

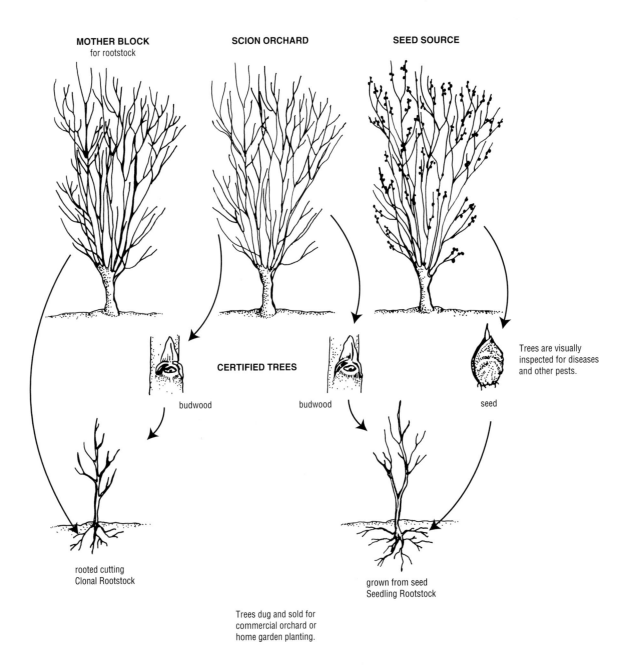

MOTHER BLOCK
for rootstock

SCION ORCHARD

SEED SOURCE

CERTIFIED TREES

budwood

budwood

seed

Trees are visually
inspected for diseases
and other pests.

rooted cutting
Clonal Rootstock

grown from seed
Seedling Rootstock

Trees dug and sold for
commercial orchard or
home garden planting.

Figure 17. Nursery progagation of stone fruits during the production of certified planting stock.

are also visually inspected for diseases and disorders by CDFA and FPMS. Foundation stock is also available from the United States Department of Agriculture at Beltsville, Maryland, and from the Irrigated Agriculture Research and Extension Center at Prosser, Washington.

Foundation stock is used by nurseries to establish blocks of Registered stock that are used to produce Certified nursery stock. Registered stock is tested annually for the presence of prunus necrotic ringspot virus and prune dwarf virus. Certified nursery stock is inspected for disease symptoms in late summer or fall, while leaves are still on the trees, and at harvest. Nursery orchards must be kept free of weeds and other pests. Nursery sites must be inspected and approved by CDFA in advance of planting.

Nematode Certification. Nursery stock can also be certified as free from nematodes, at the request of the nursery. In this case the soil must be prepared and fumigated according to guidelines specified by CDFA, which tests soil and plant samples for the presence of nematodes. As an alternative to fumigation, every acre of the planting block can be sampled for nematodes and approved if free from harmful species. By using planting stock that has been certified to be free from nematodes, the grower can start with material as free from harmful nematode pests as possible.

Soil Solarization

Soil solarization is a soil-heating procedure that involves covering prepared soil with special plastic for several weeks or months during the warmest, sunniest time of the year. This allows the sun to heat the moist soil to temperatures that are lethal to many weed seeds and some soilborne pathogens. It is a nonchemical technique that may be used to control a wide variety of weed species and Verticillium wilt. Some nematode pest populations may be reduced by soil solarization, but the technique does not control root knot nematodes. Weed control with solarization is discussed in the chapter on vegetation management.

You can solarize the soil before planting or lay down the plastic at planting and leave it in place for a year or more. Use clear plastic if you solarize before planting: it heats the soil to higher temperatures. If you begin solarizing at the time of planting, use black plastic; young trees are harmed by the higher soil temperatures reached under clear plastic. For solarization to be effective, soil moisture must be at field capacity. On coarser-textured soils, you may be able to preirrigate to fill the soil profile before laying plastic. On finer-textured soils, you will need to wait and apply water after placing the solarization plastic in order to avoid soil compaction from the application equipment. You can use drip lines or gated pipe placed underneath the plastic to bring soil moisture to field capacity after laying the plastic. It is difficult to use flood or furrow irrigation underneath solarization plastic, and these irrigation methods are not recommended where water must be applied after plastic is in place.

The preplant solarization treatment should last at least 6 weeks during the hottest and sunniest time of the year: July and August in the Central Valley, and perhaps a month or more later than that in California's coastal valleys. You will realize the greatest benefit if you solarize the soil all summer. Use plastic that is resistant to UV light; although it is more expensive, it will resist deterioration and make mechanical removal easier, especially if you are solarizing for an extended period. If you work a green manure cover crop in before solarizing, especially a crop of a cereal grain or a mustard family plant, you will enhance the effect of solarization on soilborne pathogens.

If you lay solarizing plastic at planting, lay one sheet of black plastic down on each side of the tree row, cut holes around the trees, seal the inner edges, and cover the outer edges with a layer of soil in the row middle. Drip irrigation must be used with this solarization technique. You can place drip lines on top of the plastic and run drip tubes to each tree, poked through the plastic. This makes it easier to check on the functioning of the drip tubes, since the plastic will remain in place for 1 to 3 years. The soil is heated to lower temperatures than under clear plastic, but it remains heated for a longer time. This procedure is very effective for controlling weeds in the tree rows, and can reduce the trees' water requirement by 80% or more. If you use this type of solarization, cut the amount you irrigate by 80% and check soil moisture regularly to be sure the root zone does not dry out. If soil moisture under black plastic is maintained at too high a level, tree roots may be severely injured. Trees tend to begin blooming sooner if the solarization plastic remains in place.

You can find more information about soil solarization in the publication *Soil Solarization: A Nonpesticidal Method for Controlling Diseases, Nematodes, and Weeds,* listed in the references.

Establishing the New Orchard

Choice of the orchard site, design of the orchard, proper site preparation, and careful planting all affect pest management activities and can reduce problems associated with certain pests.

Site Selection. Several points need to be considered when choosing the location for your orchard, including the soil conditions, local weather history, availability of an adequate supply of good quality irrigation water when you will need it, the cropping history and past pest problems of the site, the availability of skilled labor to help manage and harvest your crop, and the availability of facilities needed to market your crop. Market conditions and prices should play major roles in your determination of what to plant and where.

Soil. Deep, well-drained, sandy loam soil that is free of salt problems is the best choice for a stone fruit orchard. With proper preparation before planting and careful rootstock selection, however, stone fruits can be grown on a wide range of soil types. Prunes are the most tolerant of marginal soils. Have your soil tested for nematodes and salts so you can take any necessary remedial steps before planting, and choose appropriate rootstocks. Map the soil profile down to at least 5 feet.

Local Weather. Be sure that the location receives sufficient chilling for the stone fruits you plan to grow. (See Table 2 in the preceding chapter.) Normal weather during bloom periods should not be too cold for proper fruit set and development. In hotter locations such as the southern desert valleys, you will need to choose varieties that require fewer than 400 hours of chilling and that produce fruit that are less sensitive to heat damage. Avoid higher-yielding varieties in these locations. Take into account the potential for frost conditions in low-lying areas when selecting the location and planning the layout of the orchard. Windy locations will have more problems with fruit scarring on fresh market fruit.

Water Supply. You will need to have ready access to an adequate supply of good quality water. Stone fruits require about 3 to 4 acre-feet of water each season. Irrigation water should not contain excessive levels of sodium, boron, or chlorides. Have well water tested each year, and take nitrate levels into account when you calculate seasonal fertilizer requirements.

Cropping History. Whenever possible, check the records of pest problems that have occurred in previous orchards grown on the site. A history of bacterial canker, Armillaria root rot, Phytophthora root and crown rot, crown gall, Verticillium wilt, or root knot nematodes will influence your choice of rootstocks and preplant soil treatments.

Production Resources. Make sure that you will have access to sufficiently skilled laborers for cultural practices such as pruning, thinning, and harvesting techniques used in the stone fruit crops you are planning to grow. Also important are the availability of packinghouse and cooling facilities and technical assistance from pest control professionals and farm advisors.

Soil Preparation. Adequate soil drainage is essential for a successful, productive stone fruit orchard. If there is a hardpan within 4 feet of the surface, rip the soil deep enough to break up the layer. If a plow pan is present and no deep ripping is needed, chisel the soil to a depth of 20 inches (50 cm) with shanks 18 to 20 inches (45 to 50 cm) apart. If there are abrupt boundaries between soil textures, use chiseling or ripping to break them up.

Infestations of perennial weeds are most easily controlled before you plant the orchard. Simple cultivation of dry soil during the summer and fall may be enough to control johnsongrass and bermudagrass. More serious infestations may require a program of glyphosate and cultivation. See the chapter on vegetation management for more information.

If you fumigate the orchard site, do it in the fall while soil is still warm and soil moisture is low. Fumigate after chiseling or ripping and before final grading and leveling.

Proper leveling of the orchard is necessary if you plan to use flood or furrow irrigation. The correct grade depends on the soil type; coarser-textured soils require steeper grades. Plan your tree and row spacings before you set up the irrigation system. Before you plant, set up the pipes and valves for flood or furrow irrigation, or the main lines and hose faucets for drip or microsprinkler systems.

Designing the Orchard. Tree spacing and the training system you use will affect management activities such as pesticide application, cultivation, and irrigation. As you design your orchard, you will need to take into account soil fertility, the available water supply, growth characteristics of the varieties you plan to grow, your fruit production goals, and how soon you want the orchard to begin production.

North-to-south rows give trees the best exposure to sunlight. The arrangement of trees within the orchard is critical in stone fruit varieties that require pollenizer trees (see Pollination, below). If you are planting more than one variety in an orchard, plan for the compatibility of bloom times and management activities such as the timing of pesticide applications relative to pruning and thinning operations and the timing of irrigations relative to harvest. Arrange the different varieties to make cultural activities as efficient as possible. Plan for adequate turning space at the ends of rows for your spray rigs and other vehicles. Take into consideration the type of orchard floor management system you will be using (see the chapter on vegetation management).

The open-center or open-vase system of training is commonly used for stone fruits in California (Figure 18A), in a low-density planting system with trees spaced 16 to 22 feet (4.9 to 6.7 m) apart. The actual spacing you use depends on the vigor of the tree you are growing as well as soil fertility and soil type. Soil that is more fertile can support more trees or less vigorous tree types. Trees grown on heavier soils can be planted closer together because they will be less vigorous.

Higher-density plantings can be used to increase early yields and increase the efficiency of orchard operations such as spray application, weed control, pruning, and harvest. Orchard establishment costs are greater for high-density plantings, and it is more difficult to control tree growth under California conditions with the available rootstocks and scions. Hedgerow systems employ closer tree spacings without trellising. Trees in hedgerow systems may be trained in a number of ways. Three of the most common are central leader (Figure 18B) with trees spaced 5 to 8 feet apart in rows 14 to 16 feet apart, parallel V (Figure 18C) with trees spaced 7 to 10 feet apart in rows 14 to 16 feet apart, and perpendicular V with trees spaced 5 to 7 feet apart in rows 16 to 22 feet apart. With central leader or parallel V training, you can use mechanized summer pruning and platforms for harvesting and pruning; the perpendicular V is less suited to mechanical pruning and the use of platforms. All stone fruits can be trained with each of these systems, some more easily than others. For more information on using hedgerow systems, consult your local tree fruit farm advisor. If you use a hedgerow system, be sure the rows are oriented north-to-south for maximum sunlight exposure. For proper light penetration into the lower canopy, the width of the alley between the canopy walls should be 3 feet less than the trees' height.

Trellis systems employing vertical or V training may be used with less vigorous, spur-bearing plums, cherries, and apricots, but they do not work as well with nectarines or peaches. A trellis system has a high yield potential because of maximum sunlight exposure, but establishment and maintenance costs are high.

Planting. Order your trees by the May before the winter you will plant. That way the nursery can plan its budding operations and you can be assured that you will get the number of trees you will need. Determine the tree and row spacings you will use, and then calculate the number of trees you will need using the following formula:

$$\text{trees per acre} = \frac{43{,}560 \text{ ft}^2 \text{ per acre}}{(\text{tree spacing in feet}) \times (\text{row spacing in feet})}$$

Hiring an experienced tree-planting crew is often the best choice to complete planting operations in a timely fashion, especially when you are planting a large number of trees.

When possible, lay out the rows, accurately mark the planting locations, and dig all holes in advance of heavy winter rains, especially when the soil is fine-textured. Sandy soils can be dug at any time. Use shovels for clay or wet loam to avoid glazing—the compaction of the sides of the hole caused by a tractor-driven auger. Make holes just wide and deep enough to accommodate the tree's root system. If you dig them too deep, the trees will settle and the tree crowns will be too low relative to the soil surface. Do not place fertilizer in the bottom of the planting hole or mix fertilizer into the backfill soil; fertilizer salts can injure the new roots.

Plant the trees as soon as possible after you get them from the nursery. If you can't plant them right away, heel them in using clean soil—preferably soil that has been fumigated—at the orchard site. Plant the trees by January or mid-February at the latest—before top growth begins. Handle the trees carefully to avoid root or trunk injuries. Treatment with a biological control agent for crown gall is a good idea, especially if the planting site has a history of the disease. This is most effective if the tree roots are treated when they are dug

A

B

C

Figure 18. Training systems used for stone fruit trees in California.

A. Peach tree trained to an open-vase or open-center shape.
B. Tree trained to a central leader.
C. Tree trained to a dual leader or V shape.

at the nursery and again just before planting. If adverse weather or other circumstances prevent planting, you can hold the trees in cold storage at 35° to 40°F (2° to 4°C) and plant them in April or May. Keep the roots covered with clean, moist wood shavings. Check frequently to make sure shavings don't dry out.

When planting the trees, make sure the roots are not curled or bent in the planting hole. Trim them if necessary. Set the trees in the hole so they are as high as or higher than they were in the nursery. Position each tree so the rootstock scar at the bud union faces away from the afternoon sun (face the budding scar to the northeast). If you plant on berms, you will reduce the likelihood of crown and root disease. All types of irrigation can be used with berm planting.

Fill around the tree roots with soil that does not contain clods. If sides of the planting hole are "glazed," crumble them into the hole. Fill the hole to within 2 or 3 inches (5 to 7.5 cm) of the top, irrigate lightly to settle the soil, and then fill the hole the rest of the way after the water has soaked in. This will settle the moist soil around the roots. Irrigate lightly after the hole is completely filled with soil. Apply about 1 to 2 gallons per tree; avoid overirrigating, which increases the chance of root rot.

To create the open-center type growth, new trees are pruned back (headed) to a height of 24 to 32 inches (60 to 80 cm). If the trees will be mechanically harvested, they should be headed no less than 32 inches (80 cm) tall. If you head the trees higher, you will get more shoots from which to choose the primary scaffold branches. Trim the side branches below the heading cut to leave one or two buds on each branch. Apply white interior latex paint, tree wrap, or cardboard cylinders to protect the trunk from herbicides as well as sunburn and subsequent damage from wood borers. Cardboard cylinders will provide some protection from vertebrate pests, and will protect the trunk from any contact herbicides that you may use. If you are planting in a location where you anticipate problems with rabbits or voles, more substantial protection is advisable. Where deer damage is expected, consider installing deer fencing before you plant (see the chapter on vertebrates).

Irrigating Young Trees. After the first watering to settle the soil around the new tree, it should require no water until the warm, dry weather of late spring. In orchards to be furrow or flood irrigated, make a small V-shaped furrow along each side of the tree row for watering. Do not irrigate the entire row middle; water is needed only where the young tree's roots are—just a short distance away from the trunk. Extra coverage will encourage weed growth. Avoid allowing the soil around the tree crown to remain wet for long periods. If you are using drip or microsprinklers, place the emitters close enough to the trees to let water penetrate to the roots. Each tree will require as much as 1 gallon of water per day in spring, and as much as 5 gallons per day in hot summer weather. Use a soil tube frequently to monitor soil moisture at root depth to be sure the soil does not dry out. Frequent, light irrigations are best for young trees.

Fertilizing Young Trees. Young trees usually do not need supplemental fertilization until after growth has begun, when they need enough nitrogen for one good season of vegetative growth. Some soils may have enough residual nitrogen for the first season's growth; some irrigation water has enough nitrogen. To ensure adequate nitrogen, add about ⅛ pound of N by placing fertilizer in the irrigation furrow next to the tree or applying fertilizer through drip or microsprinklers when new growth is 6 to 12 inches (15 to 30 cm) long. Be careful not to add too much nitrogen or the trees may defoliate.

Intercropping. Annual crops such as cotton or vegetables may be planted between the rows of a young orchard, but because of the potential for harm to the young trees, such intercropping is generally not recommended. Intercropping can interfere with proper irrigation and pest management, and other crops will compete with the trees for nutrients. If you do plant an intercrop, take care to provide adequate water and nutrients for the young trees and to manage pest problems that arise.

Managing Pests in the Young Orchard. Weed control is important in young orchards because weeds can be very competitive for water and nutrients. Weed growth that would not be harmful in an established orchard can greatly reduce the growth of young trees. Use cultivation, hand hoeing, or careful applications of pre-emergence herbicides to control weeds. Pay particular attention to perennials such as johnsongrass, bermudagrass, and field bindweed. Weed control in young orchards is discussed in the chapter on vegetation management. Vertebrate pests can cause severe damage to young trees (see discussions of gophers, voles, rabbits, and deer in the chapter on vertebrates). Monitor the new orchard frequently for arthropod pests that can cause serious damage to young trees, including peach twig borer, oriental fruit moth, cribrate weevil, wood borers, aphids, and mites.

Training. The pruning you do during the first four years of growth is called training, since it determines the shape of the mature tree. Stone fruit trees in California are trained most commonly to the open-center or open-vase system. This requires a series of pruning steps at planting and during the first four dormant seasons, as well as some summer pruning. Proper training and pruning techniques for stone fruits are discussed and illustrated in detail in *California Sweet Cherry Production Workshop Proceedings, Prune Orchard Management, Peaches, Plums, and Nectarines,* and *Pruning Fruit and Nut Trees,* all of which are listed in the references.

Pruning

Careful pruning of the trees every year maintains the strength of the scaffold and controls the amount of fruiting wood to allow high-quality fruit production with a minimum of thinning costs. Pruning also removes dead, diseased, and injured wood. In mature orchards, summer pruning is used to remove excess vegetative growth and allow more sunlight to reach lower fruiting wood and developing fruit. When you are removing a large limb, first make an undercut partway through the limb to prevent splitting, then cut all the way through the limb from above about 2 inches farther out from the trunk or main scaffold, and finally cut the remaining stub off about ½ inch out from the trunk or main scaffold (Figure 19).

The pruning techniques you will use to renew and maintain fruiting wood depend on the age and type of wood that bears fruit buds. Most fruiting buds of apricots, sweet cherries, plums, and prunes are borne on spurs—short shoots that grow less than 4 inches a year (Figure 20). Flower buds form laterally on spurs and produce fruit the following season. Fruiting buds of peaches and nectarines are formed on 1-year-old shoots that are 6 to 24 inches (15 to 60 cm) long (Figure 21).

Apricots. Spurs of apricots are relatively short-lived, and become less productive after 3 to 5 years. Therefore, it is important that you remove lateral branches throughout the tree and thereby induce the formation of new spurs (Figure 22). Remove some spurs and shoots to reduce the fruit load and the amount of thinning you will have to do later on. Top the mature trees at a height that works best for your cultural operations, such as hand harvesting. Once you have established this height, prune back all upright shoots arising from the top as close as possible to their point of origin.

Sweet Cherries. The spurs of sweet cherries remain fruitful for as long as 10 years. A minimal amount of pruning is needed each year to initiate new fruiting spurs (Figure 23). Because the growth habit of cherries is very upright, leave spreading lateral branches when you prune these trees. Vigorous upright shoots that interfere with main scaffold growth are common and require frequent pruning out.

Nectarines, Peaches. Flower buds of nectarines and peaches grow on 1-year-old shoots. The shoots can be pruned to thin out the canopy, reduce the fruit set, and stimulate shoot growth for new fruiting wood for the following season (Figure 24). Because shoots are easily shaded out, be sure to prune enough to allow sunlight to reach the lower fruiting wood on the tree without exposing the major scaffold limbs to the risk of sunburn. Thin out the fruiting wood by cutting back lateral branches and removing some shoots completely to give an even distribution of fruiting wood along the scaffold limbs. Remove upright, vigorous shoots completely. Cling peaches are often pruned less severely, with the result of shorter shoot growth the following year. Top all peaches and nectarines each year to maintain tree height.

European Plums, Prunes. Spurs on European plums are fairly long-lived, so only moderate thinning of lateral wood is needed each year to maintain fruiting spurs. By pruning lightly after a heavy crop and heavily after a light crop, you will help compensate for European plums' tendency to be alternate bearing. Varieties that are more vigorous and upright growing should be topped each year.

French prunes need to be thinned back to a few large, lateral branches to encourage upward, outward growth and to replace older fruiting wood. Remove interfering and broken limbs. Long pruning, where secondary branches are not headed back when selected during the second dormant pruning, may be used to increase early fruit production. There are potential problems associated with long pruning, however. A heavy fruit load may bend or break the long branches, the production of lateral branches may suffer, and the branches' increased wind resistance may be a problem in some locations.

Japanese Plums. The fruit set of Japanese plums varies widely among varieties. Those varieties that set heavy crops require extensive pruning of spur wood each year to reduce the crop. You can head back lateral branches after extensive spur growth has developed. You need not remove so much fruit wood from Japanese plums that set lighter crops, but a thorough pruning is necessary each year. Top the trees to a constant height each year by cutting the upright shoots back without leaving stubs.

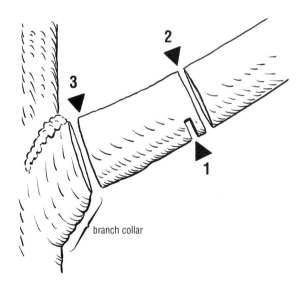

branch collar

Figure 19. When removing limbs larger than about 2 inches (5 cm) in diameter, make three cuts in the order shown here. Make the first cut about one-fourth of the way through the limb 1 or 2 feet (30 to 60 cm) out from the main scaffold. Make the second cut from above, about 2 inches farther out that the first cut. Cut off the remaining stub with the third cut at the edge of the branch collar, about ½ inch out from the trunk or main scaffold.

Figure 20. Most flower buds of apricots, cherries, plums, and prunes are formed on spurs.

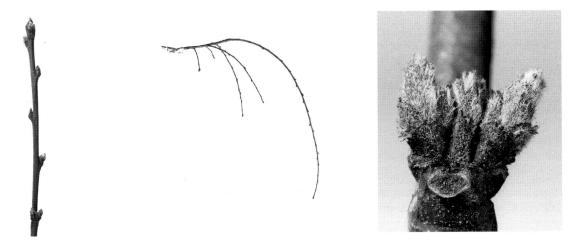

Figure 21. Flower buds of peaches and nectarines develop on one-year-old shoots.

before pruning   after pruning

Figure 22. Apricots, plums, and prunes are pruned to leave some year-old wood for production of fruit buds and to thin out lateral wood so new spurs will be produced.

before pruning

after pruning

Figure 23. Sweet cherries require only minimal pruning to renew fruiting spurs and remove interfering branches.

before pruning

after pruning

Figure 24. Peaches and nectarines are pruned every year to thin out the canopy and leave fruiting shoots positioned uniformly around the tree.

Pollination

All sweet cherries, most Japanese plums, some European plums, and a few varieties of apricot (e.g., Perfection) are not self-fruitful—their own pollen is not able to fertilize their own flowers. These trees require nearby *pollenizers*—trees of other varieties that produce compatible pollen. Some plum varieties can be self-fruitful in one growing area but not in another; for example, Santa Rosa plum is self-fruitful in the San Joaquin Valley but requires pollenizers is some locations of northern California.

Successful pollination requires the careful selection of pollenizer varieties and proper placement of pollenizer trees within the orchard. For optimum pollination, the bloom period of the pollenizer should come shortly before the bloom period of the main variety. Tables 4 and 5 list common stone fruit varieties that are compatible as pollenizers. Some self-fruitful plum varieties, such as Santa Rosa and Wickson, are considered "universal pollenizers" because they can be used as pollenizers for all other plums.

Pollenizer Placement. A common orchard arrangement when planting an equal number of two compatible varieties is to alternate four rows of one variety with four rows of the other in the orchard interior, with two rows of one variety or the other at the edge of the orchard. You need to choose two good market varieties if this arrangement is to be practical. Where one variety is preferred at market but both are to be harvested, alternate four inside rows of the preferred variety with two inside rows of the pollenizer, and plan the orchard so the two outside rows on both sides are of the preferred variety. These arrangements optimize management activities such as irrigation, thinning, and harvest. However, both

Table 4. Pollenizers for Japanese and European Plums.

Variety to be pollinated	Ambra	Autumn Rosa	Blackamber	Casselman	Durado	El Dorado	Friar	Grand Rosa	July Santa Rosa	Laroda	Late Santa Rosa	Nubiana	Queen Ann	Queen Rosa	Red Rosa	Roysum	Santa Rosa	Simka	Wickson
Angeleno								G									G		G
Blackamber	G	G	P		G	G	F			P	F			G	G		F	F	F
Black Beaut	G			F			F	F	F	F	F				F		F		F
Casselman*																			
Catalina							F			F							F		F
El Dorado			F		G	P	F			G	G	F	P	P		F	G		G
Friar†			F	F						F	F					F	F		F
Grand Rosa*																			
July Santa Rosa*																			
Kelsey			F			F					F						G		G
Laroda			P	F	P	G		G	P	G	G	F	F	F	F		G		F
Nubiana*																			
Queen Ann					G	P	F			G	G	P	P	P	F		G		F
Queen Rosa			G			G				G	F				P		G	G	F
Red Beaut	G	G			F		P	F	F	F	F				F	F	F		F
Red Rosa																F			
Red Roy													F						
Rosemary			F			F						F						F	
Royal Diamond																		F	
Royal Red		G							F	F	F					F	F		F
Roysum*																			
Santa Rosa*																			
Simka*																			
Spring Beaut	G				F		F	F			F					F	F		F
Wickson					F												G		P

Empress—*P. domestica* (European). Use President or French Prune

President—*P. domestica* (European). Use Sugar, Standard, or French Prune

G = Good fruit set most years. F = Fair fruit set most years. P = Poor fruit or no fruit set most years. * = Self-fruitful, usually does not need a pollenizer.
† = Fruitful, most years, scattered pollenizers help some years.

varieties must have good market value. Also, in such an arrangement poor weather may reduce fruit set substantially, because only the trees next to pollenizers may set fruit.

Where you have no intention of harvesting the pollenizer variety, you can use a minimum number of pollenizers placed such that every tree of the main variety is next to a pollenizer. This can be achieved with a ratio of 1 pollenizer tree to 9 trees of the main variety, such that every third tree in every third row is a pollenizer. This arrangement is common in cherries, as are ratios of 1:12 or 1:15, for which every fourth or fifth tree of every third row is a pollenizer. An alternative sometimes used for plums involves planting pollenizers down alternate alleys, between alternate pairs of trees, and staggered to be halfway between the spacings of the main variety. In such an arrangement, each pollenizer tree is trained to form a single trunk that branches 8 to 10 feet above the ground. Spaced and trained in this way, the pollenizers provide every main variety tree with adequate pollen while taking up a minimum of orchard space. The pollenizers' fruit can be knocked to the ground if harvest is impractical.

Pollenizer Limbs. The grafting of one limb of a pollenizer onto each tree of the main variety is a practical alternative to planting separate pollenizer trees. This gives each tree a pollen source while allowing solid blocks of the main variety. This is a good method to use for plum varieties that are difficult to pollinate; these trees often are not attractive to bees, so the presence of the pollinator limb will help attract bees and increase their activity within the tree, besides providing a nearby source of pollen.

Graft pollenizer limbs onto young trees after the first or second season of growth. First leave an extra limb in the northwest corner of each tree at pruning, and then whip-graft the pollenizer onto this limb 2 to 3 feet above the crotch. After the graft begins to grow in the spring, prune away interfering growth from the main limb but allow the main limb to grow toward the outside of the tree to build a fruit-bearing scaffold around the pollenizer. Train the pollenizer limb to form one or two vigorous shoots up the center of the tree. It is a good idea to mark the pollenizer limb with white latex paint so pruning crews do not remove it by mistake. Prune the pollenizer limb after bloom to allow the maximum number of pollenizer blossoms to form.

Usually it is not economical to harvest fruit from the pollenizer limbs. Unless you do intend to harvest the pollenizer fruit, have it knocked from the pollenizer limbs early in the season to prevent limb breakage. Use two or three different pollenizer varieties throughout the orchard to ensure that bloom periods will overlap. If the main variety is easy to pollinate, graft pollenizer limbs only onto occasional trees spaced evenly throughout the orchard. If the variety is difficult to pollinate, graft a pollenizer limb onto every tree. The production of some plum varieties declines after 15 to 20 years; sometimes you can improve their fruit set by grafting a pollenizer limb onto a standard near the top of the tree.

Table 5. Pollenizers for Sweet Cherries Commonly Grown in California.[1]

Variety to be pollinated	Potential pollenizers
Bing	Black Tartarian, Early Burlat, Lambert, Rainier, Royal Ann
Black Tartarian	Bing, Early Burlat, Lambert, Rainier, Royal Ann
Brooks	Bing, Early Burlat, Rainier
Early Burlat	Bing, Black Tartarian, Lambert, Royal Ann
Garnet	Ruby, possibly others
King	Bing, Brooks, Jubilee, Tulare
Lambert	Black Tartarian, Early Burlat, Rainier
Rainier	Bing, Black Tartarian, Early Burlat, Lambert, Royal Ann
Royal Ann (Napoleon)	Black Tartarian, Early Burlat, Rainier
Ruby	Bing, Lambert, Rainier, Royal Ann
Tulare	Bing, Brooks

1. Information on more varieties can be found in *California Sweet Cherry Production Workshop Proceedings*, listed in the references.

Managing Bees. Many wild insects forage for nectar and pollen in stone fruit blossoms, but honey bees are the primary pollinators for all stone fruits. You will improve fruit set greatly in sweet cherries, plums, and prunes by hiring professional beekeepers to place hives in or adjacent to the orchard. One or two hives per acre usually are sufficient. A minimum strength hive has at least six frames of bees and a queen actively laying eggs. With an active queen and at least one frame of "open brood" (larvae), the bees will be foraging more actively for pollen, which they use primarily to produce food for the queen and larvae. You can hire inspectors to verify and certify hive strength (check with your county agricultural commissioner). Follow these guidelines for placing and managing hives.

- Place hives in the orchards when first blossoms open. Bees immediately scout for food sources, and will work the first one they find until it is no longer attractive.

- One or two hives per acre of orchard usually are sufficient. Commercial beekeepers often cluster the bees in groups of 6 to 12 hives to facilitate management.

- Place hives around the perimeter of orchard blocks smaller than 20 acres. For a long orchard, place more of the hives near the middle of the long sides.

- For larger orchards, place hives along drive rows in the middle of the orchard blocks.

- Place hives in the warmest, driest locations possible, in weed-free locations away from tall grass, and preferably where morning sun will warm the hives. The sooner hives warm up in the morning, the sooner the bees will begin to forage. Bees do not fly when the air temperature is below 55°F (13°C) or when the wind velocity is at or above 12 miles per hour. You can put black plastic or tar paper under hives to increase warming.

- Control weeds, and keep cover crops mowed as needed to eliminate the presence of competing blooms in the orchard.
- Hive inserts containing pollenizer pollen, bouquets of pollenizer flowers, pollen traps, and bee attractants have been shown to improve pollination only under abnormal circumstances, and are in most cases unnecessary.
- In very high-value crops such as cherries, growers sometimes have beehives removed from the orchard before bloom has finished but after there has been enough cross-pollination to encourage fewer but larger fruit.

Africanized Bees. At the time of this writing, Africanized bees are present in southeastern California, but they have not yet moved into any of the major stone fruit production areas. In parts of the world where these bees have become established, beekeepers have adopted new practices that allow them to continue managing their hives, both for honey production and crop pollination.

Management techniques for Africanized honey bees:

- Wear adequate protective clothing when working with the hives.
- Move the hives at night to reduce agitation and reduce the likelihood that colonies will abscond.
- When foraging conditions are poor, provide the bees with syrup to reduce the likelihood that colonies will abscond. If you move a colony to a new location where food is less available, the bees usually leave.
- Keep hives replenished with European queens to dilute the Africanized bee gene pool.

Fruit Thinning

Apricot, nectarine, peach, plum, and prune orchards usually need to have some fruit removed before ripening, because they set more fruit than they can bring to marketable size. This kind of thinning increases fruit size at harvest and market quality, and reduces the likelihood that limbs will break by reducing the fruit load. Some stone fruit varieties will tend to become alternate bearing if they are not thinned. Thinning also provides an opportunity to remove misshapen or injured fruit.

As a general rule, the best time to thin fruit is when they are ¾ to 1 inch (19 to 25 mm) in diameter. At this stage, you can remove fruit that has been damaged by insects, disease, or hail, frost danger should be past, and natural thinning will have occurred for those varieties affected by June drop. The exact timing for a given orchard will depend on variety, local weather conditions, and desired final fruit size. Early-maturing varieties are thinned earlier. In some cases, blossom thinning of early varieties may be desirable, with no thinning of late-maturing or self-thinning varieties. Earlier thinning results in larger fruit. In years when fruit set is very heavy, it may be a good idea to perform a partial thinning early to remove excess fruit, and then thin again later to achieve the desired final fruit load.

Vigor and available leaf area affect the tree's ability to support fruit growth. Younger orchards tend to produce larger fruit. Fruit size tends to be less after low-chilling winters or when late season weather is hot. Balance the size and yield against the market return for the fruit. Each orchard has its own sizing potential for different fruit loads. Consult past seasons' records for your orchard to help you plan thinning operations or, for a new orchard, check the performance of other orchards of the same variety grown in the same area.

The most practical and reliable approach for thinning to a given fruit load is to use a combination of distance between fruit on a shoot and number of fruit on a tree. You want to leave more fruit on the top of the tree and on the more vigorous outer branches, so you will have less distance between fruit after thinning in these locations. Thin to a wider spacing on the shaded inner branches. When fruit set is irregular, leave more fruit in locations with a heavier set to compensate for other locations where the set is light or fruit is lacking.

Keep records of fruit loads and final yields and sizes so you can make adjustments next season. The relationship between the number of fruit per tree and the final fruit size will remain fairly constant for a number of years. Early-season peaches and nectarines are thinned to 300 to 900 fruit per tree; mid- and late-season varieties are thinned to 800 to 1,500 fruit per tree. The numbers for plums are higher, and the numbers for apricots are determined by tree spacing and market destination. Cherries are not thinned.

Begin to thin by establishing an approximate fruit spacing that will give you the desired number of fruit per tree on a few trees, and then have pruning crews use this as a guide. Check their work periodically, and have them make adjustments if necessary.

Mechanical Thinning. You can thin prunes and cling peaches mechanically using shakers. Extra care must be taken not to injure the bark on the trunk when using shakers for this purpose; because the trees are receiving ample moisture at this time of year, their bark is injured much more easily than at harvest.

Generally, the best time to thin prunes is shortly after the pits begin to harden. You can determine how long to shake each tree by testing different shake times on a few trees and noting how many seconds it takes to remove the desired amount of fruit. The number of fruit you want to leave on the tree should be based on your goal for fruit size, the sizing potential of the orchard, and the amount of fruit drop you expect will occur between thinning and harvest. For example, if the orchard can carry 5,000 fruit per tree to the desired harvest size and you expect a fruit drop of about 20%, you should shake to leave about 6,000 fruit per tree (20% more than 5,000).

In cling peaches, mechanical thinning is used to reduce the amount of time required for additional hand thinning and the overall expense of thinning operations. The best time to thin is about 45 days after full bloom. Trees should be mechanically thinned to about 150% of the final desired fruit load, and then hand thinned to the desired number of fruit per tree. As with prunes, you should determine the exact amount of time to shake each tree (generally about 3 seconds) by testing different shake times on a few trees in the orchard.

Chemical Thinning. By applying certain growth regulators to stone fruits in early summer, you can reduce fruit set the following year and reduce or eliminate the need for hand thinning. At the time of this writing a few materials are registered for this purpose. Check with your farm advisor for more information on chemical thinning.

Girdling

Girdling is the practice of removing a thin strip of bark around the trunk or the scaffold limbs to increase fruit size and yield and accelerate maturity in early-season fresh market peaches and nectarines. A strip of bark ⅛ to ³⁄₁₆ inch (3 to 5 mm) wide is removed down to the cambium layer with a grape girdling knife. This interrupts the flow of photosynthate downward for a short time, increasing its availability for fruit production. Take care not to cut deeper than the cambium or you will cut off upward water flow, severely stressing or even killing the limb or tree. In California, growers girdle trees 4 to 6 weeks before harvest for peaches and nectarines that ripen before mid-June. If trees are girdled too early, the incidence of split pits increases; if too late, there is no response. Girdling is not used for other peach and nectarine varieties or for other stone fruits.

If you plan to use girdling, be sure to have it done by workers skilled in the procedure. Determine the proper timing for your location. Make sure the trees are not stressed for water or nutrients or by pest damage. Do not girdle trees that are younger than 4 years old. Girdling may increase the risk of infection by wood decay fungi and pathogens that cause Cytospora canker and Ceratocystis canker

Fertilization

Most orchard soils in California contain adequate levels of most nutrients to support tree growth and fruit production. For most of these soils and most stone fruits, the only nutrient that must be added regularly is nitrogen. Prunes commonly need periodic supplements of potassium. In some cases zinc, magnesium, or manganese amendments may be needed.

The best way to assess the nutrient status of your orchard is to take leaf samples in July and have them analyzed. Take a leaf from each of 60 to 100 shoots or spurs, selected randomly from throughout the orchard. Sample leaves from the middle of moderately vigorous fruiting shoots of nectarines and peaches; sample leaves from nonfruiting spurs of apricots, cherries, plums, and prunes. Take separate samples from areas of the orchard that show signs of nutrient deficiency. Wash the leaves, dry them at 150° to 160°F (66° to 72°C), and send them to a laboratory for analysis. Table 6 lists leaf nutrient levels that are considered optimum and deficient.

Nitrogen. Nitrogen is the only major nutrient that needs regular amendment in stone fruit orchards. Take care to provide sufficient nitrogen to support new growth and fruit production while avoiding excess shoot growth. Excess nitrogen increases problems with peach twig borer, oriental fruit moth, and brown rot.

Stone fruit trees usually need additions of 100 to 150 pounds of nitrogen per acre each season to maintain adequate levels. The actual amount needed depends on the variety, status of the trees, soil type, ground cover, water supply, and irrigation method. Early-season varieties need less nitrogen because less is removed by the crop, and too much nitrogen

Table 6. Leaf Concentrations in Midsummer that Indicate Adequate or Deficient Levels of Nutrients in Stone Fruits.[1]

Nutrient	APRICOT Deficient if below	APRICOT Optimum range	CHERRY Deficient if below	CHERRY Optimum range	NECTARINE, PEACH Deficient if below	NECTARINE, PEACH Optimum range	PLUM, PRUNE Deficient if below	PLUM, PRUNE Optimum range
Macronutrients (levels in %):								
calcium[2]	—	>2.0	—	>1.0	—	>1.0	—	>1.0
magnesium	—	—	—	>0.25	0.25	>0.25	0.25	>0.25
nitrogen	1.8	2–2.5	—	2.0–3.0	2.3	2.6–3.0	—	2.3–2.8
phosphorus	—	—	—	0.1–0.3	—	0.1–0.3	—	0.1–0.3
potassium	2.0	>2.5	0.9	>0.9	1.0	>1.2	1.0	>1.1
sulfur[2]								
Micronutrients (levels in ppm):								
boron	15	20–70	20	20–80	18	20–80	25	30–80
chlorine[2]	—	toxic >2,000	—	—	—	toxic >3,000	—	toxic >3,000
copper	—	—	—	>4	—	>4	4	>4
manganese	—	—	—	>20	20	>20	20	>30
molybdenum[2]								
zinc	—	>16	—	>14	15	>20	18	>18

1. For peaches and nectarines, leaves from the basal half of moderately vigorous fruiting shoots 10 to 20 inches long are sampled. For apricots, cherries, plums, and prunes, leaves from non-fruiting spurs are sampled.
2. Deficiency not known to occur in California.

would trigger excessive undesirable vegetative growth after harvest. Trees that are deficient may initially need more nitrogen to overcome the deficiency, while trees that are overly vigorous should receive no nitrogen fertilizer for 1 or 2 years. Soils vary in the amount of nitrogen they make available to the trees. Ground covers may add to available nitrogen or may compete for the nutrient. A properly managed legume ground cover may contribute a substantial portion of a stone fruit crop's seasonal nitrogen requirement. Low-volume irrigation systems apply nitrogen fertilizer more efficiently; use about half the regular application rate when applying nitrogen in this way. Some water supplies contain substantial amounts of nitrate; have your water tested for nitrate, and take this into account when estimating seasonal fertilizer requirements, using the formula:

1 ppm of nitrate = 2.7 pounds of N per acre-foot of water applied.

Symptoms of nitrogen deficiency are described and illustrated in the chapter on diseases. Nitrogen deficiency is easy to correct by applying nitrogen fertilizer to the soil. Various materials are available; the best choice depends on soil characteristics of the orchard and your specific requirements. Ammonium fertilizer is least expensive, but must be incorporated immediately to avoid loss to volatilization (conversion to ammonia gas), and is taken up more slowly than other forms because it first must be converted to nitrate by soil microbes. Nitrate fertilizers are available to tree roots immediately upon application. Some forms of ammonium nitrate can be injected through low-volume sprinklers. Manure and other organic fertilizers can be useful for improving soil structure, but they release nitrogen more slowly than other forms and may add undesirable salts to the soil. When applying fertilizer to correct a deficiency, schedule the application in late summer, after harvest. In peaches, nectarines, plums, and prunes, you can also apply materials in early spring after growth has resumed. On sandy soils, split the application between late summer and early spring to minimize the loss of nitrogen to leaching. Apply nitrogen fertilizer to apricots and cherries after harvest. Do not apply nitrogen fertilizer during the dormant season, because the trees draw little water or nutrients from the soil at that time, and much of the nitrogen will be lost to leaching, volatilization, and denitrification. Late spring or early summer applications are too late to affect fruit growth, and they will just stimulate excessive vegetative growth. If you apply nitrogen through low-volume sprinklers, apply the material in smaller increments spread over an extended period.

To maintain optimum nitrogen levels, take leaf samples every year for nutrient analysis. Adjust your fertilizer program to maintain leaf nitrogen in the optimum range listed in Table 6. Avoid excessive nitrogen levels. Too much nitrogen increases pest problems, delays fruit maturity, decreases red coloration of fruit, and stimulates excessive vegetative growth that can shade out fruiting wood lower on the tree.

Zinc. Deficiencies in zinc occur commonly in stone fruits. Zinc deficiency is most likely to occur on sandy soils, where orchards are planted on old corral or feedlot sites, or where soils have been amended with large amounts of manure. Zinc applications are made routinely to fresh market stone fruit orchards. Zinc can be applied as a zinc sulfate spray at a rate of 10 to 15 pounds per acre, anytime from about 50% leaf fall until the end of the dormant season. Do not apply zinc sulfate within three weeks before or after a dormant oil spray. You can apply neutral or basic zinc with dormant oil sprays; use the same rate as for zinc sulfate. If zinc deficiency symptoms develop in the spring, apply a foliar spray of chelated zinc while leaves are still expanding. Neutral or basic zinc can be applied in spring or early summer, but may leave deposits on fruit and may damage foliage if it rains shortly after application. In orchards with chronic zinc deficiency, soil applications of zinc sulfate may be helpful; the correct application rate depends on the soil type, age of the orchard, and severity of the deficiency.

Potassium. Potassium deficiency is common in Sacramento Valley prunes, especially when the crop is heavy. Deficiencies also occur occasionally in other stone fruits. Soil applications of 3 to 4 pounds of potassium sulfate per tree each year or 20 pounds per tree every 3 or 4 years are recommended in prune orchards where deficiency is a problem. Foliar applications of potassium nitrate may be used as a supplement to maintain healthy foliage when deficiency symptoms develop, but should not be used as a substitute for soil application of potassium.

Other Nutrients. In some circumstances, you will need to apply nutrients other than nitrogen or zinc. Seasonal leaf analysis will tell you the status of most of these mineral nutrients. Phosphorus deficiency is rare in stone fruits because the trees' phosphorus requirement is low and trees recycle the nutrient from leaves very efficiently. Iron deficiency is fairly common in stone fruits, most frequently as a result of high levels of bicarbonate, caused by waterlogging or poor soil aeration, that interfere with the trees' utilization of iron. Correction of this condition, "lime-induced chlorosis," requires the improvement of soil aeration or drainage. In some cases acidification of the soil is an effective remedy. Additions of iron fertilizer may not correct the problem. Manganese, magnesium, and copper deficiencies occur occasionally. Boron deficiencies are fairly common in orchards with coarse-textured soils on the east side of the San Joaquin Valley. Foliar applications of 1 to 2 pounds of boron per acre can alleviate the deficiency. Boron toxicity is a frequent problem. Because of its potential for toxicity, boron should only be applied in small amounts. Boron toxicity is fairly common on the west side of the San Joaquin Valley, where soil levels of boron are high. Deficiency and toxicity symptoms are described in the chapter on diseases.

Irrigation

Adequate water is essential for optimum orchard growth and fruit production. If a young orchard does not receive adequate water, trees will take longer to reach their full production capacity or they may remain stunted. Early-season water stress in mature orchards can reduce fruit yields. If water stress is followed by a heavy irrigation, fruit may split. Excessive or improper irrigation can cause problems with Phytophthora root and crown rot and may create conditions favorable for diseases such as brown rot and powdery mildew.

Irrigation Methods. Surface (flood and furrow), sprinkler, or localized (drip and low-volume sprinkler) irrigation can be used for stone fruit orchards. Each method can provide adequate water when properly managed, but each may have a different effect on pest management. The best choice for a given orchard depends on soil texture, terrain, the source of water, the cost and availability of water, installation and operation costs, and the need for frost protection.

Surface Irrigation. Water can be supplied to an orchard most quickly by flood or furrow irrigation of properly leveled soil, so long as water is available at sufficient head pressure. The speed of application may be important where the rapid onset of hot weather will stress trees if they are not immediately irrigated. Energy inputs are smaller for surface irrigation because gravity is used to distribute the water. Water infiltration may be less uniform, as soil infiltration rates can vary across the orchard and water has more time to penetrate the soil at the head end of the orchard. Surface irrigation requires labor to set up and modify the temporary levees or furrows used to direct the flow of water. Where trees are on berms, you can minimize the need for this activity by using the berms themselves as levees.

Some pest problems may increase as a result of surface irrigation. Water that comes from sources such as canals or rivers may be contaminated with weed seeds or pathogens that will spread through the orchard in the irrigation water. Surface irrigation, especially flooding, may discourage ground squirrels and pocket gophers, but if trees are planted on permanent berms that remain dry during irrigations, these pests' burrowing activity may become concentrated on the berms where it is potentially more damaging to trees.

Sprinkler Irrigation. Properly designed sprinkler systems will apply water evenly to the orchard floor and can achieve greater infiltration uniformity than surface irrigation. Sprinkler systems usually apply water at a rate that is less than the soil infiltration rate, so they can be designed to achieve uniform infiltration throughout the orchard. Sprinklers allow low application rates on soils where surface irrigation would create problems involving runoff or standing water. Sprinklers require less labor than surface irrigation, but energy costs are greater. Sprinklers can also be used for frost protection and for application of some fertilizers and herbicides. Problems with diseases such as shot hole, powdery mildew, and Phytophthora pruning wound canker (aerial Phytophthora) can increase if the sprinklers keep foliage or branches wet for prolonged periods.

Localized Irrigation. Drip irrigation and low-volume sprinklers apply water to a smaller portion of the orchard floor than other methods. The root zone of a tree irrigated by these methods is smaller and the volume of water in the soil around the roots is lower than it is for other methods. For these reasons, drip and low-volume methods require that you apply water more frequently to replenish the soil reservoir. Localized irrigation uses considerably less water during orchard establishment because it applies water to a smaller surface area, so soil evaporation is reduced. Less water is usually needed by a mature orchard, because well-managed drip systems and low-volume sprinklers allow more uniform water applications. Localized irrigation interferes less with orchard management activities and works well on soils with low infiltration rates. Localized irrigation systems can easily be set up for automatic operation by time clock.

Set-up and maintenance costs are high for localized irrigation systems. Clogged emitters constitute a major problem, but this can be reduced if you use filters to remove particulates or chemical injection to control salt precipitation or growth of algae or slime. A lack of reserve soil moisture may be a problem at times of peak water demand. Drip systems must be designed to meet the maximum expected water demand; otherwise, water-stressed trees will produce less fruit.

Drip irrigation may reduce the effectiveness of preemergence herbicides, since the breakdown of these chemicals will be accelerated in the soil that remains moist around emitters. Accelerated breakdown is less of a problem with low-volume sprinklers because the soil can dry out between irrigations. Localized irrigation does not increase disease problems, since these methods do not wet the scaffold and canopy, and they generate less humidity than other irrigation methods.

Irrigation Scheduling. For orchards grown on well-drained soils, a water budget is the best tool for determining when to irrigate the orchard and how much water to apply. To make a water budget you need to know:

- the depth of the root zone
- the water-holding capacity of the soil in the root zone
- the rate of water consumption for your crop
- the irrigation efficiency of the method you plan to use

Soil is about half solid material by volume (large circle). The rest of the soil volume consists of pore spaces between soil particles. Pore spaces hold varying proportions of air and water (small circle).

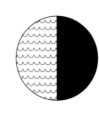

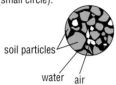

soil particles

water   air

When the soil is **saturated** after irrigation or rain, pore spaces are filled with water.

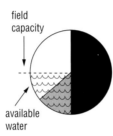

field capacity

available water

When soil has drained following irrigation, it is at **field capacity**. In most soils, about half of the pore space is filled with water. About half of this water is **available** to plants; the rest is unavailable because too much suction is needed to remove it from pore spaces. The proportion of soil water that is available is higher in clays and lower in sandy soils.

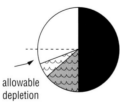

allowable depletion

The **allowable depletion** is the proportion of the available water the crop can use before irrigation is needed.

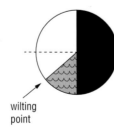

wilting point

At the **wilting point**, all available water is gone. Plants die unless water is added.

Figure 25. The soil reservoir.

A water budget is easiest to use with localized irrigation methods, because rooting zone depth and soil water-holding capacity are less important for these methods, and their irrigation efficiency is easier to estimate. The use of water budgets to schedule irrigation is not recommended for soils with high water tables or for locations where no reliable evapotranspiration (ET) data are available.

Water-holding Capacity. The soil acts as a reservoir, holding water following a rain or irrigation event (Figure 25). About half of the soil volume comprises pore spaces, and about half of these spaces are filled with water when the soil is at *field capacity* (i.e., when the soil has drained following saturation by rain or irrigation). The portion of this water that can be extracted by plant roots is the *available moisture,* and its proportion varies depending on soil texture. Table 7 lists available moisture figures for various soil types. To determine the water-holding capacity of the root zone, you need to measure the rooting depth and the thicknesses of different soil types throughout the root zone. Use a soil auger to measure the thickness of each soil type within the soil profile, and examine the soil for the presence of tree roots to determine rooting depth. You can determine the soil texture by judging its feel and appearance (Table 8) or, if available, by consulting soil maps prepared by the USDA Natural Resources Conservation Service. Multiply the available moisture for each soil type by the thickness of that soil type and total them to obtain the water-holding capacity of the root zone (Figure 26).

Allowable Depletion. Trees become stressed for water before they have withdrawn all of the available moisture within the rooting zone. The proportion of available water that can be withdrawn before trees become vulnerable to water stress is the *allowable depletion.* The actual amount of that water is the *yield threshold depletion.* The allowable depletion depends on the tree's growth stage, its rooting depth, the soil texture, and weather conditions. The allowable depletion is lower when the rooting depth is shallower, the soil is finer textured, or the rate of water loss is greater as a result of warmer, drier conditions. To prevent yield reductions, use a low allowable depletion (30% or less) during bloom and rapid fruit growth, and a higher allowable depletion (50%) for the rest of the season. Multiply the total available water content of the root zone by the allowable depletion to determine the yield threshold depletion—the amount of soil water loss you can permit between irrigations.

Rate of Water Consumption. You can measure the orchard's water consumption by keeping records of *crop evapotranspiration* (ETc), which is the combined total of the water that is taken up by the trees and the water that evaporates from the soil surface. ETc is calculated from daily reference evapotranspiration (ETo) and a crop coefficient (Kc). Daily ETo values are based on the ET of a cool-season grass under local weather conditions, and are available from some local newspapers,

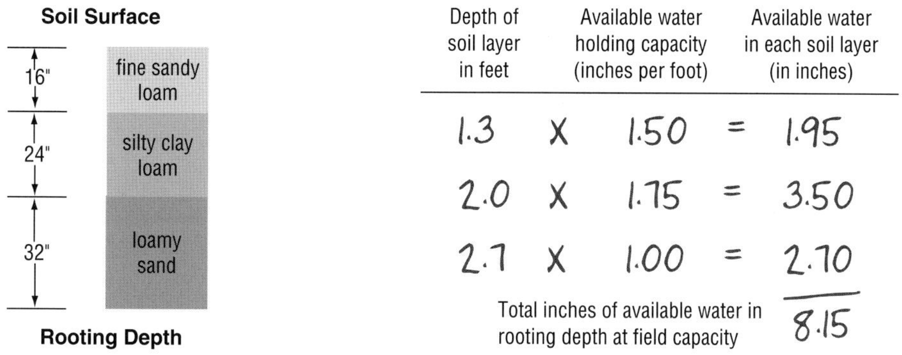

Soil Surface

16"	fine sandy loam
24"	silty clay loam
32"	loamy sand

Rooting Depth

Depth of soil layer in feet		Available water holding capacity (inches per foot)		Available water in each soil layer (in inches)
1.3	X	1.50	=	1.95
2.0	X	1.75	=	3.50
2.7	X	1.00	=	2.70

Total inches of available water in rooting depth at field capacity   8.15

Figure 26. To calculate how much water the soil can hold at field capacity, first examine the soil profile to determine the thickness of different soil textures present in the root zone. Multiply the thickness of each layer, in feet, by its water-holding capacity, and add the results for all layers to get the total water-holding capacity of the root zone.

Table 7. Available Water for Various Soil Types.

	AVAILABLE MOISTURE	
Soil type	Range (in/ft)	Average (in/ft)
very coarse to coarse texture—sand	0.5–1.00	0.75
moderately coarse-texture—sandy loams and fine-texture—sandy loams	1.00–1.50	1.25
medium-texture—very fine sandy loams to silty clay loams	1.25–1.75	1.50
fine and very fine texture—silty clay to clay	1.50–2.50	2.00
peats and mucks	2.00–3.00	2.50

Table 8. Judging Soil Texture and Water Content by Feel and Appearance.[1]

Coarse-textured soils	Inches of water needed	Medium-textured soils	Inches of water needed	Fine-textured soils	Inches of water needed
Soil looks and feels moist, forms a cast ball, and stains hand.	0.0	Soil dark, feels smooth, and will form a ball; when squeezed it ribbons out between fingers and leaves wet outline on hand.	0.0	Soil dark, may feel sticky, stains hand; ribbons easily when squeezed and forms a good ball.	0.0
Soil dark, stains hand slightly; forms a weak ball when squeezed.	0.3	Soil dark, feels slick, stains hand; works easily and forms ball or cast.	0.5	Soil dark, feels slick, stains hand; ribbons easily and forms a good ball.	0.7
Soil forms a fragile cast when squeezed.	0.6	Soil crumbly but may form a weak cast when squeezed.	1.0	Soil crumbly but pliable; forms cast or ball, will ribbon; stains hand slightly.	1.4
Soil dry, loose, crumbly.	1.0	Soil crumbly, powdery; barely keeps shape when squeezed.	1.5	Soil hard, firm, cracked; too stiff to work or ribbon.	2.0

1. Numbers in each column are inches of water needed to restore 1 foot of soil depth to field capacity when soil is in the condition indicated.

radio and television broadcasts, the California Department of Water Resources's CIMIS network, and the UC IPM computer. Your local farm advisor can help you identify a source for ETo information.

The crop coefficient (Kc) is determined primarily by the growth and development of the trees, so it changes during the season. Figure 27 shows how Kc changes for a stone fruit orchard. During the period of rapid growth that begins at leaf out (point B in Figure 27), Kc increases at a rate that is approximately linear until about 60 to 65% of the orchard surface is shaded by tree foliage (point C). Kc then remains constant until late in the season when leaves begin to age (point D), and subsequently declines at a rate that is approximately linear until transpiration stops (point E). For stone fruits, the period from the beginning of rapid growth until the beginning of decline (from B to D in Figure 27) takes up 75% of the full season (B to E). Crop coefficients are higher for orchards with cover crops; the appropriate Kc corrections are given in Table 9.

With Figure 27 as a model and using the information in Table 9, you can draw a graph or use a computer to calculate Kc values for your own orchards. Then multiply daily ETo by Kc to get crop evapotranspiration (ETc). Keep a running total of ETc, and schedule irrigations when the total approaches the allowable depletion you determined above. Figure 28 gives an example of how to calculate ETc using ETo and Kc.

The water consumption of a young orchard is less than that of a mature orchard. ETc for a young orchard can be calculated as a percentage of mature orchard ETc using the following equation:

$$P = 2G$$

where P is the percentage of a mature orchard's ETc and G is the percentage of the orchard floor that is shaded by young trees at noon. The young orchard's water consumption becomes equal to that of a mature orchard when ground shading reaches 50% (i.e., P = 100 when G = 50). You can minimize ET losses in young orchards by applying water in

one furrow on either side of the tree row. Such localized irrigation has little or no benefit in a mature orchard.

Irrigation Efficiency. Before you can calculate the actual amount of water you will need to apply, you must know the application efficiency—the proportion of the applied water that will actually be available to the tree. Application efficiency varies with the irrigation method. Table 10 lists approximate application efficiencies for different irrigation methods. You can either hire a private consultant to measure the actual efficiency of your irrigation system or learn how to measure it yourself by contacting the USDA Natural Resources Conservation Service or your local farm advisor. Divide the total ETc since the last irrigation by the percent efficiency and multiply by 100 to get the amount of water you will need to apply.

You may not be able to apply the full amount calculated by the water budget method at one time. The amount you can apply at one time depends on the intake rate of the soil. To minimize problems with root diseases, do not apply more water than the soil can take up in 48 hours. For best protection of rootstocks susceptible to *Phytophthora*, apply only as much water as can be taken up in 24 hours. Adjust the "allowable depletion" to match the soil's ability to take up water, and irrigate more often.

Midseason ET remains fairly constant from one season to the next. Therefore, when more frequent irrigations are needed, you can use historical average ETo values (available from CIMIS for locations throughout California) to predict when the next irrigation will be needed and to calculate the amount of water to apply. Keep track of actual local ET values so you can compensate at the next irrigation if you have over- or under-irrigated by using the average ET.

Measuring Soil Moisture. You can use measurements of soil moisture to confirm water budget calculations and to check that the soil profile has been replenished after an irrigation. Several techniques are available. You can use a soil tube or auger to take soil samples from the root zone, and check the soil sample's moisture content with the soil-feel technique

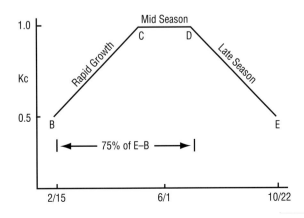

Figure 27. The crop coefficient (Kc) changes during the season. Dates given are averages for orchards in the Central Valley. Kc values for stone fruits at points B, C, and E in the graph are given in Table 9. Kc values for a date between B and C are calculated as:

$$Kc = \text{\# days after date B} \times \frac{Kc \text{ at C} - Kc \text{ at B}}{\text{doy at C} - \text{doy at B}}$$

where doy is the day of year. For the above example, Kc = (# of days since Feb. 15) × (0.5/106).

Orchard/Crop _Fantasia nectarine, Fresno Co. no cover crop_

Soil _fine sandy loam, silty clay loam, loamy sand_

Available Water _1.00 - 1.75 in/ft (from table 7)_

Rooting Depth _6 ft_

Total available Water _8.15 in at field capacity (from fig. 26)_

Allowable Depletion _30% before pit hardening = 2.4 in., 50% after = 4.1 in._

Irrigation Efficiency _70% (border strip)_

Gross Irrigation Requirement _2.4/0.70 = 3.4 in., 4.1/0.70 = 5.9 in._

Date	ETo (inches)	Kc[1]	ETc = ETo x Kc	Cumulative ETc	Remarks
3/1 - 3/7	0.51	0.56	0.29	0	Subtract 0.52 total rainfall
3/8 - 3/14	0.51	0.59	0.30	0	Subtract 1.22 total rainfall
3/15 - 3/21	0.83	0.62	0.51	0.51	
3/22 - 3/28	1.03	0.64	0.66	0	Subtract 2.36 total rainfall
3/29 - 4/4	0.97	0.67	0.65	0.65	
4/5 - 4/11	1.31	0.69	0.90	1.55	
4/12 - 4/18	1.18	0.72	0.85	2.40	
4/19 - 4/25	1.29	0.75	0.98	3.38	Irrigation (3.38/0.70 = 4.83")
4/26 - 5/2	1.69	0.77	1.30	1.30	
5/3 - 5/9	1.73	0.80	1.38	2.68	
5/10 - 5/16	1.42	0.83	1.18	3.86	
5/17 - 5/23	1.65	0.85	1.40	5.21	Irrigation (5.21/0.70 = 7.44")
5/24 - 5/30	1.59	0.88	1.40	1.40	
5/31 - 6/6	1.83	0.90	1.65	3.05	
6/7 - 6/13	1.93	0.90	1.74	4.79	Irrigation (4.79/0.70 = 6.84")
6/14 - 6/20	1.82	0.90	1.64	1.64	
6/21 - 6/27	1.47	0.90	1.32	2.96	

1. Calculated according to formula given in Figure 27.

Figure 28. Example form for scheduling irrigation using evapotranspiration data. Begin accumulating weekly total ETc at beginning of bloom (first week of March), using data from local weather station. When rainfall occurs, subtract effective rainfall from ET accumulation. Assume soil profile is returned to field capacity when rainfall exceeds ET accumulation. Schedule irrigation for week when ET accumulation is expected to exceed allowable depletion (2.4 inches before pit hardening, 4.1 inches after pit hardening).

Table 9. Early, Middle, and Late Season Kc Values for Stone Fruits in California.[1]

	No cover crop	With cover crop
Kc at point B	0.50	0.85
Kc at point C	0.90	1.20
Kc at point E	0.50	0.75

1. Use these values in conjunction with Figure 27 to estimate Kc and ET values during the season.

Table 10. Application Efficiency (Ea) of Different Irrigation Methods.

Irrigation method	Application efficiency (%)
basin	70–80
border strip	70–80
furrow	65–75
sprinkler	75–85
microsprinkler	80–95
drip	85–95

described in Table 8. Soil moisture levels can be monitored in the ground using gypsum blocks or tensiometers.

A tensiometer measures how tightly water is held by the soil. The relationship between a tensiometer reading and the soil moisture level depends on soil type, depth of placement, and irrigation method. Tensiometers are most useful when several are placed at different depths to check that water has penetrated throughout the root zone following an irrigation. They are particularly useful for verifying that a drip or low-volume sprinkler system is maintaining soil moisture in the root zone. Tensiometers work best in coarse-textured soils; in clay or clay loam soils, gypsum blocks may be more reliable.

Frost Protection

Temperatures can fall below freezing during bloom in most stone fruit growing areas of California. If temperatures are low enough in the orchard, they can injure or kill flower parts or young fruit. Table 11 lists temperatures at which low-temperature injuries begin to occur. Flower parts become more sensitive as bloom progresses, with young fruit being most sensitive. Plums are the most susceptible to frost injury, but all stone fruits can be injured. Damaging temperatures are most likely to occur when the dew point is below 35°F (2°C) at sunset. Monitor temperatures closely when the dew point drops this low during sensitive developmental stages.

The primary means of protection available to stone fruit growers are orchard floor management and irrigation with well water. The expense of maintaining and operating wind machines or orchard heaters usually is prohibitive for stone fruits, although wind machines and helicopters may help break up pockets of cold air that settle in low-lying areas of orchards in hilly terrain.

Orchard Floor Management. On cold nights, orchard temperature can vary by several degrees depending on the condition of the orchard floor. Orchards with smooth, bare, moist soil are warmest, while orchards with freshly disced, dry soil or a tall cover crop are the coldest (Table 12). Bare soil absorbs more solar radiation and moist soil stores more heat than dry soil. For maximum benefit, apply enough water to wet the upper foot of soil before frost injury conditions occur and reapply water as needed during bloom. If you are maintaining a cover crop, keep it mowed during bloom. Do not cultivate the soil

during bloom. If you are planning to turn a cover crop under before bloom, do it far enough in advance to allow yourself time to smooth and irrigate the soil before frost threatens.

Irrigation. Irrigation with well water that is 55° to 65°F (13° to 18°C) will warm the orchard air because the water releases a small amount of heat as it cools. If you are using furrow or flood irrigation, cultivate the orchard and set up the furrows or borders before bloom and apply sufficient irrigation water to smooth the soil surface and wet the upper foot of the soil. This will give the warmest orchard conditions during cold weather and will make it possible for you to apply irrigation water quickly if needed to prevent frost injury. Rapid distribution throughout the orchard gives maximum frost protection. For best protection, the system must deliver 60 to 90 gallons of water per minute per acre. If your system cannot deliver this much water to all the trees, set up the system so you can provide sufficient water to the most valuable varieties. Keep water flowing through the orchard during the frost period; standing water loses its ability to provide frost protection as it cools, and you must keep the water in the orchard from freezing. Start irrigating soon enough to allow the water to reach the ends of all rows before temperatures fall to damaging levels. Make sure the water can drain out of the orchard at the ends of runs, and do not recirculate the tail water.

Drip systems do not apply enough water to provide frost protection. Low-volume sprinklers will provide some protection and can be operated so that the water they apply freezes, releasing even more heat into the orchard. Start sprinklers well in advance of freezing conditions and keep them running throughout the frost period to keep water continuously freezing and releasing heat and to prevent water from freezing in the irrigation lines. High-volume sprinklers provide good frost protection because they can apply large volumes of water quickly to large areas; however, their use in stone fruit orchards increases disease problems and interferes with orchard cultural operations.

Harvest

Proper harvesting and handling will minimize fruit losses to postharvest disease and physical injury. Careful handling is most important for fresh market stone fruits. Be sure picking crews are trained in fruit selection criteria and proper han-

Table 11. Temperatures at Which Developing Flowers and Young Fruit Are Injured.

Stone fruit	Buds showing color	Full bloom	Small green fruit
apricot	25°F (−4°C)	28°F (−2°C)	30°F (−1°C)
cherry	27°F (−3°C)	28°F (−2°C)	30°F (−1°C)
peach, nectarine	25°F (−4°C)	27°F (−3°C)	30°F (−1°C)
plum, prune	25°F (−4°C)	28°F (−2°C)	30°F (−1°C)

Table 12. Effect of Orchard Floor Condition on Air Temperature 5 Feet (1.5 m) above the Orchard Floor.

Orchard floor condition	Relative air temperature
bare, firm, moist soil	warmest
shredded cover crop, moist soil	0.5°F (0.3°C) colder
low-growing cover crop, moist soil	1° to 3°F (0.6° to 1.7°C) colder
dry, firm soil	2°F (1.1°C) colder
freshly disced, fluffy soil	4°F (2.2°C) colder
tall cover crop	2° to 4°F (1.1° to 2.2°C) colder

dling techniques. When using mechanical harvesters, take precautions to avoid injuring the trunk and creating infection sites for the pathogens that cause Ceratocystis and Cytospora cankers.

Before or during harvest, you must sample fruit for pest damage. Examine 500 fruit (100 fruit from each of five areas of the orchard) and record the type of damage found, being as specific as possible about the cause, and the number of fruit affected. The results will help you plan the next year's pest management program.

Pick fruit at proper maturity for the market destination. If fruit is too mature at harvest, it may deteriorate before reaching market. Fruit destined for local markets can be picked more mature than fruit to be shipped long distances. If fruit is not mature enough when harvested, it may ripen abnormally or be of poor quality when ripe. Minimum maturity requirements for a large number of stone fruit varieties are published annually by the California Tree Fruit Agreement, listed in the references.

Avoid causing physical injury to fruit during harvesting and handling. Container liners can reduce abrasions. Do not overfill fruit bins. Take steps to reduce vibration of harvested fruit during transit.

Remove diseased and damaged fruit as early as possible in the harvesting and handling process. Disease organisms spread quickly, especially while fruit are still warm.

Temperature control is the most important tool for controlling postharvest losses. Cool the fruit as soon as possible after harvest. Keep the harvested fruit shaded while in the field and transport the fruit to coolers as frequently as possible, especially on hot days. Avoid harvesting during the middle of the day when temperatures are high. By cooling fruit to near 32°F (0°C), you can reduce disease development, delay ripening and senescence (thus extending the market life), reduce water loss and shriveling of fruit, and minimize the effects of mechanical injury. Forced air cooling and hydrocooling can be used for stone fruits, but vacuum cooling is not recommended. Forced air cooling can be used before or after packing. Hydrocooling is most useful before packing. The best storage temperatures for stone fruits are 31° to 32°F (−0.6° to 0°C), with a relative humidity of 90 to 95%. Chilling injury may develop if fruit are held for long periods at temperatures between 32° and 50°F (0° and 10°C). Normal ripening occurs at 60° to 80°F (15° to 27°C).

More information on postharvest handling practices can be found in *Peaches, Plums, and Nectarines* and *Postharvest Technology of Horticultural Crops*, listed in the references.

Sanitation

A number of pest problems may build up in stone fruit orchards over time. Some pests such as perennial weeds, nematodes, and soilborne diseases can be carried into orchards on contaminated equipment. Follow the sanitation practices listed below to minimize buildup and spread of pest problems in your orchards.

- Prune out brown rot fruit mummies and blighted shoots during the dormant season. If you pruned in early fall, you can leave them on the orchard floor, but you should remove them from the orchard if pruned in late fall or winter.

- Have pruning crews remove all shoots that are heavily infected with shot hole.

- Carefully remove and destroy any limbs infected with *Eutypa*.

- Clean all equipment after using it in areas infested with troublesome weeds, nematodes, or soilborne pests, and before you move it into other orchards.

- Keep the area around the tree crown free of weeds to reduce the threat of crown rot and vole infestations.

- Spot-treat perennial weeds in the orchard as soon as they are found, to keep them from spreading.

- Control weeds around the edges of the orchard to reduce the buildup of voles and prevent the production of weed seeds that will infest the orchard.

- Remove stumps, brush piles, and debris to limit refuge for ground squirrels and prevent the buildup of wood-boring beetles.

- Do not store fruit bins, which might contain pests such as oriental fruit moth and codling moth, next to susceptible orchards.

Pheromone Mating Disruption

The use of pheromones for mating disruption or confusion of males (pheromone confusion) is an environmentally benign form of chemical control used to manage certain lepidopterous (moth) pests. The technique involves placing dispensers of synthetic pheromones in the orchard to mimic the natural chemicals emitted by female moths to attract males for mating. The dispensers saturate the orchard air with pheromone so that males are unable to find females. This greatly reduces or eliminates mating and the production of fertile eggs by the target pest. In stone fruits, pheromone mating disruption can be used to control peach twig borer and oriental fruit moth. Information on available materials and recommended rates can be found in the *UC IPM Pest Management Guidelines* listed in the references.

The success of pheromone confusion depends upon correct timing, proper placement of dispensers, and use of an adequate number of dispensers to control the pest population. The technique is most effective in orchards with low pest populations and orchards that are isolated from untreated hosts of the pests being controlled. Mating disruption may not work well in windy locations, and control is poor in the upper parts of orchards grown on sloping terrain. Control also may be poor in orchards with very high pest populations. In these orchards, you can obtain better results by using higher rates of pheromone, using more point sources, and placing dispensers high in the trees. Pheromone confusion does not harm pollinators or natural enemies; it may, however, take time for natural enemies to build up significant populations in an orchard with a history of pesticide use. Some secondary pests that have been controlled by pesticides used for the target pest will not be controlled by the pheromones intended for the target pest. Monitoring for such pests is critical in orchards where you use mating disruption.

Pesticides

Properly used, pesticides provide effective, economical control for many of the pests that affect stone fruits. Preplant soil fumigation plays an important role in the protection of newly planted trees from harmful nematodes and other soil-borne pests. For most stone fruits, growers make bloomtime applications of fungicides every season to protect against brown rot and other diseases. For other pest problems, it is prudent to use pesticides only when monitoring indicates they are needed to prevent a crop loss.

Using Pesticides. Careful use of pesticides makes them more effective and reduces the likelihood of problems with pesticide resistance, pest resurgence and secondary outbreaks, crop injury, and hazards to humans and the environment. In many cases, several different chemicals or formulations are available for use to control a single pest. In some cases one chemical formulation can be used to control more than one pest problem at a time. Some materials can be applied together, while other pesticide combinations are incompatible and must be avoided. The best choice for a given situation depends on the degree of control needed, effects on other pests and beneficials, economic considerations, and legal restrictions. Use the following guidelines when selecting and applying pesticides.

- Make sure you have correctly identified the target pest or problem.

- Choose the least disruptive material whenever possible to minimize problems with secondary pest outbreaks and pest resurgence.

- Consider the history of pesticide resistance within the target pest population.

- Treat for insects and mites only when monitoring indicates that damaging populations are present or anticipated.

- Apply pesticides when the target pest is most vulnerable and natural enemies are least likely to be affected. Apply postemergence herbicides when weeds are at the growth stage recommended on the label.

- Use techniques and equipment that apply pesticides most efficiently. Calibrate application equipment properly, use correct rates, and when possible place the material selectively. By increasing the efficiency of pesticide treatments, you will reduce costs, reduce the rate of development of pesticide resistance, and reduce the likelihood of secondary outbreaks and pest resurgence.

- Before choosing a pesticide, check the latest *UC IPM Pest Management Guidelines* for the stone fruit crop.

- Be sure that all personnel handling or applying pesticides are familiar with necessary safety precautions and know what to do in case of an emergency.

- ALWAYS READ THE LABEL CAREFULLY BEFORE USING ANY PESTICIDE. Follow directions and observe all safety precautions.

Because label restrictions may change, we do not make specific pesticide recommendations in this manual. Information on pesticide recommendations can be found in the *UC IPM Pest Management Guidelines* for specific stone fruits, listed in the references. Keep up to date with label changes. Check with your county agricultural commissioner, farm advisor, pest control advisor, or chemical company representative if you have any questions about label changes or label directions.

Ground Application. Nearly all ground spraying for insects, mites, and diseases in stone fruit orchards is done with air carrier (air blast) sprayers (Figure 29). Most air carrier sprayers pump a pesticide-water mixture to a series of nozzles that direct the pesticide mixture into a blast of air from a fan that blows the spray into the tree. The air volume produced by air blast sprayers ranges from small (4,000 cubic feet per minute) to large (more than 100,000 cubic feet per minute), and the air velocity from low (80 miles per hour) to high (180 miles per hour). Both high-air-velocity/low-air-volume and low-air-velocity/high-air-volume sprayers are available.

As the sprayer moves through the orchard, the air carrying the spray must mix with the still air in the interior of the tree. If the sprayer moves too quickly or the sprayer's air output is too low, you will not achieve complete mixing with the interior air, and coverage and control will be poor. The ideal sprayer distributes the spray mixture uniformly over the entire tree surface. Low-velocity/high-volume sprayers are more effective for large or tall trees and for trees with dense canopies.

The nozzles of an air blast sprayer usually are mounted in a semicircle in or adjacent to the air stream. Most sprayers have one bank (manifold) of nozzles on each side; some have two banks. Nozzles should be arranged to deliver two-thirds of the spray volume (in gallons per minute) from the top half of the sprayer manifold. Use Figure 30 or the manufacturer's nozzle chart to arrange nozzles on the manifold. You will also need to know the ratio of air discharge, but this is not always adjustable. This arrangement prevents the sprayer from over-spraying the bottom part of the tree and underspraying the top, where most of the persistent pest problems occur. For certain pests, when you are applying a pesticide that may be harmful to beneficials, you may be able to close the bottom nozzles completely to ensure survival of the beneficials in the lower part of the canopy.

Check nozzles frequently for wear. When nozzles wear out, they cannot reliably emit the proper droplet size or the correct rate of discharge. Wettable powder formulations are more abrasive than liquid formulations, and tend to wear nozzles out faster. Hollow-cone and nonplugging types of nozzles are used for dilute sprays. These nozzles are made from common steel, brass, nylon, stainless steel, or ceramics. For conventional concentrate and semi-concentrate sprays, use only nozzles made from stainless steel, ceramic, or tungsten carbide, because they are more resistant to the abrasive wear. Low-volume air-shear nozzles operate at low pressures, and do not have serious wear problems.

Most of the air blast spray rig is made up of the spray tank. Spray tanks usually are made of coated or stainless steel; in some cases they are made from chemical-resistant plastics or fiberglass. Stainless steel or fiberglass tanks are preferable. Strainers inside the tank keep foreign material from clogging the nozzles, and agitators keep the pesticide chemicals uniformly mixed with the water during application. Most sprayers have mechanical agitators; some use hydraulic agitation. Wettable powder formulations require mechanical agitation.

Spray Coverage. THE COMPLETE COVERAGE OF ALL PARTS OF THE TREE THAT MAY HARBOR THE TARGET PEST IS ESSENTIAL FOR MAXIMUM CONTROL. The most important causes of poor coverage are improper selection and arrangement of nozzles, too fast a ground speed, inadequate pump pressure, and incorrect gallonage for the pest. Poor coverage can also be caused by failure to make adjustments when moving between orchards having different-sized trees and incorrect use of sticker-spreaders or other spray additives. Always be sure to read the pesticide label and follow directions for proper application.

Do not move ground spray rigs through the orchard more quickly than 2.5 miles per hour when applying dilute sprays or 2.0 miles per hour when applying concentrate sprays. Trees will not receive adequate coverage if the ground speed is faster. SPEEDS EVEN SLOWER THAN THIS ARE RECOMMENDED FOR DENSE CANOPIES, FOR TALL TREES, AND FOR TREATMENT OF HEAVY SCALE INFESTATIONS. To maintain proper ground speed, use a tractor with an accurate speedometer or time your travel over a set distance by counting the number of trees you pass in a minute. Figure 31 shows an example of a worksheet for calculating ground speed from tree spacings.

Gallonage. Pesticides are applied either as concentrate sprays (low-volume or no-drip sprays) or as dilute sprays (high-volume or runoff sprays). Concentrate sprays are applied in smaller quantities of water per acre, with the spray equipment adjusted to produce more, smaller droplets that are more uniform in size. Concentrate sprays usually are applied at rates of 25 to 100 gallons per acre, discharged at 2 to 5 gallons per minute from each manifold. High-volume sprays are applied at 300 to 800 gallons per acre and 12 to 40 gallons per minute from each side. The exact amount of spray you use in a given orchard depends on the target pest, tree density and size, the type of equipment, economics, and past experience.

Figure 29. Air carrier (air blast) sprayers are used for most ground applications of pesticides in stone fruit orchards.

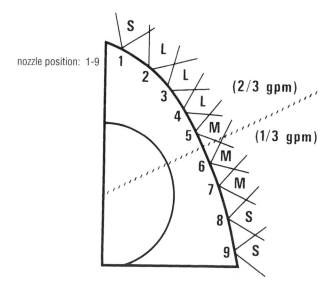

Figure 30. Nozzle arrangement on one manifold of an air blast sprayer. Arrange nozzles so that two-thirds of the spray discharge, in gallons per minute, comes from the top half of the manifold. Relative nozzle sizes: L = large, M = medium, S = small.

1. Calculate how many feet you travel in one minute
(This example is for a desired speed of 2 MPH.)

$$\text{Feet/min.} = \frac{\text{mph x ft/mile}}{\text{min/hr}} \quad \frac{2.0 \times 5280}{60} = 176 \text{ ft.}$$

2. Calculate how many tree spacings you should pass in a minute.
This example uses 22 ft. tree spacings.

$$\frac{176 \text{ ft.}}{22 \text{ ft./row}} = 8 \text{ rows}$$

If it takes you more or less than one minute to pass 8 tree spaces
adjust your ground speed.

Figure 31. Worksheet for calculating ground speed.

dilute spray droplet

concentrate spray droplet

• droplet size

◯ zone of effectiveness

**Figure 32. This diagram shows how coverage depends on droplet size of
the spray. In the diagram, each droplet is surrounded by a 100-micron
zone, in which each spray droplet is effective. The spray from a concentrate sprayer covers a much larger area (below) than the same amount
of spray from a dilute sprayer (single droplet above). A droplet 300
microns in diameter from a dilute sprayer has the same volume as 216
droplets of 50 microns discharged by a concentrate sprayer. (300÷50 =
6; 6 × 6 × 6 = 216)**

For many pests, concentrate sprays are as effective as
dilute sprays because the smaller droplets allow a smaller
volume to cover the same area as a high-volume spray (Figure 32), although the concentrate requires greater precision
during application. The advantages of concentrate spraying
are several: the equipment is smaller, may be less costly, and
is cheaper to maintain; the concentrate uses less water (70
to 90% less), so tanks need to be refilled less frequently; and
less chemical may be required (up to 25 or 30% less)
because the spray does not run off the tree as do dilute
sprays. When applied from a properly calibrated and adjusted sprayer, the small droplets of a concentrate spray stick to
the tree surface on contact.

You can modify an older spray rig designed for dilute applications so it will accommodate concentrates by adjusting the
pump pressure, the spray manifold, and the number, size, and
placement of nozzles. Newer model spray rigs designed for
dilute application are more easily adapted to concentrate
spraying because they produce pressures of 100 pounds per
square inch at the manifold and air velocities of 100 to 160
miles per hour, and are provided with a second manifold
arrangement with smaller, hollow-cone, disc-type nozzles for
concentrate sprays. Other spray rigs are available that are
designed specifically for concentrate application. Some use
the same nozzles, pressure, and air velocities as dilute application models. Others use a low-pressure system and special
nozzles designed so the air discharge shears the spray into
smaller droplets. Whatever nozzle system you use, it should
produce a relatively narrow range of droplet sizes.

Figure 33 shows how to calculate the number of gallons per
minute needed from each nozzle manifold. This formula can
be used for either dilute or concentrate sprays. Publications
with more information on the calibration and use of orchard
sprayers can be found in the references under Pesticides.

Aerial Application. Aircraft applications of pesticides to
orchards usually are not as satisfactory as ground applications. Coverage is not as thorough, especially after trees are
fully leafed out. Dormant treatments to control San Jose
scale or mite eggs cannot be applied effectively by air. Aerial
applications are useful for some dormant and delayed-dormant sprays, for bloomtime applications of Bt, and for early-
season fungicide applications when the orchard is too wet for
ground application. Aerial application may be the only alternative when a large area needs to be covered in a short period of time—for example, when a brown rot spray has to be
applied in advance of wet weather. To achieve the best coverage with an aerial application, apply concentrate sprays by
helicopter at a rate of no fewer than 25 gallons per acre and
an air speed of less than 30 miles per hour. With materials
such as Bt, for which spray drift is less of a concern, applications from 15 to 20 feet above the top of the tree canopy
might be most effective. Droplet size must be large enough to
prevent pesticide drift, yet small enough to stick to the trees
without bouncing off.

Pest Resurgence and Secondary Outbreaks. Pesticides that kill or disrupt natural enemies may cause pest resurgence or secondary pest outbreaks. In stone fruits, these problems are most likely to occur with mites, aphids, or some scale insects, which normally are kept under control by natural enemies but are able to build up rapidly when natural enemy populations are disrupted.

Pest resurgence occurs when a nonselective pesticide kills both the target pest and its natural enemies. The natural enemy populations take longer to recover because they require the pest for food and usually are more susceptible to the pesticide. Without the restraint of natural control, the few pests that survive treatment or invade the field from an untreated area quickly multiply, sometimes increasing to populations higher than those that prompted treatment in the first place. To reduce pest resurgence problems, use selective materials that are more toxic to the target pest than to natural enemies whenever possible. You can also use lower rates of selective materials to reduce pest populations well below damaging levels, and still leave some pests as a food source for the natural enemies. The relative toxicity to natural enemies and honey bees for pesticides used in stone fruits are listed in Table 13.

Pesticide applications sometimes cause nontarget pests to increase to damaging levels. These increases, called *secondary outbreaks*, occur when pesticides destroy natural enemies that have kept the nontarget pest under control (Figure 34). Mites often cause problems in stone fruits after broad-spectrum insecticides have been used to control such pests as peach twig borer, oriental fruit moth, aphids, and leafhoppers.

Pesticide Resistance. The repeated use of one type of pesticide to control a pest may result in the buildup of resistance in the pest population (Figure 35). In some cases, a pest population that develops resistance to one pesticide may also gain resistance to certain other pesticides, a phenomenon called *cross-resistance*.

Pesticide resistance is most likely to develop in pest populations that reproduce rapidly (e.g., mites) or diseases that produce large quantities of spores (e.g., brown rot fruit decay), and when multiple applications are used to control a given pest during the season. Table 14 lists the pesticides used in stone fruits for which resistance is known to occur in pest populations in California. To minimize the likelihood that resistance will develop, be sure to alternate the types of chemicals you use to control a pest, use pesticides only when needed, and keep to a minimum the number of times you use a chemical to control fruit rot.

Pesticide Hazards. Pesticides used in stone fruits may affect bees, wildlife, and humans. You must take precautions to avoid the hazards associated with pesticide application.

a. List the known criteria of your operation:

1. Row spacing (trunk to trunk, ft.)   22

2. Gallons of spray per acre (gpa)   100

3. Desired ground speed (mph)   2.0

b. To find the gallons per minute (gpm) for the nozzle manifold (one side), use the following equation:

$$gpm = \frac{gpa \times mph \times row\ spacing}{1,000}$$

$$gpm = \frac{100 \times 2.0 \times 22}{1,000} = 4.4$$

4.4 gallons per minute need to be discharged from one side (8.8 gpm from both sides) to deliver 100 gpa at 2.0 mph.

Two-thirds (2.9 gpm) should be discharged from the top $\frac{1}{2}$ of the manifold.

One-third (1.5 gpm) should be discharged from the bottom $\frac{1}{2}$ of the manifold.

Figure 33. Worksheet for calibrating air blast sprayers.

Hazards to Bees. Many of the pesticides used in stone fruit orchards are harmful to bees (see Table 13). Because bees may forage 2 to 3 miles from their hives, community-wide efforts are needed to protect bees from pesticide damage. Before you apply certain pesticides, you are required to notify the county agricultural commissioner, who then notifies beekeepers in the area. Check with your county agricultural commissioner to find out about legal restrictions before you apply any pesticides in the spring. Take the following precautions when using pesticides in the spring to minimize harm to bees:

- When applying a delayed-dormant insecticide spray, observe the minimum interval between application and placement of hives in the orchard.
- During bloom, only use pesticides—even those considered nontoxic to adult bees—when they are absolutely necessary. Pesticides, including some fungicides, can damage the honey bee brood when carried back to the hive by foraging bees.
- Notify beekeepers when you are planning to spray.
- Apply pesticides after 4 P.M. Bees collect most of their fresh pollen in the morning and early afternoon.
- Do not spray over hives or allow pesticides to get into hive entrances.

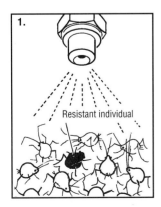

Pest A: aphids

Pest B: spider mites

Natural enemies: lacewing larvae

Predatory mites

Figure 34. Secondary outbreaks of insects or mites often occur when a nonselective pesticide kills natural enemies.

• Take precautions to avoid the drift of dormant sprays onto blooming winter annuals if there are bee hives within 2 miles of the orchard.

Hazards to Wildlife and Water Quality. Pesticides applied to stone fruits may harm wildlife if runoff or spray drift contaminates bodies of water or nearby natural areas. Nontarget wildlife may be affected by toxic baits used to control vertebrate pests. In areas where certain endangered species occur, special restrictions apply to the types of pesticides you can use and the means of application. Dormant sprays may be hazardous to raptors that roost in stone fruit orchards during the winter and may cause runoff problems when winter rains wash residues into streams and rivers. The California Department of Pesticide Regulation is developing special regulations and guidelines for dormant season applications of pesticides in orchard crops. Stay informed about pesticide regulations that are designed to protect water supplies and wildlife in your area. Take special precautions, select less-harmful materials, or avoid using pesticides where runoff or spray drift is likely to contaminate nearby bodies of water or sensitive wildlife habitat.

Hazards to Humans. Some of the pesticides applied to stone fruits are hazardous to humans. Applicators are most at risk, but orchard crews and others who enter orchards also may be exposed. Also, pesticides may drift to nearby areas where they can cause problems. Read and follow all label directions regarding the handling and application of pesticides, reentry and preharvest intervals, and disposal of pesticide containers. Special precautions are needed when you are applying pesticides near residential areas and schools. Be sure that all workers who handle or apply pesticides are trained in proper safety procedures and wear the correct protective clothing. Keep all application equipment in good working order with all necessary safety features for the materials being used. For detailed information on pesticide selection, handling, application, storage, and disposal, see *The Safe and Effective Use of Pesticides* and other publications listed under Pesticides in the references at the back of this manual.

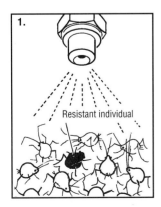
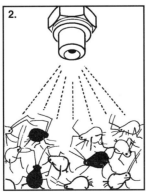

Susceptible individual

Figure 35. Repeated application of a pesticide may select for a pest population that is resistant to the pesticide.

Table 13. Relative Toxicity to Natural Enemies and Honey Bees for Pesticides Used in Stone Fruits.

Pesticide[1]	Predatory mites[2]	General predators[3]	Parasites[3]	Honey bee adults	Honey bee larvae
azinphosmethyl (Guthion)	○/◑	●	●	●	●
Bacillus thuringiensis	○	◑	○	○	○
benomyl (Benlate)	○/●[4]	○	○	○	○
Bordeaux mixture	—	○	○	○	—
captan	○	○	○	○	●
carbaryl (Sevin)	○/●	●	●	●	●
chlorothalonil (Bravo)	◑	○	○	●	—
chlorpyrifos (Lorsban)	◑	●	●	●	●
clofentezine (Apollo)	—	●	—	—	●
diazinon	○	●	●	●	●
endosulfan (Thiodan)	○	◑	◑	◑	◑
esfenvalerate (Asana)	●	◑	●	●	●
fenarimol (Rubigan)	○	—	—	○	—
fenbutatin oxide (Vendex)	○[5]	○	○	○	○
fixed copper	—	—	—	○	—
formetanate (Carzol)	○/●	●	●	◑	○
iprodione (Rovral)	○	○	○	○	—
liquid lime sulfur	—	—	—	○	—
mefenoxam (Ridomil Gold)	○	—	—	○	—
methidathion (Supracide)	●	●	●	●	●
methomyl (Lannate)	●	●	●	●	●
myclobutanil (Rally)	○	—	—	○	—
oils	○	○	○	○	—
permethrin (Pounce)	○	●	●	●	●
phosmet (Imidan)	●	●	●	●	●
propargite (Omite)	◑[5]	○	○	○	○
sulfur	○/●	○	●	○	○
thiophanate methyl (Topsin)	○	○	○	○	—
thiram	○	○	○	○	—
triforine (Funginex)	○	—	—	○	—
ziram	○	—	—	○	○

● = high   ◑ = moderate   ○ = low   — = no information

1. Check current label restrictions. Registrations may vary depending on the stone fruit crop and may change.
2. Toxicities to western predatory mite, *Galendromus occidentalis*. Where differences have been measured, these are listed as pesticide-resistant strain/native strain.
3. Toxicities are averages of reported effects and should be used only as a general guide. Actual toxicity of a specific chemical depends on the species of predator or parasite, environmental conditions, and application rate. For example, pyrethroids (esfenvalerate, permethrin) and phosmet have low to moderate toxicity to lacewings but high toxicity to predatory lady beetles.
4. Inhibits egg production by the native strain.
5. Use the lowest rates for best management of western predatory mite/ spider mite ratio.

Organic Production of Stone Fruit

Production of good-quality organic stone fruits is difficult and requires more intensive management than do conventional orchards. The pest and disease control options available to organic growers are fewer. Some chemical controls are available (Table 15); however, they tend to be less effective than conventional chemical controls. Preventive practices that reduce overwintering pest populations, inoculum, or seeds, or that enhance tree vigor and beneficial organisms are especially helpful. Increased monitoring is necessary in many cases to allow growers to target susceptible stages of a pest or control pest populations while they are still small. No effective organically acceptable chemical controls may be available for some serious pests such as brown rot. In these cases the grower must rely on less-susceptible varieties (e.g., crosses of Bolinha cling peach with current varieties) and labor-intensive cultural practices, such as removal and destruction of fruit mummies and thinned fruit, to reduce pest densities in the orchard. Despite the increased production costs, organic stone fruit orchards can be profitable.

Good-quality organic fruit generally command a premium price and consumer demand for such fruit is increasing.

New techniques have become available to organic growers in recent years to control some major pests in stone fruits. Peach twig borer can be controlled by carefully timed applications of the microbial insecticide *Bacillus thuringiensis*. Pheromone confusion techniques are available for control of peach twig borer, oriental fruit moth, and codling moth.

Some stone fruits are more difficult to produce organically than others because of their relative susceptibility to serious pests. Apricots, peaches, and nectarines tend to be more difficult to grow organically than plums and prunes because they are more severely affected by brown rot, which is hard to control in organic orchards. Some pests such as mites may not be problems in organic orchards, while others such as leafrollers and stink bugs may become more serious over time than in orchards that use conventional pesticides. For many pests, the cultural practices, monitoring, and treatment guidelines are the same for organic and conventional orchards. Management recommendations for both organic and conventional orchards are given in the *UC IPM Pest Management Guidelines* listed in the references.

Table 14. Occurrence of Resistance to Pesticides Used in Stone Fruits.[1]

Pest	Pesticide class	Pesticide
INSECTS		
caterpillars		
oriental fruit moth	organophosphate	azinphosmethyl, diazinon
codling moth	carbamate organophosphate	carbaryl azinphosmethyl, diazinon, phosmet
plant bugs		
stink bugs	chlorinated hydrocarbon	endosulfan
scale insects		
San Jose scale	organophosphate	chlorpyrifos, diazinon
MITES		
spider mites	organotin sulfite ester	fenbutatin oxide progargite
DISEASES		
brown rot	benzimidazole[2]	benomyl, thiophanate methyl
	dicarboximide	iprodione
green fruit rot	benzimidazole	benomyl, thiophanate methyl
powdery mildew	demethylation inhibitors[3]	fenarimol, myclobutanil

1. Information as of 1998. Resistance to a pesticide does not occur uniformly in all growing areas and may not be widespread. If a pesticide is not used for several years, a pest population may temporarily lose its resistance to that pesticide.
2. Resistance is widespread and stable—resistance does not decline when the pesticide is not used.
3. Resistance has developed in species that attack grapes in California and in cherry orchards in the Pacific Northwest.

Table 15. Pesticides Acceptable for Use on or around Organically Grown Stone Fruits.[1]

Pesticide	Pest controlled	Comments
INSECTICIDES, MITICIDES		
Bacillus thuringiensis (Bt)	Many caterpillar pests	Must be applied when larvae are small and feeding; short residual
Bordeaux mixture, fixed copper	Italian pear scale	Controls lichens that favor buildup of scale
pheromones	Peach twig borer, oriental fruit moth, codling moth	Pheromone mating disruption
petroleum oils	Some caterpillar pests Aphids Mites Scales	Followed by Bt sprays in spring Must be applied as eggs begin to hatch Dormant oil applications control eggs Partial control; useful only for light infestations
wettable sulfur	Eriophyid mites	—
FUNGICIDES, BACTERICIDES		
Agrobacterium radiobacter	Crown gall	Biological control agent
Bordeaux mixture	Shot hole, leaf curl	Dormant and delayed dormant applications
fixed copper	Shot hole, leaf curl	Dormant and delayed dormant applications
liquid lime sulfur	Powdery mildew, rust	Sulfur cannot be applied to apricots
sulfur dust	Brown rot ripe fruit rot, powdery mildew, rust	Sulfur cannot be applied to apricots
wettable sulfur	Powdery mildew, rust	Sulfur cannot be applied to apricots

1. For a complete current list of all organically acceptable materials, see the California Department of Food and Agriculture web site: www.cdfa.ca.gov/inspection/fvqc/organic.html

Insects and Mites

A number of different insects and other arthropods occur in stone fruit orchards. In any given orchard, only a few are likely to cause damage. Most either have no effect on crop production or are beneficial, feeding on insect and mite pests or serving as a food source for predators or parasites that feed on pests.

The relative importance of pests is generally determined by the fruit being grown, the location of the orchard, and management practices. Peach twig borer is a major "worm" pest of stone fruits in all California growing areas. San Jose scale is a major pest of stone fruits in Central Valley areas. Oriental fruit moth is a serious pest of peaches and nectarines, but is less of a problem on other stone fruits. Web-spinning spider mites attack all stone fruits and are most likely to become damaging in orchards that are stressed for water or nutrients, or where biological control has been disrupted by the use of a broad-spectrum pesticide. Wood-boring insects can become problems in any area; they are most serious on young trees and on older trees that are weakened or have sunburned limbs.

A number of insects cause problems only on certain stone fruit crops, in certain locations, or at certain times of the season. Western flower thrips is a serious pest primarily of nectarine and plum fruit, but can cause significant damage to the shoot tips of young stone fruit trees. Stink bugs and lygus bugs constitute a threat to peaches and nectarines when there are nearby crop hosts or uncultivated areas that harbor the pests. Codling moth is a problem on plums in most San Joaquin Valley areas and on prunes at a few locations in the Sacramento Valley; it rarely occurs on other stone fruits. Redhumped caterpillar is a problem primarily on plums and prunes. Orange tortrix and western tussock moth are occasional pests of stone fruits in coastal areas. At least three leafhopper species are of concern in cherries because they transmit the pathogen that causes X-disease (cherry buckskin).

These and other pests will be discussed in detail in this chapter. Photographs and drawings will help you identify the pests, the damage they cause, and their important natural enemies. Use these illustrations to help you keep track of pest problems and assess the effectiveness of biological controls as you monitor your orchards.

Monitoring

Regular monitoring is essential to detecting pests, keeping track of pest and natural enemy population densities, and identifying susceptible stages in the life cycles of some pests. You can use degree-day accumulations to schedule monitoring or control actions for several important stone fruit pests, including peach twig borer, oriental fruit moth, and San Jose scale. The use of pheromone traps to detect the BEGINNING of adult flight periods is critical to using degree-day models and scheduling monitoring and treatment activities for these pests. Monitoring during the dormant season is an important part of assessing overwintering populations of San Jose scale, aphids, and several other pest species that may cause damage. Routine monitoring throughout the season tells you how well your management activities are controlling pest populations. Regular monitoring will also help you find minor pests before they can cause significant damage. Figures 6 through 13 in the previous chapter illustrate the timing of monitoring activities for major pests in different stone fruit crops.

Details of how to monitor specific pests are given in the discussions of those pests later in this chapter. Keep written records of your monitoring results, including seasonal trap catches for each species monitored and harvest-time surveys of pest damage to fruit. For some pests, plotting a graph of your monitoring counts is an important part of scheduling management activities. A good set of records will tell you what pest problems to expect in each orchard, and will help point out differences in susceptibility among orchard blocks. Also, accurate records kept over time will help you evaluate the effectiveness of control actions and plan future management activities.

Monitoring Methods

Several methods are used to monitor for the presence of insect and mite pests, beneficials, and pest damage. Pheromone traps are used to monitor the flights of some adult insects; you use them to determine the biofix for degree-day calculations (see below). If you keep track of total seasonal trap catches, you will be able to compare year-to-year changes in pest population densities and see if they are increasing or decreasing. Other trap types include sticky tape for monitoring the crawler stage of scale insects, shelters for monitoring earwigs, and sticky barriers to monitor weevil migrations. Beating trays and sweep nets may be used to check for pests and beneficials on flowers, foliage, cover crops, and nearby weeds or brush. Visual inspection of wood, flowers, fruit, or foliage is an important component of the monitoring program for all insect and mite pests.

Pheromone Traps. Pheromones are chemicals that animals produce to communicate with other members of their species. The pheromones used in insect traps mimic the sex attractants emitted by females of a given species to attract males. These attractants are highly specific, but insects other than the target species are sometimes caught in the traps. San Jose scale pheromone traps also monitor for parasitic wasps that attack female scale, because the wasps use the pheromone scent trail to find their prey. Pheromone traps come in various shapes and sizes and are made from a variety of materials. Inside the trap is a plastic or rubber dispenser impregnated with synthetic pheromone. Traps and pheromone dispensers are available from a number of suppliers (see the references).

Control actions for several important stone fruit pests, including oriental fruit moth, peach twig borer, codling moth, and San Jose scale, can be scheduled based on pheromone trap data used in conjunction with degree-day calculations. Use these traps to help schedule your treatments to target the most susceptible time in the pest's life cycle. Pheromone traps are good indicators of the PRESENCE of a pest but not of the NUMBER of pests present; therefore, you should not use trap data alone to make your treatment decisions. Use other monitoring guidelines in conjunction with pheromone traps to decide if treatment is necessary.

Pheromone traps are used to establish a *biofix*—an identifiable point in the life cycle of the pest at which you can begin a degree-day accumulation or take a management action. For example, the biofix for peach twig borer and oriental fruit moth is the date when you first begin catching adult moths of each generation. When using pheromone traps, follow these guidelines:

- Place traps in each orchard for which you will need to make pest management decisions.

- Use at least 2 traps per block for moths, and 3 or 4 per block for San Jose scale. (The best number of traps to use for monitoring the efficacy of mating disruption or for quarantine field certification is 1 trap per 5 acres for orchards of less than 20 acres, 1 trap per 10 acres for orchards of 20 to 80 acres, or 1 trap per 20 acres for orchards of over 80 acres. Reduce these numbers by half if you are monitoring just to establish a biofix for spray timing. The actual number of traps you use will be determined by the time available and the number of orchards being sampled within a given area.)

- Distribute the traps uniformly throughout the orchard. Use the same locations each year so you can make accurate comparisons from one season to the next. Remember that changing to lures from a different manufacturer or to different trap designs may affect the relative number of moths caught, making year-to-year comparisons difficult.

- Place additional traps in hot spots where you expect to see more pest damage.

- Hang traps 6 to 8 feet high, 1 to 3 feet inside the canopy in the north quadrant of the tree, in the shade, and at least 5 trees in from the edge of the orchard.

- Check the traps twice a week until the biofix is established; thereafter, check traps weekly.

- Clean trapped insects and other material from the trap bottom after you count and record the trap catch.

- Replace trap bottoms monthly or when they become covered with dirt, plant debris, or moth scales. Trap bottoms may need more frequent replacement when moth catches are high; for instance, after 75 (peach twig borer or codling moth) to 150 (oriental fruit moth or omnivorous leafroller) moths have been caught by and removed from a trap.

- Follow the manufacturer's recommendations for replacing pheromone dispensers.

- Store pheromone dispensers in a refrigerator or freezer. Remove them from storage and open the packages to allow them to air out for 2 days at room temperature before you place them in traps.

Beating Trays. You can use beating trays to monitor adult western flower thrips, plant bugs, green fruitworm larvae, adult weevils, and beneficial predators during the season. Make your beating tray by stretching a piece of white cloth across the frame of a window screen about 18 inches (45.5 cm) square or an embroidery hoop 18 to 20 inches (45 to 50 cm) in diameter. You can also use a light-colored garbage can lid of similar size. While holding the beating tray underneath, shake flowers or foliage with one hand or beat the branch with a piece of PVC pipe wrapped with foam and duct tape or some other material that is unlikely to injure the bark.

Visual Inspection. Monitor for eggs of mites, aphids, and some caterpillar pests by examining wood or buds during the dormant season. Careful examination of flowers is critical to monitoring the activity of western flower thrips in susceptible crops. Monitoring for foliar damage is an important part of IPM programs for peach twig borer, oriental fruit moth, leafrollers, and several other caterpillar pests. Leaf sampling is a means of monitoring populations of webspinning spider mites and their natural enemies. Take fruit samples regularly to monitor for damage by peach twig borer, oriental fruit moth, leafrolling caterpillars, codling moth, San Jose scale, plant bugs, western flower thrips, and katydids; for peach twig borer and oriental fruit moth, which first appear in the upper canopy, knock fruit down from high in the tree and examine it for pest damage. During pruning operations, check branches cut from the tree tops for presence of San Jose scale. Examine trunks and scaffold limbs periodically for signs of wood-boring insects.

Taking Samples. When monitoring for pests and beneficials, you need to gather your samples in a way that is representative of the entire orchard. To do this in a comprehensive way, divide the orchard into sampling blocks. As a general rule, make each sampling block no larger than 20 acres. Make sure conditions such as soil type, type of stone fruit, age of trees, and orchard floor management are as uniform as possible with-

in the sampling block. Each block should include no more of the orchard than you will treat at one time. When selecting your sampling blocks, be sure to include all areas of the orchard. SAMPLE EDGES OF THE ORCHARD SEPARATELY; certain pests such as webspinning mites, stink bugs, and thrips are more likely to be concentrated at the edges. Walk through the sample block and select trees at random such that your sample will be representative of the entire block. Do not choose trees that are obviously different from the rest of the trees in the block. An example of a sampling walk is given in Figure 36.

Management Methods

Biological Control

Every important arthropod pest of stone fruits is attacked by one or more biological control agents. These natural enemies often suppress pest populations, and in some cases they are able to keep pests from reaching damaging levels. Arthropods that are natural enemies of pest species are called parasites (parasitoids) or predators, depending on their life cycle. *Parasites* spend part of their life cycle living in or on a certain stage of the pest. Often the adult parasite lays its egg in the egg or larva of the pest, the parasite larva feeds on the pest, and by the time the parasite pupates the pest has been consumed. Some typical parasite life cycles are illustrated in Figure 37. In general, each parasite larva kills one individual pest, although the adult parasite may lay eggs on dozens or hundreds of pest individuals, and in some cases several parasite larvae may develop on one individual pest. By contrast, a *predator* devours many individuals of the pest species. Some predators feed on only a certain type of pest; for example, the spider mite destroyer, *Stethorus picipes*, feeds on webspinning spider mites and a few related mite species. However, many

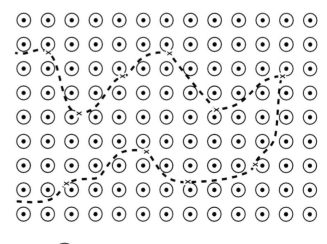

KEY ● tree   X sample   - - - - path

Figure 36. Example of a sampling walk.

Adult parasitic wasp lays one or more eggs on larva of caterpillar pest.

Parasite larvae develop on the caterpillar, killing it.

Parasites pupate on the shell that is all that remains of the pest larva.

Adult wasps emerge to mate and lay eggs in more pest larvae.

Adult parasitic wasp lays an egg beneath female scale.

A single parasite larva consumes the female scale.

Parasite pupates beneath the scale covering.

Adult cuts exit hole in scale covering and emerges to mate and attack more scales.

Adult parasitic wasp lays an egg inside the egg of a pest.

A single parasite larva consumes the contents of the egg.

Parasite pupates inside the egg shell.

Adult cuts exit hole in egg shell and emerges to mate and attack more pest eggs.

Figure 37. Three examples of parasite life cycles. Top: *Goniozus legneri* on navel orangeworm. Middle: *Aphytis* sp. on San Jose scale. Bottom: *Trissolcus* sp. on consperse stink bug eggs.

predators feed on a wide range of pest species. These are called general predators. Some insects, such as certain thrips species, can be both predators and plant feeders. Important natural enemies of stone fruit pests are listed in Table 16.

Predators. General predators such as lacewings, minute pirate bugs, and assassin bugs feed on a variety of insects and mites. Each individual predator can often consume a large number of prey. Because they survive on a number of different pest species, general predators often are present in and around stone fruit orchards before harmful pests build up. Some predators feed exclusively on one type of prey. For example, most lady beetle species feed on aphids, while some feed on scale insects or mealybugs. Several predators that help control stone fruit pests are described and illustrated in

this section. A number of predators that feed exclusively on one type of pest are described and illustrated in the section on their prey later in this chapter. For example, predatory mites, which play a key role in keeping pest mites from reaching damaging levels in undisrupted orchards, are discussed in the section on webspinning mites.

Lady Beetles. The convergent lady beetle, *Hippodamia convergens*, commonly moves into stone fruit orchards in the spring to feed on aphids. Adults are small beetles, about 1/4 inch (6 to 8 mm) long, with red wing coverings that usually have several black markings. Two converging white markings behind the head distinguish it from other similar lady beetle species except *H. quinquesignata*. The spindle-shaped, yellowish orange eggs are laid on end in clusters of

Table 16. Natural Enemies of Insect and Mite Pests of Stone Fruits.

NATURAL ENEMIES

Pest	Parasites	Predators
peach twig borer	*Bracon gelechiae, Hyperteles lividus, Macrocentrus ancylivorus, Paralitomastix varicornis, Spilochalcis, Toxophoroides,* tachinid fly (*Erynnia* sp.)	gray ant, grain itch mite, lacewings, minute pirate bugs, assassin bugs, damsel bugs, *Phytocoris* spp., spiders
oriental fruit moth	*Ascogaster quadridentata, Apanteles, Bracon, Macrocentrus ancylivorus*	lacewings, minute pirate bugs, assassin bugs, *Phytocoris* spp., spiders
obliquebanded leafroller	*Macrocentrus iridescens, Glypta variegata*	—
green fruitworms	*Apanteles, Eulophus, Meteorus, Ophion*	lacewings, minute pirate bugs, assassin bugs, damsel bugs, spiders
codling moth	*Ascogaster quadridentata, Macrocentrus ancylivorus, Trichogramma* spp.	lacewings, minute pirate bugs, assassin bugs, *Phytocoris* spp., spiders, ground beetles
redhumped caterpillar	*Hyposoter fugitivus, Apanteles*	spiders
western tussock moth	*Hyposoter fugitivus, H. exiguae, Iseropus, Spilochalcis*	spiders
orange tortrix	*Apanteles aristoteliae, Exochus nigripalpis,* tachinid fly (*Actia interrupta*)	brown lacewings
San Jose scale	*Aphytis* spp., *Encarsia (Prospaltella) perniciosi*	lady beetle (*Chilocorus orbus*), lacewings, *Cybocephalus californicus, Phytocoris* spp.
Parthenolecanium scale	*Aphytis* spp., *Coccophagus* spp., *Encarsia* spp., *Metaphycus* spp.	lady beetles (*Chilocorus orbus, Hyperaspis* spp., *Rhyzobius lophanthae*), lacewings, *Cybocephalus californicus, Phytocoris* spp.
aphids	*Praon* sp., *Aphidius, Ephedrus*	lady beetles (*Hippodamia* spp., *Olla v-nigrum, Harmonia axyridis*), lacewings, syrphid larvae, aphid fly (*Leucopis* sp.), soldier beetles
western flower thrips	—	minute pirate bugs
stink bugs	*Trissolcus basalis, T. euschisti*	—
lygus bugs	*Anaphes iole*	minute pirate bugs, lacewings, damsel bugs, assassin bugs
webspinning mites, European red mite	—	western predatory mite and other predatory mites, spider mite destroyer, sixspotted thrips, minute pirate bugs, lacewings, western flower thrips, *Phytocoris* spp.

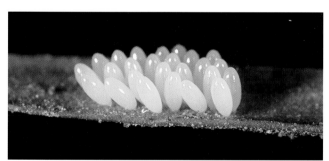

Lady beetle eggs are elongated, yellow to orange, and laid on end in clusters of 10 to 50.

Lady beetle larvae are dark gray or black with orange or yellow markings and have an elongated, alligatorlike shape. A convergent lady beetle larva is shown here.

Ashy gray lady beetle adults are tan or gray with black markings. Both larvae and adults of this species and the convergent lady beetle feed primarily on aphids.

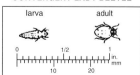

CONVERGENT LADY BEETLE

larva   adult

The twicestabbed lady beetle adult is black with two prominent red spots on the back. Larvae and adults of this species feed on mealybugs and scale.

TWICESTABBED LADY BEETLE

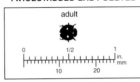

The Asiatic lady beetle is larger than most other lady beetle species. Adults usually are red, with or without several black spots, but some are black with red spots. Larvae (*right*) have prominent, forked spines. This species feeds primarily on aphids.

10 to 50 on leaves or bark. Larvae are alligator-shaped, dark gray or black with orange markings, and about ½ inch (12 mm) long when full grown. Both larvae and adults are voracious feeders; each individual convergent lady beetle can consume a thousand aphids or more. The lady beetle *H. quinquesignata* occurs commonly in prune orchards. It is very similar to the convergent lady beetle, but always lacks black spots on the wing covers.

The ashy gray lady beetle, *Olla v-nigrum*, is another species found in stone fruits that feeds primarily on aphids. Adults of this beetle may be tan or grayish with black markings on the back. The alligator-shaped larvae are black with yellow markings and reach ⅘ inch (20 mm) in length.

The twicestabbed lady beetle, *Chilocorus orbus*, occurs on a variety of woody hosts, where it feeds on mealybugs and scale. It is smaller than the convergent lady beetle, about ⅕ inch (4 to 5 mm) long, and shiny black with two red spots on the back. Larvae are alligator shaped, black with a yellow band, and covered with long spines. Young larvae will get under the cover of female scale insects to feed on eggs and crawlers. Older larvae and adults feed mainly on nymphs that have settled to start feeding. This species overwinters as adults in sheltered locations on tree hosts.

The Asiatic lady beetle, *Harmonia axyridis*, is an introduced species that is becoming a major predator of aphids in prunes. Adults usually are orange to orange-red. They may have many black spots on the wing coverings or no black spots, and occasionally are black with few to many reddish spots. The Asiatic lady beetle is larger and wider than *Hippodamia* species. Larvae are black and orange with long spines that are forked at the tip.

Lacewings. Several green and brown lacewing species occur commonly in stone fruit orchards. Lacewing larvae feed on any insects that are small enough for them to capture, including aphids, small caterpillars, scale crawlers, lygus bugs, and leafhoppers, as well as insect eggs and mites.

Adult green lacewings, *Chrysoperla* and *Chrysopa* spp., are bright green, about ¾ inch (15 to 20 mm) long, and slender, and have four delicate wings that fold over the body like a tent when at rest. These insects typically overwinter as adults. *Chrysopa* adults are predaceous; *Chrysoperla* adults are not predaceous, feeding instead on honeydew and plant nectar. Lacewings lay their eggs on leaf surfaces either singly or in groups depending on the species. Each egg is attached to the leaf by a long, threadlike stalk that helps protect against predation. Larvae are mottled gray or yellowish gray and reach a length of about ⅜ inch (10 mm). They are flat, tapered at each end, and have long curved mandibles with which they grasp and withdraw body fluids from their prey. In feeding studies, individual larvae have consumed as many as 400 aphids or 11,000 spider mites each before they pupate.

Brown lacewings such as *Hemerobius* spp. are similar in shape to green lacewings, but adults are smaller and dull brown in color. The oblong eggs do not have stalks and are laid singly on the undersides of leaves. Larvae are similar to

Adult green lacewings are long and slender with delicate wings that are folded over the body when at rest. Adults of some species are predaceous.

Adult brown lacewings are similar in shape to green lacewings, but are smaller and brown. Larvae are similar in size and shape to green lacewing larvae. Both adults and larvae are predaceous.

The green lacewing egg is attached to a leaf surface or twig by a long stalk. Some species lay eggs singly; others lay eggs in groups as shown here.

Brown lacewing eggs are laid singly on the undersides of leaves, and do not have stalks.

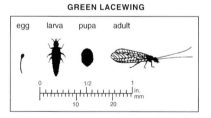

GREEN LACEWING

egg   larva   pupa   adult

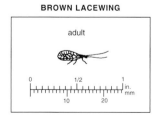

BROWN LACEWING

adult

Larvae of both green and brown lacewings have an elongated, flattened shape, and long curved mandibles that they use to grasp prey. They feed on a wide range of small arthropods and arthropod eggs.

green lacewing larvae in their appearance and feeding habits, but unlike green lacewing larvae they have a habit of moving their heads rapidly from side to side when searching for prey. Brown lacewings overwinter as larvae or pupae. Both adults and larvae are predaceous. Brown lacewings are active under cooler conditions than are green lacewings.

Minute Pirate Bugs. Minute pirate bugs, *Orius* spp., feed on thrips, all stages of mites, insect eggs, nymphs of lygus and stink bugs, aphids, and small caterpillars. Adult pirate bugs are black and about ⅛ inch (3 mm) long. They have white or silvery triangular markings on their back that form a black **X**.

Eggs are inserted into leaf tissue, mostly along veins on the undersides of leaves, leaving tiny whitish caps that protrude from the leaf surface. Nymphs are yellow-orange with prominent red eyes. Both nymphs and adults have prominent beaks and both feed on the same prey. Minute pirate bugs appear early in the spring and are attracted to flowers, where they feed on western flower thrips.

Assassin Bugs. Assassin bugs, *Zelus* spp. and other genera, are common in stone fruit orchards, and are predaceous both as nymphs and as adults. They have a long narrow body, very long legs, and a long needlelike beak. Adults are about ½

Minute pirate bug nymphs are yellow-orange with prominent red eyes.

Eggs of assassin bugs (*Zelus* spp.) are barrel-shaped and brown with a white caplike secretion on top, and are laid in clusters on leaves.

Adult minute pirate bugs are black with white or silvery triangular markings that make a black X-shaped pattern on their back. Both adults and nymphs feed on mites, small insects, and the eggs of insects and mites. Thrips are a favorite food.

An assassin bug has a long narrow body, long legs, and a long needlelike beak. Both nymphs and adults feed on a wide variety of insects.

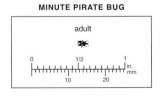

MINUTE PIRATE BUG

adult

0   1/2   1 in.
10   20   mm

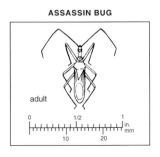

ASSASSIN BUG

adult

0   1/2   1 in.
10   20   mm

inch (10 to 12 mm) long. Assassin bugs are poor fliers but will attack a wide variety of insects. The eggs are barrel-shaped and brown, with a whitish secretion on top. Adults lay them on end in clusters on leaves.

Damsel Bugs. Damsel bug nymphs and adults, *Nabis* spp., feed on lygus and other plant bugs, aphids, and small caterpillars. A single damsel bug can consume as many as 30 lygus bugs. The damsel bug is grayish brown, about ⅜ to ½ inch (10 to 12 mm) long and slender, with a narrow head, bulging eyes, and long antennae and legs. The adult lays eggs by inserting them into leaf tissue.

Spiders. Spiders are general predators that are common in orchards. They may play an important part in suppressing pest populations in stone fruits, but their role is not fully understood. Sac spiders, *Cheiracanthium* spp. and *Trachelas pacificus*, are common and sometimes abundant in orchards from spring through fall. These species may be important predators of moth larvae. Jumping spiders, *Phidippus* spp. and *Sassacus vitis*, are commonly found in the canopy and can be active when peach twig borer hibernacula are present. *Phidippus* is an important predator of codling moth larvae in European orchards. Another spider found in abundance in stone fruit orchards is the dwarf spider, *Erigone dentosa*. This species is known to feed on mites and a variety of small arthropods, including newly hatched caterpillars. Other spider species that frequently occur in orchards include *Neoscona*, *Nodocion*, *Oxyopes*, and *Theridion*.

Gray Ant. The California gray ant, *Formica aerata*, occurs commonly in Central Valley orchards. The adult is about ¼ inch (6 mm) long. Gray ants forage at the nectaries of stone fruit leaves and will attack small caterpillars on shoots. The gray ant is the most effective predator of peach twig borer in Central Valley orchards. It is not an effective predator of oriental fruit moth, since the pest larva regurgitates a substance that repels the ant.

Soldier Beetles. Adult soldier beetles, *Cantharis* spp. and other genera, also called leatherwings, are springtime aphid predators in stone fruit orchards. They also feed on insect eggs and larvae. Larvae live under bark or in the soil, feeding on eggs and larvae of a variety of insects. Adults are about ½ inch (12 mm) long and red, orange, or yellow, with dark wing covers. Their presence in an orchard can be a signal of the presence of aphid infestations.

Damsel bug nymphs (*above*) and adults are long and slender with prominent eyes and long legs. They feed on plant bugs, aphids, and small caterpillars.

Sac spiders such as *Trachelas pacificus* (*shown here*) and *Cheiracanthium* spp. occur commonly in orchards and may be important predators of moth larvae.

Certain species of the dwarf spider, *Erigone*, occur in stone fruit orchards, where they feed on mites and small insects, including newly hatched caterpillars. Pollen grains can be seen on the legs of the dwarf spider in this photo, to give you an indication of the spider's small size.

DAMSEL BUG

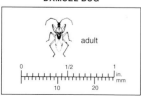

adult

0   1/2   1 in.
        mm
    10   20

The California gray ant, *Formica aerata,* is the most effective predator of peach twig borer in Central Valley orchards.

Soldier beetles, also known as leatherwings, are slender beetles that feed on a variety of insects and insect eggs. They also feed on nectaries at certain times of the year.

Predaceous ground beetles are shiny, dark, fast-moving beetles that live on the ground, feeding on soil-dwelling insects and the larvae and pupae of tree-dwelling insects such as codling moth and citrus cutworm, which pupate on the ground.

Phytocoris species occur commonly in orchards, where they apparently feed on scale, mites, aphids, and moth eggs. They can be serious pests of pistachios, but are not harmful to stone fruits.

GRAY ANT

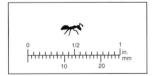

PREDACEOUS GROUND BEETLES
Size varies depending on species

adult

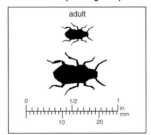

SOLDIER BEETLE

adult

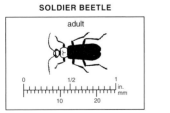

PHYTOCORIS

adult

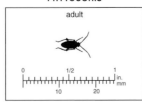

Predaceous Ground Beetles. Predaceous ground beetles, family Carabidae, live on or in the soil where they feed on soil-dwelling insects and the larvae and pupae of insects such as codling moth and citrus cutworm that crawl to the ground to pupate. Adults are fast-moving, shiny beetles with long legs. Most are black or dark reddish, but some may be brilliantly colored. The larva is elongated and somewhat flattened, with a large head and distinct mandibles. Both larvae and adults are predaceous.

Phytocoris. Species of the genus *Phytocoris,* bugs of the Miridae family, are commonly found in orchards. They are small, elongated, and mottled dark gray and dark brown, with long antennae and long hind legs. When disturbed they move quickly to protected places on the tree. *Phytocoris* spp. appear to be general predators that attack scales, mites, and moth eggs. They are active mostly at night. Their impact on tree crop pest species has not been studied or documented.

Cultural Practices

A number of cultural practices play important roles in the management of insect and mite problems in stone fruits. Pruning properly and painting exposed wood to prevent sunburn reduce the susceptibility of trees to wood-boring insects; improper summer pruning promotes sunburn and infestation by flatheaded borer. Sanitation plays an important role in population reduction for some pests. Destruction of infested wood prevents the spread of wood-boring insects. Proper irrigation and fertilization practices help reduce certain pest problems. Adequate water and sufficient fertilization reduce the trees' susceptibility to web-spinning mites and help reduce the incidence of dry conditions that favor mite buildup. Too much nitrogen fertilization can increase problems with peach twig borer and oriental fruit moth by increasing shoot growth and providing more host sites for these insects; the same conditions also encourage buildup of mites. If you thin fruit so they do not touch, you may help reduce fruit damage from peach twig borer and codling moth.

Pheromone Mating Disruption

Growers can use pheromone mating disruption or pheromone confusion to control populations of oriental fruit moth and peach twig borer in stone fruits, and this means of control may soon be available for omnivorous leafroller as well. The success of pheromone confusion requires correct timing and proper placement of dispensers. The technique is most effective in orchards with lower pest populations and orchards that are isolated from untreated hosts of the pests being controlled. Mating disruption does not work well in windy locations, and control is poor in the upper parts of orchards situated on sloping terrain. In orchards with high pest populations, it is necessary to use higher rates of pheromone and more point sources, and to place dispensers high in trees. New methods for dispensing pheromones are continually being developed to improve the technique. More specific information on materials and rates can be found in the *UC IPM Pest Management Guidelines* listed in the references. BE SURE TO FOLLOW MANUFACTURERS' INSTRUCTIONS CLOSELY WITH REGARD TO THE PLACEMENT AND NUMBER OF DISPENSERS.

Pesticides

The proper application of an effective pesticide is an important part of insect and mite pest management in stone fruits. Treatments can be applied during the dormant period or in season, during or after bloom. The potential effect of a pesticide on beneficial organisms is an important consideration when planning pesticide treatments. Table 17 lists the relative effects on beneficials of pesticide treatments made at different times of the year.

Table 17. Relative Effect of Pesticide Applications on Natural Enemies of Stone Fruit Pests.[1]

Natural enemy	Dormant oil	Dormant oil+ OP	Dormant oil + pyrethroid	Bt at bloom	In-season OP	In-season pyrethroid	In-season carbamate
caterpillar parasite (*Paralitomastix*)	○	○	○	○	●	●	●
caterpillar parasite (*Macrocentrus*)	○	○	○	○	●	●	●
scale parasites (*Aphytis*)	○	◑	—	○	●	●	●
predatory mites (*Galendromus*)	○	○	●	○	◑	●	●
lady beetles (*Chilocorus*)	○	○	○	○	●	●	●
lacewings	○	◑	○	○	◑	◑	●
minute pirate bugs	○	◑	◑	○	●	●	●
spiders	○	◑	○	○	●	○	●

○ = least harmful   ◑ = moderately harmful   ● = very harmful   — = no information

1. OP = organophosphate, Bt = *Bacillus thuringiensis*

Dormant treatment with oil plus insecticide is used, when monitoring records indicate the need, to kill mite eggs and reduce overwintering populations of scale and several other insect pests that may be present during the dormant period. If you are not using a program of bloomtime Bt sprays to control peach twig borer, you should include an insecticide in the dormant spray to control overwintering peach twig borers and scales. A suitable rate of oil alone will control mite eggs and the eggs of some insects. It also will reduce the scale population, but will not effectively control aphid eggs unless applied after the eggs hatch. Dormant oil applications may injure stone fruit trees. Prunes are the most sensitive to oil, and Queen Ann plums are also highly susceptible to injury. You can reduce the likelihood of injury by delaying oil treatment until bud break. Oil treatments may injure any stone fruit tree that is stressed by pest damage, inadequate water, heat or sudden temperature change, wind, or girdling. Avoid applying oil to any stone fruit trees that are stressed. READ AND FOLLOW LABEL DIRECTIONS CAREFULLY TO REDUCE THE LIKELIHOOD OF INJURY. More information on the use of oil sprays can be found in *Managing Insects and Mites with Spray Oils*, listed in the references.

In many orchards, peach twig borer and San Jose scale must be controlled annually, either with an oil + organophosphate treatment during the dormant season or with high label rates of superior-type oil treatments for scale and bloomtime applications of the bacterial insecticide *Bacillus thuringiensis* (Bt) for peach twig borer. Bt has the advantage that it is not disruptive of natural enemies that control other insects and mites. You may need to make in-season pesticide applications following bloom to control some pest populations, including later generations of peach twig borer. You will find guidelines to help you determine when applications may be needed in the discussions of specific pests that follow. Specific pesticide recommendations can be found in the *UC IPM Pest Management Guidelines* listed in the references. When using pesticides, choose materials that are least harmful to natural enemy populations. For instance, the microbial Bt is effective against all leaf-feeding caterpillars and peach twig borer; for peach twig borer, however, timing is more critical, more treatments may be needed to achieve the same level of control, and later generations of the pest will be more difficult to control because egg hatch is spread out over a longer period. Besides Bt, a new microbial pesticide called spinosad is registered for control of peach twig borer in nonbearing orchards. Like Bt, spinosad is highly selective. Insecticidal oils also are somewhat selective by virtue of their lack of persistence. Table 13 in the previous chapter lists the toxicity of various pesticides to natural enemies in stone fruits.

CATERPILLARS

The larvae ("caterpillars" or "worms") of several moth species are important pests in stone fruits. They overwinter as eggs, larvae, or pupae. Larvae of most species feed on both foliage and fruit; the most serious damage usually results from fruit feeding. Peach twig borer and oriental fruit moth are two of the most serious stone fruit pests in all growing areas. Other caterpillar pests that may cause damage include several species of leafrollers, green fruitworms, codling moth, and redhumped caterpillar.

Peach Twig Borer
Anarsia lineatella

Peach twig borer is a major pest in most stone fruit orchards and a minor problem in cherries. It is a major pest of almond orchards, and can spread to adjacent stone fruit orchards. Peach twig borer management involves a program of standard dormant sprays or bloom sprays using *Bacillus thuringien-*

The peach twig borer adult is a small, mottled gray moth with a snout-like projection from the head.

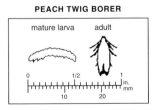

PEACH TWIG BORER

sis and regular monitoring to determine if insecticide treatments may be needed during the season. Pheromone confusion can be an effective tool in some locations.

Description and Biology

Peach twig borer overwinters as a first or second instar larva inside a chamber called a *hibernaculum* that the larva bores in thin bark—usually in crotches of 2- or 3-year-old wood, but also in pruning wounds or deep cracks. Each hibernaculum has a chimneylike pile of frass at its entrance when first made. These piles make hibernacula easy to find, but they can be washed away by fall and winter rains. When larvae are active on warm days in winter, they rebuild the piles of frass.

Larvae emerge from hibernacula in the spring about the time blossoms open. They migrate up branches to feed on newly emerging shoots and flower buds. Several shoot tips or buds may be damaged by a single larva. When shoot tips are large enough to support their growth, larvae bore into the shoots, usually penetrating less than 1 inch (2.5 cm) into the tip. Larvae feed inside the shoot tips until mature, then leave the shoots to pupate.

Adults from this overwintering generation emerge in late March through May and lay their eggs on twigs, leaves, or young fruit. The adult peach twig borer is a mottled, gray moth about ⅜ inch (9 mm) long with a snoutlike projection from the head. Eggs are yellowish white to orange, oval, and heavily sculptured. They are laid singly on shoots, fruit, or the lower surface of leaves, and hatch in 4 to 18 days depending on temperature.

The smallest larvae are whitish with light brown rings and black heads. As they grow larger, they take on a more pronounced ringed appearance as the segments turn dark brown while the membranes between segments remain white. This pattern of light and dark rings distinguishes peach twig borer larvae from other larvae found on stone fruits. Larvae are about ½ inch (12 mm) long when mature.

Larvae from the first generation to hatch from eggs laid in the spring feed inside shoot tips or on early ripening fruit. A second flight of adults from this generation comes in late June or early July. Larvae that hatch from the eggs laid by these adults may feed in shoots or on fruit. When they mature in August, they make up a third flight of adults. A fourth flight occurs in September or October. Most overwintering larvae hatch from eggs laid by the third and fourth flights. Figure 38 shows a diagram of the generations of peach twig borer.

Damage

Feeding by peach twig borer larvae inside shoots kills shoot tips, resulting in "shoot strikes" that are easily identified by the dead, drooping leaves at the tip. Similar damage is caused by oriental fruit moth larvae. Shoot strikes are most damaging on young trees. Terminal growth is killed, resulting in misshapen trees and increased pruning costs.

The peach twig borer larva forms a chimneylike pile of frass when boring a hibernaculum into the bark in the crotch of 2- or 3-year-old wood.

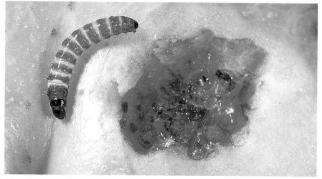

The darker body segments of an older peach twig borer larva gives it a distinctive ringed appearance. When they bore into fruit, peach twig borer larvae usually feed just under the fruit surface.

Feeding by peach twig borer larvae inside shoot tips causes terminal leaves to wilt and die, resulting in what is commonly called a shoot strike. Oriental fruit moth larvae cause similar damage.

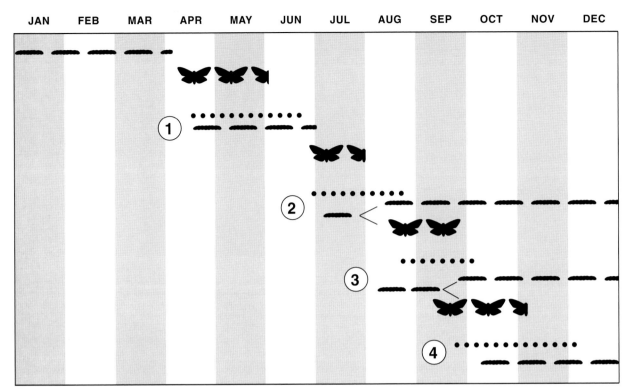

Figure 38. Seasonal development of the peach twig borer. (Timing of moth flights will vary from one season to the next and from one growing area to another. Symbols represent the time during which a moth flight usually will occur. In any given location, the actual length of a moth flight will be shorter.)

Although green fruit may be subject to attack, fruit are most susceptible to peach twig borer larvae after fruit color begins to develop. Ripening fruit are very attractive to female moths, which may fly from nearby blocks to a block of an earlier ripening variety. Larvae bore into the fruit and usually feed near the surface. Larval feeding causes fruit to be culled at harvest. A high peach twig borer population can result in complete crop loss.

Management Guidelines

Biological control agents usually do not keep peach twig borer populations from reaching damaging levels. Apricot, nectarine, peach, plum, and prune orchards should be treated each year with bloomtime sprays of *Bacillus thuringiensis* (Bt) or a dormant spray with an insecticide. Within an IPM program, the Bt spray is preferred because of its reduced impact on nontarget organisms compared to the organophosphate or pyrethroid insecticides commonly used in dormant sprays. Bloomtime or dormant sprays should be followed up with a regular monitoring program to determine if in-season insecticide sprays are needed to prevent significant fruit damage. Pheromone mating disruption initiated when moths begin to fly may eliminate the need for in-season insecticides, but should not be used as a substitute for bloomtime sprays of Bt (or a dormant spray program).

Biological Control. Peach twig borer larvae are attacked by several parasitic wasps. *Paralitomastix varicornis* and *Macrocentrus ancylivorus* are the most common, parasitizing high percentages of peach twig borer in untreated orchards in some areas. Other parasites include *Hyperteles lividus, Bracon gelechiae, Toxophoroides albomarginatus,* and *Spilochalcis* spp. The gray ant can be an important natural enemy in some orchards. Other general predators such as lacewing larvae, minute pirate bugs, assassin bugs, and spiders feed on larvae before they bore into shoots or fruit.

Bloomtime Applications of Bt. The microbial insecticide *Bacillus thuringiensis* (Bt) applied twice during bloom is sufficient to keep peach twig borer below damaging levels in many orchards. This treatment is a preferred alternative to traditional dormant applications of conventional insecticides, which may have negative environmental impacts. The bloomtime Bt treatments target the overwintering larvae, which feed on exposed shoots and buds before boring into the shoots. The larvae must consume the Bt; once larvae begin feeding inside shoots, Bt treatments are ineffective. Treatments applied before new shoot tissue is present are also ineffective. For best control, make two applications timed to larval emergence. Monitoring the percentage of larval emergence from hibernacula is time consuming, but allows the most accurate timing of Bt applications and determines the length of the emergence period, which can be affected by temperature. Starting at popcorn, examine at least 10 hibernacula each week in an orchard that has not been treated with a dormant insecticide to determine the percentage that have emerged. Make the first application when 20 to 40% of the larvae have emerged, and the second application 7 to 10 days later or when emergence has reached 80 to 100%. If emergence is spread out, a third spray may be needed when emergence finally reaches 80 to 100%. Alternatively, Bt applications can be timed according to bloom, but this approach is less precise than monitoring emergence. Make the first treatment at early bloom, just beyond the popcorn stage. Make the second treatment 7 to 10 days later. A third application may be needed at petal fall if bloom is extended due to cool weather.

Early-season applications of Bt will also control larvae of other caterpillar pests such as leafrollers or green fruitworms that may feed on flowers and foliage at this time. If possible, apply the Bt from the ground. If you must make aerial applications, use a total of 15 gallons of water or less per acre, and apply high enough above the canopy to ensure the material will stick to twigs and branches.

If you apply Bt during and after bloom instead of using dormant-season application of insecticide, you should apply dormant oil at high label rate for control of San Jose scale and mite eggs. In orchards where aphids are a problem, the oil treatment can be timed for the beginning of aphid egg hatch (see the section on aphids, below).

Other microbial insecticides and fermentation by-products are being developed for peach twig borer control. Watch for new registrations for these materials.

Dormant Treatments. Dormant or delayed dormant insecticide sprays can be used to control overwintering peach twig borer larvae. Dormant sprays of insecticidal oils alone will not control peach twig borer. An organophosphate insecticide used in combination with dormant oil also controls San Jose scale, European red mite and brown mite eggs, overwintering aphid eggs, and some other insect pests. However, the insecticide may be harmful to some natural enemy populations, raptors such as red-tailed hawks that roost in orchards during winter months, and water quality in watersheds that receive runoff from orchards. You can reduce the potential for harm to raptors by using half the rate of organophosphate, but then you may not control the target pests. If you use lower rates, be careful to achieve good coverage and follow up by monitoring for shoot strikes to determine the efficacy of the treatment. Do not use this approach in orchards where San Jose scale is a known problem. In some locations where there is particular concern with regard to organophosphates, you can substitute carbaryl or synthetic pyrethroids. If you use pyrethroids, be sure to watch scale and mite populations: pyrethroids are not as effective at controlling dormant scale insects, and are very harmful to the overwintering predators that normally prevent mites from reaching damaging levels the following season.

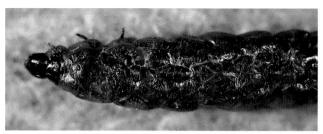

Paralitomastix varicornis is a common parasite of peach twig borer larvae, especially in northern California orchards. A parasitized larva eventually becomes an empty shell filled with a large number of parasite pupae, as shown here, that developed from a single egg.

Counts of male peach twig borer moths caught in pheromone traps like the one shown here are used to monitor the development of successive peach twig borer generations in an orchard.

To monitor for peach twig borer emergence, cut out small wedges of bark around the small, reddish piles of frass that mark the entrances of hibernacula (top arrow). Pinch each wedge of bark to open the hibernaculum and use a hand lens to look for a peach twig borer larva (bottom arrow). Beginning at popcorn, regularly check at least 10 and preferably 30 hibernacula from an orchard that was not sprayed with insecticide during the dormant season. Make at least one survey during the dormant season to get a baseline that represents 0% emergence.

Formatted degree-day calculation report
   Organism: Peach Twig Borer
   Lower threshold: 50°F
   Upper threshold: 88°F
   Calculation method: Single sine
   Upper cutoff method: Horizontal

Weather Station: KHFS32.L (Local Touchtone, #501)
   Latitude: 36 deg 35 min N, **Longitude:** 119 deg 30 min W,
      Elevation: 337 ft
   IPM records begin: January 1, 1982, **IPM records end:** on-going
   Soil type: Fine Sandy Loam, **Ground cover:** Bare Soil
   Additional information about KHFS32.L variables:
      Air temperature: Daily max/min

Note: All data were retrieved from station KHFS32.L.
Time period: March 30, 1997 to May 24, 1997, retrieved on April 6, 1998

Date	Air Temp (F) Min	Air Temp (F) Max	Daily Degree-Days	Accumulated Degree-Days
3/30/97	46.0	82.0	14.57	14.57
3/31/97	48.0	66.0	7.29	21.86
4/01/97	38.0	65.0	5.07	26.93
4/02/97	38.0	69.0	6.81	33.74
4/03/97	38.0	72.0	8.15	41.89
4/04/97	41.0	75.0	10.02	51.91
4/05/97	38.0	70.0	7.25	59.16
4/06/97	38.0	71.0	7.70	66.86
4/07/97	42.0	74.0	9.74	76.61
4/08/97	45.0	74.0	10.40	87.00
4/09/97	40.0	66.0	5.75	92.75
4/10/97	41.0	71.0	8.16	100.92
4/11/97	42.0	72.0	8.80	109.72
4/12/97	41.0	74.0	9.55	119.27
4/13/97	48.0	77.0	12.72	132.00
4/14/97	49.0	80.0	14.58	146.58
4/15/97	51.0	85.0	18.00	164.58
4/16/97	52.0	86.0	19.00	183.58
4/17/97	52.0	85.0	18.50	202.08
4/18/97	55.0	82.0	18.50	220.58
4/19/97	64.0	79.0	21.50	242.08
4/20/97	55.0	80.0	17.50	259.58
4/21/97	58.0	84.0	21.00	280.58
4/22/97	58.0	78.0	18.00	298.58
4/23/97	56.0	74.0	15.00	313.58
4/24/97	47.0	74.0	10.93	324.51
4/25/97	50.0	82.0	16.00	340.51
4/26/97	53.0	89.0	20.93	361.43
4/27/97	56.0	82.0	19.00	380.43
4/28/97	49.0	77.0	13.08	393.51*
4/29/97	51.0	76.0	13.50	407.01

*Begin monitoring for shoot strikes

Figure 39. Example from a degree-day calculation for peach twig borer obtained from the UC IPM Web site (www.ipm.ucdavis.edu).

Pheromone Mating Disruption. Place pheromone mating disruption dispensers in orchards in mid-March or as soon as you begin to catch the first moths in pheromone traps. FOLLOW THE MANUFACTURER'S RECOMMENDATIONS FOR DISPENSER PLACEMENT AND FOR THE NUMBER OF DISPENSERS TO USE. Use higher rates of pheromone application per acre for orchards with heavy infestations. Pheromone traps placed in disrupted orchards may catch a few moths during the first flight. Reapply the pheromones at the biofix timing for the third flight or after 90 days, whichever comes first. If moth response to the pheromone exceeds 5 moths per trap per week within one generation of harvest, use an insecticide treatment rather than replacing the dispensers. However, if your expected harvest date is within a week of the day you observe the increase in moths, a significant egg hatch may not occur before fruit is picked.

When using pheromone disruption, monitor the orchard regularly for shoot strikes toward the end of each generation (see Figure 38) to verify that the disruption is effective. If you find shoot strikes, examine them to find out whether the damage is being caused by peach twig borer or by oriental fruit moth. Also, monitor fruit from the tops of trees regularly for signs of larvae or damage; monitor more frequently during the final 4 weeks before harvest. Treat with insecticide if there are more than 3 to 5 shoot strikes per tree after the first moth flight, or if you find larvae in green fruit.

Monitoring. Monitor trees from mid-March through early April for shoot strikes caused by overwintering peach twig borer larvae. Twig strikes are often easiest to see near the tops of the trees and on vigorously growing shoots. Begin monitoring for the first flight of adults in late March by placing pheromone traps in the orchard. Follow the guidelines on pages 52 and 53, and place the traps about two feet into the tree canopy. Check the traps twice a week while you are trying to find the biofix for each generation—when an increasing catch of adults is found at least two counts in a row. After establishing the biofix, monitor the traps once a week. Remove any trapped moths each time and record the number caught. When you have established the biofix for each generation, begin a degree-day accumulation, using a lower threshold of 50°F (10°C) and an upper threshold of 88°F (31°C) (Table 32 in Appendix II). Use the degree-day accumulation to schedule other monitoring for damage and for treatment if monitoring indicates it is needed. A sample degree-day accumulation for peach twig borer is given in Figure 39. Continue trapping moths throughout the season and keep a record of the total number of moths trapped for the season.

A plot of the moth catch will tell you when each subsequent moth flight begins (Figure 40). Determine each biofix, start a new degree-day accumulation for that generation, and use it to schedule monitoring and any necessary treatments. This is especially important on later-season varieties of peaches and nectarines. A generation time for peach twig borer requires about 1080°D. Knowing this, you will find it easier to interpret trap catches and identify the biofix for the next generation (see Figure 40).

Begin monitoring for shoot strikes when the degree-day accumulation approaches 400. Check at least 10 trees in each orchard, selecting them at random from throughout the orchard (see Figure 36). Try to spend at least 5 minutes on each tree searching for shoot strikes. They will be easier to find on vigorously growing shoots near the tops of trees. Shoot strikes are very difficult to see from the ground on windy days. Begin to sample the ripening fruit about four weeks before harvest. Check fruit from the top of the tree, where damage occurs first, by knocking them out with a pole and looking for larvae or signs of larval damage.

Seasonal Treatments. If you find 3 or 4 shoot strikes per tree, treatment of the next generation of larvae is warranted. However, if harvest will occur before one more generation of peach twig borer have a chance to develop, treatment is probably unnecessary. Compare the forecast date for the next treatment time and the estimated harvest date before you make a decision. Use data from your trap catches and degree-day accumulations to schedule the treatments. Treatments must be timed to kill larvae before they bore into shoots or fruit, but after enough of the larvae have emerged. The optimum treatment time comes 400° to 500°D after the moth flight begins. One or two applications of Bt can be used for these later generations as an alternative to more broad-spectrum insecticides. When you use Bt, apply the first treatment at or slightly before 400°D and the second 4 to 7 days later. Good coverage of the shoot tips is critical.

Treatments may be needed later in the season to prevent fruit damage. Fruit are very susceptible to damage after they begin to show color. If treatment is needed at this time of the season, make applications at 400°D to make sure you avoid early fruit damage. Monitor fruit regularly and apply a spray immediately if you find any larvae entering fruit.

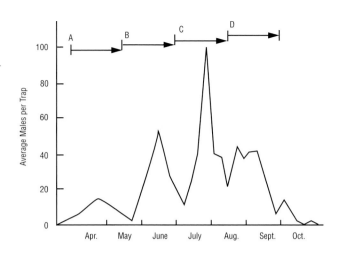

First biofix (A)	Start accumulating degree-days when you first begin trapping adults consistently. (A series of two or more successive counts at 2- to 3-day intervals; biofix is the first date in the series.)
Monitor damage	Begin monitoring the orchard for shoot strikes when the degree-day accumulation approaches 400.
Monitor next flight	Begin checking pheromone traps twice weekly when the degree-day accumulation reaches 900. Each generation (represented by an arrow in the graph) takes about 950–1,080 degree-days.
Second biofix (B)	Start accumulating degree-days when there is a consistent increase in the number of moths trapped.
Treatment	If monitoring following the first biofix indicated damaging levels are present (3–4 shoot strikes per tree or more), treat 400–500 degree-days after the second biofix.
Third biofix (C) Fourth biofix (D)	Start accumulating degree-days when there is a consistent increase in the number of moths trapped.
Treatment	If monitoring indicates treatment is necessary, treat 400 degree-days after the biofix to prevent fruit damage.

Figure 40. Keep track of peach twig borer flights in your orchard with a graph like this, which is a plot of trap catch data from an unsprayed peach orchard in the southern San Joaquin Valley. For each date that traps are checked, plot the average number of moths per trap. Use the graph to establish the biofix for each generation of adults (A, B, C, D). As outlined in the text, use degree-day accumulations to schedule monitoring and treatments, if dormant or bloomtime treatments have not kept the pest from reaching damaging levels.

Oriental fruit moth adults are dark gray with alternating black and gray markings that form a chevron pattern on the folded wings. This moth is smaller than the peach twig borer moth and lacks the snoutlike projection at the front of its head.

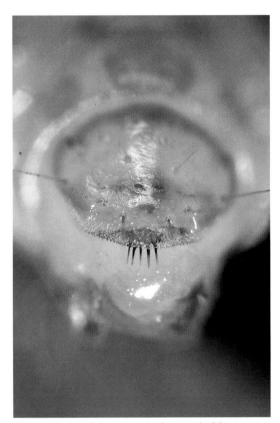

Oriental fruit moth larvae can be distinguished from codling moth larvae by the presence of an anal comb, visible with a hand lens, that protrudes from underneath the sclerite of the last abdominal segment.

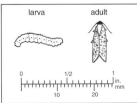

ORIENTAL FRUIT MOTH

Oriental Fruit Moth
Grapholita molesta

Oriental fruit moth is one of the most serious pests of peaches and nectarines in California. Larvae attack young shoots and fruit, causing damage similar to that caused by peach twig borer. Oriental fruit moth occasionally causes significant damage to apricots, cherries, plums, and prunes. Young trees are especially susceptible to serious damage. This pest is rare in central coast orchards. Other hosts for oriental fruit moth include almond and quince. Damage from oriental fruit moth can be kept to a minimum through the use of pheromone mating disruption or carefully timed pesticide sprays based on monitoring and degree-day accumulations. Intensive monitoring for oriental fruit moth with pheromone traps (and chemical treatment if necessary) is part of several phytosanitary (quarantine) work plans for certification and shipment of California stone fruits to export markets. For more information on phytosanitary work plans, contact the California Tree Fruit Agreement or California Grape and Tree Fruit League (listed in references).

Description and Biology
Oriental fruit moths usually go through five generations a year in California stone fruits. They sometimes complete a sixth generation if weather is warm in early spring. Oriental fruit moths overwinter as prepupae inside cocoons that they spin in protected places on the tree or on the ground around the base of the tree. After early-spring pupation, the first generation of adult moths emerges in February or early March. Adults are dark gray with alternating black and gray markings that form a chevron pattern on the wings, which are folded tentlike when the moth is at rest. The moths are smaller than codling moth or peach twig borer, with a wingspan of about ½ inch (12 mm). Adult moths of the lesser apple worm are caught from time to time in oriental fruit moth pheromone traps during spring. This moth is smaller than the oriental fruit moth and has a coppery sheen.

The white or cream-colored eggs are disc shaped, about ¹⁄₂₅ inch (1 mm) in diameter, and laid singly on the undersides of leaves near the fastest-growing shoot tips. Some eggs may be laid on upper leaf surfaces and, later in the season, on fruit. Eggs hatch in anywhere from 3 days to 3 weeks, depending on temperature. The larva's black head becomes visible shortly before hatch.

When they first hatch, the larvae are white with a black head, and about ¹⁄₁₆ inch (1.5 mm) long. At this stage they are hard to distinguish from codling moth larvae. Oriental fruit moth larvae turn pinkish as they get larger, and grow to about ½ inch (12 mm). They are similar in appearance to codling moth larvae, but can be distinguished by the presence of an anal comb on the last abdominal segment, which can be seen easily with a hand lens. This feature also is present on peach twig borer larvae.

First-generation larvae bore into the tips of shoots where they feed on xylem tissue. They tend to penetrate farther into shoot tips than do peach twig borer larvae. When mature, the oriental fruit moth larva leaves the shoot to pupate inside a cocoon under bark or on the ground. Second-generation larvae usually emerge during the first two weeks of May. Larvae of this generation feed primarily inside shoot tips, but the ripening fruit of early peaches or nectarines may be attacked. Later generations may attack shoots, but the females prefer to lay eggs on or near ripening fruit if it is present. Larvae of the fifth or sixth generation spin cocoons in September for overwintering. Some individuals of the third and fourth generations also may overwinter as dormant larvae inside cocoons. The seasonal development of oriental fruit moth is illustrated in Figure 41.

Damage

Larvae feeding inside new shoots kill the shoot tips. This kind of "shoot strike" is difficult to distinguish from one caused by peach twig borer unless the larva is present. Oriental fruit moth tends to kill more of the shoot tip, and peach twig borer tends to leave more frass on the surface of the damaged shoot. However, the shoot strikes of the two can be distinguished reliably only by identifying the larva inside the shoot, if it is present. As is the case for peach twig borer, oriental fruit moth shoot strikes are most apparent on vigorously growing shoots at the tops of trees. Old strikes that have dried can be confused with brown rot twig blight.

The most serious damage caused by oriental fruit moth is its damage to fruit. Small larvae usually enter fruit near the stem end, but may enter anywhere on the surface, especially where two fruit touch. The larvae bore into the fruit and feed around the pit. When mature, they leave the fruit to pupate. Fruit feeding causes processing fruit to be off grade and fresh market fruit to be culled. Feeding wounds can serve as infection sites for brown rot.

Management Guidelines

You can use pheromone confusion as a management technique to disrupt the mating of oriental fruit moth adults. Disruption is especially important for the first two generations in the spring. In most cases, pheromone disruption can eliminate the need for insecticide sprays. Alternatively, a program of pesticide sprays targeting the second and third generation before they bore into shoots or fruit can be employed, but this program is likely to disrupt biological control of other pests. Additional pesticide applications may be needed for later-maturing varieties if your monitoring for damage indicates they are necessary. Schedule spray applications using degree-day accumulations. Dormant sprays do not control this pest. Natural enemies do not keep oriental fruit moth below damaging levels in California.

If you do not use pheromone disruption, use pheromone traps to monitor moth flights during the season. Follow the guidelines on pages 52 and 53 for placement of pheromone

Oriental fruit moth larvae tend to bore deeper into shoot tips than peach twig borer larvae. However, the only reliable way to identify the cause of shoot damage is to find and identify the larva. Oriental fruit moth larvae do not have the dark banded appearance of older peach twig borer larvae.

Oriental fruit moth larvae bore into fruit and feed around the pit.

Macrocentrus ancylivorus is a common parasite of both peach twig borer and oriental fruit moth. An adult is shown here next to the remains of an oriental fruit moth cocoon.

JAN   FEB   MAR   APR   MAY   JUN   JUL   AUG   SEP   OCT   NOV   DEC

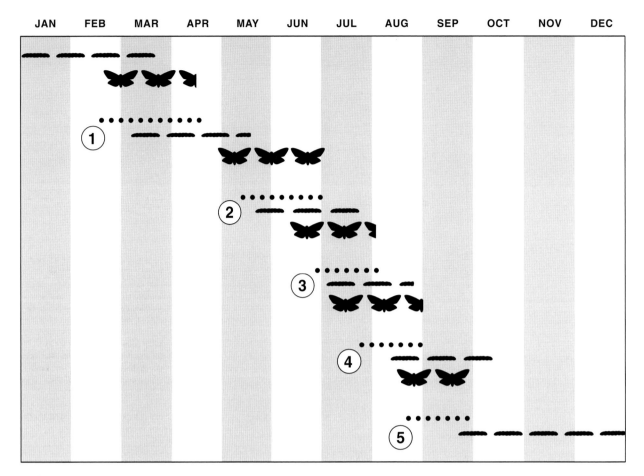

Figure 41. Seasonal development of oriental fruit moth. (Timing of moth flights will vary from one season to the next and from one growing area to another. Symbols represent the time during which a moth flight usually will occur. In any given location, the actual length of a moth flight will be shorter.)

Formula for bait to trap Oriental fruit moth adults:

5 quarts water
1 pound dark brown sugar
½ tsp (2.5 ml) terpinyl acetate
5 drops emulsifier

traps in orchards. In orchards where you are using mating disruption, these traps can monitor the effectiveness of pheromone dispensers: they should not catch males unless the dispensers are depleted of pheromone. Bait pan traps (see bait formula in box at left) can be used to keep track of moth flights in disrupted orchards. Although more difficult to use than pheromone traps, bait traps catch both male and female moths, giving a more accurate representation of population densities. It is also possible to determine if the females captured in the bait traps have mated by carefully dissecting their sex organs. You also can use pheromone traps placed in nearby, nondisrupted orchards to determine when flights are occurring, and as an indicator of when to look for shoot strikes in the pheromone-treated orchard.

Pheromone Mating Disruption. Place pheromone dispensers in orchards in late February, before the first generation of moths emerges. Follow the manufacturer's recommendations for placement, number of dispensers to use, and replacement timing and frequency. Use more dispensers for heavily infested orchards. If pheromone traps placed in disrupted orchards begin catching moths before the second flight, reapply the pheromones and apply an insecticide at the recommended timing for the second flight. If moth response to pheromone traps resumes within one generation of harvest, use an insecticide treatment instead of replacing dispensers.

When using pheromone disruption, monitor the orchard regularly for shoot strikes at the end of each generation (see Figure 42) to verify that the technique is having the desired effect. Use degree-day accumulations to schedule monitoring, as outlined under "Pesticide Spray Program". Also monitor fruit from the tops of trees regularly for signs of larvae or damage; monitor more frequently during the final 4 weeks before harvest. Treat the orchard with insecticide if there are more than 3 to 5 shoot strikes per tree or if larvae are found in fruit. If you observe shoot strikes, you can verify which species is causing them by monitoring for larvae 500°D after the next biofix.

Pesticide Spray Program. If you choose to follow a pesticide spray program, you must time treatments very carefully to reach the newly hatched caterpillars before they bore into shoots or fruit. When the number of trapped moths begins to increase in the spring, start accumulating degree-days using a 45°F (7°C) lower threshold and a 90°F (32°C) upper threshold (Table 33 in Appendix II). The second flight begins about 920 to 1010 degree-days after the first moth is trapped. Begin monitoring for the second moth flight about 800°D after the first flight. The second biofix is established when trap catches begin increasing, indicating the first moths from the second flight are being trapped (sometime in May). Begin a second degree-day accumulation using the same thresholds. It is always advisable and recommended to update and validate the biofix and degree-day accumulation for each moth generation by continuing to monitor with traps until harvest. DO NOT RELY ON ONLY A SINGLE EARLY-SEASON BIOFIX FOR MANAGEMENT DECISIONS ABOUT MID- AND LATE-SEASON GENERATIONS.

Start monitoring for shoot strikes 500°D after the beginning of each moth flight. Follow the procedure outlined for peach twig borer. If the presence of shoot strikes indicates that treatment is necessary, make the application 500°D after the beginning of the next moth flight. Figure 42 illustrates the relationship between trap catches, degree-day accumulations, monitoring, and treatment timing.

Begin monitoring fruit for worm damage after the first fruit begin to color. Sample at least once a week, and take fruit samples from the tops of trees, where fruit are most likely to be attacked. Treat immediately if you find larvae or damaged fruit.

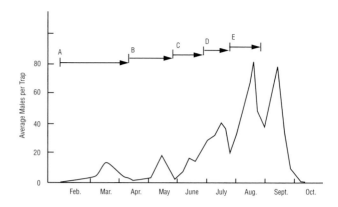

First biofix (A)	Start accumulating degree-days when you first begin trapping adults consistently.
Monitor damage	Begin monitoring the orchard for shoot strikes when the degree-day accumulation approaches 500.
Monitor next flight	Begin checking pheromone traps twice weekly when the degree-day accumulation reaches 800. Each generation (represented by an arrow in the graph) takes about 920–1,010 degree-days.
Subsequent biofixes (B, C, D, E)	Start accumulating degree-days when there is a consistent increase in the number of moths trapped.
Monitor damage	Begin monitoring the orchard for shoot strikes when the degree-day accumulation approaches 500.
Treatment	Treat 500 degree-days after the biofix if monitoring during the previous generation found more than 3–5 shoot strikes per tree.

Figure 42. A graph of trap catch data for oriental fruit moth can be used to schedule monitoring activities and treatments if needed. The example here is from an unsprayed peach orchard in the southern San Joaquin Valley. For each sampling date, plot the average number of moths per trap, and use the graph to establish the biofix for each generation (A, B, C, D, E). Use degree-day accumulations to schedule monitoring and treatments, if necessary, as outlined in the text.

All leafroller larvae have the habit of dropping on a silken thread when disturbed.

The fruittree leafroller larva is green with a dark head. Larvae of all leafroller species feed inside the protective shelter of leaves that they web together or to the surface of fruit.

Leafrollers

The larvae of several moths in the family Tortricidae are potentially damaging pests of stone fruits. They are similar in appearance and they often web leaves into rolled, protective shelters while feeding. They feed on blossoms and leaves and on the surface of fruit, sometimes webbing one or more leaves to the fruit for protection. They chew shallow holes in the fruit surface, often near the stem end. All have the characteristic behavior of wriggling backward when disturbed and dropping from a silk thread attached to the leaf or fruit surface. Some cause damage by feeding on flowers, young leaves, or small fruit during and just after bloom; others cause damage when later generations feed on fruit. Most serious damage results from fruit feeding. Young fruit may be destroyed, and scars on older fruit will cause them to be culled or downgraded at harvest. Feeding injury also may increase the incidence of brown rot and other fruit decays.

A number of parasites, including species of *Macrocentrus*, *Apanteles*, and *Exochus*, attack leafroller larvae. General predators such as lacewings, assassin bugs, and minute pirate bugs may feed on eggs and larvae. Preservation of natural enemy populations is an important part of keeping leafroller numbers low. Use selective materials that are least disruptive of biological control when treating other pests.

Dormant treatments and bloomtime Bt applications for other pests help keep leafroller populations under control. However, regular monitoring each season is important so that prompt action can be taken if damaging populations develop. Begin monitoring for the presence of larvae before petal fall, looking for any species that may cause fruit damage. Continue watching for the presence of leafrollers while monitoring for other pests during the season. This is especially important in orchards where bloomtime Bt sprays and pheromone confusion are used to control peach twig borer and oriental fruit moth. Bt applications will control leafroller larvae while they are small, before they have rolled leaves.

OMNIVOROUS LEAFROLLER

mature larva

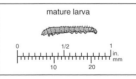

FRUITTREE LEAFROLLER

egg mass   larva

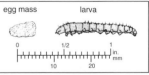

Omnivorous Leafroller, *Platynota stultana*

The omnivorous leafroller attacks a wide variety of woody plants, ornamentals, and weeds. It is a pest of stone fruits, especially nectarines, primarily in the San Joaquin Valley. It occurs in the Sacramento Valley, but seldom causes damage. Omnivorous leafroller larvae overwinter in various stages of development without entering dormancy. Larvae are light colored with dark brown or black heads. When mature they are about 0.6 inch (1.5 cm) long and have two slightly raised, oblong, whitish spots on the upper surface of each abdominal segment. Abdominal segments may have a greenish brown tinge. They pupate inside a webbed shelter.

Adults of the overwintering generation emerge in March. They are small, dark brown moths, ½ to ⅜ inch (9 to 12 mm) long with a dark band on the wing and a long snout. Eggs are laid in overlapping rows that resemble fish scales. The first generation of eggs usually is laid on weed hosts, and adults from this generation emerge in May or June to lay eggs in orchards on leaves and fruit. Larvae that hatch from this generation of eggs can cause significant damage in stone fruits.

To determine if control action is needed for omnivorous leafroller, you must know the orchard history and you must monitor for fruit damage. Pesticides applied for other pests such as peach twig borer and oriental fruit moth help reduce omnivorous leafroller populations. Remove fruit mummies and destroy potential overwintering weed hosts by clean cultivation. In some cases omnivorous leafroller may require separate pesticide treatment.

Fruittree Leafroller, *Archips argyrospila*

A common pest of apples and pears, fruittree leafroller also attacks stone fruits. It occurs in all growing areas and is the most important leafroller pest of apricots and cherries in the central coast. Fruittree leafroller overwinters as eggs, laid in masses on branches or tree trunks. Eggs hatch in early spring, around bloom time. Larvae are green with dark heads and are 0.8 to 1 inch (2 to 2.5 cm) long when mature. They pupate inside a webbed leaf shelter. Adults are about ½ inch long and reddish brown with white and gold markings on the wings. They emerge in May or June and lay eggs. There is only one generation a year.

Omnivorous leafroller eggs are laid in overlapping rows that resemble fish scales.

The omnivorous leafroller adult is a brown moth with dark brown bands on the forewings and a snoutlike projection from the head.

The larva of the omnivorous leafroller is light-colored with a brown or black head. Older larvae have light-colored oblong spots on each abdominal segment.

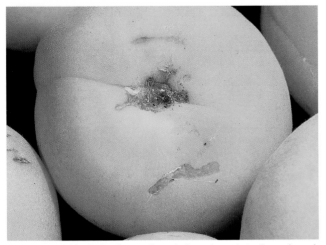

Obliquebanded leafroller larvae chew shallow channels in the surface of green or ripe fruit, such as the apricot shown here.

The orange tortrix larva is pale yellow or green with a light brown head. It has light-colored round spots on each abdominal segment.

Obliquebanded Leafroller, *Choristoneura rosaceana*

Obliquebanded leafrollers occur on a wide range of plants. They occasionally reach damaging levels on apricots, cling peaches, plums, and fresh market prunes. These leafrollers overwinter as larvae inside cocoons spun in protected places on trees. The overwintered larvae pupate in the spring, and the first generation of adults emerges in late March or April. Larvae are green, usually with black heads but sometimes with lighter-colored heads. Adults are reddish brown moths with dark brown bands on the wings. There are two or three generations a year in the Central Valley. Feeding by second-generation larvae causes small surface scars on fruit. Oblique-banded leafrollers seldom require control treatment, since bloomtime applications of Bt usually keep them from reaching damaging levels.

Orange Tortrix, *Argyrotaenia citrana*

Orange tortrix is a cyclical pest of stone fruits in coastal valleys. Several parasites and predators attack orange tortrix. The parasitic wasps *Apanteles aristoteliae*, *Exochus*, and *Hormius basalis*; the tachinid fly, *Nemorilla pyste*, spiders, and brown lacewings are the most important. These natural enemies usually keep orange tortrix populations under control, but damaging levels occur every few years.

Orange tortrix survives the winter as larvae inside fruit mummies or on alternate hosts. Mustard family weeds are a favored host. Adults of the overwintering generation emerge

Orange tortrix larvae chew shallow holes in the surface of fruit, often within fruit clusters where fruit touch.

OBLIQUEBANDED LEAFROLLER

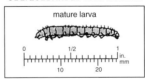

ORANGE TORTIX

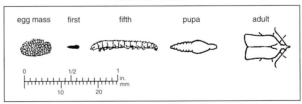

in January. They are light tan or gray moths with dark mottling on the forewings. Eggs are laid on leaves in overlapping rows that resemble fish scales. Larvae feed on leaves and buds, and chew shallow holes in fruit. Most damage occurs between fruit that are touching or where old flower parts or leaves are attached to fruit, providing a protected area where larvae can feed.

In coastal orchards where orange tortrix occurs, natural enemies and insecticide treatment in May for peach twig borer usually keep the pest controlled. Remove mummy fruit during the dormant season to help reduce overwintering populations. Control of mustards and other orange tortrix hosts also is helpful.

Green Fruitworms

The larvae of several species of noctuid moths, collectively referred to as "green fruitworms," occasionally cause economic damage to apricots, cherries, plums, and prunes. They are major pests of cherries in San Joaquin Valley and central coast orchards. The citrus cutworm, *Xylomyges curialis*, is the most damaging in the San Joaquin Valley, especially on plums, and also occurs in Sacramento Valley orchards. The species most frequently encountered in the Sacramento Valley and coastal areas are the humped green fruitworm, *Amphipyra pyramidoides*, and the speckled green fruitworm, *Orthosia hibisci*. Damage is similar for all.

Description and Biology

Adults of all green fruitworm species are fairly large, grayish or brownish moths. Most species overwinter as pupae; *Amphipyra* overwinters in the egg stage. For those species that overwinter as pupae, adults emerge and lay eggs over an extended period beginning in January. Eggs are laid singly or in clusters on branches and twigs; eggs are highly reticulated. Egg hatch begins when buds start to open and continues until after petal fall.

Green fruitworm larvae have pale green heads and bodies with white lines on the back and sides. They begin feeding from February to April. Young larvae feed on foliage; older larvae feed on leaves, flowers, and fruit. Green fruitworm larvae hide during the day. They do not web leaves together as do leafrollers. Larger larvae are more easily identifiable. Fruit damage usually begins after petal fall. When mature, larvae fall to the ground to pupate in the soil, where most species remain until the following spring. *Amphipyra* adults emerge in summer or fall and lay eggs on twigs or branches. For all species, there is only one generation a year, but because egg hatch occurs over a long period, all sizes of larvae may be present at the same time.

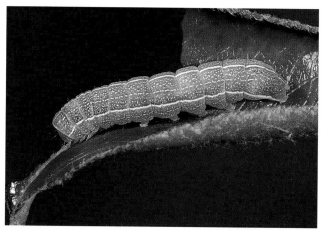

Green fruitworm larvae are light green with a pale green head and white lines on the sides and back. The speckled green fruitworm is shown here.

Green fruitworms feed on young fruit, resulting in large corky lesions and distorted growth as the fruit enlarge. The same symptoms can develop following early-season leafroller injury.

SPECKLED GREEN FRUITWORM

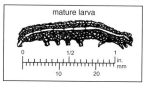

mature larva

The citrus cutworm larva has a wide white stripe down each side.

A cankerworm moves by arching its back in a characteristic inchworm fashion.

Green fruitworms and cankerworms may chew deep holes in small green fruit.

CITRUS CUTWORM

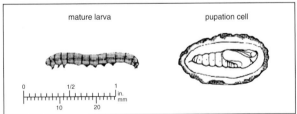

mature larva   pupation cell

CANKERWORM

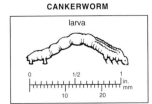

larva

Damage

Small larvae feeding on foliage and blossoms usually do not cause significant damage. Young larvae of citrus cutworm may tunnel into fruit, but the most important damage is caused by large larvae feeding on fruit surfaces. Individual larvae tend to feed for a short time on one fruit then move on to another. This means that a small population can cause significant damage. Damaged fruit usually remain on the tree until harvest, developing deep scars at the site of feeding injury. Thinning costs can increase if the thinners have to take time to remove damaged fruit.

Management Guidelines

Monitor for green fruitworms from the beginning of bloom until after petal fall. Carefully check young leaves and shoots for the presence of larvae and leaf damage. Use a beating tray to catch larvae that drop from the tree as you shake blossom clusters, young fruit, and foliage, or hit limbs with a beating stick. Check green fruit for the presence of larvae. Certain parasitic wasps (*Apanteles, Eulophus, Meteorus,* and *Ophion* spp.) help keep green fruitworm populations under control, but regular monitoring still is necessary to detect the development of damaging populations. If damaging populations are present, prevent fruit damage by treating with insecticide. A treatment threshold of 1 worm per 100 fruit clusters per 20-acre block or 1 worm per 50 beat tray samples has been developed for pears, and probably is applicable to stone fruits. *Bacillus thuringiensis* formulations are safe to use during bloom and are effective on small larvae. Bloomtime applications of Bt for peach twig borer may control green fruitworms and cankerworms as well. If you use other materials, make applications during or shortly after petal fall. Spot-treat localized infestations. Continue to monitor for the pest after treatment. If you find no more young larvae, you need take no more control action that season. Delayed dormant applications of oil plus organophosphate insecticide control green fruitworms.

Cankerworms

Two species of cankerworms occasionally cause damage in apricots, plums, and prunes. Fall cankerworm, *Alsophila pometaria,* and spring cankerworm, *Paleacrita vernata,* are similar in appearance. They cause fruit damage similar to that caused by green fruitworms.

Cankerworms overwinter as eggs and larvae hatch in spring to feed on leaves and sometimes fruit. They move along twigs and leaves in a characteristic inchworm fashion, and have a habit of standing upright on the prolegs that are at the tip of the abdomen and remaining motionless so that they resemble a leafless twig. Cankerworms go through one generation a year. They usually are controlled by dormant sprays and treatments made for other caterpillar pests during bloom. Young larvae can be controlled with *Bacillus thuringiensis.*

Codling Moth
Cydia pomonella

A major pest of apples, pears, and walnuts, codling moth also can be a serious pest of plums in the San Joaquin Valley and prunes in a few locations of the Sacramento Valley. It rarely attacks other stone fruits, even if they are adjacent to preferred hosts that are heavily infested. Peach orchards using pheromone mating disruption sometimes sustain codling moth damage in a few rows adjacent to unmanaged walnuts. Where codling moth damage is a problem, you can use monitoring and degree-day accumulations to schedule treatment.

Three generations of codling moth a year is typical for Central Valley apple, pear, and walnut orchards. In years with mild winters and warm springs, a fourth generation may occur. Codling moths overwinter as mature larvae in cocoons under loose bark or in other protected places on trees or beneath trash on the orchard floor. Adults emerge in March in Central Valley locations and in late March in coastal valleys. They are mottled gray, about ½ to ¾ inch (12 to 18 mm) long—a little larger than oriental fruit moths. Wings are folded tentlike over the body when the moths are at rest. They are distinguished by the presence of a coppery-colored spot near the tip of each forewing.

Adult females return to lay eggs on the same crop they fed on as larvae. Flattened, oval eggs are laid singly on the surface of leaves and fruit. Larvae hatch in 4 to 15 days, depending on temperatures. When they first emerge they are white with black heads, nearly identical to the young larvae of oriental fruit moth. Codling moth larvae may feed on leaves or other plant tissue for a short time, but unlike oriental fruit moth and peach twig borer, they enter fruit soon after hatching and remain there until they mature. Larvae attack green or ripe fruit, feed on the inside around the pit, and leave a conspicuous pile of frass at the entrance hole on the surface of fruit. The abundant frass and deeper penetration into the fruit distinguish codling moth fruit damage from that caused by peach twig borer. When mature, the larvae leave the fruit to pupate in protected places on or near the tree. A mature larva is pinkish white, has a mottled brown head, and is ½ to ¾ inch (12 to 18 mm) long. The absence of an anal comb distinguishes the codling moth larva from that of the oriental fruit moth.

Adults of the first spring generation emerge in late May or early June in the Central Valley, and mid-July in central coast areas. Second-generation adults emerge in late July or early August. Third-generation larvae usually spin cocoons and overwinter, but in years with above-average temperatures a fourth generation of larvae may be produced. In central coast orchards, second-generation larvae usually overwinter.

Some plum and prune orchards require treatment to prevent economic damage from codling moth larvae. In orchards where significant damage is expected, use pheromone traps and degree-day accumulations to schedule

The adult codling moth is mottled gray, larger than the oriental fruit moth, and characterized by a copper-colored spot near the tip of each forewing.

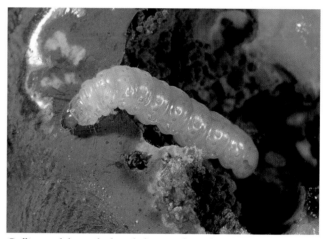

Codling moth larvae feed inside fruit, producing large piles of frass on the fruit surface. The codling moth larva is very similar in appearance to the oriental fruit moth larva, but has a mottled head and lacks an anal comb.

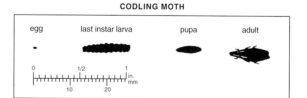

CODLING MOTH

egg   last instar larva   pupa   adult

Redhumped caterpillar larvae are yellow with black spots, with the fourth abdominal segment enlarged to form a red hump. They feed in groups, skeletonizing leaves.

Hyposoter fugitivus, a major parasite of redhumped caterpillars, forms a white or gray pupal case with a dark band around the middle. Each of the pupal cases in this photograph is still surrounded by the remains of its caterpillar host.

The redhumped caterpillar parasite *Apanteles* sp. forms a fluffy white mass of pupal cases (*left*). The young caterpillars on the right are not parasitized.

REDHUMPED CATERPILLAR

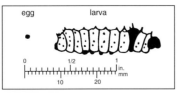

treatment. Place pheromone traps in orchards early in March to capture males from the first flight of overwintering codling moths. Start accumulating degree-days when you first begin to consistently trap moths. Calculate degree-days using the same temperature thresholds as for peach twig borer: 50°F lower and 88°F upper (Table 32 in Appendix II). In orchards where codling moth damage has been heavy in the past, apply insecticide when the degree-day accumulation reaches 250° to 300°D; if damage has been light, wait until 400° to 500°D to make the application. One treatment usually is all that is needed in plum and prune orchards.

Redhumped Caterpillar
Schizura concinna

Redhumped caterpillar attacks a number of tree crops. In stone fruits, it is important primarily on prunes and plums in Central Valley orchards. It occurs on apricots and cherries, but rarely is a serious pest. This pest may cause severe defoliation if natural enemies fail to prevent the buildup of large populations, so it is important that you monitor regularly to check for population increases.

Redhumped caterpillars overwinter as larvae in cocoons in the soil. They pupate in the spring and emerge as adults in May. The adult is a brownish gray moth with a wingspan of about 1½ inch (3–4 cm). The females lay spherical white eggs in clusters on the underside of leaves.

Larvae are yellowish orange with black spots when small, and they tend to feed in groups on the undersides of leaves, skeletonizing the leaves or leaving only the clear upper epidermis of the leaf clinging to the veins. The mature caterpillar is yellow with black and white stripes, black spots, and a red head. The fourth body segment is red and enlarged to form a hump, with two prominent black spines. Shorter spines are present on the other body segments.

First-generation larvae drop to the ground to pupate, and adults emerge in July to lay a second generation of eggs. Second-generation larvae usually are heavily parasitized. When this generation matures some of the larvae remain in the soil until the following spring, but most pupate. Adults emerge in September. Larvae of the third generation can destroy large amounts of foliage if populations have not been kept in check by natural enemies. When mature, third-generation larvae drop to the ground to overwinter in the soil.

Begin looking for redhumped caterpillars in May, when eggs or larvae of the first generation may be present. Check trees throughout the orchard, looking at the undersides of leaves for egg masses or groups of small larvae. Skeletonized leaves that turn brown may indicate the presence of redhumped caterpillars.

If you find larvae of the first generation, do not treat. Prune out and destroy localized infestations. Monitor again in July for second-generation larvae and for the presence of parasites before you make a treatment decision. Look for parasite pupae among larval colonies. The most common parasite species are *Hyposoter fugitivus*, which forms a single pupal case that is white with a black band around the middle, and *Apanteles* sp., which forms a fluffy white mass of pupal cases. If 80% or more of the larval population is parasitized, no treatment is needed. If parasitization is very low, prune out and destroy infestations or treat infested trees. Infestations tend to be very localized, so spot treatments usually suffice. Formulations of Bt are effective against the larvae.

Western Tussock Moth
Orgyia vetusta

Populations of western tussock moth occasionally build up to damaging levels in apricot or cherry orchards in coastal areas. This caterpillar pest attacks a wide variety of deciduous trees. It feeds on leaves and fruit; damage becomes significant when large numbers of larvae chew shallow holes in the surface of fruit. Natural enemies usually keep tussock moth under control.

Tussock moths survive the winter as fuzzy egg masses that females cement to their pupal cases and cover with hairs. Larvae first appear in March. They are showy caterpillars, black or dark green with red and yellow spots along the body and long hairs. Two long tufts of black hair are present on the head and one on the tail. Four prominent tufts of hair show on the back. Adults are active from May through July. Males are gray moths; females are grayish white and lack wings. Adult tussock moths are sometimes mistaken for gypsy moths, which have a blue coloration.

Watch for tussock moth egg cases on leaves and twigs as you monitor orchards in the spring before and during bloom. Begin to look for larvae in March. Infestations can be controlled with *Bacillus thuringiensis* while larvae are small. You can control localized infestations by pruning them out and destroying them. Population buildups tend to be localized because the females are flightless.

Western tussock moth egg masses are laid in a protected place on the tree and have a fuzzy appearance because they are covered with hairs deposited by the ovipositing female.

Western tussock moth larvae are colorful caterpillars with prominent tufts of hair on the back and two long tufts of black hair on the head. They feed on leaves and chew shallow holes in fruit.

WESTERN TUSSOCK MOTH

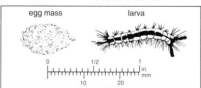

egg mass   larva

0   1/2   1 in.
mm
10   20

The forest tent caterpillar has prominent blue stripes along the side and white, keyhole-shaped spots on the back. Tent caterpillars form mats or tents of webbing. They feed outside these tents, skeletonizing leaves.

Tent caterpillars overwinter as egg masses encircling twigs or small branches of host trees.

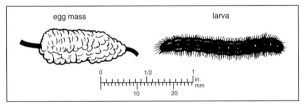

WESTERN TENT CATERPILLAR

egg mass   larva

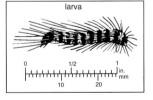

FALL WEBWORM

larva

Tent Caterpillars
Malacosoma spp.

Infestations of tent caterpillars occur occasionally in stone fruits. They tend to be concentrated in individual trees scattered throughout the orchard. Tent caterpillars overwinter as eggs laid on host branches in masses that are covered with a hard brown material. Larvae hatch in spring and early summer, then colonies of larvae build large silk nests. Western tent caterpillar, *Malacosoma californicum*, is yellowish brown with adjacent rows of blue and orange spots along the back. The western tent caterpillar builds a silk tent in a branch crotch and feeds outside the tent. Forest tent caterpillar, *M. disstria*, is grayish with yellow stripes along the side, separated by a broad blue stripe, and a row of white, keyhole-shaped spots on the back. Larval colonies of this species build a mat of webbing rather than a tent, and the larvae move away from the webbing to feed. Both species skeletonize leaves, and each has one generation each year.

Localized treatment usually is all that is needed when tent caterpillar infestations appear. Whenever possible, prune out and destroy infestations. Otherwise, spot-treat infested trees with the least disruptive material available as soon as you find caterpillars. *Bacillus thuringiensis* is effective on small caterpillars.

Fall Webworm
Hyphantria cunea

Larvae of the fall webworm feed on a variety of deciduous trees, forming large colonies inside tents of silk that they spin over the branch tips. They occasionally attack plums and prunes, but rarely occur on other stone fruits. Treatments applied for other pests usually keep fall webworms under control.

Fall webworms overwinter as pupae in sheltered places on bark or on the ground. Adults are large moths and most are pure white, though some have black specks on their wings. They emerge in late spring and lay eggs in masses of several hundred on the undersides of leaves.

Webworm larvae are pale green or yellowish with long grayish hairs that grow from black, yellow, or reddish orange warts. Larvae are about 1 inch (2.5 cm) long when mature. As soon as they hatch, the larvae from an egg mass spin silk to enclose several leaves. They feed inside the silk tent, which they keep enlarging to enclose more and more foliage. When mature, they leave the tent and crawl to secluded locations to pupate. There are two generations a year in the southern Sacramento and San Joaquin valleys and one generation in other locations.

Watch for the occurrence of webworm tents. Usually they are first seen on the edge of the orchard. If you find a few tents, prune them out and destroy them. If there are too many to prune, use a handgun applicator to spot-treat infestations with biological insecticide mixed with a spreading agent that will penetrate the silken tent. A number of natural enemies attack fall webworm, but they cannot control established colonies.

PLANT BUGS

Stink bugs and lygus bugs can cause serious damage when they move into stone fruit orchards from uncultivated areas, riparian habitats, nearby host crops, or orchard floor hosts. These insect pests overwinter on host plants on the orchard floor or outside of the orchard, and cause their most serious damage when large numbers move into an orchard to feed on fruit. Stink bugs and lygus bugs are true bugs with piercing and sucking mouthparts that they use to feed under the surface of fruit, on developing seeds of some plants, and sometimes on foliage. True bugs hatch from eggs as *nymphs*, which resemble adults but are smaller and lack wings. Nymphs increase in size as they progress through a series of *molts*, finally reaching the adult stage after the last molt. In stone fruits they are damaging to peaches, nectarines, and plums, causing discoloration and distortion of both green and ripening fruit. Lygus bugs may also damage shoot tips. Problems with plant bugs are related to the proximity of overwintering plant hosts and year-to-year fluctuations in populations. These pests can be particularly troublesome where legume cover crops are grown. Plant bugs can migrate into orchards quickly, so it is important to check for bugs or their damage regularly when fruit are present.

Stink Bugs

Several stink bug species may invade stone fruits to feed on green or ripening fruit. The most common is the consperse stink bug, *Euschistus conspersus*, but others that may cause damage in stone fruits include the green stink bug, *Acrosternum hilare*, the redshouldered stink bug, *Thyanta pallidovirens*, and Uhler's stink bug, *Chlorochroa uhleri*. Stink bugs attack a wide range of tree fruit, vegetable, and field crops, and build up on broadleaf weeds, especially mustards, legumes, blackberries, Russian thistle, and curly dock. Populations tend to follow cycles, building up to damaging levels once every few years. When stink bugs feed on fruit, they distort fruit growth or discolor small areas below the fruit surface. They are most serious as pests of peaches and nectarines, but may also damage plums. Stink bugs are most likely to cause major damage in orchards with legume or sod cover crops, or in orchards

Fall webworms are pale green or yellow with tufts of long gray hairs growing from black, yellow, or orange warts.

Fall webworm larvae feed inside silken tents, which are enlarged to cover more and more foliage as available food is consumed.

Adult consperse stink bugs are brown or gray. The consperse stink bug is one of the most commonly occurring stink bug species in stone fruit orchards.

The rough shield bug occurs commonly in stone fruit orchards, but is considered beneficial because it feeds on other insects and does not harm fruit. It can be distinguished from harmful species by its rough, sculptured appearance.

Feeding by stink bugs, such as the green stink bug shown here, causes dark sunken spots or patches on the fruit surface. Beneath the surface, tissue at feeding sites may be white and pithy or brown and corky.

Stink bug eggs are barrel-shaped and laid in clusters. They may be attacked by any of a number of parasitic wasps, such as *Trissolcus euschisti*, shown here attacking a cluster of consperse stink bug eggs. Parasitized eggs turn dark brown or black.

A parasitized stink bug egg has a jagged exit hole where an adult parasite has chewed through the shell. A normal hatched egg has a circular exit hole with smooth edges.

STINK BUG

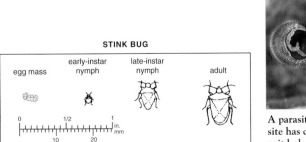

egg mass   early-instar nymph   late-instar nymph   adult

0   1/2   1 in.
          10   20 mm

near wild areas or levees. Growers can usually prevent damage by monitoring weeds and cover crops and making spot or border treatments when populations begin to build up. When monitoring indicates significant fruit damage throughout the block, treatment may be needed. Be sure to check cover crops for the presence of stink bugs, and avoid mowing cover crops when fruit are young if stink bugs are present.

Description and Biology

Adult stink bugs are about ½ inch long and shield shaped. They may be grayish, brown, or green, depending on the species. The adults overwinter under leaf litter, in boxes, around the crowns of host plants, and in clumps of grass on the orchard floor or in uncultivated areas. They may be seen flying around on warm days, but they do not begin to feed until late March or early April.

In the spring, the overwintered adults begin feeding on broadleaf hosts in orchards or other locations. They may lay eggs on broadleaf weeds or cover crops in the orchard or may move out of the orchard in search of suitable hosts. The barrel-shaped eggs are laid in clusters on leaves. Egg coloration and markings are distinctive for most species. Young stink bugs (nymphs) are similar in shape to adults, but in many cases have very different coloration.

Adults from the first generation of eggs laid in the spring feed on broadleaf hosts until May or early June in uncultivated areas, or within orchards if suitable hosts are available. As hosts begin to dry up the bugs move into irrigated areas. They may feed on broadleaf weeds or cover crops on the orchard floor, but they will also attack developing fruit. Eggs are laid on broadleaf hosts or on the leaves of orchard trees. The second generation hatches in late July or early August and can cause severe damage to fruit before harvest. Adults of this generation migrate to overwintering sites when temperatures fall in the autumn.

The rough shield bug, *Brochymena sulcata*, is a beneficial insect, and should not be confused with harmful stink bug species. This stink bug is common in Central Valley orchards, especially on apricots and prunes. Adults are ½ to ⅔ inch long, brownish or gray, with a very rough and angular shape. Both nymphs and adults feed on caterpillars and other insects.

Damage

Stink bugs feed on green or ripe fruit, using their tubelike piercing mouthparts to withdraw fluid from tissue near the fruit surface. In the process they kill small patches of tissue at the feeding site. Damage usually is first seen in May or June, when the first hatch of the season begins feeding on fruit; Say's stink bug may begin feeding on fruit in April. On green fruit, small, bluish green spots develop at feeding sites. Fruit tissue under the peel turns gray, whitish, or brown and corky. Gum may ooze from the feeding wounds on green peaches and nectarines. As fruit continues to expand, damaged areas become dimpled or depressed because fruit tissue at the feeding site does not continue to grow. The resulting growth distortion is sometimes called *catfacing*. When stink bugs feed on ripe fruit, the only visible damage takes the form of whitish pithy spots under the surface at feeding sites. Stink bug injury usually penetrates deeper into the fruit than damage from lygus bugs, and the presence of whitish areas is more characteristic of stink bug injury. Stink bugs do not feed on shoot tips or leaves of stone fruits.

Management Guidelines

An important objective in stink bug management in stone fruits is to keep damaging populations from moving into the fruit trees. Begin looking for consperse stink bugs on broadleaf weeds in March when you are monitoring for other insects in the orchard. Favored hosts include curly dock, common mullein, and Russian thistle. The sweep net is the best tool for monitoring weeds and cover crops for stink bugs. If you find the bugs, apply spot treatments to kill adults before they can move to other locations. Orchards with legume cover crops are more likely to harbor stink bug populations. You may want to keep the floors of peach and nectarine orchards free of vegetation or choose a cover crop that is least favorable for stink bugs, such as cereal grain turned under in the spring as a green manure cover crop (see the discussion of cover crops in the chapter on vegetation management). If you grow legume cover crops such as vetch or clover in peach or nectarine orchards, monitor them carefully for stink bugs in the spring. If stink bugs are present, cultivate or mow closely before green fruit are present to help prevent stink bug damage. Check nearby locations where stink bugs may build up, such as uncultivated areas with blackberry vines or adjacent fields of alfalfa or tomatoes.

Look for stink bugs moving into trees from cover crops or adjacent wild areas in mid-May. Monitor orchards where pheromone mating disruption is in effect by sampling weekly with a beating tray along any edge of the orchard that is adjacent to habitat that favors stink bugs. In early June begin to check fruit for damage. Look for discolored spots and specks of brown excrement left by feeding stink bugs. If you find damage, remove the fruit's peel and look for the characteristic discoloration of fruit tissue near the surface. If you find damaged fruit and see stink bugs, you may need to treat with insecticide. No specific treatment thresholds are currently available, but just a few bugs per tree can do substantial damage. Use a beating sheet or tray to verify that stink bugs are present before you apply a treatment. Some orchards seem to have chronic stink bug problems. In these cases, the greatest problem often is in a particular portion of the orchard. Concentrate your sampling in these areas to delineate the infested area; it may be possible to limit your treatment to the infested area and still achieve control.

A pheromone lure and trap is available commercially for consperse stink bug, and research is under way to develop pheromone lures for other species as well. The pheromone trap can be useful in detecting an infestation. Place the trap on a brick at the base of the tree or in the crotch of the tree.

An adult lygus bug is characterized by a conspicuous yellow or light green triangle in the middle of the back.

Early instars of lygus bugs are tiny (*left*) and may be confused with aphids, although they move much faster than aphids. Later instars (*right*) have conspicuous black dots on the back.

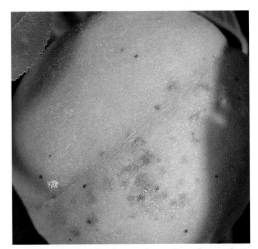

Small bluish spots develop on the surface of green fruit where lygus bugs and other true bugs have fed. Gum deposits may form. Cracks often develop at these spots as the fruit expands.

Do not hang the traps from the tree; the bugs must crawl into the traps. Pheromone traps are particularly useful for early-season (May and June) detection of stink bugs.

If stink bugs have been a problem in your orchard, clean cultivation in fall will reduce their overwintering populations.

Lygus Bugs
Lygus hesperus, L. elisus

Lygus bugs may damage shoot tips and fruit of peaches and nectarines. They are not significant pests of other stone fruits. Damage is most likely to occur in orchards near alfalfa, cotton, safflower, or uncultivated areas.

Description and Biology

Adult lygus bugs are $3/16$ to $1/4$ inch (5 to 6 mm) long and variable in color. *Lygus elisus* adults are pale greenish and *L. hesperus* adults are yellowish to reddish brown. Both species are characterized by a conspicuous yellow or pale green triangle in the middle of the back. Adult lygus bugs overwinter in plant debris, in the crowns of host plants on the orchard floor, or in uncultivated areas outside of the orchard. They may be difficult to see because they fly or hide when disturbed. Eggs are inserted into the tissue of host plants and hatch in 1 to 5 weeks. First- and second-instar lygus nymphs are tiny, light green, and may be mistaken for aphids. However, young lygus move much more quickly than aphids and the tips of their antennae are reddish. Nymphs of the third and later instars are pale green with conspicuous black dots on the back. Lygus bugs prefer to feed on the flower buds of legumes and a number of weed species.

When weed hosts begin to dry up in April, lygus adults fly to irrigated hosts such as alfalfa, cotton, and safflower, or into peach and nectarine orchards. The adults may begin to feed on orchard trees at this time or may feed and reproduce on preferred host plants on the orchard floor. Lygus adults may also move into orchards when nearby host crops such as alfalfa are mowed. Lygus adults feed on shoot tips and may lay eggs in soft shoot growth or in green fruit, but lygus nymphs are rarely found in stone fruit trees.

Damage

Feeding damage from lygus bugs on green fruit resembles that caused by stink bugs: small, bluish green spots on the fruit surface. Gum may be present. On ripe fruit, feeding causes small spots to appear on the surface. Beneath the skin, small cavities

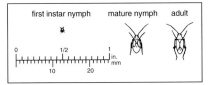

form when damaged cells collapse. Affected areas are shallower than is the case with stink bug damage because the mouthparts of lygus bugs are shorter and do not penetrate as deeply into the fruit. Gum deposits do not form on ripe fruit. Cracks may develop as damaged fruit continues to expand, and fruit may become misshapen or "catfaced." Fruit damage from lygus bugs is sporadic. Lygus bugs also may feed on growing shoot tips, killing the terminals and causing shoots to become bushy as the lateral buds push. Thrips and another plant bug, *Calocoris norvegicus*, cause similar damage on shoots, so check for the presence of bugs or thrips to determine the cause. This type of shoot tip damage can be confused with shoot strikes caused by peach twig borer and oriental fruit moth.

Damage in peaches and nectarines appears to be caused by adult lygus bugs, and not nymphs. Lygus damage tends to be worse in orchards near uncultivated areas or orchards adjacent to preferred host crops such as alfalfa, cotton, potato, safflower, or tomato, and in years when weather conditions favor lush spring vegetation in and around orchards. More damage occurs in outer orchard rows nearest the source of migrating adults.

Management

Lygus bugs prefer flowering weed hosts or flowering crops such as alfalfa, vetch, and safflower. In locations where it is hard to prevent lygus migrations, you can help prevent fruit damage by maintaining a vigorous cover crop in or adjacent to your orchard. If you are growing alfalfa near peaches or nectarines, strip mowing will keep lygus bugs from migrating out of the alfalfa. As an alternative, you can leave a strip nearest the orchard unmowed. Otherwise, lygus bugs are likely to migrate into the orchard when the alfalfa is cut. Where weed hosts are present near orchards, try to destroy them early in the spring before lygus bugs have reached the adult stage.

Clean cultivation or a weed-free cover crop that is not a lygus bug host will reduce the potential for damage. If weed hosts are present in the orchard, use a sweep net to check for lygus bugs in spring. If any are found, treat the weeds before they dry up. Do not disturb infested weeds during or immediately after bloom in the orchard. If you are maintaining a cover crop on the orchard floor that may host lygus bugs, avoid water stress, which will drive the lygus into the trees, and do not mow the cover crop when adult lygus bugs are present.

Monitor fruit regularly for damage during the season. It is a good idea to monitor orchards regularly near lygus weed hosts or near uncultivated areas such as levees. Weekly sampling with a beat tray will work, with sampling concentrated on the side of the orchard nearest the lygus bug hosts. If you begin to see lygus bugs in the trees or lygus bug damage, treatment may be warranted. Check for the presence of lygus bugs in the orchard before treating. Lygus bug damage sometimes goes unseen until the bugs have migrated out of the orchard.

A Plant Bug
Calocoris norvegicus

The plant bug *Calocoris norvegicus*, which occurs in Central Valley orchards north of Visalia, is easily confused with lygus bugs. Adult *Calocoris* are green and can be distinguished from lygus bugs by the presence of two black dots on the back just behind the head. They cause the same kind of damage as lygus bugs if they feed on fruit. *Calocoris* populations may build up on cover crops, especially purple vetch. When populations are high, nymphs may move into trees to feed on the tender new shoot growth, killing shoot tips. This damage may be confused with peach twig borer or oriental fruit moth damage, but in this case there is no tunneling inside the green twig, and small, green *Calocoris* nymphs may be seen if you shake the shoot tips onto a beating tray. These nymphs do not have red-tipped antennae and black spots on the back as do lygus

The plant bug *Calocoris norvegicus* occurs commonly in stone fruit orchards and can cause the same kind of fruit damage as lygus bugs. The two prominent black dots on the segment behind the head distinguish it from lygus bugs. Nymphs are similar to lygus nymphs but lack black dots on the back.

Nymphs of *Calocoris norvegicus* may feed on developing shoot tips low in the tree, causing damage that may be confused with shoot damage caused by peach twig borer or oriental fruit moth. However, there is no tunneling in these shoot tips, and nymphs can usually be found if you shake damaged shoots onto a beating sheet. Lygus bugs can cause the same type of damage.

nymphs. *Calocoris* nymphs tend to be longer and narrower, and have fine, black hairs on the body.

SCALE INSECTS

San Jose scale is a serious pest of stone fruits in Central Valley growing areas. Other scale insects that may occasionally cause problems include European fruit lecanium, black scale, and Italian pear scale. These insects spend much of their life cycle settled in one spot under a protective shell, with a tiny mobile stage called a *crawler* that hatches underneath the covering of the female and moves to another feeding site. Scale insects feed on twigs and branches; San Jose scale and European fruit lecanium also feed on fruit.

San Jose Scale
Quadraspidiotus perniciosus

San Jose scale attacks a wide range of woody plants, and is a serious pest of all stone fruits. It damages developing twigs, older wood, and fruit. Dormant oil sprays and natural enemies may keep San Jose scale from reaching damaging levels, but regular monitoring is necessary to determine the need for additional treatments.

Description and Biology

The mature San Jose scale female is covered by a dark grayish, flattened, circular shell, about 1/12 inch (2 mm) in diameter, with a lighter raised area in the center called the *nipple*. Underneath the shell-like covering the flattened, somewhat pear-shaped body of the female is yellow. An immature male scale has an elongated covering. Mature males are tiny, yellow, winged insects about the size of the parasitic wasp *Aphytis*, which attacks San Jose scale and frequently is caught in traps used to monitor male scale. The male scale can be distinguished by its small black eyes, a black band across the back, and its long beadlike antennae.

Eggs hatch almost immediately after they have been laid. The crawlers that hatch from the eggs are tiny, yellow, and oval, with visible legs and antennae. They emerge from under the female's shell and move about in search of suitable feeding sites. After settling down to feed, the crawler inserts its mouthparts into the host surface, loses its eyes, legs, and antennae, and secretes a white waxy covering. This is the white cap stage. After several days of feeding, the scale secretes a dark wax that at first forms a dark band around the edge of the white cap and eventually covers the entire scale. This is the black cap stage.

After the first molt, the waxy covering becomes dark gray. At this stage males are distinguishable because their covering is elongated while the female's covering remains circular. Females continue to enlarge their covering and remain legless, reaching maturity without a third molt. Males molt to a prepupa stage and then to a pupa that has well-developed legs. They emerge as winged adults after a fourth molt.

Mature female San Jose scale have a circular shell-like covering less than 1/10 inch in diameter. If you turn the shell over, the flattened yellow body of the scale insect can be seen. A healthy female is shown on the right, and a female parasitized by *Encarsia perniciosi* on the left.

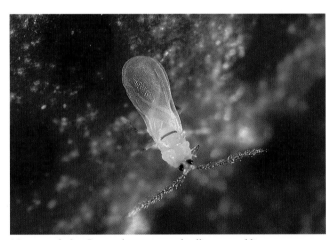

Mature male San Jose scale are tiny and yellow, resembling some parasitic wasps. The black band across the back and the black eyes help distinguish the male scale.

The tiny yellow "crawlers" that hatch from San Jose scale eggs move to new feeding sites, settle down to feed, and then secrete a white waxy coating. This stage is called the white cap stage, several of which are shown here next to a crawler.

As the white cap stage of San Jose scale develops further, secretion of dark wax turns the scale covering black. This is called a black cap, and is the primary overwintering stage. Both white cap and black cap stages are susceptible to oil sprays.

Several parasitic wasp species attack San Jose scale. The most common are *Aphytis* species (such as the one shown here attacking a female scale) and *Encarsia perniciosi.*

Red halos develop around San Jose scale on green twigs and fruit. Fruit with this type of damage are culled at harvest.

The tiny nitidulid beetle *Cybocephalus californicus* is an important predator of armored scale insects such as San Jose scale.

Longitudinal cracks form in bark that is heavily infested with San Jose scale. Gum deposits often form on the cracked bark.

SAN JOSE SCALE

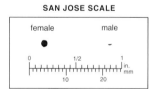

female   male

0   1/2   1 in.
mm
10   20

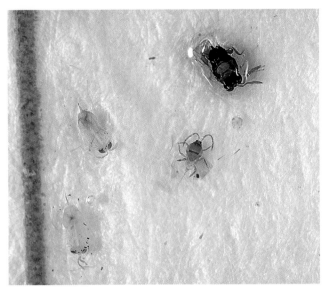

San Jose scale pheromone traps will trap parasites as well as male scale, all of which are attracted to the pheromone. Shown here are two *Aphytis* sp. (*left*), a male scale (*center*), and *Encarsia perniciosi* (*upper right*).

San Jose scale overwinters predominantly in the black cap stage on infested twigs and branches. The overwintering generation matures in March and first-generation crawlers begin emerging in late April or early May. There are four or five generations a year. The later generations overlap, so crawlers can be found throughout the summer and fall.

Damage

San Jose scale attacks twigs, leaves, bark, and fruit, feeding on plant juices and weakening trees when infestations are heavy. On fruit and green twigs, a red halo develops around each scale. Scale-infested fruit are culled at harvest to meet cosmetic or quarantine standards. On mature trees, most scale are on the bark where they may be difficult to see except in the white cap stage. Heavy infestations cause the bark to develop longitudinal cracks. Severe infestations on twigs may cause gumming and kill twigs, branches, or entire trees if left uncontrolled.

Management Guidelines

A number of natural enemies help keep San Jose scale populations suppressed. Species of the parasitic wasps *Encarsia* (formerly *Prospaltella*) and *Aphytis* lay an egg under the scale cover. The parasite larva consumes the scale body, and the new adult parasite cuts a circular hole in the scale cover to emerge (see Figure 37). Both larvae and adults of the twice-stabbed lady beetle, *Chilocorus orbus*, and the small nitidulid beetle, *Cybocephalus californicus*, feed on scale crawlers and settled nymphs. Broad-spectrum pesticides applied during the summer may destroy natural enemy populations and result in increased scale infestations. Dormant sprays are

recommended to keep scale populations suppressed, followed by regular monitoring to see if populations are increasing and to assess the presence of biological control. Dormant oil without organophosphates is effective against the white cap and black cap stages, but will not control more mature scale. GOOD SPRAY COVERAGE AND SUFFICIENTLY HIGH APPLICATION RATES ARE ESSENTIAL FOR EFFECTIVE CONTROL; DO NOT REDUCE DORMANT OIL RATES IF SCALE IS PRESENT.

Monitor for scale regularly throughout the orchard. During the dormant season, check prunings from tree tops to see if scale infestations are developing. Look for dead leaves clinging to branches, a sign of heavy scale infestations. (Dead leaves may also cling to twigs killed by brown rot or other diseases.) You can assess the level of parasitism by taking 100 samples of second-year wood and estimating the proportion of scale insects that exhibit parasite exit holes. Because female parasites are attracted by the pheromone traps used to monitor for male scale (see next paragraph), you can use counts of parasites caught in these traps to assess the level of parasitism. During the season you can keep track of the appearance and development of scale populations by trapping crawlers with double-sided sticky tape. Choose at least 10 trees at random from each orchard and place tape on 1 or 2 limbs of each tree. Place tape around scaffold limbs that are 1 to 2 inches in diameter; be sure the tape is wrapped snugly around the limb (Figure 43) so the crawlers cannot crawl beneath the tape. Try to select limbs that are very nearly the same size to keep the lengths of all the sample tapes more or less the same. Remove each tape weekly for counting and replace it with a fresh piece of tape. Keep a record of the number of crawlers trapped at each location so you will know when populations peak. During harvest, check fruit for red spots caused by scale.

If dormant sprays are not effective at controlling San Jose scale populations, or if they could not be applied, treat for the pest when the first generation of crawlers reaches a peak (usually early in May) as indicated by sticky tape traps or degree-day accumulations. Use pheromone traps for male scale, beginning by the end of February. Place the traps well within the canopy to keep them out of the wind (Figure 44). When the traps begin to catch males consistently, start accumulating degree-days using a 51°F (10.5°C) lower threshold and a 90°F (32°C) upper threshold (Table 34 in Appendix II). Apply a treatment for crawlers 600° to 700°D after you catch the first males (Figure 45). The traps may fail to catch any adults if the weather is cold, rainy, or windy while they are active. Alternatively, you can monitor for crawlers using double-sided tape wrapped as described above. Place these sampling tapes adjacent to known scale infestations; the objective is not to monitor population changes, but to determine when crawlers begin to hatch. Begin to monitor with sticky tape early in April. Treat 200°D after you detect the first crawlers.

Figure 43. When applying double-sided tape to monitor for San Jose scale crawlers, choose scaffold limbs that are 1 to 2 inches in diameter and be sure the tape is wrapped tightly around the wood so the crawlers cannot get underneath.

Figure 44. Place pheromone traps for San Jose scale well within the canopy to keep them out of the wind.

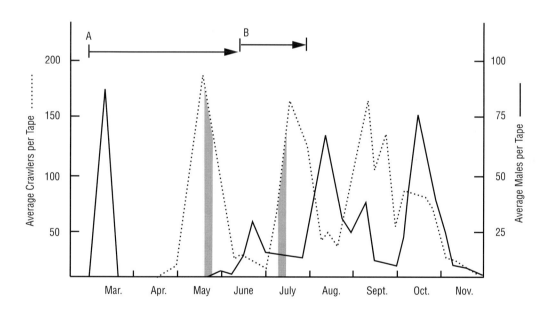

Figure 45. If dormant treatments for San Jose scale were ineffective or could not be applied, you can use pheromone trap catches and degree-day accumulations to schedule an in-season treatment to control the crawler stage. This graph shows the relationship between pheromone trap catches of adult males and sticky tape catches of crawlers in an untreated orchard in the southern San Joaquin Valley. Begin accumulating degree-days when traps begin catching male scales consistently (A, B). The first flight usually occurs in early to mid-March (A). The majority of the first male flight often occurs in only 2–7 days. Treat for crawlers when the degree-day accumulation reaches 600–700 degree-days (shaded area of graph). Alternatively, you can begin accumulating degree-days when the first crawlers are caught on sticky tapes, and treat when the accumulation reaches 200 degree-days.

Second stage nymphs of European fruit lecanium (*shown here*) are susceptible to oil treatment before they have settled down and secreted a covering.

European fruit lecanium scale have shiny, brown, dome-shaped coverings.

European Fruit Lecanium
Parthenolecanium corni

European fruit lecanium may occur on all stone fruits. It is most often seen on apricots and prunes, and is also known as brown apricot scale. This scale usually is not a problem on California stone fruits; populations are kept under control by natural enemies and dormant sprays used for other pests.

The adult European fruit lecanium has a shiny brown, oval, smooth-surfaced covering. It is larger than San Jose scale, about 1/8 to 3/16 inch (3 to 5 mm) in diameter, and has a domed appearance. The pests overwinter as flattened second instar nymphs on twigs and branches. They grow rapidly in spring and mature from mid-April through May. During rapid spring growth, the insects produce large quantities of honeydew.

The mature female lays her eggs under her protective cover. They hatch from late May through July. Crawlers are flattened, oval, and yellowish or brown. They move to leaves and feed there until October, when they return to the twigs and branches. There they molt to the second instar, settle down, and secrete a covering. There is one generation a year. There are no males in this species.

Damage from European fruit lecanium usually results from honeydew production by the feeding scales, which causes russeting on smooth-skinned fruit and sooty mold on fruit and leaves. Heavy infestations can reduce tree vigor. Look for immature scales on leaves in the spring and summer, or on twigs when monitoring for San Jose scale, mite eggs, and aphid eggs in the winter. If you find large numbers, check for parasitism. Look for parasite emergence holes in scale covers. If a large proportion of the scale insects is parasitized, do not treat. If parasitization is low, treat with a dormant oil formulation without insecticide. Dormant oil treatment is the most effective, least disruptive way to reduce lecanium populations. Treatment is advisable after a season when sooty mold has been a problem.

EUROPEAN FRUIT LECANIUM

adult

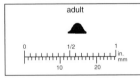

BLACK SCALE

female

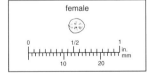

European fruit lecanium nymphs turn black when parasitized. An adult parasite, *Coccophagus lecanii*, is shown here next to the circular exit hole it made in the scale covering. Look for these emergence holes when monitoring scale populations.

Black Scale
Saissetia oleae

Black scale may occasionally build up to damaging levels on cherries. Damage is the result of honeydew secretion and the subsequent development of sooty mold on leaves and fruit.

The adult female black scale is covered with a black or dark brown, hemispherical shell, about ⅛ inch (3 mm) in diameter, with a conspicuous H-shaped ridge on top. Males are narrow and flat. Black scale insects overwinter as immature crawlers. Adults are present from May through July. The female lays eggs under her shell, and crawlers emerge and migrate to foliage and green twigs to feed and remain there through the winter.

If sooty mold from black scale is a problem in your orchard, apply a narrow-range oil the following winter to control the immature scale. Black scale seldom requires treatment on stone fruits because a number of parasites and predators usually keep the pest's populations low. Two encyrtid wasps, *Metaphycus helvolus* and M. *bartletti*, are the most important parasites. The larvae of lacewings and some lady beetles feed on black scale crawlers.

Italian Pear Scale
Epidiaspis leperii

Italian pear scale occurs widely on tree fruits but rarely constitutes a problem. These scale insects are found on shaded parts of trees, under moss or lichens. The covering of the female scale is circular, white or gray, and about ¹⁄₁₆ inch (1.5 mm) in diameter. The scale body under the shell is reddish. Little is known about the life cycle of Italian pear scale. There appears to be one generation a year.

Light populations of Italian pear scale do not harm trees. Bark cracking and reduced tree vigor have been reported when populations are heavy. Damaging infestations are rarely seen in California. Look for Italian pear scale on mossy or lichen-encrusted parts of the main scaffold and larger limbs. Treatment of large limbs with a copper material to kill mosses and lichens will reduce scale populations.

OTHER INSECT PESTS
Western Flower Thrips
Frankliniella occidentalis

Western flower thrips feed on the flowers of a wide variety of tree fruits and other flowering plants. They may cause scarring of smooth-skinned fruit, especially nectarines, if they feed on the fruit early in its development. Shoot tips may be damaged early in the season. Thrips feeding late in the season can cause a discoloration or silvering of ripening fruit. You need to monitor regularly for damaging populations. Thrips cause significant damage primarily in nectarines and plums.

Adult female black scales have an H-shaped ridge on the top of the covering.

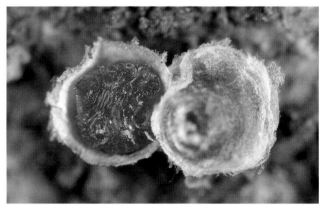

The covering of this Italian pear scale has been turned over to show the red coloration of the scale body underneath. Italian pear scales usually are found on branches infested with moss or lichens.

Description and Biology

Adult thrips are tiny and slender, about ¹⁄₃₂ inch (1 mm) long. They have featherlike, fringed wings that fold lengthwise along the insect's back when at rest. Different forms of western flower thrips vary in color from light yellow to brown. Immatures are similar in appearance, but are smaller and lack wings. Adult sixspotted thrips, an important predator of mites, can be distinguished from western flower thrips by the presence of three dark spots on each wing. Immature western flower thrips are yellow or brown and opaque, whereas immature sixspotted thrips have a clear white appearance. Sixspotted thrips usually are not found in trees early in the season.

Adult western flower thrips overwinter on weeds or other hosts on the orchard floor, in nearby wild areas, or on crop hosts such as alfalfa that remain green during the winter. Thrips are attracted to flowers; if disturbed or when hosts dry up, adults move into orchards that are in bloom.

Adult females insert their eggs into the soft tissue of developing shoots, leaves, and fruit. The nymphs that emerge use

Adult western flower thrips are tiny and slender, ranging in color from yellow to almost black. The wings have featherlike fringes and are folded lengthwise along the back when the insect is at rest.

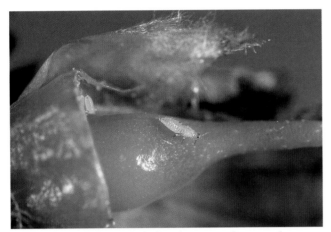

Western flower thrips nymphs feed inside nectarine flowers on the young developing fruit.

Thrips injuries to young fruit appear as corky patches on the surface of mature fruit.

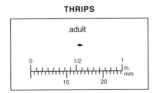

their rasping mouthparts to feed on soft tissue such as the growing points of shoots or blossoms, or the surface of young fruit underneath the calyx. They drop to the ground before molting to the adult stage. Adults usually fly a short distance to find hosts, but may fly farther if no hosts are nearby. There are 5 or 6 generations a year; populations in stone fruit orchards reach their peak in May or June.

Damage

Feeding by adult thrips on flowers does not cause significant damage to stone fruits. However, the nymphs that hatch from eggs laid by these adults can cause serious injury when large numbers feed on young fruit. Areas injured by nymphs develop into corky scars that cause fruit to be culled at harvest. Nectarines are the most seriously affected. Sometimes plums are damaged, especially when spring weather is cool and bloom is prolonged. Thrips feeding on plums causes holes or depressions surrounded by halo spots. Blotches or "pansy spots" may develop on the plums' surface at egg-laying sites. Peaches usually are not damaged unless thrips populations are sufficiently high to cause feeding injuries that result in malformed fruit. Whitish or silvery discoloration may develop on highly colored nectarines when large numbers of thrips feed on the surface of fruit after it begins to ripen.

Thrips feeding on young shoot tips sometimes kills one or two small leaves, resulting in a flagging that may be confused with peach twig borer damage. Bushy growth usually develops just behind the affected shoot tip, similar to the growth that follows shoot tip injury caused by lygus bugs, oriental fruit moth, or peach twig borer. Check for the presence of thrips or lygus bugs to determine the cause of the injury.

Management Guidelines

Begin to monitor nectarines and plums for thrips at the beginning of bloom. It is a good idea to monitor for thrips in fresh market peaches and apricots, where surface blemishes are of concern. Check for the presence of nymphs and adults by shaking or slapping flower clusters onto a light yellow painted board or a sheet of yellow paper on a clipboard. Monitor at least 3 or 4 areas in each orchard, shaking one blossom cluster from each of 10 or 12 trees selected at random. Keep a count of the number of flowers shaken and the number of thrips found. Take a separate sample from edges of the orchard adjacent to potential sources of thrips such as wild areas, ditchbanks, or alfalfa fields. Records of the number of thrips you find, the control actions you take, and the subsequent damage levels will help you make decisions about future management actions.

Also monitor for early-instar nymphs, which are not easily dislodged, by dissecting flowers and examining them with a hand lens. Examine at least 50 flowers from each orchard, checking flowers from the same blossom clusters that you shake-count. Carefully remove the outer flower parts and examine the ovary with a hand lens. First instar nymphs are white. Be sure you can distinguish them from eriophyid mites and predatory mites, which are described and illustrated later in this chapter.

No specific treatment thresholds have been developed for western flower thrips on stone fruits. As a general guideline, you may need to treat if shake sampling reveals more than 2 thrips per 50 blossoms or if flower sampling reveals the presence of young nymphs. Treatments are most effective if applied before petal fall. Most of the materials available for thrips control are harmful to natural enemy populations and may result in severe outbreaks of pest mites. Be sure to take precautions to avoid injuring honey bees (see the section "Pesticide Hazards" in the previous chapter).

To reduce thrips migration to blossoms, avoid discing or mowing orchard cover crops or allowing them to dry out when trees are in bloom. Disc well in advance of bloom if there is a danger of frost. Avoid discing any adjacent weedy areas or mowing any adjacent host crops such as alfalfa when the stone fruit orchards are in bloom.

Aphids

A number of aphid species occur on stone fruits. Some species overwinter as eggs laid on or adjacent to buds, while others overwinter as nymphs and adults on alternate hosts. Several to many generations are produced during the season by *parthenogenesis*, where females give birth to live young without mating. Colonies that develop in the spring cause distorted growth of leaves and shoots. Heavy infestations early in the season can stunt shoot growth. Honeydew produced by the aphids may cause developing prunes and plums to crack, and sooty mold that develops on the honeydew may blacken the surface of leaves or fruit. In late spring, most aphid species migrate from tree hosts to reeds, cattails, grasses, weeds, oilseed crops, or vegetable crops, and then return to fruit trees in the fall to lay eggs adjacent to buds. Dormant season organophosphate treatments to kill overwintering eggs usually keep aphids from reaching damaging levels in stone fruits. Oil sprays timed to kill hatching eggs in early spring may be used as an alternative to dormant oil plus organophosphate. If infestations develop in early spring, monitor them frequently for population increases. Treat when leaf injury begins to develop if aphid numbers are increasing. A number of natural enemies, including lady beetles, soldier beetles, lacewings, and several species of parasitic wasps, help keep aphid populations controlled. Infestations that appear in mid- to late summer usually do not cause significant damage; however, you may need to treat young trees in order to prevent damage to new growth.

Mealy Plum Aphid, *Hyalopterus pruni*
Leaf Curl Plum Aphid, *Brachycaudus helichrysi*

Mealy plum aphid and leaf curl plum aphid are the most important aphid pests of plums and prunes. Mealy plum

A number of aphid species that occur on stone fruits cause severe curling and distortion of foliage. The damage to these peach shoots was caused by peach aphid, *Brachycaudus schwartzi*.

Sooty mold that grows on honeydew secreted by aphids can disfigure fruit. Honeydew may cause developing plums and prunes to crack.

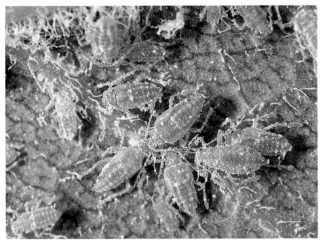

Mealy plum aphids are pale green with a characteristic white coating of wax. Other aphids commonly found on stone fruits do not produce such a waxy coating.

Most of the aphid species that occur on stone fruits survive the winter as eggs laid next to buds in the fall.

Leaf curl plum aphids are yellow-green, green, or yellow-brown and shiny. Unlike green peach aphids, with which they are easily confused, they do not have converging tubercles (tiny projections that point inward toward each other) on the inside of the base of the antennae.

Aphids that have been attacked by parasitic wasps become swollen and tan colored as the parasite develops inside them. Several individuals in this colony of peach aphids are parasitized.

aphid is pale green with three dark green stripes running lengthwise on its back, and is covered with a mealy, whitish coating of wax. Colonies develop on the undersides of leaves, which become curled and distorted. High-density populations may reduce tree vigor and the sugar content of fruit. A tentative damage threshold of three eggs per tree has been established for mealy plum aphid on prunes. Summer hosts of mealy plum aphid include common cattail and common reed, and may also include giant reed.

The leaf curl plum aphid is shinier than mealy plum aphid and is yellow-green. Leaves infested with this aphid curl tightly perpendicular to the midvein, and the aphids feed inside the curled leaves. This aphid may be confused with green peach aphid. Most summer hosts are weeds in the sunflower and fiddleneck families.

Three to thirteen generations of these aphids develop on the stone fruit host before winged adults develop and migrate to summer hosts. Aphids seem to leave mature orchards sooner than they leave young, vigorous orchards, where they build up through midsummer. Aphids migrate back into orchard trees in the fall and produce one generation before laying eggs. Some aphids remain on trees all summer, but are then unable to lay eggs in the fall. In the spring, eggs begin to hatch around the time of 5% bloom, and most have hatched by petal fall. An oil spray applied at this time will help control the newly emerging aphids. The degree of control depends on the proportion of eggs that have hatched.

You can monitor for aphids in the fall at 75% leaf fall; they are easiest to find at this time because they move to the last leaves remaining on the tree. If you find aphids, use a dormant treatment to kill eggs and prevent damage in the spring. Alternatively, you can use oil during bloom, but the control will be less effective than a dormant insecticide.

The black cherry aphid causes leaf curling and distortion of young shoot growth on cherry. This damage can be especially severe in young orchards.

Green peach aphids are light green and less shiny than leaf curl plum aphids. They have converging tubercles between and at the base of the antennae.

Black Cherry Aphid, *Myzus cerasi*

The black cherry aphid causes leaf curling and distortion of young cherry shoots. This aphid is one of the most serious insect pests of cherries in central coast orchards. It is not a pest of other stone fruits. Black cherry aphids are large, shiny, and black. They overwinter as shiny black eggs on twigs and fruit spurs. Eggs hatch shortly before bloom, and the aphids go through several generations in the spring. High populations cause severe damage to developing shoots. The aphid survives on mustard family weeds in the summer. Where aphid populations have been observed, use a dormant or delayed dormant treatment to kill overwintering eggs. If you make no dormant treatment, monitor for aphids during bloom and treat shortly after petal fall, as soon as you find aphids.

Green Peach Aphid, *Myzus persicae*

The green peach aphid is the most important aphid pest of peaches and nectarines. It lives all year on a wide variety of vegetable crops and weed hosts, moving from one host species to another as new hosts become available and others dry up or are killed by frost. This aphid goes through 20 or more generations a year, but there is no egg stage in the major stone fruit growing areas of California. Green peach aphids may move into orchards in spring to feed on developing foliage. Wingless forms are teardrop shaped and light green. Winged forms have a dark head and thorax and a green abdomen with a dark spot on the back.

Other Aphids

Other aphids that may be found on stone fruits include the peach aphid, *Brachycaudus schwartzi*; the rusty plum aphid, *Hysteroneura setariae*, which is found most often on plums and prunes; the waterlily aphid, *Rhopalosiphum nymphaeae*; and the spirea aphid, *Aphis spiraecola*.

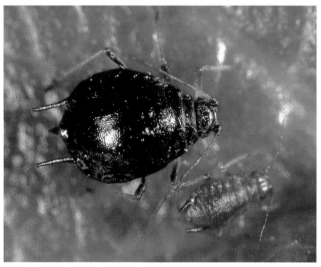

Adult black cherry aphids are large, shiny, black aphids. Immatures are not so darkly colored.

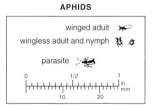

APHIDS

winged adult

wingless adult and nymph

parasite

0   1/2   1   in.
                              mm
          10   20

The mountain leafhopper adult (*right*) is dark brown or black with yellow markings and red eyes. The nymph (*left*) is light colored with red eyes.

Flor's leafhopper, also known as the cherry leafhopper, is bright green in the nymphal stage (*right*). The adult (*left*) is dark brown.

Prune leafhoppers are white and often become abundant in prune orchards. Their feeding causes a pale stippling of leaves. However, this does not result in significant damage, and treatment for prune leafhoppers is unnecessary.

LEAFHOPPER

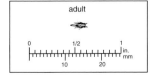

adult

```
0          1/2          1
|+++++++++|+++++++++|  in.
                       mm
     10         20
```

Leafhoppers

Mountain leafhopper, *Colladonus montanus*, and Flor's leafhopper, *Fieberiella florii* (often referred to as the cherry leafhopper), are of concern to Central Valley cherry growers because they are vectors of the pathogen that causes X-disease (cherry buckskin). *Scaphytopius acutus* is an important X-disease vector in Sierra foothill orchards. Because management of these insects is intended to prevent spread of the disease to cherries, it is discussed in the section on X-disease in the next chapter. Prune leafhopper occurs commonly on prunes, but does not require management.

Mountain leafhopper adults are dark brown to black, with red eyes and yellow markings on the back and wings. Nymphs are cream colored with red eyes. Mountain leafhoppers overwinter as adults on a variety of weeds. They commonly congregate in sugar beet fields during the winter, feeding on weed hosts that are common there, and move out when the sugar beets are harvested. Leafhoppers may invade orchards to live and reproduce on curly dock, California burclover, sweetclovers, and other weeds or cover crops (clovers are hosts). Burclover is a host for the X-disease pathogen. Cherry is not a preferred host, but the mountain leafhoppers that move into trees and feed on leaves usually are the most abundant leafhopper vectors found on cherry.

Flor's leafhopper is not as active as the mountain leafhopper and does not travel as far in search of hosts. However, cherry is a preferred host for this species. Nymphs are bluish green. Adults are dark brown, and their shape and color mimic the buds of their woody hosts. Flor's leafhoppers overwinter as eggs or nymphs on a range of hosts, including pyracantha, privet, boxwood, myrtle, hawthorn, *Cotoneaster*, *Ceanothus*, crabapple, and apple.

Scaphytopius acutus lives on a wide range of grasses, broadleaf weeds, and woody hosts. Adults are brown, and some have light spots on the wing covers. These leafhoppers overwinter as eggs on the fallen leaves of woody hosts. It appears to be the major vector of X-disease in foothill orchards, where it may spread the pathogen from weed hosts and wild *Prunus* hosts, chokecherry and bitter cherry, into cherry orchards.

Prune leafhopper, *Edwardsiana prunicola*, occurs commonly in prune orchards. This leafhopper may become abundant on foliage, and its feeding causes a pale yellow stippling on leaves. It does not cause significant damage, however, and no treatment is needed.

Wood Borers

The wood-boring insects that attack stone fruits are moth and beetle larvae that feed underneath the bark on the cambium. They are most threatening to young orchards because young trees are more susceptible to attack, and because feeding by wood borers can quickly girdle and kill small trees.

Sunburned limbs of larger trees and trees under stress are also vulnerable to attack. You can minimize problems with wood borers by pruning carefully, protecting wood from injury, and disposing of infested wood. Summer pruning often results in sunburn and subsequent attack by wood-boring beetles. Insecticide applications are not effective against wood-boring beetles, but can be used against the larvae of wood-boring moths if conditions warrant.

Pacific Flatheaded Borer, *Chrysobothris mali*

The Pacific flatheaded borer attacks all stone fruits and can be damaging to young orchards. The larvae of this beetle attack the cambium and may kill individual branches or entire trees.

Larvae overwinter in the prepupal stage in chambers in the wood of infested trees. They pupate in the spring, and adults emerge from April through July. Adult beetles are dark, about 4/10 inch (10 mm) long, with a copper-colored spot on each wing cover. Females are attracted to injured wood. They lay eggs on the bark, usually near pruning wounds or on weakened limbs, in areas exposed to the sun. The eggs are circular, flattened, and whitish. When the larvae hatch, they bore directly through the bottom of the egg and into the bark. Larvae feed in the cambium layer, and when mature they either bore into the wood to construct a pupal chamber or pupate under the bark. Full-grown larvae are about ¾ inch (18 mm) long and have characteristic large, flattened segments just behind the head. There is one generation a year, but because adults emerge over a prolonged period, larvae of many different sizes may be present at any time.

Watersoaked areas develop on the bark at the site of larval feeding. Eventually the bark splits, revealing frass-filled galleries. Flatheaded borers preferentially attack sunburned wood. Newly planted trees are the most susceptible to serious damage; they tend to be weaker, are more susceptible to sunburn, and can be girdled quickly by feeding larvae. Flatheaded borer larvae may attack sunburned limbs of larger trees; they rarely kill the trees, but may weaken them sufficiently to make them susceptible to attack by other borers.

You can minimize damage from flatheaded borers by maintaining healthy trees and preventing sunburn. Use tree wraps on newly planted trees or paint them with a white latex paint. Apply paint so that the trunk is covered from at least 2 inches (5 cm) below the soil line to 2 feet (60 cm) above the soil. Prune trees such that the scaffold remains shaded as much as possible. Apply a mixture of 1 part interior white latex paint and 1 part water to limbs of older trees that are exposed to potential sunburn. Pruning, topping, or girdling of trees in the spring or summer can predispose them to attack by flatheaded borers. If you find flatheaded borer injury, prune out and destroy the affected branches or trees. Remove or destroy these prunings before bloom to help prevent reinfestation of the orchard.

The larva of the Pacific flatheaded borer has a characteristic broad, flattened segment behind the head. It feeds underneath the bark on the cambium, and can girdle small branches and the trunks of young trees.

The Pacific flatheaded borer adult is a dark beetle with a copper-colored spot on each wing cover. It leaves an oval hole in the bark surface upon emerging.

PACIFIC FLATHEADED BORER

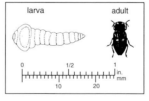

larva   adult

0   1/2   1
|||||||||||||||||||||||| in.
                              mm
        10   20

The shothole borer adult is a small, dark brown beetle.

Adult peachtree borers are bluish black clearwing moths that resemble wasps, both in their appearance and in their flight behavior. A male is shown here. Females have a single orange band around the abdomen.

The shothole borer leaves a small circular hole in the bark when it emerges. Several usually emerge from the same area of a branch, giving a "shot hole" appearance.

Gum mixed with frass can be found around the base of a tree with an active peachtree borer infestation.

If you remove the bark from where shothole borers have emerged, numerous shallow grooves left by feeding larvae are visible in the surface of the wood.

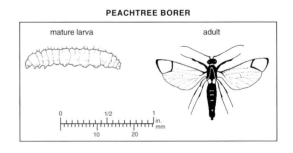

PEACHTREE BORER

mature larva   adult

0   1/2   1 in.
          10   20   mm

SHOTHOLE BORER

larva   adult

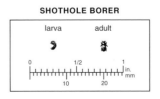

0   1/2   1 in.
        10   20   mm

AMERICAN PLUM BORER

larva

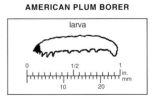

0   1/2   1 in.
        10   20   mm

Shothole Borer, *Scolytus rugulosus*

Shothole borer attacks the wood of trees that are stressed, diseased, or low in vigor. This insect overwinters as mature larvae or pupae in chambers in the wood or under the bark. Adults emerge from April through June. They are small, dark brown beetles about ⅛ inch (3 mm) long with reddish brown antennae, legs, and wing tips. Each adult leaves a single emergence hole about 1/16 inch (1 to 2 mm) in diameter in the bark. Several beetles emerge from the same area, giving a "shothole" appearance.

After mating, the female beetle bores into the bark and forms a straight gallery in the cambium, along which she lays eggs. The larvae tunnel away from the egg gallery as they feed, each larva forming one channel. The result is a characteristic pattern of shallow grooves in the surface of the wood, usually perpendicular to the grain, that may be seen to radiate away from a single, deeper groove. Larvae are white or yellowish, lack legs, and are about ⅛ inch long when mature. There are as many as four generations in a season, with adults of later generations emerging in July or August and September or October. Beetles remain active until October.

Shothole borers often attack trees at the base of buds on 1- or 2-year-old wood. The most serious damage is usually caused by larval feeding that girdles limbs or the trunks of small trees. Healthy trees usually can resist attack by producing enough sap to prevent female beetles from forming egg galleries. However, high populations of shothole borer can overcome the resistance of healthy trees, especially if the trees are small.

Follow good cultural practices to keep your trees healthy. Remove and destroy dead trees and prunings before bloom to prevent the emergence of beetles from infested wood. Do not store infested firewood or freshly cut wood near orchards. Watch for evidence of shothole borer activity when monitoring for other pests. Gum exudates usually are present around entrance holes. Prune out and destroy infested wood, or remove heavily infested trees, being sure to destroy the wood or remove it from the vicinity of orchards before spring.

Peachtree Borer, *Synanthedon exitiosa*

Peachtree borer attacks all stone fruits, but is of importance primarily on apricots and cherries in coastal areas and on peaches in the Sacramento and northern San Joaquin valleys. Larvae attack the crown and trunk and can girdle and kill trees if left uncontrolled. The adult is a clearwing moth.

Peachtree borers overwinter as larvae inside infested trees. They emerge in the spring and pupate at the base of the tree just beneath the soil. Adults emerge in late spring and early summer; they are present from May through September. They are clearwing moths about 1 inch (2.5 cm) long with bluish black bodies, and closely resemble wasps both in appearance and in flight behavior. Males have narrow yellow bands on the abdomen, females have a single orange band. Eggs are laid on the tree trunk, and larvae bore into the tree near its base and feed in the cambium until the following spring. Gum mixed with frass exudes from active bore holes in the spring. The mature larva is pinkish white with a dark head, and 1 inch or more in length. Each new generation tends to return to the same tree to lay eggs, so if the pests are not controlled, trees may eventually be killed by the continued activity of boring larvae.

Look for the presence of frass and gum at the bases of trees when monitoring orchards in the spring. Also check trees in the fall for signs of peachtree borer activity. At this time, you can kill larvae by carefully using a knife or wire to probe the trunk. Mark any that you find, and return to treat them the following spring. Treat affected trees with insecticide by spraying the trunk from the scaffold to the soil line. Remove suckers and pull soil away from the base of the tree before treating. Two applications are recommended to protect during the prolonged period when adults are active, one in mid-May when adults are first detected and one in the middle of July. Be careful to observe preharvest intervals and use low-pressure sprays to avoid contaminating fruit.

You can use pheromone traps to monitor adult emergence. They are useful for determining the presence of peachtree borers. Place them in trees when flights are expected. If they catch large numbers of male peachtree borers (approximately 10 or more per week), return later and examine the trees carefully for signs of feeding activity. Be sure to properly identify the moths that are trapped; other clearwing moths may be attracted by the peachtree borer pheromone.

Keep tree bases free of vegetation to help reduce problems with peachtree borer, especially in the Central Valley. Heat and dryness reduce the survival of eggs and larvae.

American Plum Borer, *Euzophera semifuneralis*
Prune Limb Borer, *Bondia comonana*

Prune limb borer and American plum borer are sporadic pests of young stone fruit orchards. They usually attack young trees and may cause severe damage, weakening limbs or girdling the tree. Injury is restricted primarily to the trunk and main scaffold limbs. Adults are gray moths with a wingspan of about ¾ inch (2 cm) and brown and black markings on the wings. They lay eggs near where callous tissue has developed, such as at pruning wounds, crown galls, or scaffold crotches. Larvae bore into the tree to feed on cambium tissue. Webbing and frass accumulate around feeding sites, and gum deposits may form. Young larvae are white with very large dark heads. They are about 1 inch (2.5 cm) long when mature and dull green or pinkish. They overwinter inside protective cocoons spun in sheltered locations on the tree and pupate in the spring. Adults emerge in April and May to lay eggs of the first generation. The oval eggs are laid singly or in small clusters, usually in crevices in the bark. There are 3 or 4 generations a year.

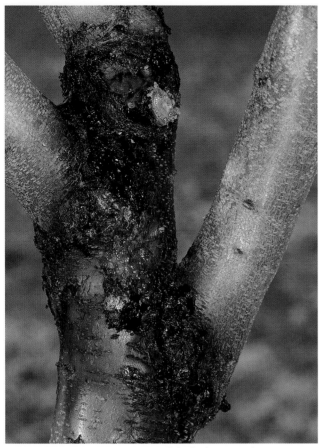

Extensive gumming may occur around the feeding sites of American plum borer larvae.

American plum borer larvae may be pinkish or dull green in color. They feed on cambium tissue, often in the scaffold crotches of young trees.

BRANCH AND TWIG BORER

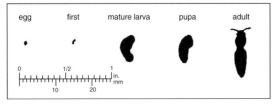

Look for piles of frass and gum deposits when monitoring young orchards in the spring. If you find borer activity, treat the trees with an approved insecticide. Apply material from 1 foot below the scaffold crotch to 1 foot above. Make two applications 6 weeks apart, with the first one in mid- to late April. Remove and destroy infested wood or heavily infested trees.

Branch and Twig Borer, *Melalgus confertus*

Many woody plants are hosts for branch and twig borer. Weakened or injured stone fruit trees, especially prunes, are sometimes attacked. Cultural practices usually keep this pest from becoming a serious problem.

Adults are slender, dark brown beetles, about ½ to ⅔ inch (12 to 16 mm) long. They normally bore into the dead wood of trees and shrubs outside the orchard or brush piles. They lay eggs in the wood, and their larvae live inside the heartwood for a year or more. Pupation occurs inside the wood, and adults emerge in early summer. At this time they may invade stone fruit orchards. Females bore into wood at the axils of small twigs or branches that have been weakened by sunburn or other injury. They leave small round holes, and one of the branches usually dies later on from larval feeding.

Maintain healthy vigorous trees, using proper irrigation techniques and sunburn protection as needed. Destroy brush piles or remove them from the vicinity of orchards by early spring. Remove and destroy infested branches and badly infested trees.

European Earwig
Forficula auricularia

Earwigs may damage ripening cherries and apricots when they climb into trees to feed on ripening fruit. These shiny brown insects are easily identified by the pair of pincers at the tip of the abdomen. They are active at night, and hide during the day under debris, under loose bark, or in weedy areas in or near the orchard. As fruit begin to ripen in the spring, they will climb into trees and remain there until harvest. They will feed on the surface of fruit, chewing shallow, irregular holes. Earwigs also will enter ripening apricots near the stem end and feed inside the fruit, around the pit, where they remain until fruit is harvested. Damage results from surface feeding injury and the presence of earwigs in fruit at harvest.

Management requires the removal of daytime harboring sites and prevention of earwig access to fruit before ripening. Remove weeds and debris from the bases of trees and prune out limbs that come in contact with the soil, offering earwigs access to the trees. Monitor for earwigs by placing boards or rolled up newspapers in the orchard early in the spring. Earwigs will hide in these locations during the day. Check for earwigs weekly and treat tree trunks as soon as you begin finding earwigs. Apply carbaryl to the trunk from the base of the scaffold to the soil line. To be effective, this treatment must be applied as soon as earwigs become active and before they have entered the tree canopy. You can also use carbaryl baits. If earwigs are present in the canopy, place bait in the crotches of the tree.

Cribrate Weevil
Otiorhynchus cribricollis

The cribrate weevil occasionally becomes a serious pest in newly planted orchards of the central coast and Sierra foothills when adult weevils move in from adjacent infested areas or ornamentals that harbor them. Adults are flightless, dark brown weevils about ½ inch (12 mm) long with longitudinal striations on their backs. They feed on the foliage of a variety of woody plants. The larvae are legless white grubs that feed on the roots of host plants but are not thought to cause significant damage to stone fruit trees. Cribrate weevils survive the winter in the larval stage. There is one generation a year.

Adult weevils are active during spring and summer. They crawl up from the ground to feed on the foliage at night, chewing scallop-shaped notches or holes in leaves. If large numbers are present, leaves may be skeletonized and bark on young twigs may be consumed. During the day they hide in the soil near the bases of host trees. Mature trees can tolerate feeding injury, but young trees may be killed if weevils are not controlled.

To monitor for the presence of adult weevils, use a sweep net or beating tray to check foliage 1 or 2 hours after dark. You can also look for feeding damage, and then dig around the base of the tree where you find damage; weevils should be present in the upper few inches of soil, and are easy to find because they "play dead" during the day. Apply a sticky barrier around the trunks of young trees at the first sign of weevil feeding injury. Renew the sticky material as it dries up or becomes clogged with dust and dirt.

Earwigs chew irregular shallow holes in the surface of ripe apricots. They will also crawl inside ripe fruit near the stem end to feed around the pit.

Cribrate weevils are dark brown, flightless weevils that climb into trees at night to feed on foliage and sometimes bark. During the day they can be found near the soil surface at the base of trees that exhibit feeding damage.

Cribrate weevils chew jagged holes in the edges of leaves. Leaves may be skeletonized if large numbers of weevils are feeding, and the bark of new shoots may be consumed.

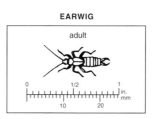
EARWIG
adult

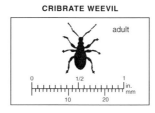
CRIBRATE WEEVIL
adult

Katydids chew small, shallow holes in the surface of fruit. On green fruit, these holes heal over and expand as the fruit grows. Small fruit may become severely distorted, and may resemble fruit injured by green fruitworms or early-season leafrollers. A forktailed bush katydid nymph is shown here.

Katydids

Katydids occasionally become damaging pests in orchards that have not been treated with broad-spectrum pesticides. Two species are found in California stone fruit orchards. The angularwinged katydid, *Microcentrum retinerve*, occurs most frequently. Both nymphs and adults of this species have a distinct humpbacked appearance. The forktailed bush katydid, *Scudderia furcata*, is smaller and is not humpbacked. Nymphs of both species have very long antennae that are banded black and white.

Katydids lay disc-shaped eggs in the fall. The eggs of the angularwinged katydid are ⅛ to ¼ inch (3 to 6 mm) long and laid in two overlapping rows on the surface of twigs and leaves. Forktailed bush katydid eggs are about ⅛ inch (3 mm) long and are inserted into the edges of leaves. Eggs of both species hatch in April and May. Nymphs feed on leaves or fruit. Katydid nymphs tend to take one bite out of a fruit before moving on to another feeding site. Hence, a few katydids may damage a large number of fruit in a short time. Feeding wounds heal over and enlarge into corky patches as the fruit expands. The most serious damage occurs when katydids feed on young fruit, which become severely distorted as they develop. Nymphs and adults also chew holes in foliage. Damage to fruit and foliage resembles that of green fruitworms. Adult katydids appear in midsummer and lay eggs in the fall. There is only one generation a year.

Look for katydid damage when monitoring for leafrollers and green fruitworms in the spring. If you find feeding damage, look for nymphs. Shaking foliage onto large beating sheets may be helpful; nymphs can be difficult to see on the tree because they jump readily when disturbed. Treatment is recommended if you find katydid damage early in the season. Katydids are easily controlled by most of the insecticides used at this time of year to control caterpillar pests; Bt is ineffective.

Katydids also chew irregular holes in the middle of leaves. This type of injury usually is more common than fruit injury, and can help identify the cause of fruit damage.

Larvae of the pear sawfly (cherry slug) leave the lower epidermis and leaf veins when feeding on foliage. Larvae are encased in a dark, slimy coating that gives them a sluglike appearance (*right*). Larvae do not have this coating during the last instar (*left*).

CHERRY SLUG

larva

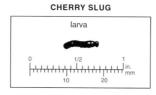

Cherry Slug
Caliroa cerasi

The cherry slug is a foliage pest of cherries in coastal areas. It is the larva of a sawfly that commonly attacks apple, quince, and pear, where it is known as the pear slug or pear sawfly.

Cherry slug overwinters as a pupa in the soil. Adults emerge about the time trees leaf out in the spring. They are small, stout wasps, about ⅕ inch (5 mm) long, that resemble flies. The female has a sawlike ovipositor that she uses to lay eggs inside slits in the leaf surface. Newly hatched larvae are white with brown heads and inconspicuous legs. They secrete a dark olive green or shiny black slimy material, giving them a sluglike appearance. Mature larvae are about ½ inch (10 to 12 mm) long and are more caterpillar like in appearance. They drop to the ground to pupate in the soil. A second generation of adults emerges in July to lay eggs of the generation that overwinters.

Cherry slug larvae skeletonize leaves as they feed, leaving a network of fine leaf veins. Look for skeletonized leaves and the presence of larvae when monitoring orchards. Treat infested trees if the number of larvae is high. In backyard trees you can wash them off by spraying foliage with a hose.

MITES

Several mite species occur on stone fruits. Some mites found in stone fruits are predators that feed on other mites. Webspinning mites can cause serious problems when orchards suffer from water stress or when broad-spectrum pesticides used for other pests destroy mite predators. European red mite, brown mite, and several species of eriophyid mites occur commonly in stone fruits, but seldom reach damaging levels unless pesticides destroy the predators that normally keep them under control.

Webspinning Spider Mites
Tetranychus spp.

Two species of webspinning spider mites are important in stone fruits. The twospotted spider mite, *Tetranychus urticae*, and Pacific spider mite, *Tetranychus pacificus*, are similar in appearance, life cycle, and the damage they cause. Management practices for the two species are the same, although Pacific spider mite is more tolerant of the selective miticide fenbutatin oxide. Predators play an important role in keeping mites under control; outbreaks often follow the use of broad-spectrum insecticides, particularly pyrethroids and carbamates. Regular monitoring for both mites and their predators will tell you when populations may be building to damaging levels.

Description and Biology

Spider mites are very small, about ¼₀ inch (0.5 mm) long when full grown, and look like pale moving dots on leaves. When viewed with a hand lens, they are pale greenish or yellow with a large dark spot on each side and a tiny red eyespot on each side toward the anterior end. Youngest forms of both species do not have the dark spots. Pacific mites may have an additional dark spot on each side near the posterior end; however, the two species cannot be distinguished reliably in the field.

Spider mites overwinter as mature females in protected places on the trunk near the base of the tree or on the orchard floor. Overwintering mites are reddish orange and lack the dark spots. As trees leaf out in the spring, mites move up from lower parts of trees. Eggs are spherical and translucent. They usually are laid on the undersides of leaves, but may be laid on upper leaf surfaces when mite population densities are high.

Spring mite populations usually decrease or disappear during periods of cool or wet weather and as predator populations increase. Treatment for thrips on nectarines and plums often causes increased spring mite populations. Spider mites are favored by hot, dry conditions, and they build up as weather becomes more favorable in late spring or summer.

Viewed through a hand lens, spider mites are pale green or yellowish with dark blotches on the sides and two red eyespots at the anterior end.

Overwintering female spider mites are reddish orange. Several spherical spider mite eggs can be seen here.

SPIDER MITES

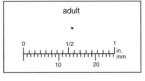

Spider mite feeding causes pale stippling of leaves. Webbing becomes visible when mite populations reach high levels. Heavily infested leaves drop from the tree.

The western predatory mite is the most important mite predator in stone fruit orchards. This mite and several other predatory mite species are pear shaped and translucent white or orange. They do not have spots.

Adult spider mite destroyers are small black lady beetles that feed on webspinning spider mites, European red mites, and mite eggs.

Adult sixspotted thrips have three distinct dark spots on each wing. Both nymphs and adults feed on mites and mite eggs.

They then move up into trees and may infest the entire tree. Spider mites go through a number of generations each season. When temperatures decrease in the fall, females move down the tree to secluded places on the trunk or on the ground near the base of the tree, where they overwinter.

Damage

Twospotted spider mites feed on lower leaf surfaces, whereas Pacific spider mites feed on both sides of the leaves. Spider mites withdraw nutrients from leaf cells, destroying chlorophyll and causing a pale stippling of leaves. When mite populations reach high levels they spin webbing on leaves, hence the names webspinning spider mites. High mite populations reduce tree vigor. Tree canopies may turn pale or yellow when infestations are heavy, and severe infestations cause leaf drop. If defoliation occurs early in the season, fruit size and quality are reduced and the limbs and fruit are exposed to sunburn. Defoliation in mid- to late season may reduce the following year's crop.

Management Guidelines

Successful mite management requires regular monitoring both for pest mites and for predators, and good cultural practices to maintain healthy trees. In many orchards with adequate predator populations, no treatments for spider mites are necessary. Follow fertilizer recommendations to avoid overfertilization, which may increase problems with mites as well as other pests. Because dry, dusty conditions favor spider mites, regular irrigation and watering or oiling of orchard roads to minimize dust will help prevent mite buildups. Certain particularly disruptive pesticides should be avoided when possible, because their use can trigger

The spider mite destroyer larva, which also feeds on mites and mite eggs, is brown to nearly black. Short hairs that grow from numerous black bumps give the larva a velvety appearance.

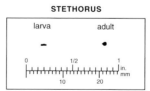

STETHORUS

larva   adult

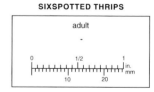

SIXSPOTTED THRIPS

adult

mite flare-ups. Specific comments regarding these points can be found in the *UC IPM Pest Management Guidelines* for each crop.

Biological Control. Several predators feed on spider mites. The most important are western predatory mite and other predatory mites, sixspotted thrips, and spider mite destroyer. Lacewings and minute pirate bugs are general predators that feed on mites. Learn to recognize these predators so you can keep track of them while monitoring. Eriophyid and European red mites (discussed and illustrated below) are food sources for predators early in the season. Whenever possible, avoid treating for eriophyids. They provide a good early food source to build up predator populations that can then control spider mites later in the spring. Some materials used to control other pests in stone fruits such as thrips, leafhoppers, and diseases also kill mite predators. Select the pesticides that are least harmful to predators whenever possible (Table 13 in the previous chapter).

Western predatory mite, *Galendromus* (*Metaseiulus, Typhlodromus*) *occidentalis,* is the most important mite predator in stone fruit orchards. It is about the same size as a spider mite but is pear shaped, translucent white or orange, and lacks spots. Predatory mites move more quickly than spider mites, and their eggs are oval rather than spherical. Populations of the western predatory mite build up quickly at low pest mite densities. When commonly present (i.e., on at least 1/20 of infested leaves), they usually can keep spider mites under control.

Other native predator mites also occur in orchards. One of these, *Typhlodromus caudiglans,* often occurs in large numbers in prune orchards. It looks very much like the western predatory mite: the two cannot be distinguished in the field. Predator mites also feed on eriophyid mites, European red mite nymphs and adults, and certain other non-pest mites. *Typhlodromus caudiglans* also feeds on pollen, and may therefore be present in large numbers in the absence of other mites. The western predatory mite and some other predator mites are available for purchase from commercial insectaries. Augmentative releases may be useful for restoring biological control after a broad-spectrum pesticide has destroyed native populations of the predator. The commercial insectaries often offer guidelines for releases in such situations.

Sixspotted thrips, *Scolothrips sexmaculatus,* is a tiny, slender insect, similar in size and appearance to western flower thrips. It has three dark spots on each forewing. Sixspotted thrips often are able to quickly reduce spider mite infestations, but they usually do not move into orchards until pest mite populations are high. If sixspotted thrips are present on most of the mite-infested leaves in a sample, no treatment will be needed.

The spider mite destroyer, *Stethorus picipes,* is a tiny black lady beetle that feeds on spider mites, including European red mites, and their eggs. The elongated larva is dark brown to nearly black, with numerous black bumps. Short hairs growing from the warts give the larva a velvety appearance. Both larva and adult are predaceous. Spider mite destroyer populations usually do not build up until spider mites reach damaging levels, but once they are established they quickly bring mite infestations under control.

Monitoring and Treatment Guidelines. Regular monitoring will tell you if biological control is keeping spider mites under control, or if treatments are needed. A presence/absence monitoring scheme developed for almonds can be used for stone fruits and is explained in Figure 46, which includes an example of a sampling form. Begin monitoring leaves for mites in March. From March through May, monitor every other week; monitor weekly from May through August. Check trees at random throughout the orchard, and separately sample trees along dusty roads, areas of the orchard that are stressed, and areas that have had mite problems in the past. Sample at least 15 leaves from each tree, taking leaves from inside the canopy on the lower part of the tree. Record the number of leaves with pest mites and the number of leaves with predators. If the number of leaves with pest mites is low or if the number of leaves with predators is nearly the same as the number with pest mites, no treatment is needed. Return in a week or so and sample again. If the number of leaves with pest mites is increasing and the number with predators is not, then treat. Presence of a large number of mite eggs is a good indication that the population is increasing.

Spot treatments may be sufficient because heavy infestations usually start in dusty or stressed areas of the orchard. Use materials that are least harmful to natural enemies (Table 13). Spray oils can be used as long as trees are not stressed, but oils are not effective on mite infestations that have developed heavy webbing. Oil sprays reduce mite populations about 50% in two weeks, so monitor mite numbers again two weeks after a treatment to see if an additional spray is needed. For those stone fruits for which the fruit finish (bloom) is important at the intended market, make sure the finish will not be adversely affected by an oil spray.

If treatment is needed early in the season and predators are present, you can use below-label rates of a miticide to reduce the pest population and help preserve predators. Treatments are not needed after the first of September, mite populations decline naturally at this time.

European Red Mite
Panonychus ulmi

A close relative of the webspinning spider mites, European red mite usually is not a pest in stone fruits, but it can become a serious problem if pesticide sprays disrupt biological control. European red mite is considered beneficial when present

Date: _____   Orchard: _____

Tree number	Total no. leaves sampled	Number leaves with mites	Total leaves with mites	Predators Present		Predators Absent		Number of leaves with western predatory mite and/or sixspotted thrips
				Don't treat if accum. total less than or equal to	Treat if accum. total more than or equal to	Don't treat it accum. total less than or equal to	Treat it accum. total more than or equal to	
1	15	_____	_____					_____
2	30	_____	_____					_____
3	45	_____	_____					_____
4	60	_____	_____					_____
5	75	_____	_____	27	40	12	24	_____
6	90	_____	_____	33	48	15	28	_____
7	105	_____	_____	39	55	18	31	_____
8	120	_____	_____	45	62	21	35	_____
9	135	_____	_____	51	69	23	39	_____
10	150	_____	_____	57	76	26	43	_____
11	165	_____	_____	63	83	29	46	_____
12	180	_____	_____	70	90	32	50	_____
13	195	_____	_____	76	97	35	54	_____
14	210	_____	_____	82	104	38	57	_____
15	225	_____	_____	88	111	41	61	_____
16	240	_____	_____	94	118	45	65	_____
17	255	_____	_____	101	125	48	68	_____
18	270	_____	_____	107	132	51	72	_____
19	285	_____	_____	113	139	54	75	_____
20	300	_____	_____	119	146	57	79	_____

Stop Sampling

Figure 46. A presence/absence sampling scheme developed for webspinning mites in almonds can be used for stone fruits. To use this form, sample 15 leaves from each of a minimum of 5 trees from each sample block, selecting leaves at random from inside and outside the canopy and from all four quadrants. Examine the leaves with a hand lens and record the presence or absence of webspinning mites and eggs, as well as predators. Continue sampling until you have reached a treatment decision or sampled 20 trees. If a decision to treat is reached but the number of leaves with predators is about equal to the number with pest mites, sample again in a few days to see if the pest mite population is decreasing.

In apricots and cherries, treat if the majority of sample leaves have pest mites and the proportion with pest mites is greater than the proportion with predators.

in low numbers because it serves as a food source for some mite predators. Important predators that feed on European red mite include spider mite destroyer, lacewings, and minute pirate bugs.

Adult female European red mites are similar in size and shape to spider mites, but are a dark brick red in color. They have long curved hairs (setae) that arise from whitish spots on the back. Immature mites and adult females that have not fed may be greenish. Eggs are red and slightly flattened, with a long, spinelike projection (called a stipe) at the top.

European red mites overwinter in the egg stage. Eggs hatch about the time the trees leaf out, and the mites feed on leaves. Populations build slowly through the spring, and go through 8 or 10 generations before overwintering eggs are laid in the fall. Feeding by these mites causes pale green or yellowish stippling of leaves similar to that caused by webspinning mites, but rarely causes leaf drop. European red mites are favored by shady, humid conditions, and tend to be more abundant in vigorous, well-managed orchards. As with webspinning mites, their numbers may be increased by excessive nitrogen fertilization.

Look for European red mite eggs when monitoring samples of dormant twigs for other pests such as San Jose scale and aphid eggs. During the season watch for mottling or bronzing of leaves. European red mite probably does little damage unless populations get very high. The predators that feed on webspinning spider mites also feed on European red mite, but they do not reduce European red mite populations as quickly

The adult European red mite is similar in size and shape to webspinning spider mites, but is dark red and has long, curved hairs growing from white spots on the back.

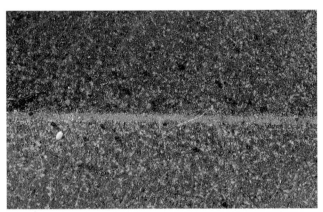

Feeding by European red mites causes pale stippling of leaves similar to that caused by spider mites. Leaves do not drop unless damage is extreme.

European red mite eggs are red and somewhat flattened, with a projection (stipe) on the top. They often are laid in masses around dormant buds or in bark cracks, and the stipe usually is absent following rainy weather.

as they do pest mite populations. Western predatory mite is not able to feed on European red mite eggs. Treatment with adequate rates of oil will control overwintering eggs and help keep populations low in most orchards. A key strategy in an IPM program in stone fruit orchards is to permit low spring populations of European red mite, which serve as food for predators that will later control the more troublesome web-spinning mites.

Brown Mite
Bryobia rubrioculus

Brown mites may cause problems on apricots, cherries, plums, or prunes if very high numbers build up on the foliage.

The brown mite is greenish brown with a flattened body and two front legs that are noticeably longer than the other legs. Immature mites are red. They overwinter as red eggs on wood. Eggs are similar in appearance to European red mite eggs, but have no stipe. Brown mites attack stone fruits, almonds, apples, and pears. At first only a few trees in an orchard may be attacked. They feed on foliage during the cool part of the day and move off leaves to spurs and shoots by mid-morning. If you are sampling for brown mites, either sample leaves early in the morning or use a beat sheet to sample spurs and shoots. When high numbers are present, leaves turn a mottled yellow or brown. Extremely heavy infestations can turn entire trees to pale yellow.

Brown mites do not require control unless numbers are high enough to cause foliage symptoms. This pest usually is kept below damaging levels by dormant oil applied for other pests. Treatment may be needed on apricots or cherries if spring weather is cool and the dormant treatment was insufficient to control brown mite eggs. If treatment becomes necessary, use a material that is least disruptive of natural enemy populations. As with European red mite, if you permit low to moderate spring populations of brown mites, they will serve as food for predators that will later help to control webspinning mites. High temperatures usually cause brown mite populations to decline naturally in summer.

Eriophyid Mites

The species of eriophyid mites that occur most frequently on California stone fruits are peach silver mite, Aculus cornutus, plum rust mite, A. fockeui, and big-beaked plum mite, Diptacus gigantorhynchus. Peach silver mite most frequently occurs on peaches and nectarines, but sometimes is found on other stone fruits. All three species are tiny (about 0.2 mm long) and teardrop shaped, with four short legs at the larger, anterior end. They are yellow, pinkish, or purplish, depending on species. To see them easily, you will need a hand lens with at least a 10× magnification.

Adult brown mites are flattened and dark greenish brown, with very long front legs. Eggs are similar in appearance to European red mite eggs but lack a stipe when freshly laid.

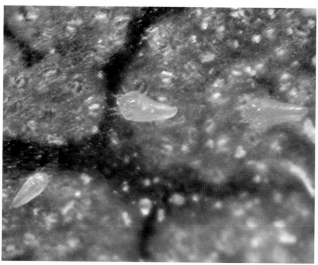

Peach silver mites are pale yellow and teardrop shaped with four short legs at the larger (anterior) end.

Eriophyid mites overwinter as females under bud scales, next to buds, or in bark crevices. They begin to feed on leaves or small fruit after buds open in the spring. If overwintering populations are very high, infested young leaves may develop yellow spots and curl upward along the edges. Later in the season they feed primarily on the undersides of leaves. Heavy infestations of plum rust mite or big-beaked plum mite later in the season cause leaves to turn rusty brown and curl at the edges. Late-season infestations of peach silver mite, which usually follow the use of a disruptive pesticide, cause nectarine and peach leaves to take on a silvery appearance.

Eriophyid mites rarely require treatment. If you observe damage and populations exceed 200 to 300 per leaf early in the season, you can use narrow-range oil, insecticidal soap, or sulfur to control them. However, such treatments may trigger later outbreaks of spider mites, since eriophyid mites are an important food source for predatory mites. Broad-spectrum pesticides applied for other pests may cause outbreaks of eriophyid mites.

Plum rust mites are reddish yellow and, like other eriophyid mites, are teardrop shaped with four short legs at the larger (anterior) end.

Several big-beaked plum mites are shown here next to a European red mite egg.

Diseases

A number of diseases may cause serious problems in stone fruits; those that require management action in a given orchard depend on the stone fruit crop being grown, local weather and soil conditions, past and current cultural practices, and the history of disease problems in and around the orchard. Some diseases, such as brown rot and Phytophthora root and crown rot, have the potential for damage in most stone fruit orchards. Others, such as leaf curl and Eutypa dieback, are specific to one or two stone fruit hosts.

Disease development requires the presence of a disease-causing agent, a susceptible host, and favorable environmental conditions. Diseases caused by biological agents or *pathogens*, which include bacteria, fungi, nematodes, and viruses, are called *biotic diseases*. (Nematodes that attack stone fruits are discussed in the next chapter.) Diseases caused by physical factors such as nutrient deficiencies, environmental conditions, or toxic agents are called *abiotic disorders*. Genetic disorders are inherited anomalies of growth and development that do not spread to unaffected scion wood or rootstocks. In this chapter, genetic disorders are discussed in the section on abiotic disorders. Diseases that may require management in California stone fruit orchards are listed in Table 18.

The successful management of biotic diseases requires knowledge of where the causal agents originate (sources of *primary inoculum*), how the agents move from one place to another, how host plants are infected, and what environmental conditions favor spread, infection, and disease development. Management of abiotic disorder requires knowledge of what conditions cause the disorders, and how these conditions may be avoided.

By classifying biotic diseases according to the parts of the tree affected and how the pathogens are dispersed, we can help identify disease problems and better understand management techniques. Foliage and fruit diseases are caused by pathogens that are spread by wind, splashing water, or insects, and mainly infect leaves, fruit, and current season wood. Root and crown diseases are caused by soil-inhabiting pathogens that infect the roots or crown either directly or through injuries resulting from cultivation and the removal of suckers, and slowly or quickly debilitate the whole tree. Root and crown pathogens spread via surface water, soil on contaminated equipment, and infected planting stock. Branch and trunk diseases are caused by pathogens that usually invade the tree

Table 18. Relative Importance of Diseases Affecting Stone Fruits in California and Available Management Options.

Disease	Apricot	Cherry	Peach/ Nectarine	Plum	Prune	Management options	Page
Foliage & Fruit Diseases							
brown rot	●●	●●	●●	◐	●	fungicides, orchard sanitation	115–120
powdery mildew	●●	●●	●●	●	⊙	fungicides, removing alternate hosts	120–125
shot hole	●●	⊙	●●	⊙	⊙	fungicides, orchard sanitation	125–127
jacket rot, green fruit rot	●●	●●	●●	●	●	fungicides, orchard sanitation	128
leaf curl	⊘	⊙	●●	⊘	⊘	fungicides, orchard sanitation	129–130
rust	⊙	⊙	●	⊙	●	fungicides, irrigation management	130–132
scab	⊙	⊘	●	⊙	⊘	fungicides	132
"fog spot"	●	⊘	⊘	⊘	⊘	(possibly fungicides)	132–133
anthracnose	⊘	⊘	◐	⊘	⊘	vegetation management, fungicides	133
leaf spot	⊘	◐	⊘	⊘	⊘	fungicides	133
Root & Crown Diseases							
Phytophthora root & crown rot	●●	●●	●●	●	●	site selection and preparation, rootstock selection, irrigation management, fungicides	134–136
crown gall	●●	●●	●●	●●	●●	nursery sanitation, biological control agent, careful planting, bactericide	136–137
Armillaria root rot	●●	●●	●●	●●	●	site selection, rootstock selection, soil fumigation	137–139
Verticillium wilt	●	◐	●	⊙	⊙	site selection. choice of rootstock/scion, soil treatment	139
Trunk & Branch Cankers							
bacterial canker	●●	●●	●●	●●	●●	site selection, roostock selection, delayed pruning, nematode control	140–142
Eutypa dieback	●●	●●	⊘	⊘	⊘	summer pruning, orchard sanitation, removal of nearby hosts	142–143
Ceratocystis canker	⊙	⊘	⊙	●	●	avoiding trunk injury	143–144
Cytospora canker	⊙	⊙	◐	●	●	site selection, adequate nutrition, avoiding sunburn	144–145
Phytophthora pruning wound canker	◐	◐	◐	◐	◐	timing of pruning, fungicide application, proper irrigation	145
silver leaf	◐	◐	◐	◐	◐	summer pruning, orchard sanitation	145–146
Virus & Phytoplasma							
X-disease	⊘	●●	◐	⊘	⊘	certified planting stock, vector control, removing diseased trees	148–151
peach yellow leafroll	⊘	⊘	●●	⊘	⊘	site selection (maybe vector control)	151
tomato ringspot virus	◐	◐	◐	◐	◐	certified planting stock, rootstock selection, nematode control, removing diseased trees	153–155
cherry stem pitting	⊘	●	⊘	⊘	⊘	certified planting stock, rootstock selection, removing diseased trees	155
prunus necrotic ringspot virus	◐	●	●●	◐	◐	certified planting stock, removing diseased trees	157
prune dwarf	◐	●	●●	◐	◐	certified planting stock, removing diseased trees	158
Abiotic Disorders							
crinkle leaf	⊘	●	⊘	⊘	⊘	remove diseased trees from scion source orchards	159
deep suture	⊘	●	⊘	⊘	⊘	remove diseased trees from scion source orchards	159
russet ("Lacy") scab	⊘	⊘	⊘	⊘	●●	fungicide application	160
wind scab	⊘	⊘	⊘	◐	◐	none	160
nectarine pox	⊘	⊘	◐	⊘	⊘	avoid susceptible varieties	161
noninfectious plum shot hole	⊘	⊘	⊘	◐	⊘	none needed	161
plum rusty blotch	⊘	⊘	⊘	◐	⊘	remove from propagation programs	162
peach false wart	⊘	⊘	◐	⊘	⊘	none needed	161

Table 18 continued.

Disease	Apricot	Cherry	Peach/ Nectarine	Plum	Prune	Management options	Page
nitrogen deficiency	◖	◖	◖	◖	◖	fertilizer application	163
zinc deficiency	●	●	●	●	●	foliar zinc application	163
potassium deficiency	◖	◖	◖	◖	●●	fertilizer application	164
iron deficiency	◖	◖	◖	◖	◖	soil amendments, fertilizer application	164
herbicide injury	◖	◖	◖	◖	◖	careful application procedures	166–168

●● = major problem
● = common problem
◖ = occasional problem
⊙ = rarely occurs
∅ = does not occur

THIS KEY IS USED THROUGHOUT THIS CHAPTER TO INDICATE THE RELATIVE IMPORTANCE OF DISEASES ON DIFFERENT STONE FRUITS

through injuries to bark or wood, but in some cases they infect uninjured trees; these pathogens are spread by wind, splashing water, and insects, and by contaminated cultivation and harvest equipment. Virus diseases are spread in infected budwood and by insect, mite, or nematode vectors, or in pollen; symptoms may appear on foliage, fruit, or wood.

Orchard Monitoring and Diagnosis

The disease descriptions and illustrations in this chapter are designed to help you recognize problems that may occur in your orchard. Become familiar with the diseases that are likely to affect the stone fruits that you manage. Watch for disease symptoms when you monitor for other pests or during other routine orchard activities. Many pathogens cause symptoms on different parts of the tree. The Pest Damage Table after the last chapter of this book lists symptoms that occur on different stone fruits along with the diseases that may cause them. Use these tables and the disease descriptions and illustrations that follow to help you identify the possible causes of the problems you observe. When trying to identify a disease, be sure to look for symptoms on all parts of the tree that may be affected. Observe how the symptoms change over time. For many diseases, you must observe several symptoms before you can make an accurate diagnosis. Field symptoms alone may not be enough to identify the cause of a disease. Check with qualified professionals if you are not sure of a diagnosis. Laboratory analysis is usually needed to confirm the cause of a disease. Tissue analysis is often necessary to confirm the cause of a nutrient deficiency or pesticide injury symptom. In all cases, a good set of field records will help confirm your diagnosis.

Keep records of what diseases you find and how much disease is present. These records, along with records of weather conditions, soil conditions, and management activities, will help you make future diagnoses, plan management strategies, and assess their effectiveness.

Prevention and Management

Begin a disease management program before you plant the orchard. Whenever possible, consult previous crop records for the site. Past problems with certain soilborne pathogens such as *Phytophthora* spp., *Armillaria mellea*, *Verticillium dahliae*, nematodes, or tomato ringspot virus will affect your choice of rootstock, scion, and preplant site preparation practices. You can have soil samples analyzed for some soilborne pathogens and nematodes that transmit viruses and predispose trees to bacterial canker. If potentially harmful levels of pathogens are present, you may want to fumigate the soil before planting to reduce the inoculum level, or you may want to avoid planting stone fruits in these locations. Soil analysis can also indicate the need for fertilizer supplements to prevent nutrient deficiencies. Choose high-quality planting stock from a reputable nursery to minimize disease problems.

Rootstock Selection. Stone fruit rootstocks vary in their susceptibility to some diseases. Choose rootstocks that are best-suited to the soil conditions of the orchard and that have the greatest resistance to pest problems that are known to be present or are likely to develop. Table 3 in the third chapter and Table 19 list rootstock recommendations for those diseases that you can reduce or prevent by planting resistant rootstocks.

Certified Planting Stock. Virus-free planting stock is the major tool for controlling most of the virus diseases that affect stone fruits. Clean stock programs provide virus-free material for propagation by nurseries. The production of certified planting stock is discussed in more detail in the third chapter, "Managing Pests in Stone Fruits." By planting certified stock, you greatly reduce the likelihood that virus diseases will be introduced. You still must take precautions, however, such as removal of diseased trees and control of vectors, to reduce the spread of those viruses that can be carried by vectors or in

Table 19. Relative Resistance of Stone Fruit Rootstocks to Some Diseases.

Disease	Resistance of rootstocks
Phytophthora root and crown rot	**apricot, nectarine, peach, plum, prune:** Myrobalan seedlings are most resistant; Myrobalan is more resistant than Marianna 2624; Nemaguard and Lovell peach are highly susceptible. **cherry:** Mazzard, Colt, Stockton Morello and Gisela 5, 6, and 7 are more resistant than Mahaleb; some Mahaleb selections relatively resistant.
bacterial canker	**apricot, nectarine, peach, plum, prune:** Lovell and Nemaguard peach are most resistant; plum most susceptible. **cherry:** scions multiple-bud grafted high onto Mahaleb, Stockton Morello, or F12/1 Mazzard scaffold are less affected.
Armillaria root rot	No true resistance to *Armillaria mellea*; apparently rootstocks that grow more slowly are infected more slowly. **apricot, nectarine, peach, plum, prune:** Marianna 2624 plum is least affected; Myrobalan 29-C plum, Damson plum, and St. Julien plum are somewhat less affected. **cherry:** Mazzard is less affected than other rootstocks.
X-disease	**cherry:** Multiple-bud grafting high onto Mahaleb scaffold may prevent loss of entire tree to cherry buckskin.
tomato ringspot virus	**apricot, plum, prune:** Marianna 2624 plum is immune to infection.
cherry stem pitting	**cherry:** Colt is resistant to infection.
cherry rasp leaf	**cherry:** Colt slows movement of the virus into the scion wood.

pollen from infected trees. Certified planting stock also helps prevent introduction of nematodes and soilborne diseases such as Phytophthora root and crown rot and crown gall because of the strict pest management requirements for certified orchards.

Cultural Practices and Sanitation. Cultural practices play an important role in disease management. Use pruning techniques that discourage the development of dense canopies, which favor powdery mildew and other foliar diseases. Select planting sites with good soil drainage or else provide good drainage, and use irrigation practices that avoid prolonged periods of soil saturation in order to minimize problems with Phytophthora root and crown rot. If you follow recommended practices for mechanical harvest of prunes, you can keep Ceratocystis canker from becoming a problem. Pruning apricots and cherries in July, August, or early September instead of during the dormant season will greatly reduce the likelihood of Eutypa dieback. For all stone fruits, pruning in spring or late summer instead of in winter reduces the risk of Phytophthora pruning wound canker and silver leaf, and may help reduce problems with bacterial canker. Follow recommended practices for nitrogen fertilization (see table 6 in the third chapter, "Managing Pests in Stone Fruits"); too much nitrogen increases problems with brown rot and other diseases. If you use sprinkler irrigation, set the heads to avoid wetting the foliage, branches, and trunk.

Removing diseased trees from the orchard is critical to preventing the spread of several virus and phytoplasma diseases, and to limiting the spread of Armillaria root rot. Avoid moving soil from sites known to be infested with *Phytophthora* spp., *Armillaria mellea*, *Verticillium dahliae*, or tomato ringspot virus. Always work the cleanest orchards first to minimize spread of soilborne diseases by workers or field equipment. Whenever possible, prune out and destroy shoots infected

with brown rot, shot hole, and powdery mildew. This will help make other management actions for these diseases more effective. You can reduce the spread of *Eutypa lata* by carefully removing infected limbs and removing abandoned apricot trees and grapevines in the vicinity of apricot orchards.

Inspect nursery stock for signs of diseases such as crown gall and root rot before you plant in order to avoid introducing pathogens into the newly planted orchard. In nurseries, grow seedlings and heel-in trees in clean media, and destroy any diseased trees as soon as symptoms appear.

Pesticides. Fungicides play a key role in the management of several stone fruit diseases. Soil fumigation is recommended in certain instances to reduce soilborne disease inoculum or to control nematode vectors of some pathogens. Under certain circumstances, insecticide applications are used to prevent the spread of X-disease by leafhopper vectors.

Correct timing is critical to the effectiveness of fungicide treatments. Chemicals must be applied before infection occurs, or in some cases within the first few days of disease development. Thorough coverage is essential. Recommended timings for treatments are given in the discussions of specific diseases that follow. Keep track of weather predictions before and during bloom, when you may need to take control actions for several diseases in advance of rainy weather. In the fall, treatments for shot hole and leaf curl are recommended before rainy weather begins. Throughout the season, monitor orchards regularly for disease symptoms.

The development of pesticide resistance in pathogen populations (see Table 14) is a major concern when using fungicides, especially systemic materials. Resistance to benzimidazole fungicides is fairly widespread in populations of the two brown rot pathogens. To minimize resistance problems, avoid using materials in locations where resistance has been observed, alternate the types of chemicals you use, and apply fungicides only when orchard history, monitoring, weather conditions, and stage of development indicate that treatment is needed. Follow recommended procedures for making each application as effective as possible; by increasing the effectiveness of the treatments you do make, you decrease the likelihood that resistance will develop. More specific pesticide recommendations can be found in *UC IPM Pest Management Guidelines* for the different stone fruit crops, listed in the references at the back of this book. Check with local authorities for the latest information on available materials. ALWAYS FOLLOW LABEL DIRECTIONS CAREFULLY WHEN USING PESTICIDES.

FOLIAGE AND FRUIT DISEASES

Some of the most serious diseases of stone fruits are caused by pathogens that attack blossoms, leaves, young twigs, or fruit during wet or humid weather. The pathogens survive from one season to the next in infected leaves, fruit mummies, or twigs that remain on the tree or orchard floor. They are spread by splashing rain, wind, or insects. Infection and disease development are most prevalent during and shortly after bloom, so this is the most critical time for control actions against several of the most important diseases. Successful management of foliage and fruit diseases requires the carefully timed application of fungicides that reduce the amount of inoculum surviving from one season to the next or that protect susceptible plant tissues, such as opening buds. Removal or destruction of diseased plant parts during routine orchard activities will help reduce problems. Choosing the right stone fruit scion wood is a good way to reduce problems with some foliage and fruit diseases.

Brown Rot
Monilinia fructicola, M. laxa

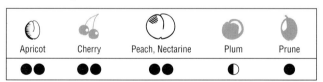

Apricot	Cherry	Peach, Nectarine	Plum	Prune
●●	●●	●●	◑	●

●● = major; ● = common; ◑ = occasional; ⊙ = rare; ∅ = does not occur

Brown rot is one of the most serious diseases in stone fruits. Brown rot pathogens blight blossoms and young shoots, rot ripening fruit, and may attack very young green fruit. Blossom and twig blight are most severe in years when mild, wet weather occurs during bloom. The disease has the potential to be worse in orchards with a history of the disease or where nearby orchards have had brown rot problems. Brown rot is managed primarily with carefully timed fungicide applications. Sanitation practices to eliminate inoculum sources and measures to control insects such as peach twig borer and oriental fruit moth that feed on fruit help reduce brown rot on ripening fruit.

Symptoms and Damage

There are two phases of brown rot in stone fruits: blight of blossoms and twigs, which occurs during bloom, and fruit rot, which mostly affects ripe fruit later in the season. Brown rot pathogens may attack green fruit early in the season, causing green fruit rot (sometimes called jacket rot), which is discussed later in this chapter.

Blossom Blight and Twig Blight. The pathogen primarily responsible for blossom and twig blight on apricots is *Monilinia laxa,* although M. *fructicola* also may be involved. On peaches and nectarines, blossom blight and twig blight are almost always caused by M*onilinia fructicola*. Both species attack the blossoms and twigs of cherries, plums, and prunes. M. *fructicola* is a less aggressive pathogen of woody tissue, so twig blight symptoms are less common on peaches and nectarines than on other stone fruits, although twig blight can accompany the rot of ripe fruit.

In all cases, the disease first develops on the blossoms. Affected flower parts turn brown, wither, and die. Anthers usually die first on peaches and nectarines, and the rest of the blossom soon follows. Sepals usually are affected first on apricots, plums, and prunes. In apricots, cherries, plums, and prunes, the pathogen commonly moves into the shoots, causing extensive blighting of twigs. Blossom blight on peaches and nectarines usually does not spread into the shoot; however, extensive twig blight can occur on more susceptible peach and nectarine varieties. The leaves on blighted shoots wilt,

Flowers with brown rot blossom blight turn brown and die.

Leaves remain attached to shoots killed by brown rot. Blighted shoots may serve as inoculum sources if left on the tree.

Fruit mummies left on the tree or on the orchard floor are important sources of brown rot inoculum in the spring.

Gum deposits form on brown rot twig lesions. The presence of grayish tan spore tufts on the dead flower parts helps distinguish brown rot.

Grayish tan tufts of spores form on the surface of brown rot fruit lesions.

die, and will continue to cling to the dead shoot throughout the following winter if shoots are left on the tree. Gum deposits frequently form on the surface of blighted shoots and at the base of blighted blossoms. Shoot blight usually affects only 1-year-old wood.

Tan or grayish brown tufts of spores develop on the surfaces of blighted blossoms and twigs during damp weather. The presence of spores helps distinguish brown rot from twig and shoot blights associated with other diseases such as bacterial canker.

Fruit Rot. Fruit rot first appears as small, dark spots on the fruit surface. Dark brown discoloration spreads rapidly, and grayish brown tufts of spores develop on the surface of the rotted area. Rotted tissue is relatively firm, compared to that caused by other fruit pathogens such as *Rhizopus*. Rotted fruit may remain on the tree, eventually drying up to become mummies that may serve as a source of pathogen inoculum the following spring. Brown rot most often occurs on fruit after they have started to ripen, but the pathogen sometimes invades young green fruit from infected flower parts or green fruit that has been injured by insects or physical abrasion. This disease, known as green fruit rot or jacket rot, can be caused by other pathogens as well and is discussed in more detail later in this chapter. Alternatively, quiescent (latent) infections may occur on green fruit. In these cases, spores produced on blighted twigs or blossoms infect young, green fruit, but the infections remain dormant. Quiescent infections may be invisible or may appear as brown or black flecks on the fruit surface, or sometimes as red spots on the surface of apricot and cherry fruit. Some quiescent infections develop into rot when fruit begins to ripen.

Seasonal Development

Brown rot pathogens survive from one season to the next either in fruit mummies on the orchard floor or in twig cankers and fruit mummies on the tree. Cankers on blighted twigs or small branches may retain their ability to produce brown rot inoculum for a number of years, although in some cases brown rot infections on the tree do not survive.

At the time of year when many stone fruits begin to bloom, fruit mummies infected with M. *fructicola* that are in contact with the soil may produce cup-shaped, spore-forming structures called *apothecia*. Spores (*ascospores*) produced by apothecia are forcibly discharged into the air and carried by wind to opening blossoms. In some years, asexual spores called *conidia* produced on twig lesions and mummified fruit in trees may serve as the primary inoculum; in other years, ascospores may serve as the primary inoculum in orchards such as peach and nectarine where M. *fructicola* is the dominant brown rot pathogen. Apothecia of M. *laxa* have been observed only rarely, and not in North America. In orchards where this species is the dominant brown rot pathogen, such as apricot and almond orchards, conidia produced on twig cankers or fruit mummies during wet weather are the primary inoculum for blossom blight. M. *fructicola* apothecia have been reported on cherry and plum, but the fungus is also reported to survive in twig cankers on these hosts. Either form of inoculum may function as primary inoculum in the spring on cherry or plum when conditions are favorable for spore production and disease development. On prune, both species have been reported to cause blossom blight. *Monilinia laxa* is the dominant fungus causing blossom blight, whereas M. *fructicola* is the dominant cause of fruit rot on prune. *Monilinia laxa* conidia from twig cankers or M. *fructicola* conidia and ascospores may be involved in initiating blossom blight of prune. Conidia are spread to opening blossoms by splashed water and wind. The seasonal cycle of brown rot is diagrammed in Figure 47.

Most flower parts are susceptible to infection by both brown rot pathogens; the specific parts that become infected and lead to brown rot, however, differ among the stone fruit crops (see Table 20). Blossom blight in peaches and nectarines is caused almost exclusively by anther infection; if petals are infected, they fall before blossom blight can occur. In apricots and prunes, all tissues including sepals can lead to blossom blight. Therefore when fungicides are being used, apricots and prunes generally need treatment at an earlier bloom stage (Table 20). Be aware that the stamens and stigma of some peach varieties protrude from the blossom before petals open, making them susceptible to brown rot blossom blight at an earlier stage.

Wetness from fog, rain, or dew is necessary if infection is to take place. Brown rot is most severe in years with frequent wet weather (rain or fog) and moderate temperatures during bloom. If it is cold (below about 50°F) during the wet weather, there is little or no brown rot. Cherries and prunes tend to be less seriously affected by blossom blight because they bloom later in the spring, when wet weather is less common.

Later in the season, blighted twigs and blossoms and decaying thinned fruit on the orchard floor are the sources of inoculum for fruit infections. Spores from these sources are spread by wind, splashing rain, or insects. Green fruit is

Quiescent (dormant) brown rot infections may appear as small, dark spots on the surface of fruit before they ripen.

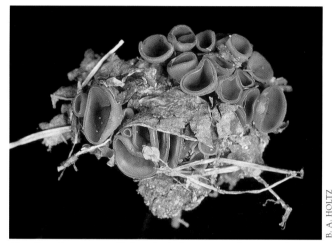

Cup-shaped structures called apothecia form on some brown rot fruit mummies in contact with soil.

Peach blossoms are susceptible to brown rot blossom blight infection as soon as the stigma or anthers are exposed.

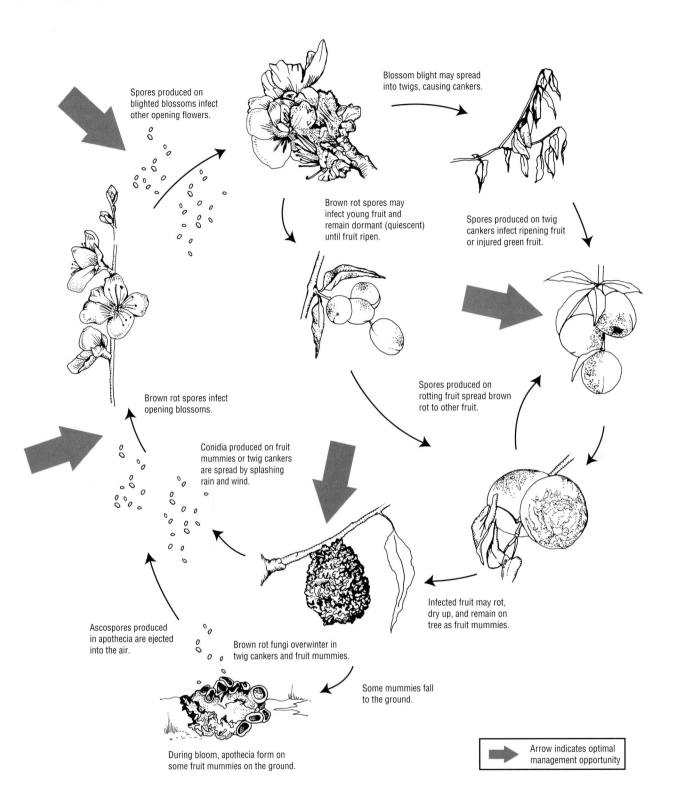

Spores produced on blighted blossoms infect other opening flowers.

Blossom blight may spread into twigs, causing cankers.

Brown rot spores may infect young fruit and remain dormant (quiescent) until fruit ripen.

Spores produced on twig cankers infect ripening fruit or injured green fruit.

Brown rot spores infect opening blossoms.

Spores produced on rotting fruit spread brown rot to other fruit.

Conidia produced on fruit mummies or twig cankers are spread by splashing rain and wind.

Infected fruit may rot, dry up, and remain on tree as fruit mummies.

Ascospores produced in apothecia are ejected into the air.

Brown rot fungi overwinter in twig cankers and fruit mummies.

Some mummies fall to the ground.

During bloom, apothecia form on some fruit mummies on the ground.

Arrow indicates optimal management opportunity

Figure 47. Seasonal cycle of brown rot pathogens. All stone fruits are affected. Control actions are aimed at preventing blossom and fruit infections

somewhat resistant to infection, but there may be infections that remain quiescent until fruit begins to ripen. Insect damage and other injuries increase the likelihood of green fruit infection. In late summer, driedfruit beetles and fruit flies may spread the disease from decaying fruit to ripening fruit. Fruit infection is most common in the last few weeks before harvest. Fruit rot is more likely to be a problem when fruit is allowed to ripen fully on the tree.

Management Guidelines

Good orchard sanitation helps reduce the amount of brown rot inoculum in spring. Have pruning crews remove all fruit mummies and blighted shoots. Remove the mummies from the orchard and destroy them. If left on the orchard floor, mummies will produce inoculum in the spring. You can cultivate the orchard floor to bury fruit mummies and reduce inoculum production. Dense ground cover maintained during bloom favors the production of inoculum by fruit mummies, and may also increase the risk of frost injury. Removing or turning under thinned fruit helps reduce fruit brown rot. Thinned fruit can be a source of inoculum for brown rot on ripening fruit, especially if you leave them where they will come in contact with irrigation water.

Appropriate levels of nitrogen fertilization and water reduce the severity of brown rot on ripening fruit and increase fruit quality. Apply only enough nitrogen to maintain the optimum level recommended for your crop, based on leaf analysis: 2.0 to 2.5% for apricots, 2.0 to 3.0% for cherries, 2.6 to 3.0% for nectarines and peaches, 2.3 to 2.8% for plums and prunes. By controlling fruit-feeding insect pests such as peach twig borer and oriental fruit moth, you can help reduce brown rot fruit infections.

Fungicides. Treatment before and during bloom can prevent substantial losses to blossom blight when weather is wet during bloom. Bloomtime treatment is recommended every season to prevent blossom and twig blight in apricot, nectarine, and peach orchards. Treatment early in bloom is recommended in cherry and prune orchards that have a history of blossom and twig blight, or if you expect to have unusually wet weather during bloom. Most plum varieties do

not need treatment; exceptions include La Roda, Wickson, and Santa Rosa.

Treatment during Bloom. Most years in California, a single application will provide sufficient protection against blossom and twig blight. The application can be made either at pink bud, with a systemic fungicide, or at full bloom (when about 80% of flowers have opened), with either a contact fungicide or a systemic fungicide. No treatment is recommended if weather during bloom is dry. If weather conditions are favorable for disease, you must time fungicide application to protect susceptible flower parts. For example, apricot and prune sepals are susceptible to infection, so treatment for those fruits must be applied as soon as buds begin to open. The susceptibility of flower parts and recommended timings for first treatments are listed in Table 20. When you are expecting rain, make applications far enough ahead of time to allow the spray to dry before rain starts. Repeat treatments at 7- to 14-day intervals (see label directions) as long as bloom continues and weather remains favorable for disease. More-frequent treatments may be necessary in unusually wet weather. After a low-chilling winter, a prolonged bloom period may require protection over a longer time. Your choice of fungicidal material may depend on the need to control other diseases such as powdery mildew or rust.

Treatment of Ripening Fruit. Control of blossom and twig blight greatly reduces brown rot inoculum in the orchard and the threat of fruit rot later in the season. Whenever practical, remove blighted twigs as soon as possible to reduce the threat of fruit rot later on. In apricots, cherries, nectarines, and peaches, you may have to treat ripening fruit to prevent losses; recommended preharvest treatment timings are listed in Table 20. Treatment is recommended for apricots, especially if you expect it to rain before harvest, because the fruit are highly susceptible to brown rot. Cherry, nectarine, and peach fruit are less susceptible to brown rot, but preharvest treatment will reduce postharvest decay. Monitor orchards for brown rot as fruit begin to ripen, especially where blossom blight and twig blight were a problem early in the season, and treat if you observe significant

Table 20. Flower Parts Susceptible to Brown Rot Infection that Can Lead to Blossom Blight and Recommended Timing of Fungicide Application for Different Stone Fruit Crops.[1]

Stone fruit	Susceptible flower parts	Timing of first treatment	Timing before harvest to protect fruit
apricot	sepals, petals, anthers, stigma	red bud	2–3 weeks
cherry	petals, anthers, stigma	first white	1–10 days
nectarine	anthers, stigma	first pink to 5% bloom	last 4 weeks
peach	anthers, stigma	first pink to 5% bloom	last 4 weeks
plum	petals, anthers, stigma	first white	not recommended
prune	sepals, petals, anthers, stigma	green tip	5 weeks

1. See Figures 75–79 in Appendix I for color photographs that illustrate bloom stages.

Whitish fungal growth develops on leaves infected with powdery mildew. In many cases leaf growth is distorted.

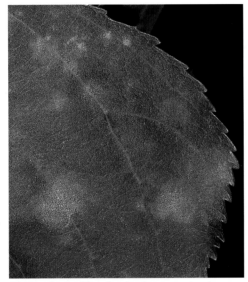

The powdery mildew that develops on apricot leaves in summer does not distort leaf growth.

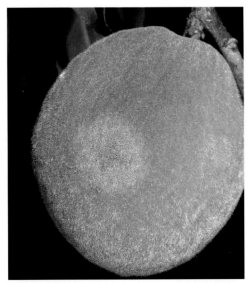

Powdery mildew appears as white, powdery patches on green fruit.

amounts of fruit brown rot. Techniques under development will allow you to monitor fruit a few weeks before harvest for quiescent brown rot infections and predict the need for pre-harvest fungicide applications.

Fungicide Resistance. Strains of *Monilinia fructicola* resistant to benzimidazole fungicides (benomyl and thiophanate methyl) occur commonly in California. To avoid problems with resistance, use these materials only once during a season, preferably as the first application, and only in combination with products of a different chemistry. Do not use them at all in orchards where resistance has been observed. Resistance to the systemic dicarboximide fungicide (iprodione) has been reported in California, but is not common. Resistance to the systemic sterol biosynthesis inhibitor fungicides (myclobutanil, propiconazole, and tebuconazole) has not been reported in California. To reduce the likelihood that resistance to these materials will develop, keep the number of applications to a minimum and follow recommendations to make each application as effective as possible. Use a systemic material for the first application of the season and a contact fungicide if treatment must be repeated. It is important that you rotate the types of chemicals used, especially for preharvest sprays, because the buildup of resistance is more likely with preharvest sprays than with bloomtime sprays. Be aware that most fungicide labels restrict the total number of applications you can make in one season.

Powdery Mildew
Sphaerotheca pannosa,
Podosphaera spp.

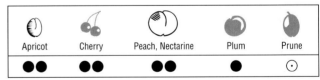

Apricot	Cherry	Peach, Nectarine	Plum	Prune
●●	●●	●●	●	⊙

Powdery mildew is a fungal disease that occurs on all stone fruits, affecting foliage, fruit, and (rarely) flowers. The disease is most often damaging to the fruit of apricot, nectarine, and peach. Plums also may be damaged and cherry fruit occasionally are affected. Foliage infections are of concern primarily in nurseries and as a source of inoculum for fruit infections, especially in cherry orchards since the fruit there remain susceptible until harvest.

Symptoms and Damage
Powdery mildew usually appears first as a netlike white growth on leaves, most often on the terminals of new shoots, or as whitish patches on young green fruit. Affected leaves become powdery white when spore production begins, and their growth is distorted. Leaves may turn yellow and then brown, and if severely affected may curl and fall off. The

powdery mildew that develops on apricot leaves in the summer does not distort the foliage.

White patches of powdery mildew develop on the surface of young fruit. As apricots and peaches ripen, infected areas may remain green or turn reddish with powdery white growth on the surface. After pit hardening, the surface of most stone fruits becomes resistant to powdery mildew; if attacked by the pathogen, a netlike pattern or scabby patch of corky tissue may develop on the fruit surface. Cherry fruit remain susceptible after pit hardening, and if infected after they begin to ripen they become distorted and covered with white fungal growth similar to that seen on leaves. Yellow areas develop on the surface of plums infected with one of the powdery mildew pathogens, *Sphaerotheca pannosa*, and the affected areas later turn into scabby lesions. A disease called rusty spot may develop on peaches growing near apples that are severely affected by powdery mildew. Tan to orange lesions form on the fruit surface and become irregular in shape as the fruit enlarges. This symptom is caused by the apple powdery mildew pathogen *Podosphaera leucotricha*.

Seasonal Development

Several different species of powdery mildew fungi attack stone fruits. *Sphaerotheca pannosa* attacks plum fruit and the foliage and fruit of apricot, nectarine, and peach; *Podosphaera tridactyla* attacks the foliage of apricot and plum; *P. clandestina* attacks the foliage and fruit of cherry; *P. leucotricha* attacks peach fruit; and an unidentified species (probably a species of *Podosphaera*) attacks fruit of certain plum varieties. All powdery mildew pathogens grow on the surface of their host, using specialized structures to penetrate the plant surface and withdraw nutrients from host cells. They differ in the details of their life cycles and in some of the host plants they attack (Table 21).

Sphaerotheca pannosa overwinters as mycelium inside infected buds of peach and on certain roses. Young peach leaves are infected as they emerge from infected buds, after shoot extension begins in the spring. Air movement spreads the spores produced on these leaves to other foliage and young fruit. Older leaves are resistant to infection, as are fruit after the beginning of pit hardening. The disease continues to spread to other peach trees, infecting young leaves or developing fruit, and may spread to apricots and plums from peaches. The most important source for infection of apricot foliage and fruit and for plum fruit is thought to be powdery mildew on nearby roses. Plum foliage is not affected, and the pathogen apparently does not spread to other plum trees from infected plums. Figure 48 illustrates the seasonal cycle of *Sphaerotheca pannosa*.

Podosphaera tridactyla and *P. clandestina* survive winter as spore-forming structures called *cleistothecia* on the surface of shoots, on dead leaves on the orchard floor, and on bark where they lodge after falling from foliage. Cleistothecia are resistant to adverse environmental conditions. Ascospores produced in cleistothecia are ejected after a spring rain, and

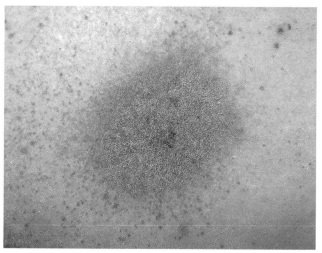

Powdery mildew on ripe fruit may appear as reddish areas with white, powdery growth on the surface.

An unidentified species of powdery mildew attacks the green fruit of Ambra (*shown here*), Red Beaut, and Black Beaut plums.

The powdery mildew pathogens *Podosphaera clandestina* (*shown here*) and *P. tridactyla* overwinter as tiny, dark, spore-forming structures called cleistothecia.

are spread by air movement to susceptible hosts. They infect young foliage or fruit of cherry and developing foliage of apricot and plum. Fruit infections on cherry are rare except when foliage disease becomes severe before harvest. *Podosphaera tridactyla* does not appear on apricot or plum foliage until summer (usually after harvest on apricot). In late summer or fall, cleistothecia form. These appear as small black dots on the surface of mildewed leaves and shoots. Figures 49 and 50 illustrate the cycle of powdery mildews caused by *Podosphaera* species.

Powdery mildew development on stone fruits is favored by warm, humid conditions—temperatures of about 70° to 85°F (20° to 30°C) and relative humidities of 70 to 100%. The disease tends to be worse inside tree canopies, in shady, humid orchards, and during overcast weather. Infection of ripening cherries is favored by damp weather; powdery

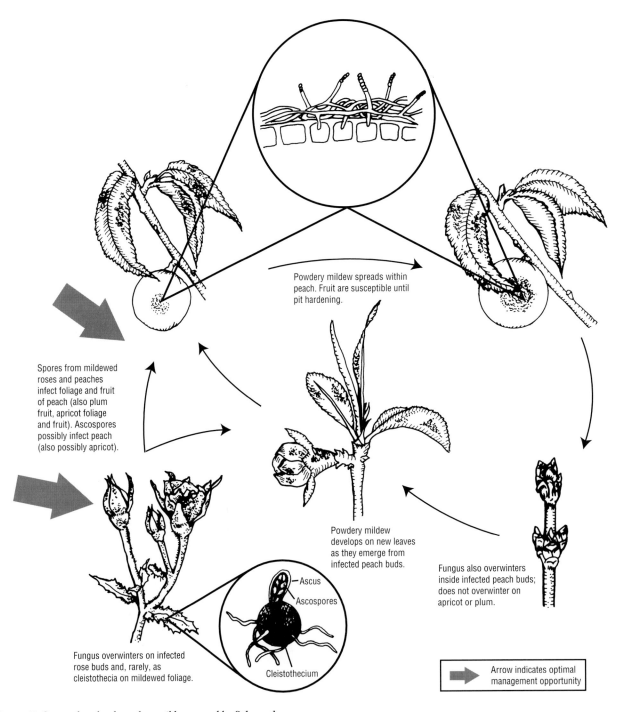

Powdery mildew spreads within peach. Fruit are susceptible until pit hardening.

Spores from mildewed roses and peaches infect foliage and fruit of peach (also plum fruit, apricot foliage and fruit). Ascospores possibly infect peach (also possibly apricot).

Powdery mildew develops on new leaves as they emerge from infected peach buds.

Fungus also overwinters inside infected peach buds; does not overwinter on apricot or plum.

Fungus overwinters on infected rose buds and, rarely, as cleistothecia on mildewed foliage.

Ascus
Ascospores
Cleistothecium

Arrow indicates optimal management opportunity

Figure 48. Seasonal cycle of powdery mildew caused by *Sphaerotheca pannosa*. Affects apricots, peaches, and plums. Control needed to prevent fruit infections.

mildew can become severe if there is rain or overcast weather after cherries start to ripen.

Management Guidelines

Management of powdery mildew in stone fruits focuses on protecting fruit from infections. The removal of nearby roses helps reduce the incidence of powdery mildew in apricot, and may control the disease sufficiently in plums. Specific control actions depend on the weather conditions, the type of stone fruit, and in some cases the variety.

Apricot. Remove nearby rose bushes to reduce powdery mildew inoculum. Apply fungicide at redbud, and if bloom is prolonged and weather conditions remain favorable (overcast or damp) make a second application 2 to 4 weeks after bloom. Some of the materials that may be applied at this

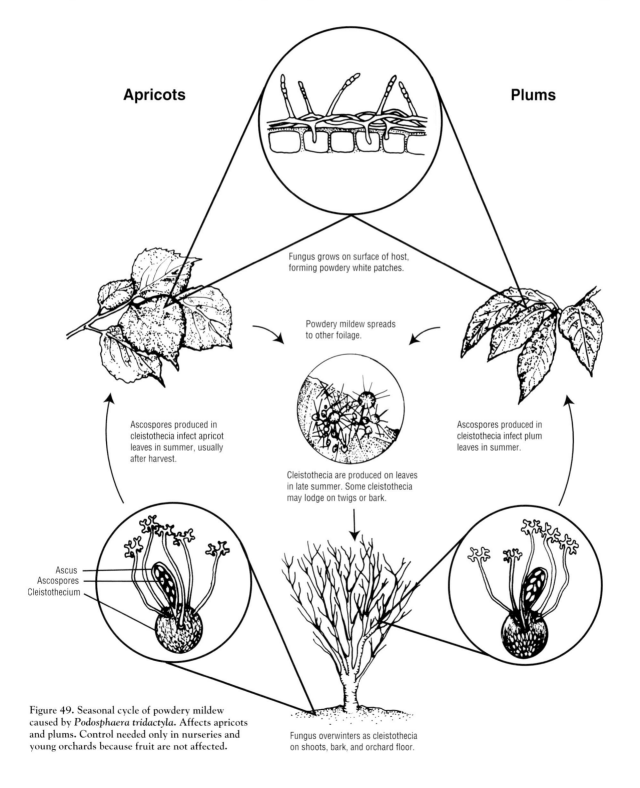

Apricots

Plums

Fungus grows on surface of host, forming powdery white patches.

Powdery mildew spreads to other foilage.

Ascospores produced in cleistothecia infect apricot leaves in summer, usually after harvest.

Ascospores produced in cleistothecia infect plum leaves in summer.

Cleistothecia are produced on leaves in late summer. Some cleistothecia may lodge on twigs or bark.

Ascus
Ascospores
Cleistothecium

Fungus overwinters as cleistothecia on shoots, bark, and orchard floor.

Figure 49. Seasonal cycle of powdery mildew caused by *Podosphaera tridactyla.* Affects apricots and plums. Control needed only in nurseries and young orchards because fruit are not affected.

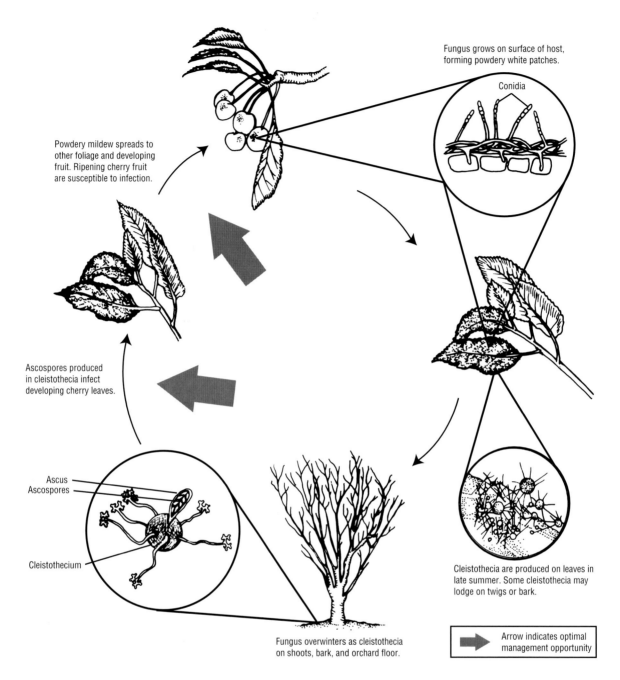

Fungus grows on surface of host, forming powdery white patches.

Conidia

Powdery mildew spreads to other foliage and developing fruit. Ripening cherry fruit are susceptible to infection.

Ascospores produced in cleistothecia infect developing cherry leaves.

Ascus
Ascospores

Cleistothecium

Fungus overwinters as cleistothecia on shoots, bark, and orchard floor.

Cleistothecia are produced on leaves in late summer. Some cleistothecia may lodge on twigs or bark.

Arrow indicates optimal management opportunity

Figure 50. Seasonal cycle of powdery mildew caused by *Podosphaera clandestina*. Affects cherries but not other stone fruits. Control needed to prevent fruit infections.

time for brown rot control also control powdery mildew. Sulfur cannot be used on apricots because of phytotoxicity. The removal of highly susceptible roses or the control of powdery mildew on those roses usually is sufficient to control powdery mildew on backyard apricots.

Cherry. Bing, Black Tartarian, and Rainier are the most susceptible cherry varieties, but all varieties are affected. In orchards where powdery mildew has been severe, treat with a fungicide at shuck fall and repeat at 7- to 14-day intervals until harvest. In other orchards, watch for the appearance of mildew on new foliage and treat with a fungicide as soon as you see disease. Research on cherries in the State of Washington indicates that you can expect the first mildew to develop after the first spring rain that exceeds 0.1 inch, when the temperature is above 50°F (10°C). Whenever possible during the season, remove water sprouts that develop powdery mildew. Before harvest, watch for powdery

Table 21. Seasonal Cycle of Powdery Mildew Pathogens Attacking Stone Fruits in California.[1]

Stone fruit	Pathogen	Seasonal cycle
Apricot	*Sphaerotheca pannosa*	Inoculum from roses and possibly peaches infects leaves and fruit in spring, little or no spread within apricot; overwinters on peach and rose.
	Podosphaera tridactyla	Infects leaves in mid- to late summer; overwinters as cleistothecia on shoots, leaves, bark.
Cherry	*Podosphaera clandestina*	Infects young leaves and shoots all season, both young and ripening fruit; overwinters as cleistothecia on shoots, leaves, bark.
Peach	*Sphaerotheca pannosa*	Infects fruit before pit hardening, young leaves all season; overwinters in infected buds of peach and rose (*Rosa* spp.).
	Podosphaera leucotricha	Infects ripening fruit in orchards next to heavily infected apples; does not survive on peach, must move into peach from nearby apple trees.
Plum	*Sphaerotheca pannosa*	Inoculum from roses and possibly peaches infects young fruit, not foliage; overwinters on peach and rose.
	Podosphaera tridactyla	Infects leaves in summer or fall; overwinters as cleistothecia on shoots, leaves, bark.
	Unidentified species	Infects Red Beaut, Black Beaut, Ambra plums.

1. These cycles are illustrated in figures 48–50.

mildew on foliage in the inner canopy during routine monitoring, and treat if mildew begins to develop. Pay special attention to susceptible varieties when they are interplanted as pollinators. Either treat or prune out and destroy localized infections that develop on these trees to prevent powdery mildew from spreading to the rest of the orchard. Later in the season, prune out and destroy any localized infections that appear. By treating late-season mildew with a fungicide, you will substantially reduce overwintering inoculum, but whether this has a significant effect on disease the following year is unknown. Do not use a systemic fungicide at this time of year, because the potential for resistance development is much higher. Follow cultural practices that reduce orchard humidity.

Peach. Peach varieties that lack leaf glands are more susceptible to powdery mildew than are varieties that do possess leaf glands. Apply a fungicide at petal fall. If conditions remain favorable for powdery mildew (cool, damp nights and warm days), treat two weeks after petal fall and again before pit hardening. No treatment for powdery mildew is necessary after pit hardening. Watch for the disease during routine monitoring, and remove and destroy infections as soon as they appear on foliage later in the season. Avoid growing peaches near apple varieties that are highly susceptible to powdery mildew, such as Jonathan, Gravenstein, and Rome Beauty. If you expect powdery mildew on nearby apples to cause disease problems for your peach trees, either control mildew on the apples or apply a fungicide to the peaches at jacket split.

Plum. The removal of nearby roses or the control of powdery mildew on nearby roses may be all that is needed to keep the disease from becoming a problem in plums, especially in

backyard situations. Some highly susceptible varieties may need protection; Black Beaut, Gaviota, Kelsey, and Wickson are the most susceptible. If you anticipate a problem with powdery mildew, apply fungicide at jacket split.

Fungicide Resistance. Powdery mildew populations on cherries in some orchards of the Pacific Northwest appear to be developing resistance to demethylation inhibitor (DMI) fungicides (e.g., fenarimol and myclobutanil). If you are using fungicides to control powdery mildew, especially on cherries, it is a good idea to limit the number of times you use a DMI fungicide each season and to alternate with non-DMI fungicides. This will reduce the likelihood that DMI resistance will develop. Never use a DMI fungicide to treat late-season powdery mildew; such treatments greatly increase the likelihood that resistance will develop. Sulfur is an alternative treatment material that you can use to control mildew on all stone fruits except apricot.

Shot Hole
Wilsonomyces carpophilus

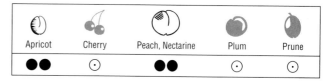

Shot hole is a major disease of apricots, peaches, and nectarines as well as of almonds. In years with unusually wet weather during winter and spring, the disease will develop on cherries, plums, or prunes growing near more susceptible stone fruits. To manage shot hole, you apply a fungicide in

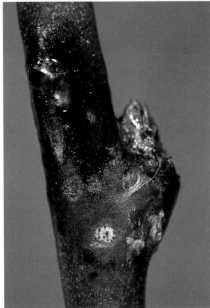

Buds killed by shot hole are dark and covered with a shiny layer of gum. Tan twig lesions with dark spots in the center help identify this as shot hole.

Shot hole lesions on leaves have tan centers and dark brown margins. Fruit lesions have dark reddish margins.

Shot hole lesions on fruit become rough and corky.

fall to control inoculum during the dormant season. Additional treatments may be needed in wet years.

Symptoms and Damage

Symptoms of shot hole may appear on buds, twigs, leaves, or fruit. In apricots, symptoms develop mainly on leaves and fruit. Twig and bud blight are the main symptoms on peaches and nectarines, but fruit lesions may develop when spring weather is wet.

Twig symptoms first appear as small purplish black spots. These turn brown as they enlarge, often having a light center with a purplish brown margin. Tiny, dark brown bumps develop at the center of each lesion. These bumps are spore-forming structures called *sporodochia*, and are easily seen with a hand lens. When buds are affected, the scales turn dark brown or black and the buds may be covered with a shiny layer of exuded gum. Buds killed by bacterial blast have a similar appearance, but tend to be much blacker, and nearby foliage of the affected shoot is wilted. Shot hole can be distinguished on peach and nectarine by the presence of tan twig lesions with dark margins, usually accompanied by profuse gumming.

Fruit and leaf symptoms look much like those of twig lesions. They are small spots, purplish at first, and turning light brown in the center as they enlarge. Sporodochia form in leaf lesions but not in fruit lesions. Leaf lesions may be surrounded by a light green or yellowish zone; in many cases the brown tissue in the center will fall out, leaving the "shot hole" that gives the disease its name. Lesions on fruit become rough and corky. Fog spot on apricot fruit may be confused with shot hole, but fog spot lesions are more numerous and there are no accompanying leaf symptoms.

Shot hole on peaches and nectarines does its primary damage by killing twigs and buds. On apricots, most damage is from leaf and fruit infections, but some buds are killed.

Seasonal Development

The seasonal cycle of shot hole in stone fruits is illustrated in Figure 51. The fungus that causes shot hole overwinters in infected buds and twig lesions. Infected buds are the most important sources of inoculum in apricot, peach, and nectarine. Spores are produced throughout the winter during periods of wet weather and are spread by splashing rain and wind. If left on the tree, blighted buds may continue to produce spores for more than a year.

Twigs and buds can be infected during rainy weather any time from fall through spring. At least 24 hours' continuous wetness is needed for twigs to be infected; the infection period is shorter for leaves and fruit in the spring. Spores can survive for several months during dry weather.

In the spring, developing leaves become infected during wet weather. Spores produced on blighted buds, twigs, and leaves infect developing fruit. Fruit lesions apparently do not produce spores. The disease cycle stops with the onset of

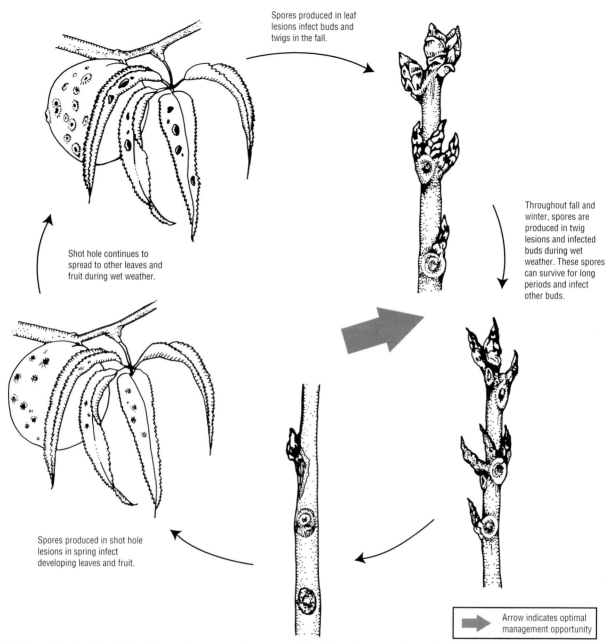

Spores produced in leaf lesions infect buds and twigs in the fall.

Throughout fall and winter, spores are produced in twig lesions and infected buds during wet weather. These spores can survive for long periods and infect other buds.

Shot hole continues to spread to other leaves and fruit during wet weather.

Spores produced in shot hole lesions in spring infect developing leaves and fruit.

Arrow indicates optimal management opportunity

Figure 51. Seasonal cycle of shot hole. Affects apricots, nectarines, and peaches. Control action is designed to destroy inoculum and prevent bud infections during fall and winter.

warm, dry weather, but the pathogen survives inside infected buds and twig lesions until wet weather resumes in the fall.

Management Guidelines

Treat apricots, peaches, and nectarines with a fungicide before rainy weather begins in the autumn, after leaf fall if possible. This treatment usually is sufficient to control twig and bud infections during the winter and to prevent significant losses in the spring. If rainfall is higher than normal, repeat the treatment in late winter, before buds begin to swell. The objective of this program is to protect buds and twigs from infection. In apricot orchards with a history of severe shot hole, make an additional fungicide application between full bloom and petal fall to reduce leaf and fruit infections.

In orchards where twig infections have become prevalent, you can improve the efficacy of dormant treatments by pruning out and destroying infected wood. If you use sprinkler irrigation, make sure the heads are set at an angle low enough to keep from wetting the lower canopy.

Jacket rot is characterized by brown lesions that form underneath the diseased calyx (jacket) of young fruit. Sporulation of the pathogen can be seen on the infected jacket in this photo.

Green fruit rot can occur when brown rot spreads from diseased flower parts to young, green fruit.

Ascospores discharged by apothecia of *Sclerotinia sclerotiorum* are moved by air currents into the tree canopy, where they can infect senescing stone fruit flowers.

Jacket Rot, Green Fruit Rot
Botrytis cinerea, *Monilinia* spp., *Sclerotinia sclerotiorum*

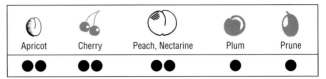

Apricot	Cherry	Peach, Nectarine	Plum	Prune
●●	●●	●●	●	●

Decay of flower parts and young green fruit, called jacket rot, calyx rot, blossom rot, or green fruit rot, is a serious problem in coastal areas if not controlled. It can become a problem in other growing areas when there is prolonged wet weather during bloom. Several fungal pathogens may be involved in this disease, and all stone fruits are affected.

The disease starts when pathogens attack the calyx and flower petals, causing them to wither. As fruit starts to develop, a brown lesion forms where the diseased calyx touched the fruit surface. The lesion quickly spreads over the entire fruit, killing it while it is still very small. If the causal agent is *Botrytis cinerea*, grayish tufts of spores form on infected plant parts. When *Sclerotinia sclerotiorum* is involved, white mycelium develops on affected fruit and flower parts. Brown rot blossom blight, caused by *Monilinia fructicola* or M. *laxa*, occasionally is followed by green fruit rot. Seasonal development and management of brown rot blossom blight is discussed in the section on brown rot.

Spores of jacket rot pathogens form on infected, dead flower parts and fruit mummies on the orchard floor, as well as on other organic matter such as dead or senescent weeds. *Sclerotinia sclerotiorum* produces apothecia, similar to those formed by brown rot pathogens, from sclerotia on infected host debris on the orchard floor, especially where cover crops or native vegetation is present. In addition, spores of *Monilinia* species are produced on twig cankers and fruit mummies on the tree. In spring, splashing rain and wind spread these spores to opening flowers. Flower parts are infected directly by germinating spores of *Botrytis* and *Monilinia* species when flowers are wet. Ascospores produced by the apothecia of S. *sclerotiorum* infect dead or senescing flower parts such as petals and sepals. The pathogens move into developing fruit from infected flower parts. Green fruit rot develops when damp weather occurs while flower shucks still cling to the surface of young fruit. Cooler weather favors retention of the shucks and increases the likelihood of green fruit rot.

Weather conditions in coastal districts usually favor jacket rot every season, and a fungicide application is recommended at full bloom to prevent serious losses. In other areas, treatment is necessary only when wet weather is expected during bloom. Fungicides applied for brown rot also control jacket rot and green fruit rot. Avoid the repeated use of benzimidazole fungicides. Resistance to these chemicals is known to occur in *Botrytis cinerea* as well as *Monilinia* species,

Leaf curl is characterized by red, distorted growth of young leaves. Young twigs become thickened and discolored. The upper surface of infected leaves turns whitish when the leaf curl pathogen produces spores.

Leaf curl symptoms on fruit appear as reddish, wartlike growths on the fruit surface.

and frequent use is likely to cause a buildup of resistant populations of these pathogens.

Leaf Curl, Plum Pockets
Taphrina spp.

![Apricot]	![Cherry]	![Peach, Nectarine]	![Plum]	![Prune]
Apricot	Cherry	Peach, Nectarine	Plum	Prune
∅	⊙	●●	⊙	∅

Peach leaf curl, caused by the fungus *Taphrina deformans*, affects foliage, young shoots, and fruit of nectarines and peaches. It can become a serious problem, especially when spring weather is unusually wet, but usually is kept under control with a dormant season fungicide application. A similar disease affecting the foliage of cherry, caused by *Taphrina cerasi*, has been reported in California only a few times. Plum pockets is a disease of plum fruit that commonly occurs in California on the native plum (Sierra plum), *Prunus subcordata*, but rarely occurs on European or oriental plums. In the Pacific Northwest, the disease occurs on French and Italian prunes. Plum pockets is caused by a different species of *Taphrina* than those that cause peach leaf curl and cherry leaf curl.

Symptoms and Damage
Leaf curl first appears as a prominent red or yellow discoloration of young leaves in the spring. Affected leaves become thickened, puckered, and tightly curled. On upper leaf surfaces, discolored areas turn whitish as the pathogen begins to produce spores. Diseased leaves eventually fall from the tree

early in the season. Young shoots, blossoms, and fruit are sometimes infected. Shoots become thickened, distorted, and discolored, and often die; blossoms shrivel and fall. Wrinkled, reddish, warty areas occasionally develop on fruit. If trees are not treated for the disease, leaf curl can become a severe problem, reducing fruit production and debilitating trees.

When affected by plum pockets, plum fruit become enlarged and bladderlike, with a leathery surface, and the pit fails to develop. The surface of diseased fruit turns whitish when the pathogen produces spores, and foliage and shoot symptoms similar to those caused by the peach leaf curl pathogen may develop.

Seasonal Development
Leaf curl is caused by species of a fungus that grows just under the surface cell layers of young, developing host tissue. The pathogen apparently survives the dry weather of summer as ascospores, which are produced in specialized structures that erupt through the surface of diseased host tissue in the spring. During wet weather, ascospores germinate and grow on plant surfaces and reproduce in a yeastlike fashion by repeatedly budding. The single cells that are formed by this budding process are called *bud conidia* or *blastospores*. They can survive several months of cold weather; the pathogen apparently survives through the winter on tree surfaces as bud conidia that actively grow and divide during wet weather.

When buds begin to open in the spring, cell division within the buds somehow activates bud conidia of *Taphrina* species. As new growth begins to emerge, it is infected by germinating bud conidia during humid or wet weather. Only juvenile host tissue can be infected. The pathogen develops just beneath the surface of young leaves and twigs,

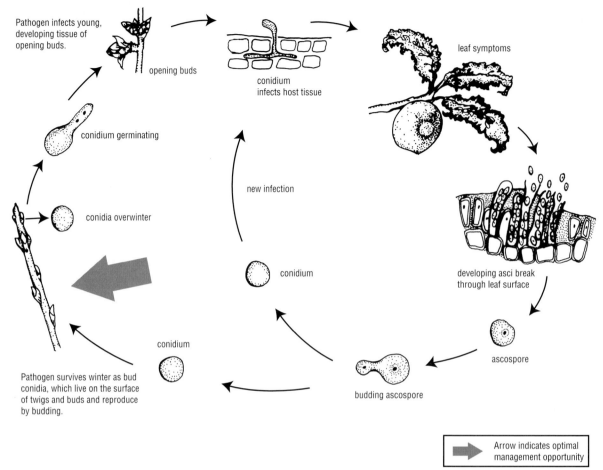

Figure 52. Seasonal cycle of peach leaf curl. Affects peaches and nectarines. Control action needed to prevent infection of opening buds.

inducing abnormal cell growth that results in distorted growth. Discoloration results as the pathogen destroys the green pigment chlorophyll in leaf cells and stimulates red pigment production.

The seasonal cycle of peach leaf curl is illustrated in Figure 52. The life cycles of the cherry leaf curl and plum pockets pathogens are the same.

Management Guidelines

Leaf curl usually is controlled effectively by fungicide applications during the dormant season. Fall treatment for shot hole also controls leaf curl when you use a fungicide that is effective against both pathogens. If winter weather is unusually wet, additional treatment is recommended because heavy rain washes off the protectant fungicide and increases spore production by the pathogen. Make the second application before buds begin to swell. Where rainfall is not high and no treatment for shot hole is needed, a single fall treatment is recommended for leaf curl control.

Remove wild plums that show symptoms of plum pockets if they are near plum orchards. If the disease becomes a prob-

lem in plum orchards, fungicide treatment before budswell will control the pathogen.

Rust
Tranzschelia discolor

Apricot	Cherry	Peach, Nectarine	Plum	Prune
⊙	⊙	●	⊙	●

Rust can occur on all stone fruits, but usually is significant only on peaches and prunes. The disease is caused by a fungus that attacks the foliage of prunes—rarely the fruit—and both foliage and fruit of peaches. The strain of rust fungus that attacks peaches is different from the strain that attacks prunes. It may become severe on peaches in wet years. Rust occurs most frequently in Sacramento Valley orchards; in San Joaquin Valley prunes, the disease may be a problem in wet years or in orchards where cover crops or nearby rivers

On the upper leaf surface (*right*) rust lesions are angular, yellow spots; on the lower leaf surface (*left*) they are rusty red from spore production.

Rust lesions on peach fruit are small, sunken spots that may be confused with stink bug damage. Presence of foliage rust helps identify the disease.

increase humidity. Rust is worse when rain occurs in spring and summer.

Symptoms and Damage

Rust usually is seen first as bright yellow, angular spots on the upper sides of leaves. On the underside of affected leaves, spores developing in lesions give the spots a rusty red appearance. Severe foliar rust can cause defoliation, which may substantially reduce yields if it occurs before harvest. In peaches, severe defoliation exposes branches to sunburn. Some late-season flowering follows defoliation and may reduce fruit set the following year.

Rust infections on peach fruit appear as small, sunken dark spots. A small area around each spot remains greenish or yellow when the fruit begins to color, and the lesion often splits open by the time the fruit is ripe. If you peel back the surface of a lesion, you will see rust-colored, spongy spore masses. As lesions mature, spores form on the surface of the fruit. Fruit lesions may be confused with stink bug damage, but rust is distinguished by the presence of leaf symptoms and spore masses within the lesions or spores on the fruit surface. Losses are caused by the downgrading of fruit quality at harvest.

In orchards where rust infections are heavy, symptoms may appear on twigs as small, lens-shaped cracks filled with rust-colored masses of spores. These lesions become obvious on second-year wood the spring after infection. Look for these in the spring in orchards where rust occurred the previous season.

Seasonal Development

On peaches, the rust fungus survives winter in twig lesions. Spores produced in these lesions during wet weather in the spring infect leaves and the disease continues to spread to other foliage and fruit during periods of wet weather. Foliage infections are dormant during the summer unless rain or irri-

Rust lesions on second-year wood are small, lens-shaped cracks with rust-colored spores.

gation creates humid conditions in the orchard. Heavily infected leaves fall early. Leaf lesions serve as sources of inoculum for fruit and twig infections. Peach fruit become susceptible to rust infection when they are nearly full-sized, and rust symptoms appear in late May or early June. New peach twig growth is infected during damp weather in summer and fall. Lesions on twigs may be apparent, but no spores are produced in these lesions until the following spring.

The strain of rust that attacks prunes survives as spores in infected leaves in leaf litter and on contaminated buds. These spores infect new foliage in spring. The prune strain of rust rarely attacks fruit.

Management Guidelines

In peach orchards where rust develops, apply fungicide in spring to reduce or prevent fruit infections. If the disease becomes severe in an orchard, begin a program of fungicide treatments the following spring as soon as trees leaf out. In prune orchards with a history of rust, apply fungicide in early and mid-summer to control leaf infections enough to delay defoliation until after harvest. Two or three applications may be needed in orchards that have had severe rust problems.

Damp conditions in the canopy favor rust development, so if you use sprinkler irrigation, set the angle to avoid wetting foliage. Drip irrigation is less favorable for the disease, since it does not increase the humidity within the orchard as much as flood or furrow irrigation.

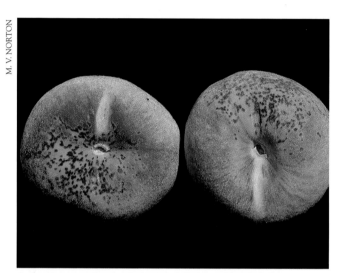

M. V. NORTON

Scab appears on ripening fruit as dark lesions with pale halos.

Fog spot develops into dark reddish, scabby lesions on the upper surface fruit.

Scab
Cladosporium carpophilum

![Apricot]	![Cherry]	![Peach, Nectarine]	![Plum]	![Prune]
Apricot	Cherry	Peach, Nectarine	Plum	Prune
⊙	∅	●	⊙	∅

Scab is a disease that affects foliage, young shoots, and fruit of peaches and nectarines, and, rarely, apricots and plums, in more humid growing areas of the world. Damage is due primarily to fruit symptoms. Historically, the disease has been important in California only on almonds; however, following a series of wet springs scab has become an important disease of cling peaches in the northern San Joaquin Valley.

The fungus that causes scab overwinters as mycelium in lesions on first-year twigs. Spores are produced in these lesions when humidity exceeds 70%, beginning in bloom and continuing for several weeks. Spores are spread by air movement and splashing water and will infect developing fruit, new shoot growth, and young or mature leaves. Symptoms usually take several weeks to appear on fruit. Small, grayish black spots develop on the fruit, most commonly on the upper surface, and may grow together to form large blotches. Lesions may have green or yellow halos after fruit begin to color. Symptoms on leaves and new shoots appear as yellowish blotches that turn grayish when spores are produced.

In orchards with a history of scab, application of a fungicide within five weeks after petal fall will reduce fruit infection. Fungicides applied during bloom for brown rot and at petal fall to control shot hole also will reduce the spread of scab.

Fog Spot
Alternaria sp. (possibly)

![Apricot]	![Cherry]	![Peach, Nectarine]	![Plum]	![Prune]
Apricot	Cherry	Peach, Nectarine	Plum	Prune
●	∅	∅	∅	∅

Apricots in coastal growing areas commonly are affected by a disorder called "fog spot." The causal agent of this disease has not been determined, but it may be the same species of the fungus *Alternaria* that causes red spot fruit blemish on peaches in other parts of North America. Fog spot may be confused with shot hole, but it affects only fruit.

Fog spot develops on exposed fruit that get wet during cool, damp weather. The disease first appears as small, reddish spots on the fruit's upper surface. The spots enlarge and darken, and may grow together to cover a substantial portion of the fruit surface. The centers of the spots may turn dark brown, but margins remain distinctly reddish. The persistent marginal red coloration and lack of leaf symptoms distinguish fog spot from shot hole and quiescent brown rot infections.

Management of fog spot is under study. The disease appears to be reduced by certain fungicides known to control *Alternaria,* but no specific recommendations are currently available.

Leaf Spot of Cherry
Blumeriella jaapii

Apricot	Cherry	Peach, Nectarine	Plum	Prune
∅	◐	∅	∅	∅

Leaf spot occurs occasionally on cherries in coastal areas and may appear in Central Valley cherries during unusually wet years. Trees can be weakened and yields reduced if the disease is allowed to cause extensive defoliation.

Leaf spot first appears as small reddish or purple spots on the upper surface of leaves. During wet weather, lesions turn white on the underside as the pathogen produces spores. Leaf lesions turn brown and may fall out of the leaf, giving a shothole effect. Diseased leaves turn yellow and fall prematurely. Severe defoliation reduces fruit set the following year.

The fungus that causes leaf spot survives winter in infected leaves on the orchard floor. Spores produced on these leaves during wet weather, from midbloom until several weeks after petal fall, are forcibly ejected and carried by wind to newly unfolding leaves. Once unfolded, leaves are susceptible to leaf spot throughout the remainder of the season. The disease continues to spread to other foliage during periods of wet weather until leaf fall.

In orchards where the disease occurred the previous season, fungicides applied about the time of petal fall will keep leaf spot under control. Some of the fungicides applied for brown rot will control leaf spot. If the disease develops later in the season, fungicide application may be used to prevent excessive defoliation.

Anthracnose
Colletotrichum acutatum

Apricot	Cherry	Peach, Nectarine	Plum	Prune
∅	∅	◐	∅	∅

Anthracnose may occur occasionally on fruit of peaches and nectarines in seasons with wet spring weather. Symptoms appear as large, orangish brown, sunken spots on ripe or nearly ripe fruit. The spots may be confused with brown

Leaf spot lesions are dark brown and angular. On the lower leaf surface (*above*), they turn white when spores are produced.

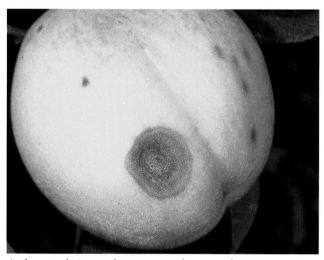

Anthracnose lesions are large, orange to brown, sunken spots.

rot at first, but the orange coloration is distinctive and the lesions do not expand beyond about 2 inches (4 to 5 cm) in diameter. The fungus that causes anthracnose attacks a wide range of broadleaf annual and perennial plants, including legumes. Fruit infections are favored by damp conditions and temperatures above about 75°F. By keeping peach and nectarine orchards free of cover crops—especially legumes—after warm weather begins, you can help minimize problems with anthracnose. If weather conditions are favorable for disease, you can apply a fungicide treatment as fruit begin to ripen.

ROOT AND CROWN DISEASES

Root and crown diseases are caused by pathogens that primarily attack the rootstocks of fruit trees. They are transported on equipment contaminated with infested soil, in infected plant parts, or in contaminated irrigation water from surface sources such as canals, ponds, and rivers. Infection occurs primarily via roots or crown tissue in contact with infested soil. Symptoms on roots and crown usually are distinctive enough to identify the disease. In contrast, aboveground symptoms of wilting, foliage discoloration, premature defoliation, and general decline are similar for most root and crown diseases and closely resemble the symptoms of water stress, girdling by vertebrate pests, and certain virus and phytoplasma diseases. Root and crown diseases are managed by proper selection of the planting site, selection of the most resistant rootstock available, use of good irrigation water management techniques to minimize conditions that favor disease, prevention of the spread of infested soil and infected plant parts, avoidance of infested planting sites when possible, and in some cases treatment of the planting site or trees before planting to reduce the pathogen's population density in the soil.

Phytophthora Root and Crown Rot
Phytophthora spp.

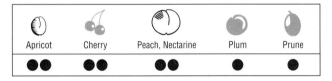

Apricot	Cherry	Peach, Nectarine	Plum	Prune
●●	●●	●●	●	●

Phytophthora species make up a potentially devastating group of pathogens that may attack all stone fruits, as well as a wide range of other woody and herbaceous plants. Depending on the species involved, the disease may affect roots only, crown only, or both. Phytophthora root and crown rot is most serious on apricot, cherry, nectarine, and peach, and relatively minor on plum and prune. The most effective ways to manage this disease are to select a good planting site, select an appropriate rootstock, and properly manage irrigation water. Other management options include proper preparation of the planting site and good sanitation practices to limit the pathogen's development and spread.

Symptoms and Damage

In nurseries, *Phytophthora* species may attack young trees if bundles are heeled-in with infested sawdust or soil. Cankers develop on trunks, crowns, and roots exposed to the wet sawdust or soil. These cankers appear as darkened patches of bark that exude copious quantities of gum. The underlying wood is dark brown.

Phytophthora root and crown rot infections interfere with the movement of water and nutrients to aboveground parts of the tree. Therefore, foliage symptoms may be confused with those caused by a lack of water or by other diseases that effectively girdle orchard trees. In orchards, the first symptom may be the failure of a tree to leaf out in the spring, or the development of sparse, pale or reddish foliage early in the season. Affected trees usually decline rapidly and die. Similar foliage symptoms can be caused by rodent damage, graft union disorders such as those caused by the X-disease pathogen or tomato ringspot virus, and Armillaria root rot. The presence of cankers in the bark at the crown area and the absence of any visible fungal mycelium on the diseased wood or bark distinguish Phytophthora root and crown rot from Armillaria root rot. Positive confirmation of infection by *Phytophthora* sp. requires laboratory detection of the pathogen from diseased tissue.

When the cankers are present around the crown of affected trees, the bark of the canker is dead and deposits of exuded gum usually are present on the surface around the margins of the canker. If the bark is removed, the underlying wood is reddish brown. Cankers extend downward into the roots and may extend upward into the trunk. At the edge of the canker there is a distinct margin between living and dead tissue that sometimes has a zonate pattern of lighter and darker discoloration.

Seasonal Development

A number of *Phytophthora* species are capable of attacking stone fruits. All survive in the soil in infected host tissue or as resistant spores that are able to survive adverse conditions. The fungus is carried from place to place on infected plants, in contaminated soil, or in surface water. Within the orchard, the disease spreads in saturated soils when the pathogen produces mobile spores called *zoospores*. Zoospores are able to move short distances and can be carried long distances in groundwater runoff and in rivers and streams contaminated by runoff from infested soil.

When the roots or crown of a tree are exposed to water or saturated soil containing *Phytophthora* zoospores, the spores germinate and infect the bark. The fungus then develops within the bark, cambium, and young xylem, killing host tissue as it advances. Infections usually remain confined to belowground parts, but cankers sometimes extend above the soil line and some *Phytophthora* species can infect limbs if spores come in contact with exposed host tissue. (See Phytophthora Pruning Wound Canker later in this chapter.) Under saturated soil conditions, more zoospores are produced on the surface of the infected host that is exposed to water. When soil moisture is low, other types of spores (*oospores*, *chlamydospores*) that withstand dry conditions for a period of time may be formed. Populations of *Phytophthora* species decline with prolonged exposure to dry soil.

Management Guidelines

To minimize losses to Phytophthora root and crown rot, you need to implement a combination of good cultural practices that include careful rootstock selection, site selection and preparation, planting on ridges or berms, sanitation, proper irrigation management, improvement of soil drainage, and in some circumstances the application of fungicides. If established trees develop aboveground symptoms of the disease, check the crown and roots for signs of decay. Clear away soil from the base of the tree and cut into the bark to look for the brown discoloration characteristic of Phytophthora crown rot. If crown rot is present and less than half the circumference of the tree is affected, you may be able to save the tree by cutting away diseased tissue and letting the affected area dry thoroughly during the summer. You will have to correct the conditions that led to the problem, however, or the disease will return.

Rootstock Selection. Some rootstocks are more resistant to *Phytophthora* species than others, although none is immune. General assessments of the relative resistance of rootstocks are given in Table 19 above and Table 3 in the third chapter, "Managing Pests in Stone Fruits." Choose the most resistant rootstock that is practical for your orchard situation. Avoid planting rootstocks that are susceptible to *Phytophthora* in soils that are poorly drained or have a history of disease losses caused by this pathogen.

Site Selection, Preparation, and Planting. Avoid locations with a history of Phytophthora root and crown rot, especially when planting on susceptible apricot, cherry, or peach rootstocks. You can use cultural or chemical methods to reduce the soil population of the pathogen, but you cannot eliminate it. Choose sites that have well-drained soils or that you can modify to provide good soil drainage. Avoid shallow soils with hardpans. Plant trees with the graft union about 6 inches above the soil line. By planting trees on 8- to 10-inch-high berms, you can improve drainage away from the crown and help reduce problems with Phytophthora root and crown rot. Maintenance of a deep-rooted cover crop such as sod will improve soil drainage and may help manage the disease, particularly on finer-textured soils, when combined with low-volume irrigation and careful water management. However, keep areas around tree trunks and root crowns free of vegetation, which increases humidity and can increase problems with Phytophthora root and crown rot.

Irrigation. Avoid prolonged and repeated periods of soil saturation. If you use flood irrigation, keep the period of soil saturation below 24 hours. Avoid using basins to irrigate trees, except for an initial irrigation immediately after planting. Whenever possible, avoid using sources of surface irrigation water that are contaminated with *Phytophthora*.

Sanitation. Avoid moving soil from areas known to be infested with *Phytophthora* species. Don't allow runoff from infested sites to contaminate noninfested sites or sources of surface

Trees with Phytophthora root and crown rot develop sparse, pale foliage.

The wood of a *Phytophthora* canker is dark, reddish brown, often with a zonate margin.

J. M. OGAWA

The galls or swellings of crown gall are most damaging when they form on the roots and crown of a young tree.

Crown galls become roughened and cracked as they get older, and may serve as infection sites for wood decay fungi.

irrigation water. When removing trees that have been killed by *Phytophthora,* be careful not to spread infested soil to other parts of the orchard; for example, use a trailer with a sealed floor to carry trees to a location outside the orchard where they can be burned. Allowing infested sites to dry out thoroughly during hot summer months will help reduce the soil inoculum of the pathogen. Use sterilized or properly fumigated soil or clean sawdust to heel-in trees in nurseries.

Pesticides. Soil fumigation, when done properly, can reduce the amount of *Phytophthora* inoculum in the soil and offer some protection for new plantings. Fungicides are available to treat the soil around newly planted trees. Use this treatment where problems are anticipated; for example, on a site with a history of Phytophthora root rot, when using more-susceptible rootstocks, or where soil conditions are favorable for the pathogen. Because a number of factors or pest problems can cause poor growth and death of trees, be sure to verify that *Phytophthora* is the causal agent before you make a decision to treat new plantings with fungicide.

Crown Gall
Agrobacterium tumefaciens

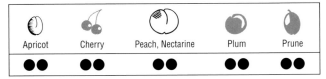

Apricot	Cherry	Peach, Nectarine	Plum	Prune
●●	●●	●●	●●	●●

Crown gall affects a wide range of woody plants, including all stone fruits. The disease is most damaging in nurseries and to newly planted trees. Young trees are severely debilitated by crown gall, but older trees can tolerate the disease. Manage the disease by selecting clean planting stock, planting carefully into clean soil, and using a biological control agent when necessary to prevent infection of new trees. If galls do develop on young trees, you can treat them with a bactericide.

Symptoms and Damage
The crown gall pathogen induces the formation of swellings or galls on the surface of roots or on the crown. These are smooth at first and become woody and rough as they grow. Galls are the same color as the bark of the affected area. As they get older and larger, galls become roughened and cracked and portions of the gall tissue die and slough off. The galls then may be invaded by secondary wood decay fungi. The gall disrupts the normal flow of water and nutrients in the tree's conducting tissue. Young trees can be girdled and killed fairly quickly by crown galls. Galls usually are not serious on older trees unless they are invaded by wood decay fungi, which can debilitate even a large tree. Environmental conditions such as strong winds and cultural practices such as mechanical harvesting can cause trees to fall over after they have been decayed by wood rotting fungi.

Seasonal Development

Crown gall is caused by the soil-inhabiting bacterium *Agrobacterium tumefaciens,* which can survive in the soil for at least 1 year in the absence of host tissue or for several years in decomposing crown gall tissue. Bacteria are released into the soil when galls are wet or when older gall tissue disintegrates. Established trees are infected only through wounds such as those caused by growth cracks, pruning, damage from cultivation equipment, or freeze injury. Seedlings are infected during germination if seeds are planted in infested soil.

Following infection, crown gall bacteria invade the host tissue, multiplying between host cells. A portion of the bacteria's genetic material becomes incorporated into that of the host cells, causing them to proliferate and produce unusual amino acids that serve as a food source for the bacteria. The proliferation of these cells results in gall formation. Where gall tissue forms, the flow of nutrients within the host plant's conducting tissue is cut off.

Management Guidelines

Follow careful sanitation practices in the nursery to prevent infections and reduce the spread of the pathogen.

- Treat seeds with sodium hypochlorite.
- Use a sterile planting medium.
- Stratify seeds directly in planting beds.
- Carefully inspect seedling trees at harvest and discard those with galls.
- Plant seedlings with little or no heeling-in.

For orchard plantings, select planting stock of the highest quality from a reputable nursery. Inspect all young trees for signs of disease before planting, and plant trees carefully to avoid root injury.

Biological Control. If planting into soil where crown gall has been a problem, treat roots with a commercial biological control agent before planting. Follow label directions carefully. These formulations contain a bacterium that is closely related to the crown gall pathogen and antagonistic to the pathogen. The material is most effective when trees receive a first treatment in the nursery at the time they are dug and a second treatment just before they are planted in the field. In some locations, strains of the pathogen have developed resistance to the biocontrol agent. If you encounter a situation where the material fails to protect against crown gall, report this to your local farm advisor or agricultural commissioner's office.

Bactericide. At the end of their first and third years in the field, examine the crown area of newly planted trees for presence of galls. If you find galls, apply a bactericide formulated for treatment of crown gall tissue during the dormant season or in spring or early summer. Before treating the galls, rinse soil away from them with pressurized water and allow the gall tissue to dry. If galls are very large, cut away some of the gall

tissue before treating. After treatment, allow galls to dry for a day before replacing soil around roots. The bactericide stops all flow of water and nutrients in the treated area. Therefore, do not treat more than one-third of a tree's circumference at a time. If more than this is galled, treat half of the diseased tissue and wait 6 to 12 months before treating the rest. Be aware that in some cases, bactericide treatment does not eliminate crown galls.

Armillaria Root Rot
Armillaria mellea

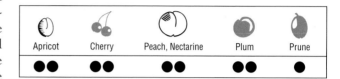

Apricot	Cherry	Peach, Nectarine	Plum	Prune
●●	●●	●●	●●	●

Armillaria root rot, also known as oak root fungus and shoestring root rot, affects a wide range of woody plants. The disease can occur on all stone fruits and is seen most often in orchards planted where forest trees or oak woodlands were recently cleared. Affected trees decline and die over a period of one or a few years. Although not a widespread, major problem, the disease is very serious where it occurs.

Symptoms and Damage

The first signs of Armillaria root rot are poor shoot growth in the spring or a premature yellowing of foliage during the season, often on one side of the tree first. Trees may suddenly wilt in hot weather. Similar aboveground symptoms develop on trees damaged by Phytophthora root and crown rot, certain viruses, X-disease, or rodents. Armillaria root rot tends to be a greater problem on coarse-textured, well-drained soils, whereas Phytophthora root rot is more serious on fine-textured, poorly drained soils. Over time, Armillaria root rot symptoms will spread outward to adjacent trees, usually in a circular pattern.

Armillaria root rot is distinguished by the presence of mycelial fans—thin white or yellowish layers of fungus mycelium that can be seen by peeling bark away from diseased wood on the trunk where it meets the soil. The mycelium has a pleasant, mushroom odor. Dark brown or black filaments of mycelium called *rhizomorphs,* which resemble thin shoestrings or small roots, sometimes are present on the surface of diseased wood and extend into the soil. The fungus causes a "white rot" type of wood rot in which the wood is bleached white or lighter than healthy wood and is soft and punky. Damage to the wood may spread into the crown and lower trunk.

After periods of rain in fall or winter, clusters of light brown mushrooms may form at the base of trees infected by *Armillaria mellea.* The stipes (stems) of these mushrooms are lighter brown than the cap and they have an annulus—a ring of tissue that remains clinging to the stipe after the

Armillaria root rot causes leaves to turn pale and wilt, often on one side of the tree first.

The presence of white mycelium underneath the bark distinguishes Armillaria root rot from Phytophthora root and crown rot.

Armillaria mellea forms dark filaments called rhizomorphs, which can extend from diseased wood to infect the roots of healthy trees. A rhizomorph is shown here (*above*) next to a light brown healthy root (*below*).

Armillaria mellea mushrooms may appear around the trunk of infected trees following rain in fall or winter.

cap opens. The gills on the underside of the cap are white, and a white spore print often can be seen on the upper surface of a cap that is beneath another cap in a cluster of mushrooms.

Seasonal Development

Armillaria mellea can survive for many years on dead roots or other fragments of woody host tissue in the soil. Rhizomorphs are closely associated with infected tree roots. The fungus grows through the soil for short distances as rhizomorphs, which infect new hosts by penetrating the root surface. The disease is spread over longer distances via the movement of contaminated soil and infected root fragments. *Armillaria* also can spread into the roots of an uninfected tree that are in contact with the roots of a diseased tree. The

pathogen moves through the root system and into the crown, killing host tissue as it progresses. Scion wood eventually is colonized by the fungus.

Management Guidelines

Avoid planting stone fruits where forest or oak woodland has recently been cleared or where there is a history of Armillaria root rot. All stone fruit rootstocks can be attacked by *Armillaria mellea*, but some rootstocks are less affected than others. Evidence indicates that rootstocks that grow more slowly are infected more slowly by *A. mellea*, giving them some resistance to root rot (see Table 19). By maintaining the trees' vigor, you can help the trees resist *Armillaria* attack. Follow the irrigation management recommendations given for Phytophthora root and crown rot.

Verticillium wilt is first observed as dying foliage on one or two branches of a tree.

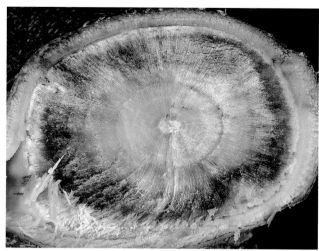

A portion of the sapwood turns dark brown or black in limbs affected by Verticillium wilt.

Infested sites can be fumigated, but often this procedure will not prevent recurrence of the disease. Remove diseased trees and adjacent, symptomless trees, which are likely to be infected with *Armillaria*. Remove the stumps, backhoe the site, and remove all root fragments that are 1 inch or larger in diameter. As with Phytophthora root and crown rot, when you remove host material from the orchard, be careful not to spread the fungus to new locations. Dry out the infested site's soil by withholding water and planting a deep-rooted cover crop such as sudangrass or safflower for one summer. After drying the soil, work it thoroughly in the fall and fumigate it before replanting. Replant with the most tolerant rootstock available.

Verticillium Wilt
Verticillium dahliae

Apricot	Cherry	Peach, Nectarine	Plum	Prune
●	◐	●	⊙	⊙

Verticillium wilt is caused by a soilborne fungus that infects through the roots but moves upward through the xylem, causing symptoms in the upper part of the tree. The disease sometimes occurs in stone fruit orchards, especially when trees are planted in ground where highly susceptible crops such as cotton, tomato, or peppers were grown for a number of years. Verticillium wilt tends to be most troublesome in the southern San Joaquin Valley. Almonds and apricots are more susceptible than other stone fruits.

The fungus that causes Verticillium wilt, *Verticillium dahliae*, produces resistant structures (*microsclerotia*) that can survive in the soil for many years in the absence of hosts. The pathogen infects the roots of host plants and invades the vascular system, moving up through the xylem and interfering with water transport. In stone fruits, the first symptom of disease is a sudden wilting of leaves on one or more branches during the first hot weather of the season. If an affected branch is cut in cross-section, a portion of the sapwood will be stained dark brown or black. Young trees may be killed by Verticillium wilt, but older trees usually are not, although growth and yield may be affected adversely. The pathogen dies out in the upper part of infected trees during hot weather, and branches put out new growth the following season. However, symptoms may recur.

Avoid planting stone fruit orchards on ground where susceptible crops have been grown, especially if they were grown there for a number of seasons. Such crops include cotton, eggplant, pepper, potato, and tomato. Verticillium wilt inoculum usually is present in these soils. Inoculum levels can be reduced by fumigating the soil, flooding the fields during summer, solarizing the soil, growing several seasons of grass cover crops (especially rye or sudangrass), or a combination of these treatments. No stone fruit rootstocks are available that are resistant to *Verticillium dahliae*. Maintenance of adequate soil fertility and soil moisture levels will help trees tolerate Verticillium wilt.

TRUNK AND BRANCH CANKERS

Certain pathogens can cause cankers—discolored areas of dead and dying bark and sapwood—on the trunk or branches of stone fruit trees. These pathogens usually are spread by splashing water and wind; most of them infect trees through pruning wounds or other injuries. The pathogen that causes bacterial canker can infect uninjured buds and twigs, causing a blight or blast of blossoms and shoot tips as well as branch and trunk cankers. Cankers also can be caused by sunburn and mechanical injury. In all cases, gum deposits form on the surface of cankers, especially at their margins. Keep canker diseases to a minimum by avoiding mechanical injury, pruning when conditions are least favorable for disease spread, and following cultural practices that promote tree health and vigor. In the case of bacterial canker, selecting the right rootstock and avoiding problem sites will help reduce disease problems.

Bacterial Canker and Blast
Pseudomonas syringae pv. *syringae*

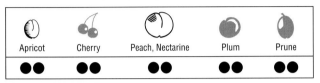

Apricot	Cherry	Peach, Nectarine	Plum	Prune
●●	●●	●●	●●	●●

Bacterial canker is a serious disease of all stone fruits. It affects scaffold and smaller branches, and may kill buds and shoot tips. Young trees are most severely affected. You can reduce problems with bacterial canker by carefully selecting the planting site, choosing the least susceptible rootstocks, and following recommended cultural practices.

Symptoms and Damage
Cankers on branches or trunks cause the most serious damage. These may be more or less elliptical in shape as they develop. Substantial gumming occurs on the bark surface around the canker margins. Underneath the outer bark cankers are reddish brown, and reddish streaks or flecks in the phloem extend beyond the margins of the canker. Cankers may girdle and kill entire branches, or if on the trunk they can kill the entire tree. When this happens, sour smelling liquid will often exude from the bark of the dead branch or trunk in early spring. The root system of the diseased tree usually is not affected; one characteristic of bacterial canker is the development of numerous suckers from the rootstock after the top portion of the tree is dead.

Branches affected by bacterial canker may fail to grow in the spring. Buds that fail to open are brown and usually exude droplets of gum; the symptoms resemble those of shot hole. In some cases blossoms turn brown after they open, and the bud and spur also may be affected, forming a small canker that exudes gum. This symptom is similar to brown rot blossom blight, but the latter can be distinguished by the presence of sporulation, which develops during damp weather. Twigs killed by *Pseudomonas syringae* usually turn black.

Young green fruit, especially of cherry, occasionally are affected by the bacterial canker pathogen. They develop small, dark brown, sunken lesions that leave the fruit severely deformed.

Seasonal Development
The bacterial pathogen that causes bacterial canker is widespread, living on the surfaces of woody hosts, orchard weeds, and plant debris. It is spread by rain and wind, but the mechanism of infection is not fully understood. Leaf scars are thought to be the primary infection sites for the development of cankers. Buds and pruning wounds also may be infected. Trees that are stressed may be more likely to be infected. Inadequate nutrition, root feeding by ring nematode *Criconemella xenoplax,* and possibly freezing injury predispose trees to infection. If the weather is cool and wet when buds are opening, blossoms and young shoots can be infected, resulting in blight or blast symptoms.

Bacterial cankers begin with infection by the pathogen in late fall and winter, and cankers develop during tree dormancy and early spring. Trees become resistant to infection and canker development in late spring, summer, and fall. During hot weather, most of the bacteria die out, and cankers usually do not resume growth when cool weather returns.

Management Guidelines
No control actions are available that will prevent bacterial canker, but a number of cultural practices can be used to reduce the likelihood of the disease and its severity.

Site Selection. Avoid planting stone fruits on acidic soils (soil pH below 5.5), shallow soils over hardpan, and coarse-textured soils. These soil characteristics increase the incidence and severity of bacterial canker. Avoid planting stone fruits on a site that has a history of bacterial canker.

Rootstock Selection. Whenever feasible, choose the most resistant rootstock (see Table 3 in the third chapter, "Managing Pests in Stone Fruits").

Budding and Grafting. Scaffold budding or high grafting of susceptible cherry, plum, and prune scion wood may reduce the severity of bacterial canker.

Soil Fertility. Provide optimum levels of key nutrients to maintain tree vigor without overfertilizing. Although acidic soil conditions favor bacterial canker, there appears to be no benefit from adjusting soil pH in California.

Pruning. Pruning in late spring or in late summer or early fall may help reduce problems with bacterial canker.

Pesticides. Bactericide applications have no reliable effect on bacterial canker or blast in stone fruits. Their use is not recommended. Preplant soil fumigation reduces the severity of bacterial canker in newly planted orchards, apparently by reducing ring nematode populations in the soil. For best results, work the planting site and fumigate in the fall, while

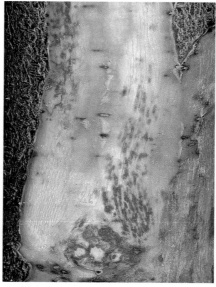

Removal of the outer bark from a tree with bacterial canker exposes the reddish brown inner bark of the canker.

Reddish flecks can be seen in the phloem at the margins of active bacterial cankers. This symptom helps distinguish bacterial canker from cankers caused by other pathogens.

Shoots growing from the rootstock are characteristic of trees girdled by bacterial canker, since the pathogen does not invade belowground portions of the tree.

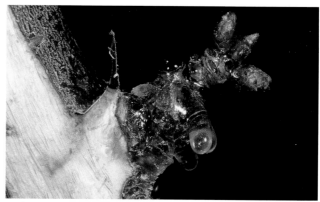

Buds killed by bacterial canker are brown and exude droplets of gum. This phase of the disease is often called bacterial blast. The presence of red discoloration in the phloem helps distinguish bacterial blast.

Bacterial canker may girdle and kill entire branches.

This shoot tip was killed by bacterial blast when the young leaves were expanding. Blackening of the affected tissue helps distinguish the bacterial disease from symptoms of brown rot twig blight.

Dead leaves remain attached to limbs killed by Eutypa dieback.

Gum forms around the margins of a Eutypa canker. Notice the association of the canker with an old pruning wound.

The darkened wood of a Eutypa canker is U- or V-shaped in cross-section.

the soil is still warm, and plant in the spring. Soil fumigation helps provide protection during the young orchard's most vulnerable years. Proper application of a postplant nematicide in mid-October can effectively control bacterial canker the following spring. Follow label directions and use a high enough rate to reduce ring nematode numbers at least by half. You can check effectiveness of the nematicide by having soil samples analyzed for ring nematode 60 days after the treatment, and comparing the results with samples from a small area of the block left untreated or with samples taken immediately before treatment.

Eutypa Dieback
Eutypa lata

Apricot	Cherry	Peach, Nectarine	Plum	Prune
●●	●●	∅	∅	∅

Eutypa dieback is an important disease of apricots and grapevines in California, and also occurs on sweet cherries, where it is increasing in importance. Besides these hosts, the pathogen is known to attack apple, kiwifruit, *Ceanothus* species, and chokecherry. Eutypa dieback is most serious in coastal areas, where weather conditions are more favorable for spread of the disease. However, it does occur in Central Valley locations as well. Mature trees are affected more severely because Eutypa dieback infections accumulate over time, and more pruning cuts usually are made on older, larger trees than on younger, smaller trees.

Symptoms and Damage
On newly infected trees, the first symptom of Eutypa dieback usually is the wilting and death of leaves on individual branches during the summer. The dead leaves usually remain attached throughout the following winter. Affected limbs have a canker that can be traced back to a pruning wound or other injury that has exposed the sapwood. Globs of gum usually are present around the margins of the canker. The bark of the canker is dark and may be swollen and cracked; the underlying wood is light or dark brown. Discoloration of the wood may extend for some distance beyond the edge of the bark canker and into the heartwood of the branch. The darkened wood tends to be V-shaped or U-shaped when viewed in cross-section. Affected branches become brittle and break easily because the wood has been decayed by the pathogen.

Several years after infection, a dark layer of fungal tissue (*stroma*) forms on the surface of the sapwood of cankered areas where dead bark has sloughed off. This gives the limb a blackened, burnt appearance. In wet locations, spore-forming structures called *perithecia* form in stroma on wood that has been dead at least 2 years. The small, black, globe-shaped perithecia are visible when you slice into the stroma. Perithecia are produced where mean annual rainfall is at least 14 inches. They also occur in lower-rainfall areas in sprinkler-irrigated orchards and vineyards. Spores (ascospores) produced in perithecia are the only known infective stage of *Eutypa lata*.

Seasonal Development

Ascospores produced in perithecia are discharged during periods of rain, primarily in fall, winter, and spring. They can be spread across long distances by wind, and can infect pruning wounds or sapwood-exposing injuries that have not healed. The spores are drawn by capillary action into the xylem vessels of unhealed sapwood. In cold weather, pruning wounds may take 6 weeks or more to become resistant to infection; in warm weather, they take 2 weeks or less to become resistant. *Eutypa* develops within the vascular tissue, killing the cambium, and then invades the heartwood, rotting and weakening it. Dieback symptoms become evident 1 or 2 years after infection.

Eutypa dieback infections often continue to advance for many years and eventually may kill the entire tree. In a few cases, infections stop spreading and the fungus dies out.

Management Guidelines

To manage Eutypa dieback, restrict pruning activities in apricots to the months of July and August in the Central Valley and to August in coastal areas. It's a good idea to follow this guideline for cherry trees, especially where Eutypa dieback is known to occur on cherries. This pruning schedule allows tree wounds to heal before spores are likely to be present. Pruning intended to shape apricot trees should always be done at this time. If trees must be pruned outside of these times, flaming the cut surface with a propane torch for 5 to 10 seconds may render the pruning wound immune to infection. This technique is not practical for routine pruning of commercial orchards, but is useful for backyard trees and when a small amount of pruning is needed in a commercial orchard at a time of year when conditions favor infection.

Sanitation helps prevent the spread of existing infections. Remove and burn cankered branches during the summer months. Make cuts at least 8 inches below the margins of affected wood. Make sure no discolored, diseased wood remains below the cut. If you can still see discolored wood, make another cut further down the limb and repeat, if necessary, until the wood of both faces of the cut appears healthy. Heavily infected trees should be removed and burned. Remove and destroy any abandoned grapevines or apricot trees in the vicinity of apricot orchards.

Follow recommended irrigation and fertilization practices to maintain adequate tree vigor. Eutypa dieback appears to be more severe in orchards stressed for water or nutrients. If you use sprinkler irrigation, keep the sprinkler angle low enough to avoid wetting the tree branches. Schedule irrigations to allow as much time as possible for pruning cuts to heal before irrigating.

Ceratocystis Canker
Ceratocystis fimbriata

Apricot	Cherry	Peach, Nectarine	Plum	Prune
⊙	∅	⊙	●	●

Also known as "mallet wound canker," Ceratocystis canker occurs most frequently on almonds and prunes when bark is injured by mechanical harvesting equipment. The incidence of the disease has been reduced greatly through the modification of shakers to reduce or eliminate bark injury. Ceratocystis canker occurs rarely on apricots and peaches.

Ceratocystis canker is always associated with bark injury. Cankers first appear as water-soaked, sunken areas on the bark. Gum deposits usually form around the edges of the canker. The inner bark of the canker on a prune tree is reddish brown, with purplish areas in the wood. On other stone fruits, the inner bark of the canker is brown. Cankers expand

Ceratocystis cankers develop where bark has been injured. The diseased inner bark of a Ceratocystis canker is reddish brown.

Ceratocystis cankers eventually girdle affected trees.

Cytospora cankers appear as depressed areas in the bark, and always are associated with sunburned areas or other injuries.

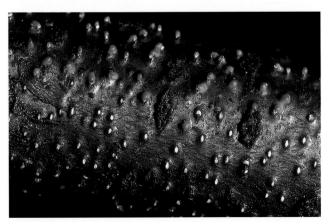

The white specks of pycnidia are diagnostic for Cytospora canker. Reddish orange spore masses are exuded by some pycnidia during wet weather.

most rapidly in summer, in contrast to branch cankers caused by *Phytophthora*, which stop growing in the summer. Cankers eventually girdle the affected trunk or branch.

The pathogen produces spores on and in bark cankers. Ceratocystis canker is usually spread by bark beetles that become contaminated when adults emerge from cankered wood and fly to injured wood on other trees. Some species of vinegar flies, *Drosophila* spp., also may spread *Ceratocystis* spores.

Among *Prunus* species, almond, apricot, and French and Imperial prune are the most susceptible to Ceratocystis canker. Peach and nectarine trees are less susceptible, and cherry appears to be resistant. The best way to control the disease is to take precautions to avoid tree injury during mechanical harvest or other field operations. Avoiding irrigation for 3 weeks before harvest reduces the susceptibility of bark to injury. Remove severely cankered limbs by cutting them off at least 6 inches below the canker. You can cut small cankers out by removing all diseased tissue and at least 1 inch of healthy tissue all around the canker. Flag the treated branch and check it again in a year to be sure the canker is gone. Burn all diseased wood so it will not attract beetles and serve as a source of inoculum.

Cytospora (Leucostoma) Canker
Cytospora leucostoma

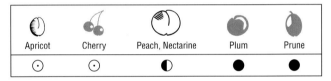

Apricot	Cherry	Peach, Nectarine	Plum	Prune
⊙	⊙	◐	●	●

Cytospora canker is a branch canker that occurs on prunes and European plums, *Prunus domestica*, but not on Japanese plums, *Prunus salicina*. It is not important on other stone fruits.

The pathogen forms cankers that girdle limbs. This causes the death of individual branches, which becomes evident in mid- to late summer. A darkened, depressed canker is present, and is always associated with a sunburned area, an old bacterial canker, or sometimes other bark wounds. Gum deposits form around the edges of the canker. Under the outer bark, the canker has a margin of light- and dark-colored zones.

Black spore-forming structures (pycnidia) develop underneath the outer bark of Cytospora cankers. They give the surface of the bark a pimpled appearance. Eventually the tips of the pycnidia turn white; the white specks on the bark surface are characteristic of Cytospora canker. In humid weather following rain, amber tendrils that contain spores exude from the pycnidia.

Cytospora leucostoma is spread by rain and wind and possibly by wood-boring beetles. The pathogen can infect only injured or dead wood. Most infections occur on wood injured by sunburn, bacterial canker, insects, or rodents. Vigorous trees are less susceptible. Moisture stress, freezing injury, nutrient deficiency, and infestations of ring nematode, *Criconemella xenoplax*, predispose trees to infection by *Cytospora*.

Cytospora canker can be kept to a minimum with good cultural practices. Avoid planting trees on heavy clay or shallow soils. Avoid moisture stress and provide adequate levels of nutrients, especially potassium. Prune trees in a way that will minimize or prevent sunburn, and apply whitewash to limbs that are exposed to the sun. Follow recommended management practices for wood-damaging insects such as peachtree borer and wood-boring beetles. Control of ring nematodes may help prevent problems with Cytospora canker.

Phytophthora Pruning Wound Canker (Aerial Phytophthora)
Phytophthora syringae

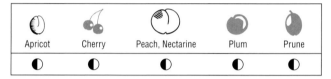

Apricot	Cherry	Peach, Nectarine	Plum	Prune
◐	◐	◐	◐	◐

Phytophthora cankers on aboveground parts of the scaffold are typically caused by *Phytophthora syringae*, and are called "aerial Phytophthora." The disease is most serious in almonds but can occur on all stone fruits. On cherry, the disease is sometimes called "brown rot gummosis."

Cankers on branches usually are associated with pruning wounds. They exude globs of sour-smelling, amber gum. Underneath the bark, the canker is a dark reddish brown or greenish; the margin has zones of alternating light and dark discoloration. Cankers are active in winter and spring, and the pathogen dies out in summer. Branches may be girdled by cankers and killed, especially on younger trees.

Phytophthora syringae infects pruning wounds that have not yet healed. Inoculum apparently comes from the orchard floor, when *Phytophthora* spores produced in wet soil are moved up onto the scaffold by splashing rain and wind. Pruning wound cankers are most likely to develop when heavy rains occur shortly after pruning. They also can occur where sprinklers keep the lower branches wet. In winter, pruning wounds become immune to infection after about 6 weeks. Aerial Phytophthora infections have been widespread in orchards flooded by breaks in river levees.

You can reduce the likelihood of pruning wound canker by pruning early in the fall. In young, nonbearing orchards, it may help to delay pruning until late winter. If you prune at a time of year when wet weather is likely to occur before wounds heal, apply a fungicide registered for *Phytophthora* to the fresh pruning cuts. When using sprinkler irrigation, make sure the angle is low enough to keep tree branches from being wetted; the development of pruning wound

Gum deposits form around the margins of Phytophthora pruning wound cankers, and the margin of the reddish brown canker has zones of alternating light and dark discoloration.

cankers is favored where sprinklers keep the branches of stone fruit trees wet.

Silver Leaf
Chondrostereum purpureum

Apricot	Cherry	Peach, Nectarine	Plum	Prune
◑	◑	◑	◑	◑

Silver leaf or silver blight occurs occasionally on stone fruits in California. The disease is caused by a fungus that infects the water-conducting xylem through fresh wounds. A toxin produced by the pathogen is carried through the xylem to leaves, causing them to turn a silvery gray. Affected leaves curl upward at the edges and may turn brown.

The pathogen, *Chondrostereum purpureum*, attacks a wide range of woody plants. It invades the sapwood and may kill branches or entire trees. Dark brown discoloration of the heartwood in dead or dying limbs is a characteristic symptom of the disease. Spore-forming *basidiocarps* develop on the surface of branches that have been killed by the fungus. These are small, leathery structures that are often shelflike in shape. Their upper surface is grayish white and indistinctly zoned, and their lower surface is smooth and purplish. They may appear at any time of the year, but most often are formed in the fall. Spores are ejected from the basidiocarps' lower surface during rainy weather and are spread by wind. Sapwood-exposing wounds that have not healed over are susceptible to infection. Spores infect exposed xylem, and the pathogen remains confined to the xylem tissue until the infected branch dies.

Control actions for silver leaf rarely are needed in California stone fruits. Basidiocarps may form on infected wood after it is dead, so be sure to remove and burn or bury any prunings, branches, or stumps of diseased trees. Head back young trees in late spring and prune during late summer or early fall to reduce the likelihood of infection.

Leaves on branches infected by the silver leaf pathogen turn a silvery gray. Affected branches eventually die.

VIRUS AND PHYTOPLASMA DISEASES

Several virus and phytoplasma diseases can cause problems in stone fruits, especially sweet cherries and peaches. Symptoms develop primarily on foliage, sometimes in the sapwood, and in a few instances flowers or fruit can be affected. The types of symptoms that are caused by viruses and phytoplasmas are listed in Table 22.

Table 22. Symptoms of Virus and Phytoplasma Diseases in Stone Fruits.

CHERRY Symptom	Disease
rapid decline of whole tree: pale foliage, sparse foliage, yellowing or reddening of leaves	X-disease (on Mahaleb rootstock) cherry stem pitting
premature fall colors	X-disease prunus stem pitting
stunting and/or rosetting of foliage or shoots	X-disease (on Colt, Mazzard, or Stockton Morello rootstock) yellow bud mosaic prunus necrotic ringspot prune dwarf cherry stem pitting
yellow or reddish mottling or patterns or necrotic lesions on leaves; whole tree does not decline rapidly	yellow bud mosaic prunus necrotic ringspot prune dwarf cherry mottle leaf cherry necrotic rusty mottle
leaf curl or distorted leaf growth	yellow bud mosaic cherry rugose mosaic cherry rasp leaf cherry mottle leaf cherry necrotic rusty mottle
enations (leaflike growths from underside of leaf)	yellow bud mosaic cherry rugose mosaic cherry rasp leaf
stunted, misshapen, or discolored fruit	X-disease (on Colt, Mazzard, or Stockton Morello rootstock) cherry stem pitting cherry mottle leaf
bare limbs	yellow bud mosaic prune dwarf cherry rasp leaf
bark cankers	cherry necrotic rusty mottle
browning in wood and phloem at graft union	X-disease (on Mahaleb rootstock)
pits and grooves in surface of wood	prunus stem pitting cherry stem pitting

Table 22. Symptoms of Virus and Phytoplasma Diseases in Stone Fruits *(continued)*.

PEACH, NECTARINE

Symptom	Disease
premature fall colors	prunus stem pitting
stunted tree growth	peach stunt X-disease
stunting and/or rosetting of foliage or shoots	peach mosaic[1] yellow bud mosaic prune dwarf cherry rasp leaf
yellow, reddish, or brown mottling or patterns on leaves	X-disease peach mosaic[1] yellow bud mosaic prunus necrotic ringspot
leaf yellowing, swollen midvein and lateral veins	peach yellow leafroll
leaf curl, distorted leaf growth, small leaves, or tattered leaves	X-disease peach yellow leafroll yellow bud mosaic cherry rasp leaf
enations (leaflike growths from underside of leaf)	cherry rasp leaf
color breaks on flowers	peach mosaic[1]
stunted, misshapen, or discolored fruit	peach yellow leafroll peach mosaic[1]
bare limbs	yellow bud mosaic
bark cankers	cherry rasp leaf
pits and grooves in surface of wood	prunus stem pitting

PLUM, PRUNE

Symptom	Disease
decline of whole tree: pale foliage, sparse foliage, yellowing or reddening of leaves	prune brownline (European plum on Myrobalan or peach rootstock)
premature fall colors	prunus stem pitting
stunting and/or rosetting of foliage or shoots	peach mosaic[1]
yellow, reddish, or brown mottling or patterns on leaves	peach mosaic[1] prunus necrotic ringspot
color breaks on flowers	peach mosaic[1]
stunted, misshapen, or discolored fruit	peach mosaic[1]
browning in wood or phloem at graft union	prune brownline (European plum on Myrobalan or peach rootstock)
pits and grooves in surface of wood	prunus stem pitting

1. Known to occur only south of Tehachapi Mountains.

Viruses and phytoplasmas are microscopic organisms that multiply within infected trees. Effective management methods are aimed primarily at preventing the spread of pathogens from infected to healthy trees. Both viruses and phytoplasmas can be spread by budding and grafting; therefore, the first line of defense against these diseases is the use of certified, virus-tested planting stock. By using clean planting stock for your orchards, you will avoid accidental introduction of most of these diseases. Some viruses and phytoplasmas can be spread by insects, mites, or nematodes, or in pollen, making additional steps such as control of vectors and removal of diseased trees important control actions. Table 23 lists virus and phytoplasma diseases of stone fruits in California according to their means of spread, and gives the management methods available for their control.

Table 23. Spread and Management of Stone Fruit Virus and Phytoplasma Diseases.

Means of spread	Disease	Management options
budding and grafting	all virus and phytoplasma diseases, including those listed below	virus-free scion wood for budding and grafting virus-free root-stock certified planting material
insect vectors	X-disease peach yellow leafroll	removing diseased cherry trees vector control controlling weed hosts of pathogen avoiding planting peaches near pears
mite vectors	cherry mottle leaf peach mosaic	removing diseased trees removing wild host plant reservoirs
soilborne nematode vectors	yellow bud mosaic prune brownline prunus stem pitting cherry rasp leaf cherry stem pitting (possibly)	removing diseased trees controlling nematodes sanitation avoiding sites known to be infested controlling weed hosts of pathogen resistant rootstocks
pollen/thrips	prunus necrotic ringspot cherry rugose mosaic plum line pattern prune dwarf, peach stunt	removing diseased trees keeping ground cover and weeds from flowering during stone fruit bloom

X-Disease (Cherry Buckskin)

Apricot	Cherry	Peach, Nectarine	Plum	Prune
∅	●●	◐	∅	∅

X-disease or cherry buckskin is one of the most serious diseases of sweet cherries in California. At the present time it occurs in the northern San Joaquin Valley and in Sierra foothill orchards, but has not been detected in the southern San Joaquin Valley or in coastal orchards. X-disease is caused by a phytoplasma that may also affect peaches grown near cherries. Apricots and prunes are hosts for the pathogen, but they do not develop disease symptoms. X-disease is spread by certain leafhopper species and is managed by planting disease-free stock, removing diseased trees, and controlling leafhopper vectors.

Symptoms and Damage

Symptoms of X-disease vary depending on the stone fruit scion wood that is infected, the rootstock, and the strain of pathogen involved. Two different strains of phytoplasma cause X-disease on sweet cherry in California: the Green Valley or "common" strain and the Napa Valley strain. The Green Valley strain occurs more frequently, causing cherry buckskin and peach X-disease in northern San Joaquin Valley orchards. The Napa Valley strain rarely occurs.

Cherry. Symptoms on cherry depend primarily on the rootstock. Cherries on Mahaleb rootstock develop different symptoms than cherries on Colt, Mazzard, or Stockton Morello.

When scion wood on Mahaleb rootstock is infected, a rapid decline occurs that is similar to what may be caused by Phytophthora root and crown rot, Armillaria root rot, or rodent damage. The decline is caused by the rapid killing of rootstock cells just below the graft union. Foliage that is of

Foliage of cherry scions on Mahaleb rootstock turns pale, reddish, and wilted when infected with X-disease.

Fruit affected by the Green Valley strain of X-disease are pointed, have short pedicels, and develop a rough, leathery ("buckskin") surface.

Pits and grooves that take on a zipperlike appearance develop at the graft union of X-disease–infected cherry scion wood and Mahaleb rootstock.

Fruit infected by the Napa Valley strain of X-disease (*left*) are rounder than normal with abnormally long pedicels.

normal size turns pale with a reddish tint and curls upward. Trees die by late summer or early the following year. In trees topworked on Mahaleb scaffolds, only the infected branches develop symptoms. Fruit usually look normal or slightly enlarged, and may taste sweeter than normal. To distinguish X-disease from fungal diseases and rodent injury, examine the bark and wood at the graft union. On Mahaleb rootstock, X-disease causes pits and grooves in the wood at the graft union; often, in advanced stages of decline, it causes a browning of phloem in the bark.

On Colt, Mazzard, or Stockton Morello rootstock, affected leaves are smaller than normal, may be pale green and more upright, and foliage may be sparse. Terminals may appear more dense because of growth from normally dormant buds. Some dieback of shoot tips occurs as the disease progresses. Fruit on affected branches are smaller, lighter in color, and pointed, have short, thick pedicels, ripen more slowly than normal fruit, and have a leathery ("buckskin") surface. The fruit's sugar content is low. Fruit on trees infected with the Napa Valley strain of X-disease may be smaller, lighter in color, and rounder than normal, with pedicels that are longer than normal.

Peach. The general incidence of X-disease on peaches is low in California; however, severe outbreaks occur occasionally in orchards that are near cherries affected by the disease. One or two years following initial infection, leaves develop yellow spots that turn brown and fall out, leaving a shothole appearance by mid-May or June. In the summer, leaves turn yellow, develop a severely tattered appearance, and curl inward from the edge. Fruit on affected branches are smaller than normal and have poor flavor. Affected leaves fall prematurely throughout the summer and trees continue to decline in vigor.

Leaves on peach trees infected by X-disease turn yellow with brown patches, and curl inward from the edge.

Seasonal Development

Phytoplasmas are microbes that multiply within the nutrient-conducting tissues (phloem) of plant hosts. The X-disease phytoplasma can be spread by budding and grafting, but orchard trees most often are infected by insect vectors. The most significant spread of X-disease from one stone fruit tree to another goes from cherry to cherry and from cherry to peach. There is very little or no spread from infected peach to other peach trees or to other stone fruits. In the Sierra foothills, the disease may spread to cherry or peach from infected chokecherry and bitter cherry.

The two most important vectors of X-disease in cherry in California are the mountain leafhopper, *Colladonus montanus*, and Flor's leafhopper (cherry leafhopper), *Fieberiella florii*. The most important vector in Sierra foothill orchards appears to be the leafhopper, *Scaphytopius acutus*. The mountain leafhopper overwinters on winter annual weeds. Adults, which may be plentiful on weeds in sugarbeet fields, migrate to favored weed hosts (curly dock, burclovers) in orchards when sugar beets are harvested in the spring. Mountain leafhopper usually is the most abundant vector species found on cherry, but cherry is not a preferred host and the leafhopper does not reproduce on cherry. The mountain leafhopper is thought to be more important in introducing X-disease to cherry orchards than in spreading the disease between cherry trees. In contrast, Flor's leafhopper feeds and reproduces on a wide range of woody plants. This leafhopper is more important in spreading X-disease from tree to tree within the orchard, because cherry is a favored host. *Scaphytopius acutus* is suspected of playing a similar role in foothill orchards. Maximum spread from cherry occurs from July through October, when high concentrations of the pathogen are present in the leaves of infected trees. Hosts for the X-disease phytoplasma and leafhopper vectors are listed in Table 24.

Leafhoppers acquire the X-disease pathogen when feeding on infected plants. The most important reservoirs for the phytoplasma are cherry trees and certain weeds—California burclover, *Medicago polymorpha*, clovers, *Trifolium* spp., and dandelion, *Taraxacum officinale*. In the Sierra foothills,

Table 24. Hosts for the X-Disease Phytoplasma and Its Three Major Leafhopper Vectors in California.

	HOST PLANTS	HOST FOR			
Common name	Scientific name	X-disease phytoplasma	*Fieberiella florii*	*Colladonus montanus*	*Scaphytopius acutus*
HERBACEOUS HOSTS					
alfalfa	*Medicago sativa*	∅	∅	●	●
California burclover	*Medicago polymorpha*	●	∅	●	●
clovers	*Trifolium* spp.	●	∅	●	∅
curly dock	*Rumex crispus*	∅	∅	●	∅
dandelion	*Taraxacum officinale*	●	∅	◐	●
sweetclovers	*Melilotus* spp.	●	∅	●	●
thistles	*Cirsium* spp.	—	—	—	●
Cahaba white vetch	*Vicia sativa* × *V. cordata*	∅	∅	∅	—
other vetches	*Vicia* spp.	—	∅	◐	—
WOODY HOSTS					
bitter cherry	*Prunus emarginata*	●	●	∅	●
boxwood	*Buxus* spp.	∅	●	∅	—
ceanothus	*Ceanothus* spp.	∅	●	∅	●
chokecherry	*Prunus virginiana*	●	●	∅	●
cotoneaster	*Cotoneaster* spp.	∅	●	∅	—
lilac	*Syringa* spp.	∅	●	∅	—
myrtle	*Myrtus communis*	∅	●	∅	—
peach	*Prunus persica*	●	●	∅	●
plum	*Prunus domestica*	●	●	∅	●
privet	*Ligustrum* spp.	∅	●	∅	—
pyracantha	*Pyracantha* spp.	∅	●	∅	●
spirea	*Spiraea* spp.	∅	●	∅	●
sweet cherry	*Prunus avium*	●	●	◐	●
viburnum	*Viburnum tinus*	∅	●	∅	—

● = HOST
◐ = not a preferred host, does not reproduce
∅ = NOT A HOST
— = no information

chokecherry, *Prunus virginiana*, and bitter cherry, *Prunus emarginata*, are often infected. However, these wild cherry hosts do not occur in Central Valley or coastal production areas. After leafhoppers feed on an infected host, a certain amount of time must pass before the vector can transmit the phytoplasma to another host. During this time, called the *latent period*, the pathogen multiplies and spreads within the vector. The average latent period for the cherry buckskin phytoplasma in leafhoppers is about one month, depending on temperature and vector. After completing the latent period, the leafhopper can transmit the pathogen for the rest of its life.

Once a stone fruit tree is infected, the pathogen multiplies and spreads within the tree's phloem. In most cases the pathogen will spread downward into the trunk and rootstock and upward into the rest of the tree. Mahaleb cherry rootstock is resistant to infection. It reacts to the presence of the phytoplasma in such a way that a layer of rootstock cells is killed at the union of infected scion and rootstock, girdling the infect-ed scion, but preventing invasion of the rootstock. If scion wood has been topworked onto each of several Mahaleb scaffold branches, the pathogen will not spread from one infected scion branch to other scion branches of the same tree.

Symptoms of X-disease can appear as quickly as 2 to 3 months after infection, but it usually takes 6 to 9 months. Because the pathogen spreads mostly in late summer or fall, symptoms usually are first seen in the next growing season after infection. If a tree is infected by the X-disease pathogen in early spring, however, symptoms may develop that same season.

Management Guidelines

The effective management of X-disease involves a program of removing diseased trees, treating the orchard for leafhopper vectors, treating nearby ornamental leafhopper hosts, and controlling weed hosts that harbor leafhoppers and the X-disease phytoplasma.

Infected cherry trees are the most important source of inoculum for spread of the disease in California. On high-grafted Mahaleb rootstocks, remove diseased scaffold branches by sawing off below the graft union. Trees on low-grafted Mahaleb rootstocks or other susceptible cherry rootstocks should be completely removed. Before removing diseased trees, treat with an insecticide to kill potential leafhopper vectors that may be in the diseased tree; otherwise, they will move into healthy trees and spread the disease. If stumps of Colt, Mazzard, or Stockton Morello rootstock are not removed right away, be sure to kill any suckers immediately, since they may serve as reservoirs of X-disease inoculum. In foothill locations, remove any chokecherry or bitter cherry shrubs that are near cherry orchards. The removal of diseased peach trees is not critical, since the pathogen does not spread from them; however, infected trees will continue to decline and become nonproductive.

Begin a leafhopper vector management program if you find X-disease in your cherry orchard or in a nearby orchard. Apply an insecticide for leafhoppers immediately after harvest and repeat the treatment every 4 or 6 weeks, depending on the residual activity of the material you use. Monitor the orchard for X-disease symptoms shortly before or after harvest, mark any diseased trees, and remove them as soon as possible after the first treatment, while effective insecticide residue remains on the foliage. The materials available for leafhopper control may cause secondary outbreaks of mites, so monitor carefully for mites in orchards that you are treating for leafhoppers.

Treat ornamental shrubs in the vicinity of cherry orchards to control Flor's leafhoppers, using a material that is registered for leafhopper control on residential ornamentals. Make the first treatment at the peak of cherry bloom to control overwintering nymphs before they mature and migrate to cherry orchards. Make the second treatment in the latter half of May to control nymphs that have hatched from overwintering eggs.

A leafhopper vector monitoring program using yellow sticky traps may provide information on the type of leafhoppers present and sources of infestation, but such a program has not proven useful for making treatment decisions. You can use commercially produced yellow sticky traps or make traps out of yellow boards or rigid plastic sheets about 5 × 6 inches, treated on both sides with a sticky material such as Stickem Special or Tanglefoot. Place 6 to 10 traps throughout each orchard, hanging them as high in the tree as you can easily reach, and check them once a week.

Grafting scions onto individual Mahaleb scaffold branches is one way to manage X-disease in cherry. If an individual scion limb becomes infected, the pathogen will not spread to other parts of the tree through the Mahaleb rootstock. As soon as you observe X-disease symptoms, treat the tree for leafhoppers, remove the diseased branch by cutting it off below the graft union, and then topwork with clean scion wood.

Control weed hosts of the pathogen in and around cherry orchards; for the most part, these are burclover, dandelion, and sweet clovers. Also control curly dock, which is a breeding host for leafhoppers but not a reservoir of the pathogen.

Peach Yellow Leafroll

Apricot	Cherry	Peach, Nectarine	Plum	Prune
⦰	⦰	●●	⦰	⦰

Peach yellow leafroll is a serious problem of cling peaches in parts of the Sacramento Valley. The disease is caused by two strains of a phytoplasma, one of which is related to the X-disease phytoplasma. The other is closely related to a strain of phytoplasma that causes pear decline. Leaves of infected trees turn yellow and curl downward at the tip. Affected leaves usually remain on the tree and their midveins become very swollen and turn brown. The prominent midveins and retention of leaves distinguish peach yellow leafroll from peach X-disease. With both X-disease and peach yellow leafroll, fruit set is reduced and most fruit fall before they reach maturity. Fruit remaining on the tree are pointed, have discolored flesh around the pit, and have a bitter taste.

Pear trees appear to be the reservoir for peach yellow leafroll phytoplasma, which is closely related or identical to a strain of phytoplasma that causes pear decline. Peach yellow leafroll appears to be spread into peach orchards in the fall when pear psylla migrate from nearby pear orchards. The disease is not spread from peach to peach. Psylla migration out of pear orchards in the Sacramento Valley occurs sometime between late October and the middle of November.

On trees infected by peach yellow leafroll, leaves turn yellow with a midvein that is swollen and streaked with brown (*left*).

Peach mosaic virus causes a yellow mottling (mosaic) and distortion of infected leaves.

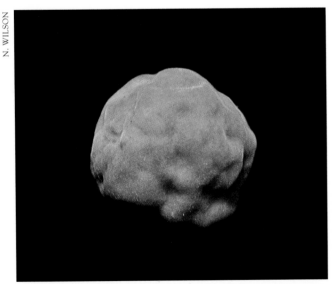

Fruit on trees infected by peach mosaic virus become lumpy and distorted.

Control of late-season psylla populations in pear orchards has greatly reduced the incidence of peach yellow leafroll in nearby peaches. Information on pear psylla management in pears can be found in *Integrated Pest Management for Apples and Pears*, UC DANR Publication 3340.

Peach Mosaic

Apricot	Cherry	Peach, Nectarine	Plum	Prune
⊘	⊘	◑	◑	⊘

Peach mosaic is a disease that occasionally occurs in California south of the Tehachapi Mountains. Quarantine procedures are in place to prevent spread of the disease via infected wood into the Central Valley. Peach mosaic has the potential to be devastating if it spreads to the Central Valley. Growers and pest control professionals should be familiar with the symptoms of the disease, and should report any suspected occurrences to local authorities.

Peach mosaic is caused by a virus that is spread by budding and grafting and by the bud mite *Eriophyes insidiosus*, and infects all stone fruits except cherry. Sensitive varieties of peach, nectarine, and plum develop mosaic symptoms. Apricot, wild plum, and resistant varieties of peach, nectarine, and plum can be symptomless carriers of the pathogen.

Symptoms of peach mosaic vary with the strain of virus and the variety of the host. Symptoms develop on flowers, foliage, fruit, and shoots. If buds are infected early in development, symptoms appear on the leaves or flowers that develop from them. If infections occur later, symptoms develop the following season.

Infected flowers may develop a mottling or streaking of lighter and darker colors. Discolored petals usually are distorted. Symptoms are more pronounced on peach and nectarine varieties that have large, showy flowers, such as Fay Elberta and Rio Oso Gem. Fruit develop surface bumps about the time of pit hardening. Infected fruit fail to reach full size, ripen late, and have poor flavor. Fruit of freestone peaches and nectarines are often deformed.

Leaves infected early in development emerge more slowly and develop irregular yellow spots or mosaic patches. These discolored areas may turn brown and fall out, leaving shot holes in the leaves, or they may turn green with the onset of hot weather in summer. Severely affected leaves drop prematurely. The internodes of infected shoots are shortened and may be thicker than normal. In some cases, large numbers of stunted twigs develop at the tips of infected branches, giving them a bushy or "witches'-broom" appearance.

On sensitive plum varieties, the primary symptoms are those of mosaic leaf discoloration. Some apricot varieties, including Blenheim, develop foliage and twig symptoms similar to those of peach; most do not develop symptoms, although they can be infected and serve as reservoirs for the disease. Sensitive peach varieties include Elberta, Fay Elberta, Hale, Red Haven, and Rio Oso Gem. The most susceptible nectarine varieties are Gower and Stanwick.

Peach mosaic is managed through the use of noninfected budwood. The movement of stone fruit rootstocks and scion wood from Southern California is restricted to prevent the pathogen's spreading to the Central Valley. Symptoms appearing north of the Tehachapi Mountains should be reported immediately to local agricultural authorities.

Cherry Mottle Leaf
Cherry Mottle Leaf Virus

Apricot	Cherry	Peach, Nectarine	Plum	Prune
∅	◐	∅	∅	∅

Cherry mottle leaf virus is spread via budding and grafting with infected wood and can be spread from infected bitter cherry, *Prunus emarginata*, or infected but symptomless peach trees to sweet cherry by the bud mite *Eriophyes inaequalis*. Spread by mite vectors in the field is rare, however, in California. Cherries grown in foothill locations where bitter cherry occurs are at greater risk of infection. Leaves developing from buds infected with cherry mottle leaf virus are distorted and mottled with yellow. The margin between yellow and green is not as sharp as it is with other viruses. Fruit on these spurs may be stunted and may ripen later than normal. Mottle leaf is controlled through the use of certified nursery stock. In nurseries, the use of virus-free budwood keeps the disease from becoming a problem. Remove bitter cherry trees near cherry orchards, and remove any orchard trees that develop symptoms.

Yellow Bud Mosaic, Prune Brownline, Prunus Stem Pitting
Tomato Ringspot Virus

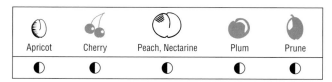

Apricot	Cherry	Peach, Nectarine	Plum	Prune
◐	◐	◐	◐	◐

Tomato ringspot virus is a soilborne virus spread by the dagger nematode, *Xiphinema americanum*. The virus is capable of infecting certain stone fruit rootstocks (peach, almond, Mahaleb and Mazzard cherry, Myrobalan plum) when virus-infected nematodes feed on the roots.

Symptoms and Damage
Depending on the combination of scion wood and virus strain, one of three diseases may result: yellow bud mosaic, prunus

Cherry mottle leaf virus causes leaf distortion and a diffuse yellow mottling.

stem pitting, or prune brownline. Because the pathogen is spread from tree to tree by nematodes in the soil, symptoms tend to appear on trees in one area of an orchard, rather than being scattered about at random.

Yellow Bud Mosaic. Yellow bud mosaic primarily affects peach, nectarine, cherry, and almond. Apricots and plums can be infected, but are not significantly damaged. In this disease, foliage symptoms slowly spread throughout the canopy as the virus moves up into scion wood. Trees grown on peach, almond, Mahaleb or Mazzard cherry, and Myrobalan plum rootstocks are affected. Yellow bud mosaic occurs on peaches, nectarines, and cherries in the Sacramento and northern San Joaquin Valleys.

Peach and Nectarine. The "mosaic" phase of the disease develops in April and May on leaves emerging from infected buds. Irregular yellow patches develop on symptomatic leaves, usually along midveins. Margins of the yellow patches often appear "feathered." Affected leaves may be distorted. The yellow areas often turn brown and drop out, leaving a shot hole or tattered appearance.

Symptoms of the "yellow bud" phase appear on foliage from buds in the second year after infection. Yellow bud symptoms are easiest to see just after the trees leaf out in the spring. The development of leaves from infected buds is retarded severely, compared to that of leaves from healthy buds. The infected buds produce tufts or rosettes of stunted, yellow leaves that stand out against the normal green growth of unaffected buds. Most of the affected leaves die and fall off after hot weather begins, leaving infected trees with a sparse canopy.

Individual branches can have both healthy and infected buds; leaves from newly infected buds show mosaic symptoms

Mosaic symptoms caused by tomato ringspot virus appear as yellow areas on distorted leaves (*left*). "Yellow bud" symptoms (*right*) appear as severely stunted, yellow leaves the second year after buds are infected by the virus.

Trees with prune brownline slowly decline as they are girdled by the disease.

and leaves from buds that were infected the previous year show yellow bud symptoms. Often, leaves and fruit are present only on the terminals of branches, which have not yet been infected by the virus. Loss of foliage makes limbs highly susceptible to sunburn and subsequent attack by wood-boring beetles. Over time, many trees infected with yellow bud mosaic become heavily infested with wood-boring beetles.

Cherry. On cherry trees, a bare-limb appearance starts at the bottom of branches and moves upward as the virus kills spurs, twigs, and small branches. Affected leaves have an elmlike appearance because the prominent, whitish veins are at right angles to the midrib. Leaflike growths (*enations*) develop along the midrib on the underside of these leaves.

Prune Brownline. Prune brownline affects French prune, Empress plum, and President plum grown on rootstocks that are susceptible to infection by tomato ringspot virus: Myrobalan plum or peach. *Prunus domestica* scions react to the tomato ringspot virus by forming a layer of dead cells at the graft union, effectively girdling the scion. Prune brownline is known to occur in Sacramento Valley and Sierra foothill growing areas, but because the virus and its nematode vector are widespread it is likely to be found elsewhere.

Foliage symptoms of prune brownline are similar to those caused by root and crown pathogens such as *Phytophthora* and *Armillaria*, some mineral deficiencies, and other graft union disorders. The first signs of the disease are poor growth of terminals, premature appearance of fall colors, and premature leaf fall. As the disease progresses, terminals die back, new growth ceases, leaves turn yellow, and leaf margins turn brown and curl upward. Affected trees may die within one year of the onset of symptoms or may decline over a period of several years.

Prune brownline is characterized by a dark brown layer that forms between the rootstock and scion of affected trees.

Prune brownline is characterized by the development of a dark brown layer of tissue at the junction of scion wood and rootstock. You can see this by removing a plug of bark from the graft union; the dark line can be seen on the inside surface of the bark as well as in the wood along the graft line. The brownline symptom is not present all the way around the trunk at first, so you may need to remove bark from several locations to find it. Take samples from all four quadrants of the trunk. Usually there is a swelling or overgrowth of scion wood at the graft union on affected trees.

Prunus Stem Pitting. Prunus stem pitting affects peaches, nectarines, plums, and cherries. Infected trees leaf out later than normal. Foliage appears pale green or yellowish and wilted in early summer. In late summer, foliage may prematurely develop reddish or purple fall coloration. Fruit size and yield are reduced greatly, and fruit may fall prematurely. Foliage and fruit symptoms are caused by a reaction at the graft union that interferes with the flow of water and nutrients. Poor water availability causes foliage symptoms similar to those caused by root-destroying fungal pathogens and girdling or root destruction by rodents. A distinguishing characteristic of this disease is an abnormally thick and spongy bark at the base of the tree just above and below the soil line. The wood underneath is deeply grooved and pitted. The wood may be weakened to the point that the tree falls over.

Seasonal Development

Tomato ringspot virus is spread by budding and grafting and by dagger nematodes, *Xiphinema* spp., in the orchard soil. Strains of the virus that cause yellow bud mosaic and prunus stem pitting also cause prune brownline. The virus is seedborne in dandelion, *Taraxacum officinale*, and infects a number of other broadleaf weeds (see Table 25) as well as grapevines and cane berries. The nematode vector acquires the virus by feeding on the roots of infected weed hosts. *Xiphinema* larvae remain infective until they molt. Adults remain infective for 3 to 8 months. Disease spread in the orchard may follow the movement of soil water. Cultivation and irrigation may assist in the spread of both the nematode and the disease.

Susceptible rootstocks become infected with tomato ringspot virus when infected dagger nematodes feed on their roots. The virus moves upward in the roots until it reaches the graft union. If the scion is a variety of *Prunus domestica*, which reacts defensively to the virus, a thin layer of scion wood tissue dies at the graft union. This reaction (prune brownline) eventually girdles the tree. In susceptible scions infected with yellow bud mosaic, the virus moves upward into the scaffold slowly, infecting buds and causing symptoms as it progresses. In the case of prunus stem pitting, the virus moves up the tree slowly and causes pitting in the sapwood, but affected trees usually die before the virus reaches the lowest branches.

Table 25. Weed Hosts of Tomato Ringspot Virus.

Scientific name	Common name
Brassica kaber	wild mustard
Chamaesyce spp.	spurge
Chenopodium album	lambsquarters
Chrysanthemum leucanthemum	oxeye daisy
Cirsium vulgare	bull thistle
Daucus carota	wild carrot
Fragaria vesca	wild strawberry
Plantago lanceolata	buckhorn plantain
Plantago major	broadleaf plantain
Rumex acetosella	red sorrel
Stellaria media	common chickweed
Taraxacum officinale	dandelion
Trifolium pratense	red clover
Trifolium repens	white clover
Verbascum thapsus	common mullein

Management Guidelines

Tomato ringspot virus management requires a combination of tactics: the use of clean planting stock, planting resistant rootstocks where possible, removing diseased trees, controlling the nematode vector, and strict sanitation to avoid spreading nematodes with infested soil.

Use virus-free propagating stock in the nursery. Plant orchards with certified material to reduce the likelihood that you will introduce tomato ringspot virus.

When disease develops in the orchard, remove the affected trees and adjacent trees from the next two rows, which may already be infected with the virus. If you do not remove the stumps immediately, kill any suckers that sprout. This prevents the roots from staying alive and supporting the nematode vector. Take care to avoid moving infested soil when you remove the trees from the orchard. Leave the ground fallow for 2 years to allow all remaining root fragments and nematodes to die out. Control weeds during the fallow period, since they may host both the nematode and the virus. Fumigate the soil before replanting, or replant with a nonhost such as walnuts or resistant rootstock—for example, plums or prunes on Marianna 2624. If several sizable areas within a block are affected, it probably is best to replace the whole block.

Cherry Stem Pitting

Apricot	Cherry	Peach, Nectarine	Plum	Prune
∅	●	∅	∅	∅

Cherry stem pitting is caused by a graft-transmissible agent that has not been identified, but is thought to be a soilborne virus. Symptoms usually spread from tree to tree in a

Foliage is smaller and sparser on limbs or whole trees affected by cherry stem pitting.

Pits or grooves are present in the wood of trees with cherry stem pitting.

Leaflike growths called enations develop on the undersides of leaves infected with cherry rasp leaf virus. Affected leaves may be distorted but are not mottled with yellow.

circular pattern, which is characteristic of spread by soil-borne vectors. Trees on susceptible rootstocks will develop symptoms if replanted where diseased trees have been removed. Aboveground symptoms resemble those of root diseases and some other viruses. Buds on infected trees open later than normal. Leaves are smaller than normal and trees have a more open canopy because leaves are smaller and fewer. Fruit may be small and pointed with short stems, similar in appearance to fruit affected by X-disease (cherry buckskin). In some cases, foliage and fruit symptoms develop on one or two branches of a tree. Cherry stem pitting is characterized by pits and grooves that develop in the wood of the trunk, just underneath the bark of Bing sweet cherry on Mazzard, Mahaleb, or Stockton Morello rootstocks. The stem pitting symptoms develop on *Prunus avium* wood; that is, on Bing scion and Mazzard rootstock but not on Mahaleb or Stockton Morello rootstock. To minimize problems with stem pitting, use certified planting stock and virus-free material in nurseries. Remove diseased trees and replant with Colt rootstock, which has been found to be resistant to stem pitting when used as a replacement rootstock in affected orchards.

Cherry Rasp Leaf
Cherry Rasp Leaf Virus

Apricot	Cherry	Peach, Nectarine	Plum	Prune
⊘	◑	⊙	⊘	⊘

Leaves infected with cherry rasp leaf virus develop prominent leaflike growths (enations) on the underside, along the midrib. Affected leaves are distorted but remain green. The green color distinguishes rasp leaf from the rugose mosaic strain of prunus necrotic ringspot virus, which is discussed below. Symptoms begin on the lower part of the tree and move upward as the virus spreads. Because fewer leaf buds develop on infected wood, limbs become bare near the base of the tree while leaves higher up develop rasp leaf symptoms. The disease may develop on peach trees planted where diseased cherry trees have been removed. Diseased peach leaves are unusually dark green and narrow, with enations forming on the underside. Shoots may be stunted, and cankers may develop on the trunk and scaffold limbs. Cherry rasp leaf virus is spread by dagger nematodes, *Xiphinema americanum*, and by budding and grafting. As with other nematode-vectored virus diseases, symptoms appear in localized areas of an orchard and tend to spread outward in a circular pattern. Techniques used to manage tomato ringspot virus probably are effective against cherry rasp leaf. Colt rootstock appears to slow the development of symptoms in cherry scions.

Prunus Necrotic Ringspot, Cherry Rugose Mosaic, Plum Line Pattern
Prunus Necrotic Ringspot Virus

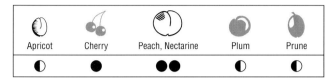

Apricot	Cherry	Peach, Nectarine	Plum	Prune
◐	●	●●	◐	◐

Strains of prunus necrotic ringspot virus cause almond calico, cherry rugose mosaic, plum line pattern, and necrotic ringspot in stone fruits. Also, a combination of prunus necrotic ringspot virus and prune dwarf virus causes peach stunt disease (see below). All stone fruits and a number of other woody species are susceptible to infection by prunus necrotic ringspot virus. The virus is spread in pollen and seed as well as via budding and grafting with infected wood. Thrips feeding is suspected to spread the virus from infected pollen into the tree; otherwise virus from infected pollen remains confined to the seed. Symptoms caused by this virus include yellowing, browning, and shot hole of leaf tissue, distorted growth, death of twigs, buds, or young foliage, and stunting of trees.

Prunus Necrotic Ringspot. Symptoms usually appear the year after infection as yellow spots or brown rings on emerging leaves. A gum deposit may form at the base of a diseased leaf cluster. On peaches, buds may be slow to open, or flowers and leaves may die shortly after budbreak. Some of the previous season's twigs may be killed. Ringspot symptoms usually do not develop on the new growth that emerges later in the season after the weather is warmer.

Cherry Rugose Mosaic. On cherry trees infected by the rugose mosaic strain of the virus, necrotic ringspot symptoms occur early in the season and are followed by yellowing and distortion of leaf tips. Discolored areas on leaves may turn brown and leaves may drop early in the summer. Enations develop from the underside of leaves near the midrib. Fruit may be deformed and may ripen later than normal.

Plum Line Pattern. Several plum varieties develop a netlike pattern of yellow veins, called plum line pattern, when infected with certain strains of prunus necrotic ringspot virus.

To manage prunus necrotic ringspot virus, use virus-free budding material and rootstock in nurseries and plant certified nursery stock in production orchards. Immediately remove trees that develop symptoms to prevent spread to other trees in the orchard. This is especially critical in blocks that are being used for scion wood. Mow or disc cover crops and weeds before stone fruits bloom in order to reduce the buildup of thrips populations on flowering weeds, as they may otherwise contribute to the spread of the virus.

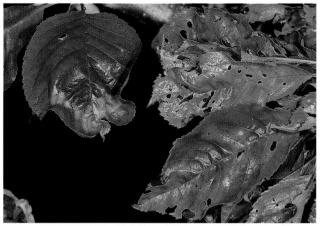

Rugose mosaic symptoms of prunus necrotic ringspot virus include leaf distortion, yellow mottling, and brown spots or patches.

Plum line pattern is a netlike yellowing of leaf veins caused by prunus necrotic ringspot virus on some plum cultivars.

J. K. UYEMOTO

Trees infected by both prune dwarf virus and prunus necrotic ringspot virus are severely stunted (*left*) compared to healthy trees (*right*). This syndrome is called peach stunt.

Prune Dwarf, Peach Stunt
Prune Dwarf Virus

Apricot	Cherry	Peach, Nectarine	Plum	Prune
◐	●	●●	◐	◐

Prune dwarf virus causes mild stunting of new shoot growth on peaches and a reduction in yield. Severe stunting, referred to as "peach stunt," results when trees are infected with both prune dwarf virus and prunus necrotic ringspot virus. On cherry trees, leaves that develop from buds infected by prune dwarf virus are narrower than normal and have a rough texture. Prune dwarf can cause severe dwarfing of plum and prune trees.

Prune dwarf virus is transmitted via budding and grafting with infected wood, and possibly by thrips that feed on infected pollen deposited by bees. The disease is usually kept under control through the use of certified nursery stock and the removal of any trees that develop symptoms. In nurseries and scion block orchards, use virus-free rootstock and scion wood, and monitor trees carefully for virus symptoms. Immediately remove and destroy diseased trees. In young fruit orchards, remove and replace symptomatic trees if they are less than 10 years old. If trees are older than that, replacement usually is not cost effective. You can eliminate the spread of the disease from tree to tree through clean cultivation, and greatly reduce its spread by keeping orchard weeds and ground covers from flowering until after the trees have bloomed.

Cherry Necrotic Rusty Mottle

Apricot	Cherry	Peach, Nectarine	Plum	Prune
⊘	◐	⊘	⊘	⊘

The causal agent of cherry necrotic rusty mottle has not been identified. The disease is transmitted via budding and grafting with infected wood. Spread from tree to tree within orchards has been observed in other states, but not in California. Brown lesions develop on leaves about one month after full bloom. Lesion tissue may drop out, leaving shot holes, and the affected leaves drop prematurely. Shortly before harvest, infected leaves may develop a yellow and dark green mottling. Terminal buds may be killed, and dead patches may develop on bark, with blisters and gum deposits. To control cherry necrotic rusty mottle, plant certified trees and remove any trees that develop symptoms.

Peach Wart
Peach Wart Virus

Apricot	Cherry	Peach, Nectarine	Plum	Prune
⊘	⊘	⊙	⊘	⊘

Peach wart occurs rarely on peach fruit in California. Symptoms may first appear on young fruit as pale bumps or welts

Cherry leaves infected with prune dwarf virus are narrower than normal and have a rough texture.

Brown patches develop on leaves infected with cherry necrotic rusty mottle. Leaves become mottled with yellow and dark green shortly before harvest.

near the blossom end shortly after shuck fall. These develop into wartlike growths that may cover most of the fruit surface. Severely affected fruit are stunted and distorted; mildly affected fruit reach full size and develop only one or a few warty growths. Wart symptoms tend to be concentrated around the blossom end of the fruit. Gumming usually is associated with the warty growths, and tissue inside the warts may be very hard, resembling that of the pit. Peach wart symptoms appear on certain trees in the orchard, and usually on individual branches.

Peach wart is caused by a virus that is transmitted via budding and grafting. To control the disease, use certified planting stock and remove any trees that develop symptoms. Be sure not to confuse the symptoms of false wart (discussed below) with those caused by this virus. Spread between trees in the orchard is not known to occur, except via budding or grafting.

ABIOTIC DISORDERS

Diseases caused by factors other than infectious agents or pathogens are called abiotic disorders. Some disorders are caused by adverse weather conditions, some by lack of essential nutrients, and some by exposure to toxic substances such as incorrectly applied herbicides. In some cases, abnormal growth may be caused by genetic factors that can be passed along in budwood. It is important to become familiar with the symptoms of abiotic disorders so that you do not confuse them with biotic diseases. Also, you need to recognize those that can be corrected—for example, nutrient deficiencies that can be treated with specific fertilizer supplements. To keep genetic disorders to a minimum, avoid the use of affected trees for budwood.

Crinkle Leaf
Deep Suture

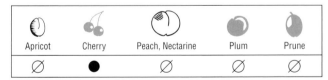

Apricot	Cherry	Peach, Nectarine	Plum	Prune
∅	●	∅	∅	∅

Crinkle leaf (cherry crinkle) and deep suture are genetic disorders that affect certain varieties of cherry. Both are serious problems of Bing and Black Tartarian, and can cause substantial yield losses. Both can develop in previously symptomless trees and can be spread when wood from affected branches is used for budding or grafting.

Crinkle leaf is caused by a spontaneous mutation that occurs within buds. Leaves that develop from affected buds have irregular, deeply indented margins and are distorted. They are light green or mottled. Leaf symptoms are most pronounced early in the season, and become difficult to see by June or July. Blossoms often are deformed, with small,

Cherry leaves with crinkle leaf disorder are distorted, with pale green or yellow mottling and deeply indented margins.

Deep suture disorder of cherry is characterized by abnormally long leaves (*foliage on the left above*) and fruit with deeply cleft sutures (*below*).

A normal fruit is shown at the top, middle.

Russet scab first appears on young prunes as shiny areas, usually around the blossom end.

As russet scab develops, corky patches appear in the shiny areas.

Corky areas may develop on the surface of plums and prunes when windy weather occurs early in fruit development, causing injury to the developing cuticle of the fruit surface.

discolored flower parts. Some flowers do not completely open. Their petals turn reddish brown and cling to the spur for several weeks. Fruit production is low, and fruit that do form are small and pointed, and have short or long stems. Sutures on affected fruit may be raised. Misshapen fruit ripen unevenly.

Deep suture is a fruit symptom that develops spontaneously on trees that were previously free of symptoms. Leaves become longer and narrower than normal, and are often thickened, with a roughened surface appearance. A deep cleft develops in fruit along the suture line. Trees may be stunted. The presence of long narrow leaves distinguishes this disorder, because deep sutures also develop on fruit doubles caused by stress during bud development the previous season.

To reduce the incidence of crinkle leaf and deep suture disorders, use symptom-free trees for budwood. In nurseries, inspect trees carefully during the season and remove any scion source trees that develop symptoms. In orchards, inspect trees closely during the first 5 years. Remove any branches that develop symptoms and topwork them with disease-free scion wood. Lambert and Napoleon (Royal Ann) are not susceptible to these disorders.

Russet Scab

Apricot	Cherry	Peach, Nectarine	Plum	Prune
⊘	⊘	⊘	⊘	●●

Russet scab, also called "lacy scab," is a disorder that develops on the surface of prunes when heavy rains occur during bloom. Shiny areas appear on the surface of green fruit, usually at the blossom end, shortly after shuck fall. These are the result of incomplete development of the waxy layer that gives the fruit surface its normal dull, grayish bloom. The shiny areas persist until fruit are harvested, and if the spots are fairly large, they become obvious russeted or corky patches on the surface after drying. The presence of russet scab at harvest can cause the fruit to be rejected for drying. Treatment with certain fungicides at full bloom will reduce or prevent the development of russet scab, apparently because they stimulate wax formation on the fruit surface.

Wind Scab

Apricot	Cherry	Peach, Nectarine	Plum	Prune
⊘	⊘	⊘	◗	◗

Windy conditions following bloom can cause the development of a corky russeting, known as wind scab, on the surface of prunes and European plums. Wind scab results from the abrasion of young fruit by leaves, twigs, or other fruit. The disorder develops when several windy days occur during the first 3 weeks after full bloom, and is most likely to occur when winds have exceeded 15 mph. Wind scab may be confused with russet scab. Wind scab tends to appear as longitudinal, corky streaks or patches on the sides of fruit, whereas russet scab usually develops on or around the blossom end of fruit. Fruit damaged by wind scab will be concentrated on the side of the tree that was exposed to the wind, so an examination of weather records for the weeks following bloom may aid your diagnosis. Wind scab increases the incidence of fruit decay and causes a downgrading of fruit at harvest.

Nectarine Pox

Apricot	Cherry	Peach, Nectarine	Plum	Prune
⌀	⌀	◑	⌀	⌀

Some nectarine varieties may develop superficial symptoms that are known as nectarine pox. The specific type of symptom varies with variety. Small, dark, scabby lesions known as "black scab" occur on Late LeGrand. On yellow-skinned varieties such as Fantasia and Spring Red, raised red bumps or pimples develop. Severe pimpling and surface cracking occur on May Red and May Grand. A combination of black, scabby lesions and red pimples sometimes occurs on Red Giant. Nectarine pox may be caused by a nutritional imbalance, but the cause is not known for certain. Historically, nectarine pox has been worse in some years and in some locations. It may be helpful to avoid excessive fertilization with nitrogen and to avoid planting susceptible varieties where the disorder has been known to occur. Otherwise, no controls are available. If symptoms develop before thinning, you can selectively remove diseased fruit.

Peach False Wart

Apricot	Cherry	Peach, Nectarine	Plum	Prune
⌀	⌀	◑	⌀	⌀

Wartlike growths occasionally develop on the fruit of some peach varieties. They resemble the symptoms of peach wart, but are not caused by any infectious agent. The symptoms develop on only a few fruit of a given tree and are not confined to one branch or spur. One or more warty growths may develop on a fruit, and the growth often is softer in texture than peach wart (see above). False wart symptoms normally do not recur on the tree. No controls are needed for peach false wart.

Noninfectious Plum Shot Hole

Apricot	Cherry	Peach, Nectarine	Plum	Prune
⌀	⌀	⌀	◑	⌀

Noninfectious plum shot hole is a genetic disorder that is transmitted in seeds and budwood. It is important only because it may be confused with the shot hole caused by the fungal pathogen *Wilsonomyces carpophilus*, which may occur on plums in wet years. Symptoms of noninfectious shot hole develop in late spring on older leaves at the base of shoots. Small, translucent spots turn brown and fall out, leaving a shothole pattern. Symptoms move upward on the shoot until much of the foliage is full of holes by midsummer.

Peach false wart is characterized by one or two warty growths on the surface of a peach. It is a noninfectious disorder that affects only a few fruit on a given tree.

Noninfectious plum shot hole appears as brown spots or patches that eventually fall out, leaving holes in the leaves. The spots do not have the light centers with dark dots that are characteristic of the fungus disease, shot hole.

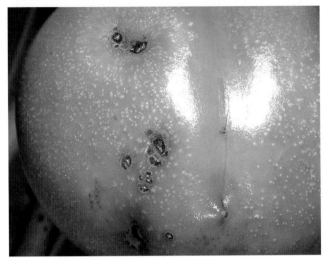

Noninfectious plum shot hole also may appear as small, corky spots or patches on fruit.

Leaves on plum trees with plum rusty blotch disorder develop yellow bands or patches.

Small, dark brown, corky patches may also develop on green fruit. If caused by the fungal pathogen, shot hole lesions on leaves are not translucent when they first appear, and as they turn brown, small black dots develop in their centers. If symptoms such as these develop on plums, have a pest control professional help confirm a diagnosis before making any management decision. Do not use trees that show noninfectious shot hole symptoms for budwood. Remove them from nursery plantings. Because the disorder does not cause significant damage, no control actions are necessary in production orchards.

Plum Rusty Blotch

Apricot	Cherry	Peach, Nectarine	Plum	Prune
⬤	🍒	🍑	🔴	🫐
⊘	⊘	⊘	◑	⊘

Plum rusty blotch appears as bands or patches of yellow discoloration that start at the base of the leaf and spread toward the tip. The yellowing may spread over most of the leaf surface. Discolored areas eventually turn reddish brown with dark red spots that may fall from the leaf, creating a shothole effect. Affected leaves are stunted and may be distorted. Symptoms usually develop on all leaves of an affected branch. Plum rusty blotch appears to be a genetic disorder. To minimize its effect, remove diseased trees from breeding programs before they can be used for propagation.

Nutrient Deficiencies

In California stone fruit orchards, deficiencies of nitrogen, iron, and zinc are common. Deficiencies of some other nutrients such as potassium, magnesium, manganese, phosphorus, and copper are less frequent. Nutrient deficiencies can be caused by low levels of nutrients in the soil or by factors that affect uptake by the tree roots, such as soil pH, temperature, and moisture. Visual symptoms often are sufficient to identify the cause, but some symptoms resemble those of certain diseases. Use the descriptions and photos in this section to familiarize yourself with common deficiency symptoms. You can use leaf analysis to diagnose a deficiency and to get an idea of how severe the deficiency is. Take leaf samples in June or July, when nutrient concentrations in the leaves are most stable. Have soil analyzed before you plant to predict potential deficiency problems. Try to avoid nutrient deficiency problems by following the recommended practices for plant nutrition discussed in the third chapter, "Managing Pests in Stone Fruits."

Nitrogen

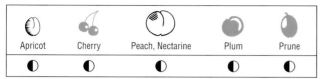

Apricot	Cherry	Peach, Nectarine	Plum	Prune

A good management program requires the regular provision of nitrogen to maintain optimum levels in the tree. Nitrogen is the only major nutrient that must be added regularly to stone fruit orchards. When trees are deficient in nitrogen, leaves near the shoot terminals are pale green and leaves at the bases of shoots are yellow. The midribs and petioles of affected leaves turn reddish. Later on, reddish brown spots develop on the yellowing leaves. Affected leaves are smaller than normal and drop prematurely. Reddish discoloration is most pronounced on peaches and nectarines. Pale foliage and premature coloration and leaf fall are the main symptoms on other stone fruits. Fewer flower buds are formed on deficient trees. Fruit are smaller and their color more intense.

Use leaf analysis to monitor the orchard's nitrogen status. You can correct nitrogen deficiency via soil applications of fertilizer. Nitrate forms are taken up by the tree more quickly, and organic forms more slowly. Foliar fertilizers will not adequately correct nitrogen deficiency. Make any nitrogen applications in early spring or in late summer, after harvest. Avoid applying too much nitrogen, as it may increase some disease and insect problems.

Zinc

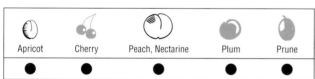

Apricot	Cherry	Peach, Nectarine	Plum	Prune

Stone fruits are sensitive to low zinc levels, and deficiency symptoms are common. Deficiency is more likely on coarse-textured soils and on soils with high organic matter, for example where orchards are planted on old feed lot or corral sites. Heavy applications of manure may cause zinc deficiency.

Zinc deficiency causes the delayed opening of flower and leaf buds. The typical symptom of zinc deficiency is known as "little leaf." Slow bud development causes leaves at the tips of shoots to be stunted and the internodes to be shortened so that the shoot tips have a rosette appearance. Leaves are yellow or pale green and distorted. Yields are substantially reduced because fewer fruit buds form and the fruit that do develop are small and misshapen.

Foliar applications of chelated zinc in the spring can be used to prevent or correct a zinc deficiency. Because zinc deficiency is so common, such applications are recommended for most fresh market stone fruit orchards. Formulations of neutral or basic zinc can be applied in spring or summer. However, these treatments may leave residues on fruit surfaces and

Lack of nitrogen causes leaves to turn yellow; reddish spots develop if the deficiency is pronounced.

On trees deficient in zinc, shoot tips are stunted and have small, pale leaves.

Potassium deficiency causes foliage to yellow, turn brown, and dry. Leaves fall prematurely, leaving limbs susceptible to sunburn.

Iron deficiency causes the youngest leaves to turn yellow except along leaf veins, which remain green.

may cause leaf burn if rain comes within a few days after zinc application. You can apply neutral or basic zinc with dormant sprays. Foliar application of zinc sulfate can also be used anytime from mid-October into the dormant season to help prevent zinc deficiency. Do not apply zinc sulfate within 3 weeks of a dormant oil application.

If zinc deficiency is a chronic problem, apply zinc sulfate to the soil, trenching it at least 6 inches deep. Rates depend on the soil type, the age of the orchard, and the severity of the deficiency.

Potassium

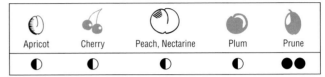

Apricot	Cherry	Peach, Nectarine	Plum	Prune
◑	◑	◑	◑	●●

Potassium deficiencies are more of a problem in prunes than in other stone fruits. Because potassium is concentrated in the upper 6 to 8 inches of the soil, deficiencies are more likely to occur where topsoil has been removed or leveled off. In early summer, leaves along the middle of shoots turn pale and curl upward at the edges. Eventually, leaf margins turn brown and crack or tear as the tissue dries. Affected leaves are smaller than normal and may drop prematurely. Fruit size and number are reduced, and development of fruit color is retarded. Terminal shoots and terminal portions of main scaffolds of prune trees may die when the crop load is heavy. Potassium deficiency predisposes prunes and European plums to Cytospora canker.

To correct a potassium deficiency, apply 5 to 10 pounds of potassium sulfate per tree, in a band at a depth of 6 to 8 inches in tilled orchards. In nontilled orchards, you can apply the potassium sulfate in a band on the soil surface near the drip line. Higher amounts are needed on fine-textured soils because the potassium is fixed by clays and other soil minerals. Potassium sulfate also can be applied through low-volume irrigation systems. It takes about 2 years for soil-applied potassium to have an effect on the trees. Foliar sprays of potassium nitrate give a quicker response, and are useful for restoring the tree while waiting for a soil application to take effect.

Iron

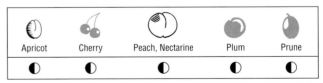

Apricot	Cherry	Peach, Nectarine	Plum	Prune
◐	◐	◑	◐	◐

Iron deficiency is common in California stone fruit orchards. It is characteristic of iron deficiency that symptoms appear first on the youngest leaves, which turn yellow while their veins remain green. Affected leaves may turn nearly white. Eventually, they turn brown and fall from the tree, leaving bare shoot tips.

Iron shortage most frequently is caused by a high level of bicarbonate in the soil solution, which makes iron unavailable for uptake by tree roots. This condition is called lime-induced chlorosis. It often is caused by poor soil aeration or waterlogging, which leads to a buildup of carbon dioxide in the soil. The addition of iron fertilizer will not correct the condition. To correct lime-induced chlorosis, change irrigation patterns to eliminate waterlogging of soils or improve soil aeration and soil drainage. The problem can sometimes be corrected by applying sulfur to reduce the soil pH or fertilizers such as ammonium sulfate that acidify the soil. Foliar applications of iron may reduce the symptoms, but they will not fully correct the deficiency. Trunk injections of ferric phosphate, iron citrate, or other compounds show promise as a means to correct lime-induced chlorosis.

Iron deficiency also may be caused by the lack of sufficient available iron in the soil. In this case, applications of chelated iron will correct the deficiency. A temporary iron deficiency may occur in the spring when low soil temperatures inhibit root growth and make iron less available to the tree. Younger foliage turns pale green or light yellow, with darker green veins. These symptoms disappear when the soil warms up.

Manganese

![Apricot]	![Cherry]	![Peach, Nectarine]	![Plum]	![Prune]
Apricot	Cherry	Peach, Nectarine	Plum	Prune
◑	◑	◑	◑	◑

Manganese deficiency may occur in trees grown on alkaline soil (pH above 7) or following a lime application. Leaves on affected trees turn yellow between the veins. More leaf tissue remains green around the veins than with iron deficiency, and older leaves are affected first. Terminal leaves often are distinctly greener than the rest of the foliage on affected shoots. Neither growth nor yield is reduced unless the deficiency becomes severe (i.e., unless more than half of the leaves show symptoms). To correct the deficiency, apply manganese sulfate as a foliar spray. Sulfur applications to reduce soil pH are effective when the deficiency is the result of alkaline soil. Temporary manganese deficiency may develop in the spring when cold or dry soil inhibits root growth and reduces the uptake of this nutrient.

Copper

![Apricot]	![Cherry]	![Peach, Nectarine]	![Plum]	![Prune]
Apricot	Cherry	Peach, Nectarine	Plum	Prune
⊙	⊙	⊙	◑	◑

Copper deficiency occasionally develops in plums and prunes, but rarely is seen in other stone fruits. Terminal leaves turn yellow about 2 months after the beginning of spring growth. Some leaf burn may occur, and growth from

Manganese deficiency causes leaves to turn yellow between veins. In contrast to iron deficiency, symptoms appear on older leaves and more of the leaf remains green around the veins.

A visible sign of copper deficiency is bunchy, distorted, yellow foliage at shoot tips.

multiple buds forms rosettes at shoot tips. Leaf growth is distorted. Bark may become roughened, and gum deposits may form. Symptoms may be confused with boron deficiency or boron toxicity; therefore, use leaf analysis to confirm the cause. To correct copper deficiency, apply copper sulfate to the soil around the base of affected trees at the rate of ¼ to 2 pounds per tree. The deficiency can also be corrected with foliar applications of chelated copper or Bordeaux mixture in early spring, or with soil applications of chelated copper.

Phosphorus

Apricot	Cherry	Peach, Nectarine	Plum	Prune
⊙	⊙	⊙	⊙	⊙

Phosphorus deficiency is uncommon in stone fruits because the trees' demand for this nutrient is low and it is recycled efficiently from leaves before they drop. Leaves on trees that are deficient in phosphorus turn dark green and develop a leathery texture. A purple or reddish tinge develops on leaves, stems, and young shoots. Leaves may be smaller than normal and may drop early. Yields are reduced. The fruit are smaller and more highly colored than normal, they ripen early, and they have poorer flavor. If a deficiency develops, you can correct it with heavy applications of phosphorus (500 pounds of phosphoric acid per acre). If you expect a deficiency at planting time, apply superphosphate to the planting hole, making sure that it does not directly contact tree roots.

Magnesium

Apricot	Cherry	Peach, Nectarine	Plum	Prune
⊙	⊙	⊙	⊙	⊙

Magnesium deficiency is rare in California stone fruits. It is most likely to be seen on young, vigorous trees. When magnesium deficiency occurs, it usually is caused by excess potassium, which results in a leaching of magnesium from the root zone. Deficiency symptoms appear first on the lowest leaves of shoots and move upward. Leaves turn yellow along the edges between veins such that the remaining green forms an inverted V along the midrib, with its widest part at the base of the leaf. Affected leaves eventually turn brown and fall off. Magnesium deficiency does not affect yield or fruit quality. You can correct it by applying magnesium sulfate, magnesium oxide, or dolomite.

Boron

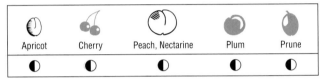

Apricot	Cherry	Peach, Nectarine	Plum	Prune
◐	◐	◐	◐	◐

Boron deficiency causes the discoloration, distortion, and death of terminal growth in the spring. Similar symptoms result from copper deficiency, but in that case they usually don't appear until summer. Boron deficiency is difficult to diagnose in stone fruits. Leaf analysis may be misleading. In almonds, the analysis of hull tissue gives a more accurate picture of boron status than leaf analysis, but this technique, which would involve analysis of fruit tissue, has not been perfected for stone fruits. To correct boron deficiency, apply ½ to 1 pound of borax per tree or apply soluble borax as a foliar spray.

Boron Toxicity

Apricot	Cherry	Peach, Nectarine	Plum	Prune
◐	◐	◐	◐	◐

Orchards on the west side of the San Joaquin and Sacramento valleys may have problems with boron toxicity. Symptoms include brown spotting along the midrib on the underside of leaves, cankers on young twigs and petioles, and misshapen fruit with sunken areas on the surface. If boron levels are very high, the leaves turn yellow and drop off, the shoot tips die, and gumming occurs. When a soil test level indicates 1 ppm or more of boron, leach boron out of the root zone by applying excess irrigation water. Leaching is more difficult on alkaline soil. If irrigation water exceeds 0.5 ppm boron, stone fruit yields will be reduced. Avoid planting stone fruits where boron in the soil or water is likely to be a problem, especially peaches and nectarines, which are most sensitive.

Herbicide Injury

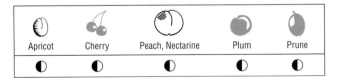

Apricot	Cherry	Peach, Nectarine	Plum	Prune
◐	◐	◐	◐	◐

Some herbicides used in or around orchards can injure stone fruit trees if they are applied incorrectly or if their spray drifts onto buds or leaves. Certain soil conditions are conducive to injury by some herbicides. Symptoms of herbicide injury usually are seen on foliage, and in some cases

C. L. ELMORE

Dichlobenil injury appears as yellowing leaf margins, with more of the leaf affected if injury is more severe.

If a fall application of glyphosate contacts buds, leaves that develop the following spring are stunted, distorted, and very narrow.

they may be confused with diseases or nutrient deficiencies. To avoid injury, be sure to follow label precautions when using herbicides.

Dichlobenil (Casoron)

When higher rates of dichlobenil are incorporated around trees growing on coarse-textured soils that are low in organic matter, yellow halos may develop on leaf margins. Symptoms may appear again the following year. Surface application of a granular formulation is less likely to injure trees.

Glyphosate (Roundup)

Symptoms of glyphosate injury depend on the time of year at which trees are exposed. If a fall application contacts stone fruit buds, symptoms will appear the following spring. Affected buds will be slow to open, and the leaves that emerge from them are small, distorted, and very narrow. If spray contacts leaf buds after they begin to open in the spring, the buds may be killed or the first 2 or 3 leaves that emerge may be malformed. Subsequent leaf growth may show yellow blotches, or may be normal. If glyphosate drift contacts mature leaves, the material will be translocated into the tree. This will cause the bark to crack on peach, sometimes on nectarine, and possibly on cherry. Bark symptoms may extend all the way to the trunk. The following spring, emerging leaves will show symptoms similar to those caused by a fall glyphosate application.

Norflurazon (Solicam)

Root uptake of norflurazon causes the veins of mature leaves to turn yellow to white. New shoot growth may be tinged purple or pink, or bleached white. Purple discoloration develops on petioles of affected leaves. Injury symptoms are most likely to be seen on coarse-textured soils where water stands or where the application is excessive, such as at row ends where spray rigs turn around.

Norflurazon injury causes veins of mature leaves to turn yellow or nearly white. Petioles of affected leaves are purplish.

Oxyfluorfen (Goal)

Oxyfluorfen can cause damage if warm weather occurs in late winter while the soil is wet. Under these conditions, the chemical can evaporate from the soil surface and cause burning at leaf edges. If the spray drift contacts new foliage, brown spots develop on the leaves.

Simazine (Princep)

Excessive application, which may occur where spray rigs turn at the ends of rows, can cause injury to stone fruit trees. A light yellow to nearly white coloration appears on leaf margins and spreads toward the midrib, affecting leaf tissue between veins. Symptoms usually appear in early to midsummer and become worse during periods of hot weather.

2,4-D

Young limbs and leaf petioles may become twisted and distorted if phenoxy herbicide drifts onto foliage. Symptoms are seen most frequently in early to midsummer. If new growth is affected, symptoms gradually disappear. Leaves turn brown and appear scorched if they have been contacted by a high concentration of phenoxy herbicide.

Simazine injury appears as a bleaching of leaf tissue along margins and between veins.

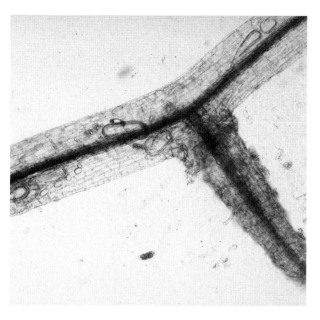

Nematodes

The nematodes that occur in orchards are tiny, unsegmented roundworms that live in the soil or inside plant roots. Some feed on or in the roots of orchard trees, interfering with their uptake of water and nutrients, diverting nutrients that would otherwise aid growth or fruit production, transmitting viruses, or making trees susceptible to certain diseases. The life cycles and feeding behaviors of nematodes depend on the species; damage symptoms are similar for all harmful nematodes, except where other pathogens are involved.

Description and Damage

Plant parasitic nematodes that damage stone fruits include root knot nematodes, root lesion nematodes, ring nematode, and dagger nematode. They use specialized mouthparts to pierce the cells of the host root and withdraw the cellular contents. Nematode feeding reduces the ability of roots to take up water and nutrients, causing nutrient deficiency and water stress symptoms in affected trees. Nematode feeding also has what is called a "sink effect"—it causes photosynthate produced in the foliage to be diverted to the roots. The overall result is a reduction in fruit size and numbers. Aboveground symptoms of nematode injury include lack of vigor, stunted growth, twig dieback (most noticeable on unpruned trees), slight yellowing of foliage, and reduced yield. All of these symptoms can have a number of causes and are not by themselves diagnostic of nematode injury. Laboratory analysis of soil samples is necessary to diagnose a nematode problem.

Damage occurs more frequently to trees growing on sandy soils and is most severe when trees are young or when their root systems are restricted by conditions such as shallow hardpans or stratified soil layers. When high nematode populations develop on the roots of young, nonbearing trees, those trees may never become economically productive.

Root Knot Nematodes, *Meloidogyne* spp.

At least four root knot nematode species occur in California stone fruit orchards: the northern root knot nematode, *M. hapla*; the southern or cotton root knot nematode, *M. incognita*; the Javanese root knot nematode, *M. javanica*; and the peanut root knot nematode, *M. arenaria*. *Meloidogyne incognita* is most often associated with damage to stone fruits. The life cycles of these four species are similar and they are managed with the same techniques. However, the resistance of some stone fruit rootstocks may vary depending on the species of root knot nematode.

The root knot nematode spends most of its life cycle inside the roots of the host plant (Figure 53). Females produce eggs in small, gelatinous masses inside the root or on the root surface. The first stage of the juvenile nematode develops inside the egg. After the first molt, second-stage juveniles hatch from the eggs and move through the soil to invade new roots.

Roots are invaded just behind the root tip or at a junction where roots branch. Within several weeks of infection, new adult females become established at feeding sites in or near the conductive tissue. Some of the root cells at the feeding site enlarge greatly to form giant cells. Other cells proliferate to form swellings or galls. The swollen adult female remains at the feeding site and produces eggs. An individual may produce as many as 2,000 eggs when conditions are favorable. Adult males remain wormlike in shape after their final molt and leave the root without feeding.

Populations may build up quickly on susceptible rootstocks, and they can occur wherever roots develop because the second-stage juveniles are able to move in any direction through moist soil to find new root sites. In many orchards grown on the susceptible Lovell rootstock, populations reach a peak after 3 or 4 years, and then decline so the trees that survive beyond 6 or 7 years have low populations and little root galling. On the other hand, root knot nematodes do remain a problem in some older orchards on Lovell rootstock. Root knot nematodes are most prevalent and damaging on coarse-textured soils (sand, loamy sand, and sandy loam). They usually do not cause severe problems in finer-textured soils.

Feeding by root knot nematodes within the roots interferes with the roots' uptake of water and nutrients. Young trees can be severely stunted when planted in sites that are already infested with root knot nematodes, even when they are grown on nematode-resistant rootstock. Root knot nematodes can invade resistant Nemaguard rootstock and feed, but they cannot reproduce there. Trees planted in heavily infested soil may grow very poorly the first year or two until the nematodes' inability to reproduce on the resistant rootstock results in a gradual reduction of the population.

Water stress will increase the severity of root knot nematode damage. If trees show symptoms that suggest root knot nematode damage, examine the roots for galling, which tends to be concentrated on young feeder roots. Have soil or root samples analyzed for nematodes to confirm your diagnosis.

Root Lesion Nematodes, *Pratylenchus* spp.

Several root lesion nematode species occur in California orchard soils. In most of the state, *Pratylenchus vulnus* is the only species that causes damage to stone fruits. *Pratylenchus penetrans* may cause damage in cooler or higher-elevation locations. Other species of root lesion nematode feed on the roots of weeds and cover crops and may reach high populations in orchard soils, but they usually do not damage stone fruits unless they occur in abundance within the roots of the trees. It is important to have the root lesion nematode species identified when you have your orchard soil analyzed.

Root lesion nematodes feed on the surface of host roots and also penetrate roots to feed inside. Females lay eggs inside roots and in the soil. After hatching, all developmental stages may feed on roots or move through the soil to find other host roots. If roots become unsuitable, those feeding inside the roots will leave to search out new host roots. *Pratylenchus vulnus* feeds on a number of woody perennial hosts; *P. penetrans* may be found on the roots of a wide range of woody and herbaceous hosts.

Feeding by root lesion nematodes restricts the flow of nutrients within larger roots and may kill smaller roots. Feeder roots are most susceptible, and a lack of feeder roots and major structural roots is one symptom of root lesion nematode infestation. In some cases, dark lesions may form on the surface of infested roots, but this symptom is not a reliable diagnostic characteristic. In any case, you should use soil analysis to confirm the presence of root lesion nematodes.

Damage from root lesion nematodes can be severe when trees are replanted in infested sites that have not been treated to reduce nematode populations. Stunting and foliage discoloration, due in part to nutrient deficiencies caused by the nematode infestation, often occur on trees within a certain area of the orchard. Root lesion nematode damage is increased by conditions that restrict root growth, such as shallow hardpans, sandy subsurface soil, herbicide injury, and poor land preparation.

Ring Nematode, *Criconemella xenoplax*

Ring nematodes, which have been known in the past by the scientific names *Macroposthonia xenoplax* and *Criconemoides xenoplax*, do not penetrate roots as do root knot and root lesion nematodes. They remain on the outside of the root and withdraw nutrients from root cells with their piercing mouthparts. Ring nematodes are characterized by the ringlike appearance of the outer body layers, as seen under a microscope.

Feeding by ring nematodes can greatly reduce the number of small feeder roots, and result in poor tree growth. These are considered especially important nematodes because high populations predispose trees to bacterial canker. If trees are replanted in infested sites that have not been treated to reduce nematode levels, they can be killed within the first year. Ring nematodes build up on the roots of orchard trees and vines growing on coarse-textured soil or clay soil; they usually do not cause problems on finer sandy loam soils.

Dagger Nematode, *Xiphinema americanum*

Dagger nematodes are relatively large nematodes that, like ring nematodes, are external parasites of roots. They are of concern because they transmit strains of tomato ringspot virus to most stone fruit rootstocks and transmit cherry rasp

Root knot nematodes may cause severe galling of tree roots.

Tree growth may be severely stunted if new trees are planted on a previous orchard site that has not been treated to reduce populations of harmful nematodes. The trees in this photo are all the same age; the larger trees were planted in sites that were fumigated.

leaf virus to cherries. Dagger nematodes occur in a wide variety of soil types in all fruit growing areas; they are most common in northern California. Dagger nematodes do not live very deep in the soil, so they ought to be more susceptible to control with nematicides; however, some nematicides are effective while others are not.

Management Guidelines

You can minimize the harmful effects of nematodes by selecting planting sites that are free of harmful nematode populations; planting resistant rootstocks; using procedures such as crop rotation, fallow, and soil fumigation to reduce nematode populations before planting; following careful sanitation practices to avoid spreading harmful nematodes from infested sites; and following practices after planting, such as proper fertilization, that help reduce nematode buildup and increase the ability of orchard trees to withstand nematode damage.

Soil Sampling

Have your orchard soil analyzed for nematodes by a professional laboratory before you select a management strategy. Soil analysis will tell you which nematodes are present and give you an estimate of their numbers. This information will help you decide if a site is suitable for planting an orchard, if preplant treatments such as fumigation or long-term rotation are needed to reduce nematodes before planting, and if you should use a nematode-resistant rootstock. Preplant soil analysis is always a good idea, but is especially important for sites where high nematode populations are most likely to occur: where tree crops have been grown, where broadleaf annual crops have recently been grown, where soil is coarse-textured or has a subsurface layer, or where bacterial canker is prevalent. Use soil analysis in established orchards to confirm a diagnosis of nematode injury.

Check with your farm advisor or local pest control professionals to find a commercial laboratory that will analyze your soil for nematodes. Some laboratories will collect the samples

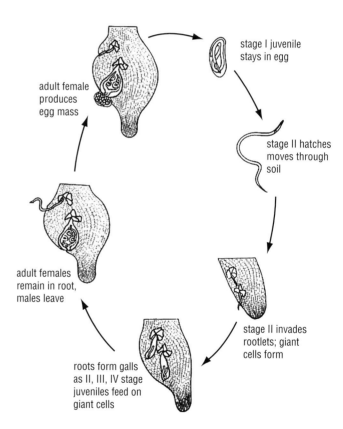

adult female produces egg mass

stage I juvenile stays in egg

stage II hatches moves through soil

adult females remain in root, males leave

stage II invades rootlets; giant cells form

roots form galls as II, III, IV stage juveniles feed on giant cells

Figure 53. Root knot nematodes spend most of their life cycle in galls on roots. Second-stage juveniles hatch from eggs and invade new sites, usually near root tips. Nematodes induce some root cells to grow into giant cells, where the nematodes feed. As feeding continues, root cells proliferate to form galls around the infection sites.

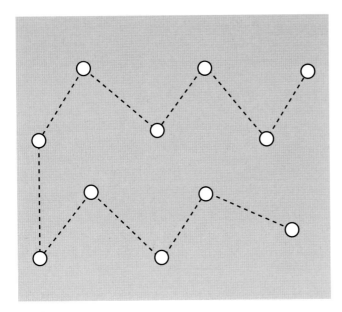

Figure 54. Recommended pattern for collecting soil samples from a sampling block in a fallow field.

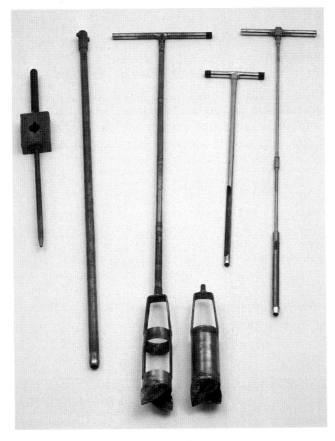

Figure 55. Tools for taking soil samples. The Veihmeyer tube (*left*) has a slotted hammer for driving the tube into the soil and removing it. Soil augers (*center*) have a variety of bits for different soil samples. Oakfield soil tubes (*right*) usually are easiest to use, especially for samples down to 2 feet (60 cm). These tools can be used for monitoring soil moisture and sampling for nematodes.

for you, or you may collect them yourself. If you take your own samples, be sure to make arrangements with the laboratory ahead of time so they will be prepared to analyze the samples promptly and to see whether they have specific recommendations about how you should take the samples and package them. It takes about 2 weeks to get the results of a soil analysis. Be sure to keep the laboratory reports as a part of your orchard's permanent history.

Before taking samples, draw a map of the orchard or field to be sampled and divide the site into sampling blocks of 5 acres or less that adequately represent differences in soil type, drainage patterns, cropping history, and crop injury. Make sure each block is an area that can easily be managed as a unit. Take a separate sample from each block. In a field that is not yet planted, collect samples from throughout each block, following the pattern illustrated in Figure 54. In an established orchard, take separate samples from the soil around trees that show symptoms and from around nearby, healthy trees for comparison; sample soil that is frequently wetted at the edge of the canopy, and include feeder roots when possible.

In fallow fields or established orchards, you can take soil samples for nematode analysis at any time of year. It is best to sample soil that is moist, preferably within a week after rain or an irrigation. If you are planning to prepare a field that has an existing crop, it is best to sample the field while that crop is still present. Be sure to sample below the root zone of that crop, where nematodes from a previous woody-rooted crop may be concentrated. You can use a shovel or various types of soil tubes or augers to collect soil samples (Figure 55). For each sample, collect subsamples at various depths, from 6 inches to 3 feet (15 cm to 1 m). Take 15 to 20 subsamples from each block or 5 subsamples from around individual trees, mix the samples thoroughly in a clean bucket and take about one quart of this mix as the sample for the block or location in the orchard that is suspected of having nematode damage.

Put the soil sample into a durable plastic bag or other moistureproof container, seal the container, label it, and place it in the shade or in a cooler while you finish taking samples. Attach a label to the outside of each sample container: include your name, address, and phone number, the crop present, the crop you intend to grow, the location of the orchard site, soil characteristics, the cropping history of the site, and any injury symptoms that were present. Use an ice chest or cardboard box insulated with newspapers to keep the samples cool (50° to 60°F) until you deliver them to the laboratory. Do not freeze the samples. Deliver them to the lab immediately.

If you want the samples analyzed for ring nematodes, request that sugar flotation or centrifugation be used for nematode extraction. Root knot and root lesion nematodes are also detected with these methods. Request that root lesion nematodes be identified to species if they are found; presence of *Pratylenchus vulnus* or *P. penetrans* indicates a need for management action.

Damage thresholds are not well established for stone fruits. As a general rule, if soil analysis identifies root knot nematodes, ring nematodes, or damaging species of root lesion nematodes on a site where tree crops have been grown, either soil fumigation or a long-term rotation to non-host crops such as grains is recommended before you plant the site to stone fruits. If root knot nematodes are present, use resistant rootstocks.

Field Selection and Preparation—
The "Replant Problem"

Whenever possible, avoid planting new orchards on land that has previously been planted to woody crops. Stone fruits planted on an old orchard or vineyard site are likely to suffer from poor vigor, often accompanied by symptoms of nutrient deficiency. This phenomenon, called the "replant problem," is caused by nonpathogenic microbes that became established on the old root system as well as by pathogens (nematodes, fungi, and bacteria) and other factors. Nematode populations build up in the soil as deep as the tree roots penetrate. For several years after the old trees are removed, the remaining roots act as food sources for nematodes and provide them some protection from fumigation. After an herbaceous crop, harmful nematode populations will be lower, will not be as deep in the soil, and will be less protected because the roots of these crops decay more quickly.

When you plant a stone fruit orchard on a site that has grown trees or vines before, proper preparation is essential to the successful establishment of the orchard. Table 26 gives an example of how to prepare an orchard site for planting after a tree or vine crop.

Soil Fumigation

Fumigation of the soil reduces nematode populations but does not eradicate them. Following fumigation, nematode populations will increase over time and eventually will reach harmful levels. Proper fumigation will keep nematodes below damaging levels for as long as 6 years, long enough for trees to develop extensive root systems that are better able to tolerate nematode damage. If soil sampling indicates that root knot nematodes are the only harmful species present and you are planting on Nemaguard rootstock, you may want to fumigate just the tree rows or, if you are replanting individual trees, just the planting sites. If lesion or ring nematodes are present, fumigate the entire orchard.

The effectiveness of soil fumigation is influenced by soil preparation, soil moisture, soil texture, soil temperature, and the quantity of chemical applied. Figure 56 diagrams the effects of soil moisture, texture, and temperature on the quantity of chemical needed for effective fumigation. As a general rule, the best time of year to fumigate is from September until mid-November. This is when soil moisture and temperature are optimum for effective fumigation. Actual time varies from one region to the next, and more flexibility in timing is possible with sandy soils. If soil conditions are

not optimal, nematode control will be less effective and populations will return to damaging levels more quickly; this can reduce the period of time new trees are protected by anywhere from 6 months to 6 years.

Soil Preparation. Table 26 includes a suggested program for preparing an orchard site before fumigation. Thoroughly work the soil to remove clods, which the fumigant cannot penetrate. Whether you are fumigating an entire orchard site or individual tree sites for replanting, remove the old tree stumps and as many of the old roots as possible that are larger than ½ inch (1 cm) in diameter; nematodes within roots can escape the fumigant's effect. Remove stumps and roots before you fumigate individual planting sites when you replace trees within an established orchard. To improve the effectiveness of fumigation of individual tree sites, backhoe to a depth of 5 feet (1.5 m) and cave in the sides of the hole. Before you fumigate, make sure to add extra soil when backfilling to compensate for the settling that will occur after you plant.

Soil Moisture. Correct soil moisture is essential for successful fumigation. If the soil is too wet, the fumigant will not disperse properly in the soil. If soil is too dry, gaseous fumigant will disperse too quickly and liquid fumigant will be tightly adsorbed by soil particles, reducing its effectiveness. Determine the soil moisture by taking soil samples from throughout the orchard, making sure to sample all areas that have different textures. You may want to follow a sampling plan such as that illustrated in Figure 54. At each sampling location, take 1-pint soil samples from depths of 1, 2, 3, 4, and 5 feet (30, 60, 90, 120, and 150 cm). Weigh each sample, dry the samples at 221°F (105°C) for 24 hours, and then weigh again. Be sure to subtract the weight of the container from each sample weight. Calculate the percent moisture by subtracting the dry sample

Table 26. Suggested Schedule for Preparing Orchard Site Following a Tree or Vine Crop.

Season	Action
summer/fall	Remove trees or vines, destroy residues, deep cultivate to remove residual roots and break up cultivation pans or soil layers. Sample for nematodes.
winter/spring	Fallow or plant a winter crop of small grains after soil temperature is below 64°F (18°C).
spring/summer	Level or grade site for irrigation and proper drainage, cultivate, and do other operations necessary to prepare site for planting. Allow soil to dry.
late summer/early fall	Rip the soil. Apply an inch of water if necessary to break up surface clods. Fumigate in September or October.
winter/spring	Observe waiting period required by fumigant label. Plant young trees on resistant rootstock if root knot nematodes are present.

SOIL AND MOISTURE CHART

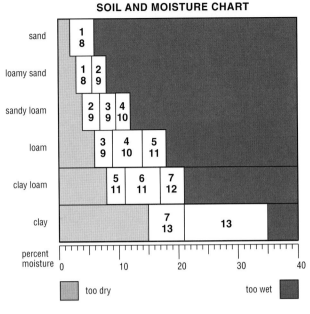

Number code from soil and moisture chart	Soil temp. (°F)	Application rates (lb/Ac)	

1,3-D Nematicides (92% 1,3-D)

		A	**B**
1	40–77	50–100	400
2	40–77	75–125	400
3	50–77	100–150	500
4	50–77	125–175	500
5	60–68	150–200	600
6	60–68	200–250	700
7	60–68	250–300	800

Tarped Methyl Bromide (98% ai)[1]

		C	**D**
8	40–77	200	400
9	40–77	250	400
10	40–77	300	500
11	40–77	350	600
12	50–77	400	700
13	50–77	500	800

Key

A: Controls soil pests, such as nematodes outside roots, throughout the surface 2.5 feet of soil.

B: Controls pests or nematodes in smaller (less than 2 in. diameter) roots throughout the surface 5 feet of soil.

C: Controls pests or nematodes in smaller (less than 2 in. diameter) roots throughout the surface 5 feet of soil.

D: Eradicative treatment to control nematode virus vectors throughout the surface 5 feet of soil.

1. Additional chloropicrin may be present.

REGISTRATION STATUS OF THESE COMPOUNDS MAY CHANGE. CHECK WITH LOCAL AUTHORITIES BEFORE USING.

Figure 56. Influence of soil texture, moisture, and temperature on application rates for preplant fumigation to control nematodes. Use the highest rate recommended for the soil conditions within the profile. For example, if a soil has a loamy sand surface layer with 5% soil moisture and a subsurface loam layer with 10% moisture, use the higher rate given for the loam. A permit is required to apply methyl bromide, and the applicator must be licensed for its use.

weight from the wet sample weight, dividing the result by the dry sample weight, and multiplying by 100. Use the result to interpret Figure 56 for your soil conditions.

Variations in soil moisture and texture within the soil profile can prevent adequate penetration of the fumigant. For example, if a layer of sandy loam with moisture in excess of 12% is at the 3-foot (1m) depth beneath a layer of loam with 12% moisture, the fumigant will not penetrate beyond 3 feet unless the sandy loam layer is permitted to dry out before treatment.

Soil Texture. Soil texture is a way of describing the proportion of different-sized particles that make up a given soil. Coarse-textured soils have higher proportions of sand and larger pores, through which fumigant can quickly disperse. Fine-textured soils have high proportions of clay and silt, with much smaller pores, and are able to hold a greater proportion of water. Fumigants move more slowly and are more readily diluted in fine-textured soils. The finer the soil texture (moving down Figure 56), the higher the application rate needed for fumigant to penetrate to the 5-foot (1.5-m) depth.

Most soils are not uniform, but vary in texture throughout the profile. Determine the soil textures present in your soil profile when you are taking samples to determine soil moisture. If you find abrupt boundaries (Figure 57), they may prevent adequate penetration of the fumigant. Use backhoeing, ripping, or deep plowing to eliminate such boundaries, hard pans, or clay pans before you fumigate.

Soil Temperature. Check the soil temperature 12 inches (30 cm) deep with a thermometer to be sure it is within the ranges specified in Figure 56. If the soil is too cold, the fumigant will not move properly through the soil, and will not penetrate soil aggregates and root fragments. If the soil is too warm, the fumigant will degrade and volatilize too quickly.

Application. Both gas and liquid nematicides are available for preplant fumigation of stone fruits. All are restricted-use materials, so you need a permit to use them. Liquid formulations may require preirrigation before fumigation, and the materials are applied with irrigation water to move them into the soil profile. Gas is injected into the soil and the treated area is immediately covered with a plastic tarp to keep the gas from dissipating. Fumigants are toxic to plant roots; be sure to observe the waiting periods specified on the fumigant's label before planting. Information on application procedures and restrictions for currently available fumigants can be found in the *UC IPM Pest Management Guidelines* for each of the stone fruit crops.

Postplant Nematicides

The proper application of a postplant nematicide can effectively reduce populations of ring and root lesion nematodes. Although costly, the expense of the application may be justified if the nematodes are causing severe damage. Successful treatment requires the uniform delivery of an adequate amount of nematicide throughout the root zone. The best way to achieve this is to deliver the nematicide via low-volume irrigation in spring or fall. The best results are obtained when you apply the nematicide to preirrigated and drained soil, using a 4-hour irrigation with 3 ½ hours of nematicide injection. More specific information on materials, rates, and restrictions are given in the UC IPM Pest Management Guidelines listed in the references.

Ring Nematode. Postplant treatment can substantially improve the trees' vigor if they are suffering from ring nematodes. Where ring nematodes are associated with bacterial canker, nematicide treatment in mid-October will greatly reduce or halt bacterial canker the following spring. This is discussed in greater detail in the section on bacterial canker in the chapter on diseases.

Root Lesion Nematode. Nematicide treatments can increase fruit sizes and numbers if root lesion nematodes are limiting the trees' productivity. However, nematicides do not kill nematodes that are inside the tree roots, so any protection will be short-lived.

Rootstock Selection

Resistance or tolerance to nematodes is one consideration in selecting rootstocks. Some rootstocks are resistant to root knot nematodes and a few have some resistance to root lesion or ring nematodes (Table 27). If you are planting in coarse-textured soil or in locations where soil analysis has shown root knot nematodes to be present, choose rootstocks that are resistant to these nematodes. For cherries, rootstock resistance depends on the root knot nematode species (Table 27).

Be aware that a resistant rootstock will not protect trees that are planted in soil that is heavily infested with root knot nematodes. These nematodes can feed on resistant roots, but cannot reproduce. By using these rootstocks, you can prevent low populations from building to damaging levels, but you cannot prevent high populations from severely damaging newly planted trees. Also, cover crops that favor the buildup of root knot nematodes may allow the nematodes to overwhelm the rootstock's resistance. Where ring nematodes are present and bacterial canker is a potential problem, you may want to use Lovell peach for compatible scions, as long as you do not expect root knot nematodes to be a problem.

Fallow and Crop Rotation

Fallowing a site before planting or replanting an orchard can reduce soil-dwelling nematode population densities. However, it may not control the nematodes remaining in live roots from the previous orchard. For a fallow period to be effective, the roots remaining from the previous orchard must somehow be killed. Weeds must be controlled by cultivation or

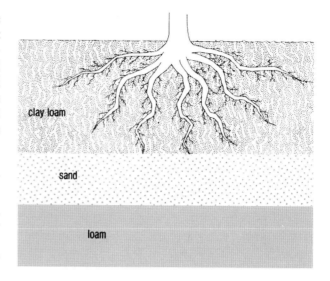

Figure 57. Abrupt boundaries between different soil textures act like pans, even though they may not be dense.

herbicide application, because many weeds are good hosts for harmful nematode species.

Grains are not hosts for the lesion nematode, Pratylenchus vulnus. Some wheat varieties, such as NK 916 and Storey, may not grow optimally under California conditions, but they are reported to reduce ring nematode populations. Sorghum–sudan grass hybrids such as Germain's SS-222 are also antagonistic to ring nematode, but they are hosts for root knot nematode species and may increase dagger nematode populations if planted too many years in succession. Piper sudangrass is a host for northern root knot nematode, M. hapla.

If a grain rotation crop is a host for root knot species that attack stone fruits, you can prevent root knot nematodes from reproducing before the crop is harvested or plowed under in the spring by planting it in the fall after soil temperatures drop below 64°F (18°C). By following this planting schedule when you use small grain rotations, you can reduce root knot nematode populations. It may take as many as four seasons of small grains to reduce nematode population densities the same amount as a soil fumigation. Preplant rotations of sudangrass or a sorghum–sudan grass hybrid in summer and barley or Cahaba white vetch in winter can be effective tools for reducing nematode populations only if the remaining roots of the old orchard have been destroyed.

Sanitation

After taking steps to prepare the orchard site and reduce nematode populations, follow good sanitation practices to avoid introducing nematodes into the orchard. Nematodes can be introduced in roots of infested planting stock, in

Table 27. Resistance of Stone Fruit Rootstocks to Nematode Pests.

Rootstock	Root knot nematodes	Root lesion nematodes	Ring nematode
Royal Blenheim apricot	resistant	resistant	susceptible
Mazzard cherry	immune to M. incognita resistant to M. javanica	susceptible	—
Mahaleb cherry	resistant to M. incognita susceptible to M. javanica	susceptible	—
Stockton Morello cherry	immune to M. incognita	susceptible	—
Colt cherry	—	—	—
Nemaguard peach	resistant	susceptible	susceptible
Lovell peach	susceptible	susceptible	somewhat tolerant
Citation plum	—	susceptible	—
Marianna 2624 plum	resistant	somewhat tolerant	susceptible
Myrobalan 29C plum	resistant	somewhat tolerant	susceptible

Immune: nematodes cannot invade roots.
Resistant: nematodes can invade and feed in roots but cannot multiply.
Tolerant: nematodes can invade, feed, and multiply, but rootstock is damaged less than susceptible rootstocks.
Susceptible: nematodes can invade roots, feed, and multiply.
— = no information.

infested soil on rootstocks or field equipment, or in runoff water from infested fields or orchards. Always use certified nematode-free rootstock. This greatly reduces the likelihood that nematodes will be introduced on the roots of the young trees. You can minimize the spread of nematodes by working noninfested orchards before you move equipment into infested orchards, cleaning roots and soil off equipment after you work infested soil, and avoiding the use of runoff water from infested sites to irrigate noninfested sites.

Cover Crops

A number of the cover crops that may be grown in orchards are hosts for nematode pests of stone fruits (see Table 28 at the end of the next chapter). It is best to avoid cover crops that are hosts for root knot nematode and to avoid inter-cropping with broadleaf crops such as cotton, lettuce, or alfalfa during the first 2 years of establishing an orchard on coarse-textured soils. Root knot nematodes may build up on these crops to levels high enough to damage trees on resistant rootstocks. Where nematodes are a concern, either choose cover crops that are not hosts for the species that damage stone fruits or choose nematode-resistant varieties of cover crops when they are available. Cover crops that are broadly useful for managing nematode pests in California orchards are barley, Blando brome, and Cahaba white vetch. Some cover crops will help reduce populations of some nematode species but increase the populations of other species. For maximum effectiveness, rotate the cover crops you use. More information about cover crops can be found in *Covercrops for California Agriculture*, listed in the references.

Vegetation Management

The management of orchard floor vegetation in stone fruits has several goals:

- controlling undesirable weed species
- encouraging desirable resident vegetation or seeded cover crops
- encouraging a shift to less competitive species
- reducing other pest problems
- minimizing interference with management activities such as pruning and harvest

A number of problems can develop if the orchard floor is not managed properly or if weed populations build up in the orchard. Weeds can compete with orchard trees for water and nutrients; competition is greatest during an orchard's first 3 or 4 years. Rank weed growth can compete with trees for sunlight in newly planted orchards, and young orchards may take longer to come into production if badly infested with problem weeds. Heavy weed growth around trees also can interfere with harvest operations and raise the orchard humidity, increasing some disease problems. Weeds and certain cover crops may serve as hosts for some problem pests such as stink bugs, lygus bugs, X-disease, and root knot nematodes. Weed growth around the bases of trees can provide shelter for voles (meadow mice), increase the likelihood of crown rot, and create a fire hazard when dry. Weeds that bloom at the same time as stone fruits, such as mustard family weeds and fiddleneck, compete with trees for pollinators. Weedy orchards and orchards with cover crops are more likely to suffer frost damage because the presence of vegetation can reduce the temperature by a few degrees, as compared with moist, vegetation-free soil. However, mowing or discing weeds and cover crops before bloom reduces both competition for pollinators and the potential for frost injury.

Weed Management

A plant's life cycle affects both its importance as a weed and the management strategies that may be needed for its control. The plants that grow in stone fruit orchards can be grouped as annuals, biennials, or perennials, based on their life cycles. Annuals complete their life cycle of germination, growth, flowering, and seed production in one season. Winter annuals germinate in the fall, grow through the winter, flower in late winter and early spring, produce seed in the spring, and die by early summer. Summer annuals germinate in the spring or early summer and produce seed in the fall, dying in late fall or early winter. Biennials complete their life cycle in two years, usually flowering and producing seed in the second year. Perennials live for 3 or more years, usually dying back in the winter and regrowing from underground parts. Some biennials, such as bristly oxtongue, little mallow (cheeseweed), and sweetclovers, behave as short-lived perennials in the mild climates of most California growing areas.

Winter annuals are the least troublesome because they grow when competition for water usually is not an issue. They may be controlled by mowing, flaming, spring cultivation, or herbicide application. Many winter annuals are desirable cover crops in stone fruit orchards. Summer annuals tend to cause more serious problems because they compete for a more limited water supply in the summer and may interfere with irrigation. Perennials usually are the hardest to control because they form extensive rhizomes, stolons, tubers, or tap roots that regrow after mowing or cultivation. Management requires a prolonged program of cultivation and herbicide treatment to destroy underground structures and control seedlings and regrowth in order to prevent seed production and the formation of perennial structures. It is best to deal with established perennials, especially field bindweed, before you plant the orchard.

Management Methods

Several methods are available for managing vegetation on the orchard floor. Cultivation, soil solarization, mowing, flame cultivation, and herbicide application can be used in combination, or you may wish to rely almost completely on cultivation or on herbicides. You can limit the scope of weed management to include vegetation around tree trunks (basal weed control), vegetation in the tree rows (strip weed control), or all vegetation on the orchard floor (total orchard floor control). The most effective methods to use depend on the type of orchard floor management (basal, strip, or total orchard floor), the irrigation method, what tools are available, and what weed problems are present.

Cultivation. Cultivation involves tilling the orchard floor in one or both directions. It may be used in the spring to turn under a cover crop or throughout the season as necessary to control weed growth. Cultivation is used in nonirrigated orchards to conserve soil moisture during the summer, and may be the most practical method for managing orchard floor vegetation where contours and checks are used for irrigation. If you turn the ground cover under and smooth the bare soil before bloom, you will end up with a warmer orchard environment, and reduced risk of frost injury. Cultivation can be combined with the application of contact or systemic herbicides for an effective way to reduce or control established infestations of perennial weeds, because cultivation cuts the perennial structures

(stolons, rhizomes, or rootstocks) into smaller pieces that are controlled more easily by translocated herbicides.

Mowing. Mowing or flailing can be used for total orchard floor vegetation management or to control vegetation only in the middles between tree rows. Specially designed mowers can be used for row middles to blow the mown vegetation into the tree rows where the resulting mulch suppresses weed growth. Cereal cover crops, especially forage oats, work particularly well for this "mow and blow" technique because the biomass does not degrade as quickly as that of broadleaf vegetation. Cereal rye is probably the best choice for lighter soils. Vetch may be combined with the cereal for added nitrogen. Plant the cover crop in October and mow in late March; the exact timing for best results depends on the location. Be sure to control vegetation in the tree rows by mowing or applying an herbicide before you blow in the mulch. Mulch around the bases of trees may increase problems with voles or crown diseases. If you use mulching for strip weed control, you may want to have the mulch moved away from the crown by hand and then use hand hoeing as needed for basal weed control.

Soil Solarization. Soil solarization involves covering prepared soil with special plastic and allowing the sun to heat the moist soil to temperatures that are lethal to plant propagules. The technique can effectively control the seeds of most weed species and shallow-growing perennial structures such as johnsongrass and bermudagrass rhizomes and stolons. As a general rule, the seeds of winter annuals are most susceptible to solarization; sweetclovers (*Melilotus* spp.) are not controlled. Seeds of summer annuals are less susceptible, but most can be controlled by correctly applied solarization. Purslane and crabgrass are harder to control. These weed species, if present, can be used as markers to indicate the effectiveness of a solarization program.

Effective solarization usually requires a period of at least 4 to 6 weeks when temperatures are highest and days longest to kill susceptible weeds. In central coast areas, the period may have to be 8 to 12 weeks. Solarization is most effective when large areas of well-worked, smooth soil are covered with plastic and soil moisture is maintained at 70% of field capacity or above. For these reasons, solarization is most effective as a preplant operation. Black plastic placed over the soil surface during planting inhibits weed growth and greatly reduces the amount of irrigation water required during the early establishment of new trees. However, this technique does not control weed propagules as well as preplant solarization with clear plastic. The susceptibility of common orchard weeds to preplant solarization is given in Figure 58. You can find more information on soil solarization in *Soil Solarization: A Nonpesticidal Method for Controlling Diseases, Nematodes, and Weeds*, listed in the references.

Flame Cultivation. Specially designed propane flamers provide an effective nonchemical alternative for strip weed

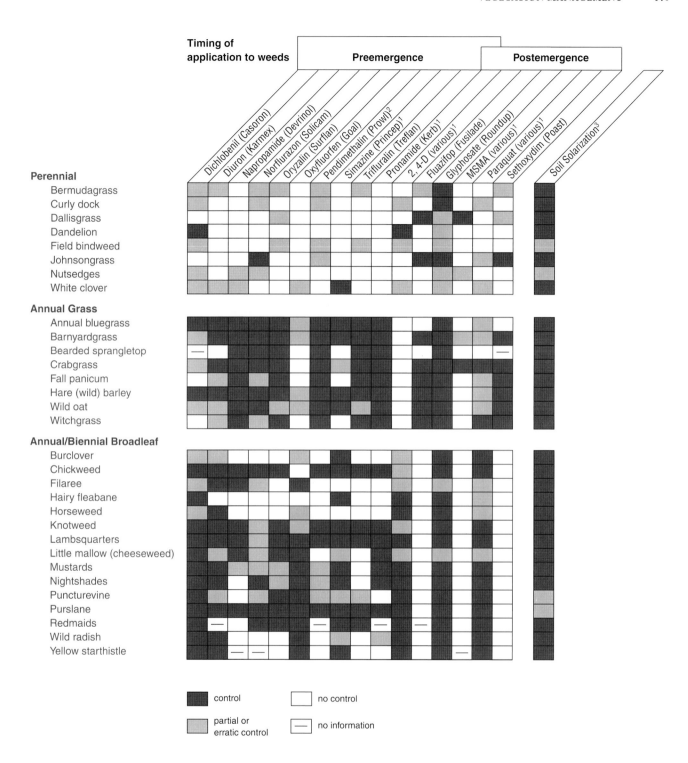

Figure 58. Susceptibility of weed species to herbicides available in stone fruits and to soil solarization.

1. Restricted-use pesticide. Permit required for purchase or use.
2. Nonbearing orchards only.
3. Solarization controls perennial structures in upper few inches of soil.

REGISTRATION STATUS OF THESE COMPOUNDS
MAY CHANGE. CHECK WITH LOCAL AUTHORITIES
BEFORE USING.

control and for basal weed control around larger trees. They can be used for total orchard floor weed control as an alternative to cultivation. Using a flamer, you can achieve successful weed control with two or three trips through the orchard, timed to kill weeds while they are still small. Flame cultivation is most effective on weeds less than 2 inches (5 cm) tall. Broadleaf weeds are more sensitive to flaming than are grasses; some grasses are very tolerant of flaming. To control larger weeds, you need to move the flamer more slowly through the orchard. Flaming is also used in conjunction with other weed control methods to reduce the number of cultivations or the quantity of herbicide needed, and to spot-treat regrowth in perennials. A higher-speed treatment used to retard weed growth has the same effect as chemical mowing. If you use flame cultivation for strip weed control in young orchards, hand hoe or apply herbicides to remove vegetation and leaves around the bases of trees to avoid injuring the trunks or burning trunk guards with the flame. Grass weeds may require additional controls such as spot-treatment with herbicides or hoeing.

The advantages of flame cultivation include broad-spectrum weed control, low cost, and lack of chemical residue. You can repeat the flame treatment as often as necessary, and you can use it when the orchard floor is too wet for cultivation. Disadvantages include a lack of residual control, poor control of some grasses, the hazards associated with handling pressurized flammable gas, and the potential for fire.

Herbicides. Herbicides used in stone fruits are classified as preemergence herbicides if they are applied before weeds emerge, or postemergence herbicides if they are applied to weeds after they have emerged. Herbicides available for use in stone fruits are listed in Figure 58. If you plan to use herbicides for basal or strip weed control, apply a residual preemergence herbicide in fall or early winter to control winter weeds as they germinate. Some orchards may require postemergence herbicide applications for weeds that were not controlled by the preemergence treatment. Postemergence herbicides are used for total orchard floor weed control.

Preemergence Herbicides. Preemergence herbicides kill the seeds of susceptible plants as they germinate. To be effective, the chemical must be mixed (incorporated) into the upper few inches of soil where weed seeds germinate. Incorporation can be accomplished mechanically, with a light irrigation, or by rain. Some preemergence herbicides must be incorporated immediately, while others may remain on the soil surface for a short time before incorporation without losing their effectiveness. Label directions specify how quickly a particular herbicide must be incorporated. As a general rule, apply preemergence herbicides within seven days before irrigation in orchards that are sprinkler irrigated or flood irrigated. In orchards irrigated with drip or when applying herbicides to berms around trees, make the application before a rain.

Most preemergence herbicides used in stone fruits are effective only against germinating weed seeds. Oxyfluorfen is effective on some weed species as a postemergence herbicide when applied to the seedlings' foliage. Preemergence herbicides may remain active in the soil for several weeks up to a year, depending on the chemical, application rate, soil conditions, and amount of rainfall or frequency of irrigation. In areas of the orchard that remain wet, such as around low-volume drip emitters, or during periods of prolonged wet weather, herbicide activity deteriorates more quickly as a result of leaching and accelerated breakdown caused by microbial activity and hydrolysis. In higher-rainfall locations or where unusually heavy rainfall is expected, you can split applications to prolong control. The use of split applications on coarse-textured soil prolongs the period of activity and reduces the risk of injury, because herbicides are leached from these soils more readily and are more toxic on these soils than on soils that are higher in organic matter.

In some cases, you can achieve adequate weed control with lower application rates than are specified on the label. Where you use herbicides for strip or basal weed control around trees planted on berms in areas with annual rainfall of less than 11 inches, lower rates may be effective on the berms. The treated soil of the berms remains drier during rains, and if it is above the level of surface irrigation water it has a lower rate of leaching and breakdown. Also, because the berms are drier, fewer weeds are likely to germinate.

Plan to discontinue the use of preemergence herbicides 1 or 2 years before you replant an orchard. This will eliminate the possibility that you will injure the following crop or the replant trees with herbicides, some of which may persist in the soil for a year or more. When replacing trees in the orchard, be sure to fill around the roots of the new tree with soil from 6 inches (15 cm) or deeper to avoid exposing the roots to herbicide residues (Figure 59).

Postemergence Herbicides. Postemergence herbicides are called foliar-applied herbicides because they are sprayed on the foliage of weeds that have emerged. They are classified as *contact herbicides* if they kill only the plant parts that are sprayed. Contact herbicides are most effective on weed seedlings and young weeds.

Translocated or *systemic herbicides* are transported via the plant's vascular system from contacted foliage to other parts of the plant, including roots and rhizomes. They are more effective on actively growing weeds, and are the best choice for control of perennials.

Use postemergence herbicides when monitoring indicates they are needed. Apply them in conjunction with the fall preemergence herbicide if weeds have already emerged. Make additional applications later in the season for weeds that are not controlled by preemergence herbicides and for spot-treatment of perennials.

Sprayers now are available that apply postemergence herbicides only where they detect the presence of weed foliage.

Often called "intelligent sprayers," they greatly reduce the amount of herbicide applied when weed populations are low. They can be used for strip weed control or for total orchard floor control.

When using herbicides, choose materials and rates according to the weed species you need to control, your soil type, the irrigation method you are using, and the age of your orchard. Combinations of materials or sequential treatment with different materials often are needed, since no single herbicide available for use in stone fruits will control all weed species. Figure 58 lists the susceptibility of common weed species to the herbicides available for use in stone fruits. More up-to-date information is available in the *UC IPM Pest Management Guidelines* for the different stone fruit crops. For current registration status of herbicides in stone fruits, check with your farm advisor or county agricultural commissioner. ALWAYS READ AND FOLLOW LABEL DIRECTIONS CAREFULLY. Be sure spray equipment is calibrated carefully and functioning properly. Proper calibration and use of spray equipment are discussed in detail in *The Safe and Effective Use of Pesticides*, listed in the references at the back of this book.

Management during Orchard Establishment

Begin your weed management program before you plant the orchard. Do a weed survey in the spring to see what species are present before you cultivate. A series of surveys made in late winter, spring, summer, and fall the year before you prepare the orchard for planting will give you the full spectrum of weed species that are present so you can plan the most effective management strategies. Soil solarization is easiest and most effective if you apply solarizing plastic as you plant the trees.

Perennials are easier to control before trees are planted. Established johnsongrass, bermudagrass, and dallisgrass plants can be destroyed by repeated cultivations during the summer before planting. This exposes rhizomes and stolons to drying, which eventually will kill the perennial structures that have been established. However, this will not eliminate the reservoir of seeds, which will continue to germinate for a period of years. Solarization will kill seeds in the upper few inches of soil, but later cultivations will bring viable seed to the surface. Control emerging seedlings with herbicides or cultivations to prevent them from forming perennial structures. In early fall, treat regrowth of perennials with glyphosate when the plants are beginning to flower, and cultivate again after 10 to 20 days to expose the root systems to further drying. Watch for regrowth the following spring, and use glyphosate to spot-treat any plants that appear. If field bindweed is present, the above program will help reduce infestations, but it is virtually impossible to eradicate this weed's deep perennial root system (Figure 60). Oryzalin and trifluralin applications will help control bindweed seedlings and reduce the infestation.

You can apply preemergence herbicides before planting in the spring to the entire orchard or to strips 4 to 6 feet wide where trees are to be planted. When planting trees into ground that has been treated with herbicide, set aside at least

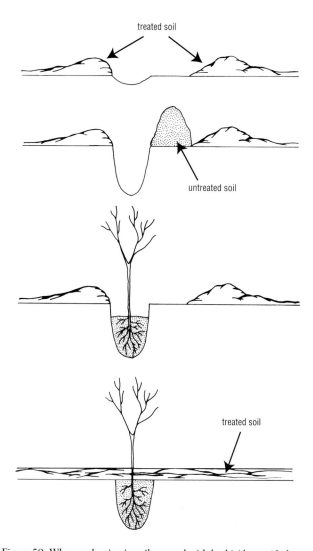

Figure 59. When replanting in soils treated with herbicide, avoid placing treated soil around the roots of the young trees.

6 inches of surface soil and be sure to place deeper soil around the roots of the young trees. This will prevent herbicide injury to the young roots. After the roots are covered, replace the surface layer so that the treated soil remains on top, where weed seeds will try to germinate (see Figure 59). Preemergence herbicides can be applied after planting and incorporated with a shallow cultivation or irrigation.

A preemergence herbicide applied in the spring will usually control germinating seedlings of susceptible weeds through the summer. Additional treatments may be needed for emerging perennials or annuals that survive the preemergence herbicide. Use spot-treatments for localized problems.

Winter annuals may be controlled with cultivation after the trees are planted or with preemergence herbicide treatments in late fall, before the first rains. Choose materials based on the weed species noted in your spring survey. Repeat the fall preemergence treatment every year, either to

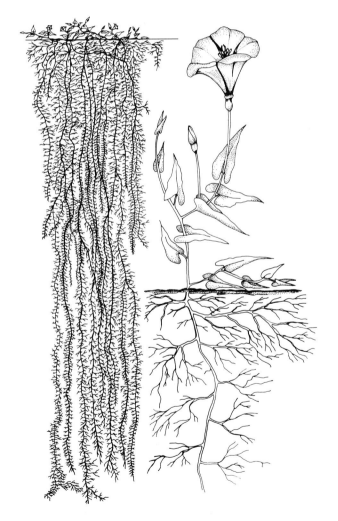

Figure 60. The storied rhizome system of field bindweed. The ability of new plants to form from the deeply penetrating root system makes established infestations of field bindweed extremely difficult to control. (Drawn from B. F. Klitz, *Journal of the American Society of Agronomy,* 22:216–234, 1930)

the tree row (if you plan to use a strip or basal weed control program) or to the entire orchard (if you plan a program of total reliance on herbicides). Use postemergence herbicides when monitoring indicates they are needed. In orchards with fine-textured soils or where rainfall is high, you can split the preemergence treatment into two applications to prolong the effective period of weed control. Make the first application in fall and the second in late winter. A postemergence herbicide can be combined with the first or second treatment to control weeds that have already emerged.

Management in Established Orchards

Several options are available for weed management in established orchards. The weed control program you choose depends on the spectrum of weeds present, tree spacing, soil type, the irrigation method you will use, the need for erosion control, the potential for frost injury, economic considerations, and your own personal preference. You may wish to rely on cultivation for most or all weed control (total cultivation), on mowing (total mowing), or on herbicides. Herbicides may be used for basal weed control, for strip weed control, or to manage the entire orchard floor (total reliance on herbicides). When cultivating or mowing to control weeds in the row middles, you also need to control weeds around tree bases with strip weed control (if you work the row middles in only one direction) or basal weed control (if you work the row middles in both directions). As an alternative to herbicides, you may use hand weeding, mulching, or flame cultivation for basal or strip weed control.

Regardless of the management strategies you adopt, you need to take steps to avoid introducing problem weeds and to eliminate conditions that favor weed development. Clean your field equipment after working infested ground to keep from spreading weed seeds and perennial weed structures. When working several orchards, be sure to work those infested with problem weeds last. Control weeds in and around irrigation ditches, and consider installing screens in canals used as surface water sources to reduce the spread of perennial structures such as rhizomes and root fragments. Provide proper drainage in the orchard to eliminate areas of standing water, which favor the development of dallisgrass, sprangletop, and curly dock. If you let the top 2 to 4 inches of soil dry out between irrigations, you will discourage the establishment of weed seedlings and increase the effectiveness of herbicides, which degrade more rapidly in saturated soil.

Total Cultivation. Total or clean cultivation can keep orchards free of weeds most of the year. Growers often use cultivation for the first few years in newly planted orchards to control weed seedlings and reduce established weeds. A combination of cultivation and herbicide applications is the most efficient way to reduce or eliminate infestations of perennials such as johnsongrass. Cultivation may be the most practical method if you are using furrow or flood irrigations, which require periodic activity to remove and replace furrows or checks. Use a cultivation when you remove fur- rows or checks to destroy weed seedlings that germinate after an irrigation.

A typical cultivation program involves discing or harrow- ing in late winter or early spring to turn the winter cover crop under, followed by additional cultivations from late spring through summer as needed to control weed growth. In non- irrigated orchards, one additional cultivation in early sum- mer may be sufficient; irrigated orchards may require four cultivations or more. If you allow resident vegetation or a seeded cover crop to grow in the winter, it will help prevent soil erosion and improve soil structure and drainage, helping to reduce problems with root and crown diseases. However, the presence of orchard floor vegetation increases the risk of frost injury. If frost is a concern, cultivate before or early in the bloom period. In summer, keep cultivations as shallow as possible to conserve moisture and reduce potential damage to the trees' feeder roots.

Total cultivation requires discing or harrowing in both directions, which may cause some problems. The heavy equipment involved can compact soil, decreasing the ability of water to penetrate the soil and increasing erosion on slop- ing land. Equipment can injure the trunk or crown, increas- ing the trees' susceptibility to certain diseases such as Ceratocystis canker and crown gall. Use hand weeding or herbicides around tree trunks to avoid injuring the trees. Cultivation destroys feeder roots in the top 6 inches of soil, rendering the nutrients and water present in the cultivated layer unavailable to the tree. Keep cultivations as shallow as possible. Cultivation can spread perennial weeds if herbicide applications aren't made before and after cultivation to con- trol rhizomes, stolons, or rootstocks. Be sure to clean all cul- tivation equipment before you move it from an infested site to an uninfested site. Cultivation of dry soil creates dusty conditions that can increase mite problems; keep the num- ber of cultivations to a minimum during summer months.

Total Mowing. A total mowing program uses mechanical or chemical mowing instead of cultivation. Begin mowing each season before frost is a concern. After that initial mowing, mow as necessary to keep problem weeds from setting seed. As a general rule, you should mow native ground cover before it is 6 to 8 inches (15 to 20 cm) tall to allow desirable winter annuals such as redmaids, chickweed, and annual bluegrass to reseed, while preventing seed production by less- desirable species. As with cultivation, use hand weeding or herbicides to control vegetation around tree trunks to avoid mechanical injury to the trees.

A program of total mowing obviates some of the problems of cultivation. Equipment is lighter, so soil compaction is less, and the roots of the cover crop maintain good water penetration and reduce soil erosion. Increased accessibility during wet weather allows the ground application of fungi- cides during bloom for more effective control of diseases such as brown rot. During dry weather, dusty conditions are

reduced. Tree roots can grow closer to the surface and make better use of water and nutrients. The equipment used for mowing is less expensive and easier to operate.

Disadvantages include a cooler orchard during frost sea- son. You can minimize this condition by keeping the ground cover mowed closely during late winter and early spring. The cooling effect can be advantageous during summer, but then the ground cover will consume more water and nutrients. Perennials tend to increase under a total mowing program, because they grow longer and outcompete annual weeds for water and nutrients. The perennials most likely to become problems are bermudagrass, field bindweed, and dandelion. Nutsedge may become a problem on coarser soils of the San Joaquin Valley. Contour checks for flood irrigation cannot be used with total mowing.

Strip Weed Control. Strip weed control involves the use of herbicides, flaming, or mulching to maintain a weed-free strip 2 to 6 feet (0.6 to 1.8 m) wide in the tree row. Hand hoeing may be a viable option for small orchards. Strip weed control can be used in both young and established orchards, with flood irrigation that uses permanent berms down the tree rows, and with drip or sprinkler irrigation. It reduces equipment travel by eliminating the need for cross-discing or mowing in two direc- tions, and prevents tree injury by eliminating the need to cul- tivate close to the trunks. Weed control in the tree rows reduces some competition for nutrients and water and keeps the tree crowns drier. Strip weed control has the advantages of total mowing and, when herbicides are used, requires a small- er quantity of chemicals than does total reliance on herbicide.

With strip weed control, perennials can get established quickly in the tree rows because there is no competition from annual weeds. Watch for their appearance both in tree rows and in row middles. Spot-treat with systemic herbicides to keep perennials from becoming established.

Basal Weed Control. Basal weed control involves the use of herbicides, hand hoeing, mulching, or flaming to control weeds in a 4- to 8-square-foot (0.4- to 0.8-square-meter) area around the base of each tree. This system uses less herbicide than strip weed control but requires more mowing or cultiva- tion. The cross-discing or mowing that is necessary to control weeds between trees prevents the use of permanent berms or low-volume irrigation systems. Basal weed control eliminates the possibility of trunk injury from mowing or tillage equip- ment. In young orchards, the safest preemergence herbicides to use around tree bases are napropamide, oryzalin, oxyfluor- fen, and pendimethalin.

Total Reliance on Herbicides. Herbicides can be used to keep the entire orchard floor free of weeds, or they can be used in a combination of basal or strip weed control and chemical mowing. Total orchard floor weed control with her- bicides requires the fewest equipment trips of any control strategy, controls perennials more easily, and greatly reduces competition for water where the annual rainfall is 11 inches or less. Initial costs are higher than with other methods.

Total reliance on herbicides has certain disadvantages. It requires more careful monitoring of the weed population and often requires the application of combinations of herbicides or sequential treatments to achieve total control. No single chemical will provide effective control of all of the weeds that infest California orchards. Soil compaction will be a problem on some soils, so periodic shallow cultivations may be needed. The orchard will be less accessible during wet weather than it would be if a cover crop were maintained during winter months. Sloping land will be subject to increased erosion of the topsoil. Perennials may become established quickly in the absence of competition, especially nutsedges and bermudagrass, both of which tolerate most postemergence herbicides. Repeated applications of some herbicides may lead to the buildup of resistant species. For example, repeated use of simazine will increase the buildup of annual grasses such as crabgrass and witchgrass that are not controlled by this herbicide.

Chemical Mowing. An alternative to mechanical mowing involves using a low rate of glyphosate to inhibit weed growth without killing them, thus maintaining a ground cover in the orchard. Chemical mowing requires fewer trips through the orchard than mechanical mowing; two or three trips per season may be sufficient, depending on the plants present. By maintaining a ground cover, you decrease erosion and increase accessibility as compared to total orchard floor weed control. Chemical mowing has advantages in orchards where irrigation water is limited or unavailable and where mechanical mowing is difficult before bloom time. If you use this technique, remove weeds around trunks by hand or with herbicides. Chemical mowing can be combined with strip weed control to reduce weed competition around trees and minimize drift hazards from the glyphosate used for mowing.

The application timing and rates used for chemical mowing depend on the vegetation present, its stage of growth, and growing conditions. Chemical mowing works best on annual weeds. Young winter annuals can be controlled with very low rates applied in January or February. Summer annuals and older winter annuals are harder to control. Weeds are harder to control in spring or summer, and when stressed by periods of drought they require even higher rates of herbicides. If you don't start a chemical mowing program until March or April, it is best to mow mechanically first. Perennials or annuals not controlled by chemical mowing may quickly take over because of the reduced competition. Spot-treat these weeds with standard rates of glyphosate as they emerge or they will become the dominant species and will be extremely difficult to manage. Continued use of low rates of glyphosate may result in a shift in the weed population, so careful monitoring is essential.

Weed Monitoring

Identification of the weed species that are present and their emergence dates is essential for making decisions about which herbicides to use and whether postemergence treatments are necessary. Knowledge of what weeds are present is also important for planning control programs that involve solarization, cultivation, flaming, or mowing, whether or not you plan to use herbicides. Monitor your orchard for weeds at least three times each year, in fall, winter, and late spring or early summer.

Fall Monitoring. After the first rains in the fall, look for winter annual weeds in tree rows to check the effectiveness of any preemergence herbicide applications, and check the ground cover in row middles for perennial seedlings. Use appropriate postemergence herbicides, flaming, or hand weeding if needed.

Winter Monitoring. An examination of untreated ground in February will show you the full range of winter annual species present. Keep a record of what you find to help you plan weed control activities for the orchard. February monitoring following a fall preemergence herbicide treatment will tell you which weeds were not controlled. Record these and use the results to plan next year's weed control program. If a large number of weeds are present, consider treating with a postemergence herbicide.

Spring Monitoring. Monitor in late spring or early summer, after summer annuals have germinated. Spring monitoring the year before you plant the orchard will indicate which species are present; after the orchard is in place, it will tell you which species have not been controlled by preemergence herbicides. Monitoring at this time also tells you what perennial weeds are present.

Where you use cultivation for weed control, monitor at least two weeks before you plan to cultivate as a check for the presence of perennial weeds. If present, treat perennials with a translocated herbicide such as glyphosate to kill underground structures so they will not be spread by cultivation. This treatment is most effective two weeks before cultivation. Monitor again a few weeks after the cultivation to check for regrowth of perennials, and treat again if necessary.

Keep records of your monitoring results. By knowing which species are present, you will be able to make correct decisions on cultural and chemical controls. Information collected over a period of years tells you how weed populations may be changing and how effective your control operations have been. When monitoring for weeds, pay special attention to perennials. It is a good idea to sketch a diagram of the orchard and mark where perennials are found. This way you can quickly return to see how well your control actions are working. Two examples of weed monitoring forms are illustrated in Figures 61 and 62.

ORCHARD LOCATION _____   **HERBICIDE(S)** _____

DATE _____   **APPLICATION** _____

COMMENTS _____

	LATE FALL		LATE SPRING	
	TREATED	UNTREATED	TREATED	UNTREATED
Annual Grass				
annual bluegrass	_____	_____	_____	_____
barnyardgrass	_____	_____	_____	_____
crabgrass	_____	_____	_____	_____
fall panicum	_____	_____	_____	_____
hare (wild) barley	_____	_____	_____	_____
sprangletop	_____	_____	_____	_____
wild oat	_____	_____	_____	_____
witchgrass	_____	_____	_____	_____
_____	_____	_____	_____	_____
_____	_____	_____	_____	_____
_____	_____	_____	_____	_____
Annual Broadleaf				
cheeseweed (mallow)	_____	_____	_____	_____
clovers	_____	_____	_____	_____
fiddleneck	_____	_____	_____	_____
filaree	_____	_____	_____	_____
groundsel	_____	_____	_____	_____
hairy fleabane	_____	_____	_____	_____
horseweed	_____	_____	_____	_____
knotweed	_____	_____	_____	_____
lambsquarters	_____	_____	_____	_____
mustards	_____	_____	_____	_____
pigweeds	_____	_____	_____	_____
prickly lettuce	_____	_____	_____	_____
puncturevine	_____	_____	_____	_____
purslane	_____	_____	_____	_____
starthistle	_____	_____	_____	_____
wild radish	_____	_____	_____	_____
_____	_____	_____	_____	_____
_____	_____	_____	_____	_____
_____	_____	_____	_____	_____
Perennial				
bermudagrass	_____	_____	_____	_____
curly dock	_____	_____	_____	_____
dallisgrass	_____	_____	_____	_____
dandelion	_____	_____	_____	_____
field bindweed	_____	_____	_____	_____
johnsongrass	_____	_____	_____	_____
nutsedge	_____	_____	_____	_____
_____	_____	_____	_____	_____
_____	_____	_____	_____	_____
_____	_____	_____	_____	_____

Figure 61. Example of form used to monitor for weed species present in the orchard. Checking in late fall, after rains or postharvest irrigation stimulates germination, will tell you what winter annuals are present. Checking in late spring or early summer will tell you what summer annuals and perennials are present. Use a scale from 1 to 5 to indicate level of infestation: 1 = very few weeds; 2 = light infestation; 3 = moderate infestation; 4 = heavy infestation; 5 = very heavy infestation.

ORCHARD LOCATION _____   HERBICIDE(S) _____

DATE _____   APPLICATION _____

COMMENTS _____

| | SUMMER | | MID-WINTER | |
	TREATED	UNTREATED	TREATED	UNTREATED
Annual Grass				
annual bluegrass	_____	_____	_____	_____
barnyardgrass	_____	_____	_____	_____
crabgrass	_____	_____	_____	_____
fall panicum	_____	_____	_____	_____
hare (wild) barley	_____	_____	_____	_____
sprangletop	_____	_____	_____	_____
wild oat	_____	_____	_____	_____
witchgrass	_____	_____	_____	_____
_____	_____	_____	_____	_____
_____	_____	_____	_____	_____
_____	_____	_____	_____	_____
Annual Broadleaf				
cheeseweed (mallow)	_____	_____	_____	_____
clovers	_____	_____	_____	_____
fiddleneck	_____	_____	_____	_____
filaree	_____	_____	_____	_____
groundsel	_____	_____	_____	_____
hairy fleabane	_____	_____	_____	_____
horseweed	_____	_____	_____	_____
knotweed	_____	_____	_____	_____
lambsquarters	_____	_____	_____	_____
mustards	_____	_____	_____	_____
pigweeds	_____	_____	_____	_____
prickly lettuce	_____	_____	_____	_____
puncturevine	_____	_____	_____	_____
purslane	_____	_____	_____	_____
starthistle	_____	_____	_____	_____
wild radish	_____	_____	_____	_____
_____	_____	_____	_____	_____
_____	_____	_____	_____	_____
_____	_____	_____	_____	_____
Perennial				
bermudagrass	_____	_____	_____	_____
curly dock	_____	_____	_____	_____
dallisgrass	_____	_____	_____	_____
dandelion	_____	_____	_____	_____
field bindweed	_____	_____	_____	_____
johnsongrass	_____	_____	_____	_____
nutsedge	_____	_____	_____	_____
_____	_____	_____	_____	_____
_____	_____	_____	_____	_____
_____	_____	_____	_____	_____

Figure 62. Example of form used to monitor for effectiveness of previous year's treatments. Checking in summer will tell you what weeds are present and not controlled. Checking in mid-winter will tell you what was not controlled by preemergence treatments. Use a scale from 1 to 5 to indicate level of infestation: 1= very few weeds; 2 = light infestation; 3 = moderate infestation; 4 = heavy infestation; 5 = very heavy infestation.

Identifying Major Weed Species

In addition to being classified as annuals or perennials based on their growth habit, weeds can be classified as broadleaf, grass, or sedge, based on botanical characteristics. Figure 63 illustrates some of the structures used to identify weeds. Broadleaf seedlings have two seed leaves (cotyledons), whereas grass and sedge seedlings have one seed leaf. The seed leaves of each broadleaf weed species have a characteristic shape, texture, and color, which makes the seedlings relatively easy to identify. Seed leaves and usually the first true leaves are different from the leaves that form later. Seedlings of grasses are more difficult to identify because the seed leaves of different species are similar, and they differ little from true leaves that form later. Characteristics of the collar region, where the leaf blade joins leaf sheath, are used to distinguish grasses. Perennial grasses may be distinguished by the appearance of rhizomes or stolons. Sedges are similar in appearance to grasses; most species found in orchards have three-sided stems that are triangular in cross-section. The most important are nutsedges, perennial sedges that form characteristic tubers or nutlets on their rhizomes.

Photographs and detailed descriptions of all the weeds mentioned in this chapter can be found in *The Grower's Weed Identification Handbook*, listed in the references.

Perennial Grasses and Sedges

Johnsongrass, *Sorghum halepense*

Johnsongrass occurs commonly in annual crops, orchards, and other locations where soil is moist. It is one of the most troublesome of the perennial grasses. Mature plants form leafy clumps that may reach heights of 6 or 7 feet (2 m). Johnsongrass reproduces from underground stems (*rhizomes*) and from seeds. Johnsongrass seeds are often spread in irrigation water and can remain dormant for many years. Repeated cultivation of dry soil the summer before planting can effectively control established infestations. Care must be taken not to move viable rhizomes to uninfested locations. If johnsongrass invades an established orchard, it is best controlled with herbicides. Control seedlings before they begin to form rhizomes, which may occur 3 to 6 weeks after germination. If rhizomes become established, repeated herbicide (glyphosate) applications will be needed to control them.

A. (*photo next page*) Johnsongrass seedlings have broad, light green leaves with smooth leaf sheaths that may have a maroon tinge. The midvein appears as a broad, white line at the base of the first leaf.

B. (*photo next page*) The johnsongrass ligule is a dense fringe of hairs. Presence of a ligule helps distinguish young johnsongrass plants from barnyardgrass.

C. (*photo next page*) Johnsongrass rhizomes are thick, fleshy, and segmented. Each segment can form roots and shoots.

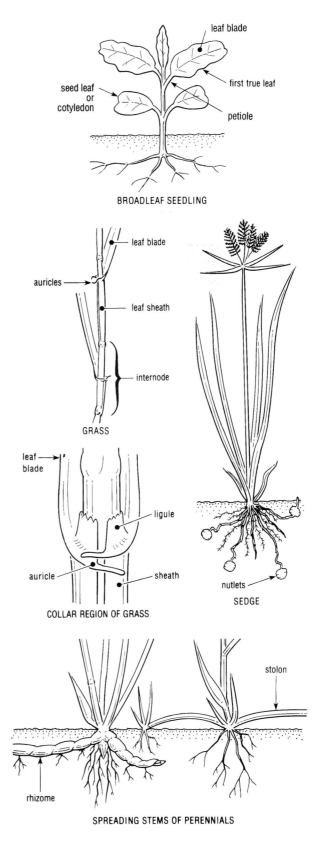

Figure 63. Vegetative parts commonly used to identify weeds.

A. Johnsongrass seedlings

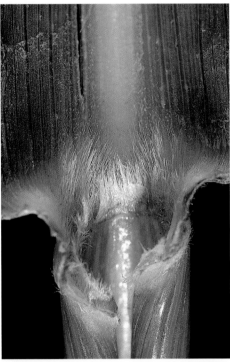

B. Johnsongrass ligule

Dallisgrass, *Paspalum dilatatum*

Dallisgrass occasionally becomes a problem in orchards. It is a bunchgrass that reproduces from seeds and very short rhizomes. Dallisgrass is undesirable in ground covers because it may inhibit the growth of other plants and is able to invade tree rows quickly. Dallisgrass is highly competitive with trees for water and nutrients. It produces large quantities of seed and tends to become dominant in mowed groundcover because mowing stimulates seed production. Seeds are transported easily in water or by machinery. Like other perennial grasses, dallisgrass can be controlled before planting the orchard by cultivation of dry soil. However, seedlings will still need to be controlled, which can be accomplished with pre-emergence herbicides or with cultivations. If dallisgrass becomes established in your orchard, you can control it with repeated applications of translocated herbicide (glyphosate).

D. Mature dallisgrass plants form loose bunches that may reach 1 to 4 feet (30 to 120 cm) in height. Flower heads often droop, and consist of three to six spikes that arise from different points along the flower stem. Dallisgrass plants often grow close to the ground in mowed orchards. Rhizomes (not shown) are very short, with shortened internodes that give the appearance of concentric rings.

Bermudagrass, *Cynodon dactylon*

Although commonly used as a turfgrass, bermudagrass is a troublesome weed in orchards. It reproduces from rhizomes, stolons, and seeds, and becomes a problem in mowed orchards because mowing provides more light to the stolons, stimulating their growth. However, exposure to direct sunlight kills stolons and rhizomes. Before planting the orchard, control bermudagrass by repeatedly cultivating the dry soil. In established orchards, use herbicides to control plants that become established. You can use cultivations to control seedlings. Solarization will control seeds, stolons, and rhizomes in the upper few inches of the soil.

C. Johnsongrass rhizomes

D. Dallisgrass

E. Bermudagrass forms dense mats of spreading, branching stolons that have short leaves and erect stems 4 to 18 inches (10 to 45 cm) tall. There is a papery sheath around the stolon at the base of each leaf. Three to seven slender flower spikes arise from a single point at the tip of the stem.

Nutsedge, *Cyperus* spp.

Nutsedge, also called nutgrass, can be distinguished from grasses by the three-sided stem, which is triangular in cross-section. Two species are found in California: yellow nutsedge, *Cyperus esculentus*, is the most common; purple nutsedge, *C. rotundus*, tends to be found in wetter locations. Nutsedges can reproduce from seed, but for the most part they reproduce from nutlets or tubers that form on their rhizomes. The tubers are spread easily by cultivation. Nutsedges may become troublesome in an orchard where herbicides are used for all weed control, since most chemicals do not control nutsedges and they spread quickly in the absence of competition. To prevent the formation of tubers, you must kill the young plants before they reach the 6-leaf stage. Some preemergence and postemergence systemic herbicides will provide partial control. Deep tillage of dry soil will reduce nutsedge populations. The tubers of purple nutsedge are more susceptible to drying than are those of yellow nutsedge.

F. Mature nutsedge plants are 1 to 3 feet (30 to 90 cm) tall with a flower head at the tip of each stem. Flowering stems are triangular in cross-section and the stiff leaves are V-shaped in cross-section. Yellow nutsedge has three long, leaflike bracts at the base of each flower head. These bracts are short in purple nutsedge.

G. Tubers or nutlets form on the extensive root system of the nutsedge plant. Tubers can sprout to form new plants and are the main means for dissemination of nutsedge. The tubers of yellow nutsedge (shown here) are produced singly, whereas the tubers of purple nutsedge are produced in chains along rhizomes. Yellow nutsedge tubers have a pleasant nutlike flavor, while purple nutsedge tubers are bitter.

Perennial Broadleaves

Curly Dock, *Rumex crispus*

Curly dock grows in wet areas and usually becomes a problem where drainage is poor or where orchards are overirrigated. It is a member of the buckwheat family, which is characterized by jointed stems and membranous sheaths surrounding the stem at the base of each leaf. Curly dock regrows from a fleshy taproot after mowing or discing. Deeper cultivation will control curly dock. Preemergence herbicides will control seedlings, but not the deep taproot of an established plant. Some foliar-applied translocated herbicides will control established plants. Curly dock is an important weed in cherry orchards because it is a host for the leafhopper vector of X-disease.

E. Bermudagrass

F. Yellow nutsedge

G. Yellow nutsedge tubers

H. Curly dock

I. Field bindweed

H. Curly dock plants regrow in the spring from a rosette of leaves. Plants remain low-growing if mowed, or if unmowed they can reach heights of 2 to 5 feet (0.6 to 1.5 m). Long, loosely branched flower heads form at the ends of stems. The flower heads turn reddish brown when mature. Stems die back in the fall.

Field Bindweed, *Convolvulus arvensis*

Field bindweed, also called perennial morningglory, is one of the most troublesome broadleaf perennial weeds in many crops. It competes with trees for moisture and nutrients during summer months, and can be a serious problem in young orchards. Bindweed plants can be prostrate or can climb vine-like up other vegetation. The showy white or reddish flowers are funnel shaped and borne singly along the stems. Bindweed is difficult to control after the seedling stage because it forms a deep, perennial rootstock and produces many seeds. Established infestations are nearly impossible to eradicate because the seeds can remain dormant for up to 60 years. Cultivation can spread bindweed infestations by moving fragments of viable rootstock. Repeated deep cultivations of dry soil may help reduce infestations, but care must be taken not to transport viable rootstock fragments on field equipment. A program of treating bindweed plants with glyphosate, cultivating, and treating regrowth when flowers begin to form will reduce infestations substantially if carried out over a period of years.

I. Seed leaves of field bindweed are nearly square, with a deep notch at the tip. True leaves are arrowhead-shaped, with petioles that are grooved on the upper surface. Young plants regrowing from rootstock lack seed leaves.

Dandelion, *Taraxacum officinale*

Dandelion is a commonly occurring perennial that is most troublesome in mowed orchards with fine-textured soils. It is of particular concern in cherry orchards because it is a host for the X-disease pathogen. It is also a host for tomato ringspot virus, which affects all stone fruits. The mature dandelion plant consists of a rosette of leaves that sends up hollow stalks 3 to 12 inches long, and topped with a single, bright yellow, disclike flower head. Dandelion reproduces from the familiar windblown seeds and regrows from a strong, deep taproot. It is difficult to control with herbicides and tolerates close mowing. Cultivation can spread fragments of the taproot, which can regrow.

White Clover, *Trifolium repens*

White clover is a desirable cover crop, especially in orchards where a perennial cover is maintained in tree middles. However, the plants are aggressive and may invade tree rows where they become difficult to control. In peach and nectarine orchards, clover may serve as a host for the buildup of stink bugs and lygus bugs. White clover plants are low-growing, and the stems root at the nodes. The trifoliate leaves have a distinctive white crescent on each leaflet.

Biennial Broadleaves

Little Mallow (Cheeseweed), *Malva parviflora*

Little mallow, also called cheeseweed, grows as a biennial or short-lived perennial in the milder climates of the Central Valley and coastal valleys. Plants may be prostrate or may grow as tall as 5 feet (1.5 m), with flowers that are purple or pink and white. The fruit is shaped like a tiny wheel of cheese, giving the weed the common name "cheeseweed." Seeds remain viable for many years and can germinate and emerge from deep in the soil. This, plus the fact that little mallow tolerates many herbicides, means that it may become predominant in orchard cover crops. Mature plants form dense bushes with woody stems that interfere with orchard activities. Under a mowing program, the plants are low-growing and thick-stemmed. Use hand weeding or herbicides to control little mallow plants while they are small; otherwise they quickly grow a deep, tough tap root, and become difficult to eliminate. Discing will control seedlings and young plants. Napropamide controls germinating seedlings. Oxyfluorfen can be used during the dormant season.

> **J.** Seed leaves of little mallow are triangular or heart-shaped. True leaves are round or kidney-shaped with scalloped edges. There is a red spot at the base of each leaf where it attaches to the petiole.

J. Little mallow

Bristly Oxtongue, *Picris echioides*

Bristly oxtongue, like little mallow, grows as a biennial or a short-lived perennial in stone fruit production areas. It tends to be most troublesome in coastal orchards. The spiny leaves and stems can be unpleasant to work around and may interfere with orchard activities. Bristly oxtongue plants produce large quantities of seed, but can be controlled by discing. Plan cultivations to uproot the plants before they set seed.

> **K.** The rough, hairy leaves of bristly oxtongue have a warty appearance. Clusters of yellow flowers form near the tips of stems.

Winter Annual Grasses

Annual Bluegrass, *Poa annua*

Annual bluegrass is an excellent ground cover in orchards. It is low-growing and because it dies out in early summer it does not compete with trees for irrigation water. Mature plants are 3 to 12 inches (8 to 30 cm) tall. Flower heads are branched with clusters of 3 to 6 flowers at the tip of each branch.

Wild Oat, *Avena fatua*

Wild oat is a tall plant that can become a problem around tree trunks, where it creates moist conditions that favor crown diseases and provides shelter for voles. This weed is difficult to control because it may emerge several times during the year, and the large seeds can germinate deep in the soil, beyond the effective zone for most preemergence herbicides. Effective

K. Bristly oxtongue

L. Wild oats

M. Mustard seedling

postemergence herbicides are available, but several treatments may be necessary to control young plants. Wild oat seedlings may be distinguished from most other grasses by their large seed coat, which usually remains attached for a long time.

L. Mature wild oat plants are 1 to 4 feet (30 to 120 cm) tall, with flowers nearly identical to those of domestic oats.

Hare Barley (Wild Barley), *Hordeum murinum* subsp. *leporinum*

Hare barley is not such a serious weed problem as wild oat. Mature plants are shorter and they dry up earlier in the summer. Seedlings are similar to those of wild oat, but lack the large attached seed coat. Mature hare barley plants are 6 to 24 inches (15 to 60 cm) tall. The long awns or bristles of the individual flowers give the flower head a bushy appearance. Long, clawlike auricles are present at the collar, but may not be prominent on the young plant. When mature, the flower head disintegrates into the familiar "foxtails."

Winter Annual Broadleaves

Mustards

Several species of mustard may occur in California orchards. Those found most commonly are black mustard, *Brassica nigra*, wild mustard, *Sinapis arvensis*, and birdsrape mustard, *B. rapa*, also known as common yellow mustard and wild turnip. Mustards frequently are used in ground covers or as green manure crops because their taproots help loosen heavier soils and their flowers attract a number of beneficial insects. However, with the exception of prunes, they are not a good ground cover in stone fruits because they bloom at the same time as the fruit trees, and so compete for pollinators. Mustard plants have large lower leaves that usually are deeply lobed. Plants are erect and may reach heights of 2 to 6 feet, depending on the species and growing conditions. Because of their large size, mustard plants can interfere with cultivation, and plants around the bases of trees create conditions that favor crown diseases and provide refuge for voles. They compete for water, and this is of special concern in lower rainfall areas (annual average less than 11 inches). In milder coastal locations, mustards may grow year-round.

M. Mustard seedlings all have broad seed leaves with a deep notch at the tip. The first true leaves are bright green above, pale green below, deeply lobed, and often hairy.

Wild Radish, *Raphanus raphanistrum*

Wild radish is similar to mustards in its growth habit and appearance. Plants reach heights of 2 to 5 feet (0.6 to 1.5 m), and flowers range in color from white to purple, or are sometimes yellow. The seed pods and seeds are much larger than those of mustards. Wild radish is undesirable as a ground cover in stone fruits for the same reasons that apply to mustards.

Redmaids (Desert Rockpurslane), *Calandrinia ciliata*

Redmaids occur commonly in Central Valley orchards. Mature plants may be from 6 to 12 inches (15 to 30 cm) tall with narrow, succulent leaves. The showy, reddish purple flowers appear in early spring. Redmaids makes a good ground cover for stone fruit orchards because it is low-growing, it dries up by early summer, and it is easy control in the tree rows.

Common Chickweed, *Stellaria media*

Chickweed is a low-growing, spreading plant that makes a good orchard ground cover when combined with other winter annuals such as bluegrass. Chickweed has thin, succulent stems that trail along the ground and root where nodes contact moist soil. The small white flowers have five deeply cleft petals. Chickweed dries up with the onset of hot weather in Central Valley orchards, although it can continue growing through the summer in shady, cool locations where moisture is adequate. Under high-nitrogen conditions, chickweed can form dense mats 12 to 14 inches (30 to 35 cm) tall. It can become a problem if it invades tree rows and forms dense, wet mats around the bases of trees.

Burclover, *Medicago* **spp.**

Two or three different species of burclover occur in California. California burclover, *Medicago polymorpha*, is most likely to be seen in orchards. Seedlings may emerge in spring in milder coastal locations. Control of this weed is important in cherry orchards because it is a host for both the X-disease pathogen and its leafhopper vector.

N. California burclover stems are up to 2 feet (60 cm) long and tend to trail along the ground, but may grow upright. The trifoliate leaves resemble those of clover and usually have reddish-tinged midveins. Small, bright yellow flowers form in clusters at the end of stems. The seed pod is a bur that contains several yellowish or tan, kidney-shaped seeds.

O. Burclover seed leaves are oblong. The first true leaf is rounded with a single leaflet. Later leaves have the characteristic cloverlike trifoliate shape.

Filaree, *Erodium* **spp.**

Several species of filaree are common winter annuals or biennials throughout California. They are desirable ground cover in orchards because they are low-growing and do not compete with trees. They dry up in the summer. Plants are erect or spreading, and the stems may be anywhere from 3 inches to 2 feet (8 to 60 cm) long. The leaves are lobed or finely divided, depending on the species. Filaree flowers may be rose, lavender, purple, or violet in color. The characteristically long, pointed fruit are borne in clusters. At maturity, the fruit separates into five parts, each consisting of a long, spirally twisted beak attached to a seed.

N. California burclover

O. California burclover seedling

P. Barnyardgrass collar

Summer Annual Grasses

Barnyardgrass, *Echinochloa crus-galli*

Barnyardgrass grows in dense clumps or patches that may be tall or may spread along the ground. It forms dense mats when mowed. Several varieties that differ in growth habit and floral appearance occur in California. Because barnyardgrass plants produce huge quantities of seed, the weed can be difficult to control without the use of herbicides.

> P. Barnyardgrass is the only common summer annual grass that has no ligule or auricles. This characteristic helps distinguish young barnyardgrass plants from young johnsongrass plants.

Bearded Sprangletop, *Leptochloa fascicularis*

Bearded sprangletop occurs in Central Valley orchards, usually on alkaline soils. It is most abundant on fine-textured soils and in wet locations where herbicides are leached or degraded more quickly. Good drainage in the orchard helps discourage this weed. Mature bearded sprangletop plants form large, upright tufts 12 to 40 inches (30 to 100 cm) tall. Flowers are elongated, upright, and highly branched, and are straw-colored when mature. The ligule is long and thin, and there are no auricles.

Large Crabgrass, *Digitaria sanguinalis*

Large crabgrass, also called hairy crabgrass, occurs commonly in orchards, especially in the San Joaquin Valley. The low-growing plants root deeply at the nodes, becoming difficult to remove once established. Flowers of large crabgrass resemble those of bermudagrass. Branches of the crabgrass flower arise separately from the stalk, whereas bermudagrass flower branches all arise from the same point. Large crabgrass has a papery ligule but no auricles; there are small tufts of hairs where the leaf blade meets the sheath. Crabgrass is easily controlled with napropamide, norflurazon, or oryzalin.

Fall Panicum, *Panicum dichotomiflorum*

Fall panicum or smooth witchgrass occurs commonly in cultivated orchards. It is found frequently in orchards where simazine is the only preemergence herbicide used. The thick, flattened stems of fall panicum may be erect, but more commonly are spreading. Leaves are rolled in the budshoot. No auricles are present. The ligule is a dense fringe of hairs.

Witchgrass, *Panicum capillare*

Witchgrass, also called tumbleweed grass, ticklegrass, and witches' hair, occurs commonly in orchards grown on sandy soils. Mature witchgrass plants are bushy and branched at the base, and have a fuzzy appearance. The large, highly branched flower heads break off easily when mature, and blow around in the wind. The stem, leaf sheath, and leaf of witchgrass are covered with long, coarse hairs. The ligule is a fringe of hairs.

Summer Annual Broadleaves

Common Knotweed, *Polygonum arenastrum*

Common knotweed, also known as prostrate knotweed, grows well in most orchards and may build up under a total mowing program. It becomes troublesome if it invades tree rows, where it competes for moisture during summer months. Mature knotweed plants may be prostrate or erect. Stems are thin, tough, and extensively branched. The tough stems may become entangled in cultivation equipment.

> **Q.** Seed leaves of common knotweed are long, narrow, and rounded at the tip, and have whitish streaks or blotches. The true leaves are much more broad, and emerge from a membranous sheath that encircles the stem. Nodes usually are swollen.

Puncturevine, *Tribulus terrestris*

Puncturevine plants are prostrate in open areas, but grow erect in dense vegetation. Single yellow flowers arise from leaf axils. At maturity, the fruit breaks apart into five nutlets, each of which has two hard, sharp spines. Puncturevine is drought-resistant and its seed burs are easily disseminated on shoes or vehicle tires. This weed frequently invades tree rows after its seed is deposited by equipment working the row middle. Mature plants are harder to control than the seedlings, but the seeds can germinate beyond the effective depth of some preemergence herbicides. A stem and seed weevil that attacks puncturevine controls populations of the weed more effectively in undisturbed areas than in cultivated situations.

> **R.** Puncturevine seed leaves are thick, elongated, and brittle. They are grayish below and green above, with a groove along the prominent midvein. True leaves have 8 to 12 leaflets.

Common Purslane, *Portulaca oleracea*

Common purslane occurs commonly in orchards on coarse-textured soils and grows rapidly under both wet and dry conditions. It forms a mat of highly branched, reddish stems up to 3 feet (1 m) long that may be prostrate or may stand up to 1 foot (30 cm) tall. The thick, succulent growth can create a moist environment favorable to crown diseases if infestations develop around the bases of trees. Yellow, cup-shaped flowers usually are open only in the morning. Horse purslane, *Trianthema portulacastrum*, is similar to common purslane but has broader leaves and purple flowers. Hand weeding or spot-treatment with a postemergence herbicide may be needed to control purslane that emerges after preemergence herbicides have broken down.

Horseweed, *Conyza canadensis*

Horseweed, also known as mare's tail, is a common weed in California orchards, cultivated fields, and disturbed areas.

Q. Common knotweed seedling

R. Puncturevine seedling

S. Horseweed

T. Horseweed seedling

U. Hairy fleabane

Because it is tolerant to most herbicides available for use in stone fruits, it may increase over time. If left undisturbed, the plants can grow big enough to interfere with orchard activities.

S. Undisturbed horseweed plants grow up to 10 feet (3 m) tall, branching near the top. Small flower heads with yellow centers form at the ends of the branches. Horseweed plants are shorter and more highly branched if mowed, and may be confused with hairy fleabane. Horseweed leaves are dark green, while leaves of hairy fleabane are grayish green. Also, horseweed flowers are yellow and more showy than the whitish flowers of hairy fleabane.

T. The seed leaves and first true leaves of both horseweed and hairy fleabane are oval, narrowing to a stalk at the base. Later leaves are narrower. These two related species are difficult to distinguish in the seedling stage.

Hairy Fleabane, *Conyza bonariensis*

Hairy fleabane is a close relative of horseweed and is often found growing in the same locations. It is more tolerant of available preemergence herbicides and can produce seed after several mowings. The stiff stems can interfere with orchard activities such as the movement of irrigation pipes or drip lines.

U. Mature hairy fleabane plants are 1½ to 3 feet (0.5 to 1 m) tall and highly branched with very narrow leaves. Numerous flower stalks form on the upper parts of branches. The small, dull white flowers are not showy.

Cover Crops

An orchard cover crop can consist of the resident vegetation, one or more seeded cover crops, or a blend of resident and seeded vegetation. Which cover crops will work best in your orchard is determined by the irrigation system, the stone fruit, the age of the orchard, the soil conditions, the location, and the weather. If you use flood or sprinkler irrigation, you will have more cover crop options than if you use drip or microsprinkler systems. For information on which cover crops are best suited to your own situation, consult with cover crop specialists and your local farm advisor.

Cover crops have a number of advantages. They can attract beneficial insects and allow natural enemies of a number of stone fruit pests to build up, but they must be managed to get the beneficials to move into orchard trees without causing problems with pests such as stink bugs, lygus bugs, and thrips that may also move into trees. Legume cover crops contribute to the stone fruit's seasonal nitrogen requirement if worked into the soil. Deep-rooted plants such as grasses improve water penetration and reduce soil erosion. Water consumption by grass cover crops helps dry the soil in late winter; this is particularly beneficial in orchards with heavy soils where root and crown diseases such as Phytophthora root and crown rot are likely to be problems. Cover crops should always be kept away from the trunks of trees, or they may increase problems with Phytophthora root and crown rot. Some cover crops may reduce populations of harmful nematode species. By providing a firmer surface, cover crops can make orchard activities such as ground spraying possible under wet conditions. Cover crops help reduce dusty conditions that favor mite pests. Competition from desirable cover crop species helps keep weeds from building up.

Cover crops can also have a negative impact on pest management in stone fruits. Legume cover crops attract pocket gophers and plant bugs that may damage stone fruits. Flowering cover crops attract flower thrips, which can damage nectarine and plum fruit and may contribute to the spread of pollen-borne viruses to stone fruit trees. By tilling or mowing these cover crops before the stone fruits bloom, you can help prevent thrips damage and virus spread. Cover crops that attract stink bugs may cause problems, especially in peaches. If you do not till or mow such cover crops before fruit are on the trees, you may need to take measures to control stink bugs on the cover crops in order to prevent damage. Some clover species are hosts to the pathogen that causes X-disease; avoid these cover crops for cherry orchards. Cover crops that allow root knot nematode populations to build up may negate the benefits of nematode-resistant rootstocks, which prevent the multiplication of root knot nematodes but are susceptible to infestation. If not properly managed, cover crops can lead to increases in relative humidity, longer periods of wetness, and lower temperatures that may be conducive to development of a number of diseases. Dense cover crops, especially grasses, favor the buildup of voles, which can cause severe damage to orchard trees. Perennial legume cover crops can be difficult to control once they are established, and they become competitive with trees.

Table 28 lists a number of cover crops, their horticultural characteristics, and their effects on pest problems in stone fruits. More information about cover crops can be found in *Covercrops for California Agriculture*, listed in the references.

Table 28. Cover Crops and Their Effects on Pest Management in Stone Fruits.

Cover crop	Horticultural benefits and requirements	Effects on arthropod pests and natural enemies	Effects on diseases and nematode pests	Effects on weeds and vertebrate pests
ANNUAL LEGUMES				
bell bean *Vicia faba*	N contribution[1]: 50–200 lb tolerates high and low pH tolerates some high mowing for frost control roots penetrate 2–3 feet depending on moisture plant early to mid-fall flowers 40–60 days after planting	populations of predaceous wasps, aphid predators may attract plant bugs flower thrips may build up	host for root knot nematodes[2] SRN[3]	not competitive with weeds; best mixed with annual grass or vetch
berseem clover *Trifolium alexandrinum*	N contribution[1]: 50–400 lb tolerates high pH and salinity tolerates close mowing; frequent mowing recommended best adapted to mild winters; can be grown as a summer annual in colder areas roots penetrate upper 2 feet plant early fall; will reseed flowers May–June	high populations of bigeyed bugs may attract plant bugs flower thrips may build up	host for root knot nematodes[2] SRN[3] host for X-disease and leafhopper vectors	highly competitive with weeds, especially when mowed frequently attractive to rabbits
crimson clover *Trifolium incarnatum*	N contribution[1]: 70–140 lb tolerates mowing to 3–5 inches tolerates wide range of climatic and soil conditions plant early fall; will reseed if moisture adequate in spring flowers April–May	high populations of minute pirate bugs and aphid natural enemies lygus bug populations lower than vetch flower thrips may build up	host for root knot nematodes[2] SRN[3] host for X-disease and leafhopper vectors	competitive with weeds
rose clover *Trifolium hirtum*	N contribution[1]: 50–100 lb tolerates mowing to 2–4 inches tolerates acid soil, poor fertility does not tolerate flooding taproot penetrates over 6 feet plant early fall; will reseed flowers March–May	high populations of minute pirate bugs high populations of lygus bugs high populations of flower thrips	host for root knot nematodes[2] SRN[3] host for X-disease and leafhopper vectors	poor competitor unless mowed frequently weed control improved by mowing to 2–4 inches will control summer weeds after seed set if mowed

Table 28 continued.

Cover crop	Horticultural benefits and requirements	Effects on arthropod pests and natural enemies	Effects on diseases and nematode pests	Effects on weeds and vertebrate pests
subterranean clover *Trifolium subterraneum*	N contribution[1]: 50–200 lb tolerates mowing to 2–4 inches plant early fall; will reseed mowing improves establishment and seed production cultivars range in maturity from April to May	buildup of bigeyed bugs relatively low populations of lygus bugs populations of spider mites may build up flower thrips may build up	host for all major root knot nematodes[2] SRN[3] host for X-disease and leafhopper vectors	competes well with weeds if mowed frequently mowing needed during establishment
sweet clovers *Melilotus* spp.	N contribution[1]: 70–165 lb does not tolerate shade strong taproot may help penetrate clay pans biennials, flower May–September seldom used as cover crop in California	populations of predaceous wasps and some general predators may attract plant bugs flower thrips may build up	host for root knot nematodes[2] SRN[3] host for X-disease and leafhopper vectors	poor weed control unless combined with other cover crops foliage toxic to rodents and livestock
annual medics *Medicago* spp.	N contribution[1]: 50–100 lb frequent mowing to 3–5 inches to increase weed competition and seed set works well in mixes with grasses or other legumes flowers February through May, depending on species	very high populations of lygus bugs high populations of spider mites	host for root knot nematodes[2] SRN[3] some species host X-disease and leafhopper vectors	competes with weeds when mowed to 3–5 inches
Cahaba white vetch *Vicia sativa* × *V. cordata*	N contribution[1]: about 100 lb tolerates low mowing in March and April for frost protection taproot penetrates 3–5 feet plant in fall, flowers April–July; will reseed may require spring irrigation to set seed performs well in prune orchards	attracts a variety of beneficials high populations of lygus bugs high populations of spider mites flower thrips may build up	non-host for most harmful nematode species host for northern root knot nematode host for ring nematode non-host for X-disease	highly competitive with weeds habitat for voles, rabbits food source and habitat for gophers
hairy vetch *Vicia villosa*	N contribution[1]: 60–100 lb tolerates mowing to 1–2 inches before flowering taproot penetrates 1–3 feet more drought tolerant than other vetches range of varieties adapted to different areas plant mid-fall; will reseed	high populations of flower thrips	host for root knot nematodes[1] SRN[3] host status for X-disease unknown	highly competitive with weeds provides habitat for voles, rabbits food source and habitat for gophers
purple vetch *Vicia benghalensis*	N contribution[1]: 50–300 lb tolerates moderately close mowing in winter persists well on heavy soils root system penetrates 3 feet plant in early fall, flowers April–May; will reseed may require spring irrigation to set seed	high populations of general predators relatively low lygus populations high populations of *Calocoris norvegicus* high populations of spider mites flower thrips may build up	rank growth increases orchard humidity and potential for foliar diseases host for root knot nematodes[2] SRN[3] host status for X-disease unknown	highly competitive with weeds provides habitat for voles, rabbits food source and habitat for gophers
woollypod vetch *Vicia dasycarpa*	N contribution[1]: 50–200 lb tolerates mowing to 5 inches tolerates a range of soil types flowers March–May; will reseed if not mowed for frost protection	aphid predators, minute pirate bugs high populations of lygus bugs high populations of flower thrips	host for root knot nematodes[2] SRN[3] host status for X-disease unknown	highly competitive with weeds provides habitat for voles, rabbits food source and habitat for gophers
PERENNIAL LEGUMES				
strawberry clover *Trifolium fragiferum*	N contribution[1]: 100–300 lb low-growing, can be mowed frequently tolerates heat, full sun, low moisture, alkaline soil root system penetrates 3 feet plant in fall or spring, flowers May–June works well in mix with white clover and grass	relatively low populations of beneficials may attract plant bugs flower thrips may build up	host for northern root knot nematode, poor host for other species host for ring nematode host for X-disease and leafhopper vector	highly competitive with weeds favors high populations of pocket gophers

Table 28 continued.

Cover crop	Horticultural benefits and requirements	Effects on arthropod pests and natural enemies	Effects on diseases and nematode pests	Effects on weeds and vertebrate pests
white clover *Trifolium repens*	N contribution[1]: 100–200 lb some cultivars are low-growing and more tolerant of frequent mowing tolerates shade root system mainly in top 2 feet plant in fall, flowers April– December	attractive to lygus bugs flower thrips may build up prone to high spider mite populations	host for root knot nematodes[2] SRN[3] host for X-disease and leafhopper vectors host for tomato ringspot virus	competitive with weeds if mowed or grazed spring planting recommended if winter weeds abundant favors high populations of pocket gophers

ANNUAL GRASSES

Cover crop	Horticultural benefits and requirements	Effects on arthropod pests and natural enemies	Effects on diseases and nematode pests	Effects on weeds and vertebrate pests
barley *Hordeum vulgare*	accumulates ca 40 lb N/acre[4] cultivars available for all growing areas, fairly drought tolerant mowing delays and prolongs flowering strong root system penetrates over 6 feet crop residue improves water infiltration rate plant in fall or winter, flowers April–July; does not reseed well	aphid natural enemies build up on grain aphids not harmful to stone fruits may reduce root lesion nematode populations	host for root knot nematodes[2] reduces *P. vulnus* populations but not other root lesion spp. host for ring nematode	highly competitive with weeds when seeded at high rate mow or till before seed set to avoid attracting rodents
Blando brome (soft chess) *Bromus mollis*	adapted to all areas below 3,000 feet tolerates mowing to 2 inches for frost protection; stop mowing by early April for seed set improves soil tilth when mowed or cultivated plant in early fall; will reseed	aphid natural enemies may build up on grain aphids not harmful to stone fruits	relatively poor host for root knot nematodes[2] host for ring nematode	highly competitive with weeds
annual fescue *Festuca megalura* *F. myuros*	adapted to wide range of soils and climates tolerates frequent mowing until flowering fibrous root system improves water infiltration and soil structure plant mid-fall, flowers March–June; will reseed if not mowed after flowering begins	harbors few beneficials		highly competitive with weeds
oats *Avena sativa*	accumulates about 12 lb N/acre[4] less tolerant of drought and cold than other cereals fibrous root system improves soil drainage plant fall to mid-winter, flowers April–May	natural enemies of aphids build up on grain aphids not harmful to stone fruits	host for root knot nematodes[2]	less competitive than barley; better as a companion crop with a legume such as vetch or bell bean
cereal rye *Secale cerealis*	accumulates ca 15 lb N/acre[4] good for reducing nitrate leaching tolerates wide range of soil and climatic conditions fibrous root system improves soil drainage, best cereal crop for this purpose tolerates close mowing in winter mow or till while stems still sweet to minimize tie-up of N plant late fall, flowers April–May	natural enemies of aphids build up on grain aphids not harmful to stone fruits	host for root knot nematodes[2]	highly competitive with weeds works well as a companion crop with legumes
annual ryegrass *Lolium multiflorum* *L. rigidum*	accumulates ca 25 lb N/acre[4] excellent for reducing nitrate leaching does well on heavy soils fibrous root system good for improving soil drainage tolerates close mowing in winter plant in fall, flowers May–June; will reseed	harbors few beneficials	reduces *Verticillium* levels in soil when grown without broadleaf companions	highly competitive with weeds works well as a companion crop with legumes

Table 28 continued.

Cover crop	Horticultural benefits and requirements	Effects on arthropod pests and natural enemies	Effects on diseases and nematode pests	Effects on weeds and vertebrate pests
Sudan grass *Sorghum sudanense*	summer annual useful for improving soil structure can be mowed or flailed several times during growing season	grain aphids and associated beneficials host for southern green stink bug	host for northern root knot nematode, M. *hapla* reduces P. *vulnus* reduces ring nematode may reduce levels of soilborne pathogens when worked in as green manure	Good suppression of summer annual weeds

1. Actual amount of nitrogen made available to orchard depends on growing conditions, how much of the cover crop biomass is worked into the soil, and when the cover crop is worked in.
2. Planting cover crops in fall after soil temperature is below 64°F (18°C) or turning under the cover crop before soil temperature reaches 60°F (15°C) in the spring will prevent increase of root knot nematode populations.
3. SRN = suspected host for ring nematode.
4. Grasses reduce soil nitrogen levels, accumulating the N in their biomass. Most of the N is released back into the soil when the grass cover crop decomposes.

Much of the information in this table was obtained from the cover crops database that is available under Cover Crop Resources at the University of California Sustainable Agriculture Research and Education Project's World Wide Web Site: http://www.sarep.ucdavis.edu/

Vertebrates

Vertebrates that can cause significant damage in stone fruit orchards include rodents (pocket gophers, ground squirrels, and voles), rabbits, deer, and birds. Mammals are potentially more serious pests than birds because they can cause long-term damage by killing or seriously stunting the growth of trees. The burrowing of pocket gophers and ground squirrels can also interfere with management activities in the orchard such as mowing and irrigating. In well-managed orchards where mammal pest problems are kept under control, birds may become the most serious vertebrate pests because they are difficult to control. Several bird species can reduce fruit yield by feeding on ripening fruit or destroying flower buds during the dormant season.

The vertebrate pest problems in a given orchard are determined in large part by the orchard's location. Rodents are potential pests in all orchards, but they are more likely to invade orchards next to rangeland or unmanaged areas, where their populations may build up unchecked. Orchards adjacent to wild areas are more likely to be damaged by species such as rabbits, deer, and birds that live in these areas and move into orchards to feed. Orchard management activities also have some effect on vertebrate pest problems; for example, flood irrigation and total cultivation may help discourage the buildup of gopher and ground squirrel populations within the orchard.

Managing Vertebrate Pests

Successful management programs for all vertebrate pests involve four basic steps:

- identifying the damaging species

- assessing management options

- implementing appropriate control actions

- monitoring to detect reinfestation or reinvasion of the orchard

Observation and Identification. If you are going to choose an appropriate control action, it is critical that you correctly identify the species causing the damage. In the case of birds, you need to use direct observation to distinguish between nonharmful species that frequent orchards and birds that actually cause damage. Deer, ground squirrels, and rabbits all may chew small branches off newly planted trees; in these cases you can observe signs such as tracks, feces, and burrows to identify the cause of the damage. The descriptions, line drawings, and photographs in the following sections will help you identify vertebrate pests that are causing problems in your orchards. Several publications listed in the references have more information on vertebrate identification and biology.

Habitat Modification. Changes to the environment in and around the orchard may affect vertebrate pest problems and their management. Brush piles near the orchard often provide shelter and resting places for ground squirrels, rabbits, and birds; by removing brush piles, you can reduce bird activity in the orchard and make it easier to observe and take control actions against ground squirrels. Weedy areas provide a habitat for buildup of vole populations; by eliminating weeds around trees and maintaining a weed-free zone around orchards, you can greatly reduce problems with voles. Certain types of flood irrigation and regular cultivation of the orchard floor discourage the buildup of pocket gopher and ground squirrel populations in the orchard, but will not eliminate them. Certain ground covers are attractive to pocket gophers and voles, so you can practice careful management of orchard floor vegetation in conjunction with other controls to reduce gopher problems.

Control Actions. For most vertebrate pests, more than one control method is available to reduce damaging populations. Table 29 lists control options you can use against important vertebrate pests in stone fruit orchards. Details on how to use these controls are given in the pest sections that follow. It is a good idea to consult your county agricultural commissioner before you use any of these controls to find out which procedures work best in your location and what the latest restrictions are on these techniques. The timing of control actions is often critical, and is determined in large part by the life cycle of the target pest. Become familiar with the biology of the vertebrate pests affecting your orchards and the available control options so you will be able to plan the most effective management strategies.

You can take a number of steps when preparing and planting the orchard to prevent or reduce potential problems with certain vertebrates. Properly installed fencing will protect young trees against deer and rabbits. Deep plowing and discing will destroy or disperse resident vole populations and destroy much of the burrow systems of pocket gophers and ground squirrels, reducing the risk of reinvasion. A vegetation-free zone around the orchard will greatly reduce the risk of invasion by voles. Take steps to eliminate pocket gopher and ground squirrel populations before you plant the orchard. Trapping, baiting, shooting, or burrow fumigation can be used, depending on the pest involved and the situation. Tree guards will protect against damage by rabbits and, to some degree, by voles.

Once the orchard is in place, you should develop and implement some type of management program to address any vertebrate pest problems that may arise.

Monitoring. Follow the recommendations in the pest sections below on when and how to monitor for specific vertebrate pests. After you take a control action, establish a routine monitoring program to assess the effectiveness of the control and to detect any reinvasion. Keep detailed records of the procedures you use and their effects on vertebrate activity. These will help you plan future control strategies.

Biological Control. Vertebrate populations are affected most by the availability of food and cover, while diseases and predators play a relatively minor role. A number of predators such as hawks, owls, foxes, coyotes, and snakes feed on some of the vertebrates species that can become orchard pests. However, natural enemies seldom keep vertebrate pests from reaching damaging levels. Take precautions to avoid harming predators when you use toxic baits or traps. Nesting boxes for raptors such as barn owls have been installed in orchards by some growers in the hope that this will increase predation of small mammal pests such as gophers. There is no evidence that this has a measurable impact on pest numbers.

Table 29. Control Methods for Vertebrate Pests of Stone Fruits.

PEST	Trapping	Baiting	Fencing	Tree protectors	Repellents	Frightening	Shooting	Fumigating
ground squirrels	■	■					■	■
pocket gophers	■	■						■
voles (meadow mice)		■		■				
rabbits	■[1]	■	■	■	■		■	
deer			■		■	■	■[1]	
birds	■[1]					■	■	

1. Useful for some species.

Endangered Species Restrictions. In some areas of the Central Valley, stone fruit orchards may be located within the range of federally protected endangered species. The species likely to be of concern are the San Joaquin kit fox, several species of kangaroo rats, and, where burrow fumigants are used, the blunt-nosed leopard lizard. See the composite map showing ranges of these species (Figure 64). Special restrictions apply to the use of toxic baits and fumigants for vertebrate pest control in these areas; these restrictions are described briefly in Table 30. Your county agricultural commissioner has the latest detailed maps that show the ranges of endangered species and the latest information on restrictions that apply to pest control activities in those areas. You also can get more information on endangered species regulations from the California Department of Pesticide Regulation's World Wide Web site (http://www.cdpr.ca.gov/).

Figure 64. Distribution of endangered species in California. This is a composite of current maps showing approximate locations of endangered species that may affect pest management options in or near orchards. Check with the county agricultural commissioner for the latest information regarding restrictions that may apply to a specific location.

Table 30. Restrictions on the Use of Toxic Baits and Burrow Fumigants within the Ranges of Endangered Species.

Control	Endangered species	Restrictions
burrow fumigants	all	Use must be supervised by someone trained to distinguish burrows or dens of target species from those of nontarget species. Contact your county agricultural commissioner for information on training.
toxic baits	kangaroo rats	Use of toxic baits is prohibited unless: • used in bait stations specially designed for kangaroo rats (see Figure 65) OR • bait stations are elevated to prevent access by kangaroo rats (Figure 66) and designed to prevent spillage OR • bait is placed in stations only during daylight hours and removed or station entrances closed by dusk OR • bait is broadcast in areas under active cultivation that are separated from native vegetation by at least 10 yards of untreated, cultivated ground.
	San Joaquin kit fox	Bait station design: openings not to exceed 3 inches in diameter, designed to control spillage, staked to prevent tipping, not filled beyond capacity and never with more than 10 pounds of bait. Bait station monitoring: must be monitored for signs of spillage, tampering, moisture, and depletion; kept replenished; bait removed immediately after feeding ceases. Resumption of baiting: minimum of 2 weeks before baiting can be resumed. Carcass survey: begin monitoring for carcasses 3 days after baiting started and until at least 5 days after baiting stopped. Handle carcasses carefully to avoid contact with parasites such as fleas and ticks. Bury carcasses deep enough to be inaccessible to wildlife. Prebaiting: prebaiting with untreated bait is recommended to make baiting more effective and shorten the time required for baiting. Broadcast baiting: active ingredient no greater than 0.01%; apply only after prebaiting with untreated bait and determining that untreated bait is taken; do not pile bait or place directly in burrows; survey for carcasses as described above. Pelletized baits: can be used for ground squirrels only in bait stations; cannot be used for rabbits. Jackrabbit control: self-dispensing bait stations, used according to above restrictions, can be used only where rabbits are active.

Information compiled from U.S. Environmental Protection Agency draft documents *Protecting Endangered Species Interim Measures for Use of Burrow Fumigants* and *Protecting Endangered Species Interim Measures for Use of Grain Bait or Pelletized Rodenticides,* October 7, 1996. Restrictions pertaining to specific locations can be found on the World Wide Web at www.cdpr.ca.gov/docs/es/index.htm and in rodenticide county bulletins available from agricultural commissioners' offices.

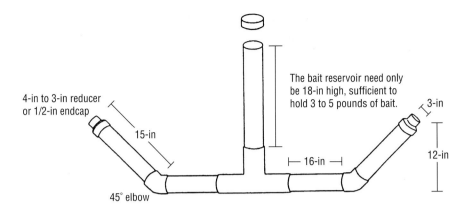

4-in to 3-in reducer
or 1/2-in endcap

15-in

45° elbow

The bait reservoir need only
be 18-in high, sufficient to
hold 3 to 5 pounds of bait.

16-in

3-in

12-in

Materials required for Modifications

30-in PVC pipe (4-in diameter)
2 45° elbows
2 4-in to 3-in reducers or 1/2-in endcaps

Figure 65. Bait station design for use within range of endangered kangaroo rats.

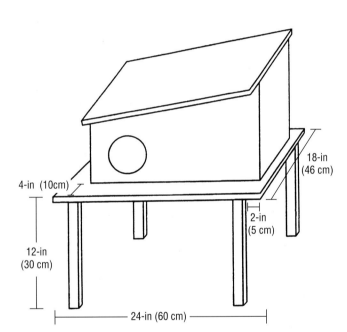

4-in (10cm)

18-in
(46 cm)

2-in
(5 cm)

12-in
(30 cm)

24-in (60 cm)

Materials (others may be substituted)
Legs: 1.5-in x 1.5-in pine
Platform: 18-in x 24-in x 3/4-in exterior plywood
Bait box: see *Vertebrate Pest Control Handbook*, J. P. Clark
(Ed.) 1994. California Department of Food and Agriculture.

Figure 66. Platform design for elevating bait station to prevent access by kangaroo rats.

The California ground squirrel has mottled dark and light brown or gray fur and a long tail that is somewhat bushy. One subspecies (*shown here*) found in northern California has a dark patch on its back.

Ground squirrels often dig burrows at the base of a tree when they invade an orchard. Their burrows have large, conspicuous openings that are not plugged.

Ground Squirrels
Spermophilus beecheyi

Ground squirrels can be troublesome vertebrate pests of stone fruits in all growing areas. Ground squirrels climb trees to take green fruit often for the seeds, and will feed on ripening fruit later in the season. Burrow systems in the orchard may interfere with the even distribution of irrigation water and the activity of orchard equipment such as mowers. Ground squirrels may damage drip lines by chewing on them, and can occasionally girdle scaffolds or trees by chewing the bark from limbs or tree trunks. Flood-irrigated orchards tend to have somewhat fewer problems with ground squirrels than orchards irrigated with drip or micro-sprinklers.

The adult California ground squirrel has a head and body 9 to 11 inches (22 to 28 cm) long and a somewhat bushy tail that is about as long as the body. The fur is mottled dark and light brown or gray. Ground squirrels dig burrows along ditches and fence rows and in uncultivated areas. In orchards, they often dig the entrances to their burrow systems near the bases of trees. Ground squirrels live in colonies that may grow very large if left uncontrolled. They are active only during the day; during warmer months, they usually are most active in morning and late afternoon.

Ground squirrels hibernate during the winter, emerging around January in warmer locations such as the southern San Joaquin Valley and in February or March in cooler locations of the northern Sacramento Valley and foothills. In spring the squirrels feed on green vegetation, including new growth on trees. They switch to seeds and fruit in early summer as vegetation dries up. Females have one litter, averaging 8 young, in the spring. The young squirrels emerge from the burrow after about 6 weeks. Adults often go into a temporary dormant state (*aestivation* or *estivation*) during the hottest part of the summer. Young ground squirrels do not aestivate their first summer, and some may not hibernate during their first winter. Figure 67 illustrates the periods of activity for the California ground squirrel.

Management Guidelines

The type of control action needed for ground squirrels depends primarily on the time of year at which the control is to be undertaken. Choice of control action is also influenced by the location of the infestation and the number of squirrels present. Watch for signs of squirrel activity within the orchard, especially the appearance of burrows, during routine orchard activities. Check the perimeter of the orchard at least once a month during the times of year when squirrels are active. Mid-morning usually is the best time of day for observing squirrel activity. Keep records of the approximate number of squirrels you see and the location and number of burrows.

To keep populations from increasing, begin to apply controls as soon as you see burrowing activity within the orchard. Select the control method best suited for the time of

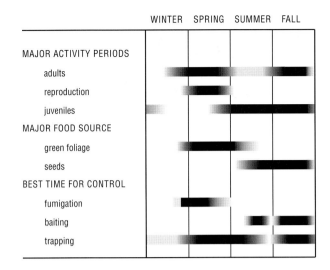

Figure 67. Activity periods and preferred food sources for the California ground squirrel. Activity periods vary somewhat from one growing area to another, depending on local climate. To choose the most effective control action for ground squirrels and the proper timing you need to know when they are active and what their preferred food sources are.

Figure 68. Conibear traps are placed over the entrance to ground squirrel burrows. Secure traps with a stake.

year. Where large numbers of squirrels are moving into the orchard to feed, baiting or trapping along the perimeter offers the most effective control. If you have access to nearby infestations, try baiting, trapping, or burrow fumigation. The most effective time of year to control ground squirrels is in early spring when adults have emerged but before they have reproduced. Begin control about 3 weeks after the first squirrels emerge from hibernation.

Removal of brush piles, stumps, and debris in and around the orchard may to some extent help limit the buildup of squirrel populations, but it will certainly make it easier for you to monitor squirrel activity. Ground squirrels quickly occupy abandoned burrow systems. After controlling squirrel infestations outside your orchard, use thorough cultivation or deep plowing to destroy burrow entrances and help slow the rate of reinvasion.

Traps. Trapping is an effective tool for controlling small populations of squirrels, and can be used any time of year when squirrels are active. The most commonly used ground squirrel traps are kill traps such as the Conibear trap or box trap. The most attractive baits to use for ground squirrel traps are walnuts, almonds, oats, barley, and melon rinds.

Conibear traps most commonly are placed unbaited over the burrow entrance (Figure 68), where they trap squirrels as they leave the burrow. Place the trap near the burrow entrance for a few days without setting so the squirrels will become used to it, and then set it. If you are using this type of trap within the range of the San Joaquin kit fox, you must place the trap in a covered box with an entrance no larger than 3 inches wide to exclude the fox. Place bait in the box with the trap, but don't set the trap for a few days until squirrels are entering the box regularly to take the bait.

Box traps are also effective against ground squirrels (Figure 69). Place the bait inside the trap well behind the trigger or tied to it. Bait the traps without setting them for several days until squirrels become used to taking the bait. Then put in fresh bait and set the traps. Box traps can be placed in pairs (Figure 69), in groups, or inside larger boxes. Place the traps so that nontarget animals are not likely to be caught—for example, inside a larger box with openings just large enough for ground squirrels.

Fumigants. Fumigation can be very effective against ground squirrel populations, used either before squirrels reproduce or when baits are relatively ineffective. The best time to start fumigation is in the late winter or early spring, after squirrels have emerged from hibernation. At this time the squirrels are active and the soil is moist. Fumigation is not effective when squirrels are hibernating or aestivating, because at those times they seal off their burrows. Fumigation is much less effective when soil is dry, because more of the fumigant can escape from the burrows through cracks in the soil. When using a fumigant, be sure to treat all active burrow systems in and around the orchard. Recheck all areas a few days after fumigation, and retreat any that have been reopened. Do not use fumigants on burrow systems that are adjacent to or may open under buildings.

Gas cartridges provide an easy and relatively safe way to fumigate ground squirrel burrows. They are available commercially and from some agricultural commissioners. Use one or two cartridges for each burrow that shows signs of activity. More than two may be needed for a large burrow system. Quickly shove the ignited cartridges into the burrow, using a shovel handle or stick, and seal the burrow entrance with soil. Watch nearby burrow entrances, and seal any that begin to leak smoke.

Aluminum phosphide* is the most effective fumigant when used early in the spring when soil moisture is high. Application personnel should be trained in the material's proper use and on its potential hazards when misused. When aluminum phosphide pellets come into contact with moist soil in the burrow they produce phosphine gas, which is highly toxic to any animal.

Baits. Poison bait is usually the most cost-effective method for controlling ground squirrels, especially for large populations. A bait consists of grain treated with a poison registered for ground squirrel control. To be effective, the bait must be used at a time of year when ground squirrels are feeding on seeds and will readily accept grain baits. In and around stone fruit orchards, begin to place bait in mid- to late spring, before squirrels begin to feed on fruit. Once squirrels start taking fruit, it may be difficult to entice them with grain baits. Before you use baits, place small amounts of untreated grain near burrows to see if the squirrels will take it. If the grain is taken, proceed with baiting. If it is not taken, wait several days or a week and try again. As the season progresses, you may have to wait until the crop is harvested before the ground squirrels will take bait again. Check with local county authorities about proper timing for your area.

Multiple-dose anticoagulant baits can be applied in bait stations or as spot treatments near burrows, or they can be broadcast over larger infested areas. For these baits to be effective, animals must feed on them for several consecutive days. Anticoagulant baits often are preferred because they are very effective, they do not produce bait shyness, and they are relatively safe for humans, pets, and livestock. Bait stations are used most commonly in orchards to provide bait for ground squirrels. You must use bait stations if spot or broadcast applications are not specified on the bait label.

Various kinds of bait stations can be used, all of them designed to let squirrels in but to exclude larger animals. One design is made of PVC pipe (Figure 70). Make the openings about 3 to 4 inches (7.5 to 10 cm) in diameter and use baffles to keep the bait inside the station. Special types of stations must be used within the ranges of the San Joaquin kit fox or kangaroo rat to ensure that these endangered species are

* Restricted-use material. Permit required for purchase or use.

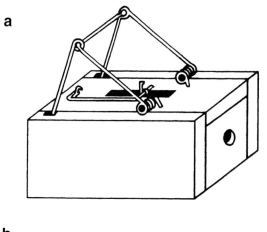

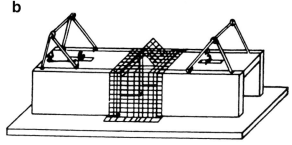

Figure 69. Single box-type traps (a) can be used for ground squirrels. They can be used in pairs by removing the backs, connecting the two traps with wire mesh, and attaching them to a board (b).

Figure 70. Four-inch plastic pipe can be used to construct a bait station for ground squirrels. Three-inch pipe must be used within the range of the San Joaquin kit fox. Place baffles inside the pipe to keep bait inside the station. Some bait labels restrict the kind of material that can be used for constructing bait stations.

excluded (see Table 30 and Figures 65 and 66). Place bait stations near runways or burrows and secure them so they cannot easily be tipped over. If squirrels are moving into the orchard from adjacent areas, place bait stations along the perimeter of the orchard where squirrels are invading, one station every 100 feet (30 m). Use more stations when the number of squirrels is high. Check bait stations daily at first, then as often as needed to keep the bait replenished. If bait feeding is interrupted, the bait's effectiveness is greatly decreased. Replace bait that is wet or moldy. Successful baiting usually requires 2 to 4 weeks. Continue to supply bait until feeding ceases and you observe no squirrels, and then properly dispose of unused bait.

When so specified on the label, anticoagulant baits can be applied as spot-treatments, which are the most economical and effective for small populations. Scatter one handful of bait (a pound is about ten handfuls) evenly over 40 to 50 square feet near active burrows. Reapply every 4 or 5 days for a total of 4 or 5 applications to make sure there is no interruption in exposure to the bait. Scattering takes advantage of the ground squirrels' natural foraging behavior and minimizes the risk to nontarget species. Never pile the bait on the ground; this would increase the hazard to livestock and nontarget wildlife.

Bait containing zinc phosphide,* an acute poison, can be applied as spot-treatments to control ground squirrels during the nonbearing season or outside of orchards. The bait can be scattered over a 2- to 3-square-foot area around each burrow opening. Be sure to check for bait acceptance before you apply the bait. Assess the potential hazards to humans, livestock, and wildlife before using this type of bait; if it is risky, use some other method to control ground squirrels. After treatment, dispose of carcasses whenever possible to prevent poisoning of dogs or scavengers.

Neither spot-treatments nor broadcast applications of poison baits can be used in orchards when fruit is present or in areas that are within the range of certain endangered species.

Pocket Gophers
Thomomys spp.

Pocket gophers are potentially serious orchard pests in all growing areas, especially in young orchards. Herbaceous cover crops, especially legumes, are their preferred food, but they also feed on the bark of tree crowns and roots, girdling and killing young trees and reducing the vigor of older trees. Gophers sometimes damage drip irrigation lines. Burrow systems may divert irrigation water, causing water stress to younger trees and increasing soil erosion. The mounds of soil pushed out of burrows may interfere with mowing or other orchard activities.

Adult pocket gophers are 6 to 8 inches (15 to 20 cm) long with stout yellowish or grayish brown bodies and small ears and eyes. They rarely are seen above ground, spending most of their time in a system of tunnels they construct 6 to 18 inches (15 to 45 cm) beneath the surface. A single burrow system can cover several hundred square feet, and consists of main tunnels with lateral branches used for feeding or to push excavated soil to the surface. The conspicuous, fan-shaped mounds that are formed over the openings of lateral tunnels are the most obvious signs of gopher infestation. Gophers feed primarily on the roots of herbaceous plants, and also clip small plants and pull them into their burrows to feed. Gophers may produce feeding holes and may come above ground to feed on vegetation a few inches from the hole. When they have finished using feeding holes, they plug them with soil, but these holes are inconspicuous because they lack mounds.

Gophers breed throughout the year on irrigated land, with a peak in late winter or early spring. Females may bear as many as three litters each year. When mature, the young may leave their mother's burrow and some may travel above ground to find a favorable location for establishment of their own burrow. Buildup of gopher populations in the orchard is favored by the presence of most cover crops, especially perennial clovers, which are a favored food. When cover crops dry up, gophers may be forced to feed extensively on the bark of tree roots and crowns. Damage to orchard trees is always below ground, and usually is not evident until trees show signs of stress.

Management Guidelines

Monitor for gopher activity in late fall, in winter, and in spring. The best times to check for gophers are in the fall and spring, when mound building activity is at a peak. Monitor monthly in the spring and pay close attention to orchard perimeters, where gophers may move in from adjacent infested areas. Monitor orchards with ground covers more closely, since they are more likely to support gophers and the presence of vegetation may make burrowing activity harder to see. Plan to monitor immediately after you mow, when fresh mounds are easier to see. Look for darker-colored mounds that indicate newly removed soil.

Begin control as soon as you see any gopher activity in the orchard. For infestations that cover a limited area, use traps or hand-applied poison bait. For infestations that cover a large acreage, use a mechanical burrow builder to place bait. Trapping and hand-baiting can be used anytime during the year, but are easier when the soil is moist and not dry and hard. Although mechanical burrow builders can be used anytime if soil conditions are right, the best time is after the first major rains in the fall, when the soil is moist enough to retain the shape of the mechanically constructed burrows. A second treatment can be made in the spring while there still is enough natural moisture in the soil to support an artificial burrow.

Clean cultivation of the orchard floor reduces the food supply and destroys some burrows, making the orchard less habitable for gophers. Clean cultivation also makes it easier

---

* Restricted-use material. Permit required for purchase or use.

Pocket gophers form conspicuous, fan-shaped mounds when excavating. Burrow openings are plugged. The darker soil on some of these mounds indicates fresh activity.

A gopher has chewed the bark from the crown of this cherry tree.

These trees have been girdled by pocket gophers. Similar aboveground symptoms can be caused by root rot and X-disease.

The mechanical bait applicator or burrow builder makes an artificial burrow into which it dispenses poison bait. It is pulled behind a tractor down the middle of orchard rows so the artificial burrow will intersect as many gopher tunnels as possible.

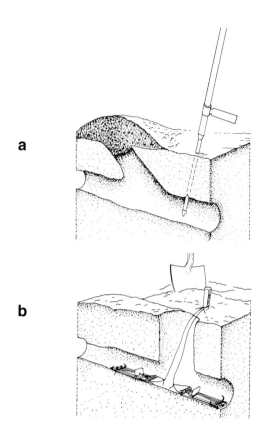

Figure 71. Use a probe to find gopher tunnels for placing traps (a). Begin probing 8 to 12 inches (20 to 30 cm) from the plug side of the mound. The probe will suddenly drop a few inches when you hit the main tunnel. Use a shovel to expose the main tunnel and place two traps in the tunnel, one in each direction (b). Tie the traps to a stake that is tall enough to be seen easily. Push each trap well back into the tunnel and cover the hole so that no light will enter.

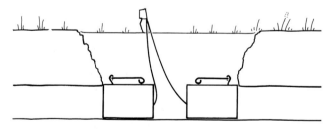

Figure 72. When placing box traps for gopher control, be sure to fill in the openings so that no light will get in after the traps are pushed tightly against the tunnel openings.

to monitor gopher activity. Flood-irrigated orchards may have fewer gopher problems than orchards that are drip- or sprinkler-irrigated. Gopher control in adjacent areas helps keep gophers from moving into the orchard.

Traps. Traps are effective against small numbers of gophers, but are labor intensive and therefore relatively expensive. Either pincer-type or box-type traps can be used.

To place traps you need to use a probe near a fresh mound to find the main tunnel, which usually is on the lower side of the mound (Figure 71a). The main tunnel usually is 8 to 12 inches (20 to 30 cm) deep, and the probe will drop quickly about 2 inches (5 cm) when you find it. If you are using pincer-type traps, place two traps in the main tunnel, one facing each direction (Figure 71b). Box traps also are best placed in the main runway, one facing each way (Figure 72). Be sure to anchor either type of trap to a stake with wire.

If a trap is not visited within 48 hours, move it to a new location. Gophers are solitary animals most of the time, but in the spring more than one gopher may enter a single burrow system. If you trap a gopher at this time, reset the traps in the same tunnel system.

Baits. Apply baits by hand for small infestations or where the use of a mechanical burrow builder is not feasible. Use a probe to find the main tunnel next to a fresh mound or between two fresh mounds, as shown in Figure 71a. Once you find the main tunnel, enlarge the opening so you can drop bait into the burrow. After you place the bait, cover the hole to keep out light and prevent soil from falling onto the bait. Place bait in two or three places along the tunnel. This hand-application method can be used for single-dose or multiple-dose baits. Reservoir-type hand probes designed to deposit single-dose baits are available. Bait application is faster with these devices because they eliminate the need to place the bait by hand. For commercial orchards, single-dose strychnine baits are by far the most cost-effective, although other baits are registered for use. Be sure to follow label directions carefully for application rates and safety considerations.

When large areas are infested, the most economical way to control gophers is to apply bait with a mechanical burrow builder. Burrow builders are tractor-drawn machines that construct artificial tunnels through infested areas, intersecting many gopher tunnels. Single-dose strychnine bait is dropped automatically into the artificial burrows, and gophers find the bait when exploring these new tunnels. Operate burrow builders down row middles within infested orchards and along orchard perimeters where gophers are moving in from adjacent infested areas. Adequate soil moisture is essential for successful burrow building. When operating the machine, periodically check to see that burrows are being formed properly. If possible, wait at least 10 days before running any other equipment over treated areas.

Mechanical burrow builders may not work well on rocky soils; in some mature orchards that have not routinely been deep cultivated, surface roots may be damaged by the burrow builder.

After you use a mechanical burrow builder, follow up with a program of trapping or hand baiting to take care of any misses and to maintain control. Begin about 10 days after mechanical baiting if there are signs of new gopher activity. If the orchard is free of gophers, concentrate your follow-up actions along orchard perimeters where gophers are moving in from adjacent locations.

Fumigants. Most fumigant materials are not effective against gophers because they quickly seal off their tunnels when they detect poison gas. However, aluminum phosphide* can be effective if applied in late winter or early spring when there is ample soil moisture to retain toxic gas, and before the gophers' major breeding period. Follow label instructions and follow all of the safety precautions given. To use aluminum phosphide, first probe to find the main burrow as with hand application of bait, then drop 2 to 4 tablets into the burrow and seal the probe hole. As with other control methods, you need to keep monitoring for signs of renewed gopher activity. Re-treat the area if you find new mounds.

Voles (Meadow Mice)
Microtus spp.

Voles, also called meadow voles or meadow mice, damage trees by feeding on the bark around the base of the tree. Small trees are most susceptible to being completely girdled and killed by voles, but even large trees can be severely damaged or killed. Voles are most likely to cause problems in orchards with year-round cover crops or where you allow dense vegetation to build up around the bases of trees. Vegetation management and the proper use of trunk guards on young trees usually keep damage to a minimum. Baiting is used to control populations that reach harmful levels.

Adult voles are larger than house mice but smaller than rats. They are active all year, both day and night. Females bear several litters each year, with peaks of reproduction in spring and fall. Populations cycle, climaxing every 4 to 7 years and then rapidly declining. Grasses and other dense ground covers provide both food and cover that favor the buildup of vole populations. You can recognize vole activity by the presence of narrow runways in grass or other ground cover and numerous shallow burrows with openings about 1½ inches (4 cm) in diameter. Voles seldom travel far from their burrows and runways.

Management Guidelines

In mid-winter, begin to monitor monthly for active runways in cover crops or weedy areas. Look for fresh vole droppings

* Restricted-use material. Permit required for purchase or use.

The vole (meadow mouse) is gray or brown, with a blunt nose, inconspicuous ears, and a short, slightly hairy tail.

Voles chew the bark off trees just above and below the soil line.

Voles make small, shallow burrows in and around vegetation on the orchard floor.

and short pieces of clipped vegetation, especially grass stems, in runways. Look for burrow openings around the bases of orchard trees. If you find any, remove the soil from around the base of the tree and look for bark damage. Voles usually start chewing on bark about 2 inches (5 cm) below the soil line then move upward. If you do not check carefully, you may not notice damage until late spring or summer, when it may be too late to prevent significant injury to the trees. Be sure to monitor fence rows, ditchbanks, and other areas near the orchard where permanent vegetation is favorable for the buildup of vole populations.

Habitat Management. Ground cover provides voles with both food and cover. Because voles travel only a few feet from their burrows, destruction of vegetation will cause them to abandon the site or die out. A vegetation-free zone 30 to 40 feet wide between the orchard and adjacent areas will help reduce the potential for invasion by voles, but such a wide area is rarely practical. If you observe vole activity within the orchard, clean cultivation or a good job of strip weed control may be sufficient to prevent extensive damage to trees.

Control the vegetation around tree trunks to reduce the likelihood of vole damage. Use hand-hoeing or herbicides to keep an area about 3 feet (1 m) out from the tree trunk free of vegetation. If you maintain ground cover in the row middles, keep it mowed fairly short.

Baiting. If you find damaging infestations within the orchard, poison baits can greatly reduce the vole populations. Baiting can also reduce populations in adjacent areas before they invade the orchard. Single- and multiple-dose baits are available. Restrictions related to endangered species are listed in Table 30. For small infestations, scatter the bait in or near active vole runways and burrows according to the bait's label directions. For larger areas, you can broadcast some baits; broadcast application must be specified on the label. For noncrop land, apply bait in fall or spring before the reproduction peak. Note that label restrictions prohibit the application of bait while fruit are on the tree. Bait acceptance will vary depending on the amount and kind of other food available. One of the most effective baits for voles is crimped oat groats treated with the single-dose poison, zinc phosphide.* Because this material has a high potential for creating bait shyness among survivors, do not apply it more than two times in one year, and space those applications several months apart.

Tree Guards. You can use wire trunk guards to protect young trees from voles and rabbits. The most effective guards are cylinders made from ¼-inch or ½-inch hardware cloth that is 24 inches (60 cm) wide and of sufficient diameter to allow several years' growth without crowding the tree. Bury the guards' bottom edge at least 6 inches (15 cm) below the

soil surface to discourage voles from burrowing beneath them. Plastic, cardboard, or other fiber materials can be used to make trunk guards. These materials are less expensive, also provide sunburn protection, and are more convenient to use; however, they do not provide the same degree of protection against vole damage. If you use any of these other materials, check underneath them periodically for evidence of voles burrowing underneath them to gnaw on the tree trunk. Good basal or strip weed control improves the effectiveness of trunk guards.

Other Controls. Trapping is not practical for voles because so many individuals have to be controlled when they are causing problems in commercial orchards. Fumigation is not effective because of the shallow, open nature of vole burrow systems. Repellents applied to tree trunks will not prevent damage, because voles gnaw the bark just beneath the soil line.

Black-tailed Jackrabbit
Lepus californicus
Cottontail and Brush Rabbits
Sylvilagus spp.

Rabbits may cause severe damage to young trees by chewing the bark off the trunk and clipping off branches within their reach to eat buds and young foliage. They also may gnaw on drip irrigation lines. Jackrabbits are the most common pests. Cottontail and brush rabbits may damage trees in orchards near the more wooded or brushy habitats favored by these species.

A jackrabbit is about the size of a large house cat. It has very long ears, short front legs, and long hind legs. Jackrabbits live in the more open areas of the Central Valley, coastal valleys, and foothills. They make depressions underneath bushes or other vegetation, where they remain secluded during the day. Jackrabbits are hares. Young are born fully haired, with open eyes, and become active within a few days. Cottontail and brush rabbits are smaller than jackrabbits and have shorter ears. They build nesting areas where thick shrubs, woods, or rocks and debris provide dense cover. Their young are born naked and blind, and stay in the nest for several weeks.

Rabbits are active all year in fruit-growing areas. They often live outside of orchards, moving in to feed from early evening to early morning. They damage trees primarily in winter and early spring, when other sources of food are limited. You can prevent damage with proper fencing or tree guards. You can also bait, trap, or shoot rabbits, depending on the species and the size of the population.

Management Guidelines

Periodically examine new plantings for rabbit damage. If you find damage, look for droppings and tracks that indicate rab-

---

* Restricted-use material. Permit required for purchase or use.

bits as the cause. Voles also chew the bark from the trunk, but the bark damage caused by rabbits extends higher on the tree, and the tooth marks are distinctly larger. If you find damage, monitor the orchard perimeters in early morning or late evening to see where the rabbits are entering and obtain an estimate of the number of rabbits involved. You can also estimate the number of rabbits at night by using a spotlight, which will produce readily observed eyeshine. Once the orchard is 4 or 5 years old, rabbits usually do not present a serious problem.

Fencing. Rabbit-proof fencing is an effective tool for preventing damage to young orchards planted where rabbits are a major concern. Make the fence of woven wire or poultry netting at least 3 feet (90 cm) wide and with a mesh diameter of 1 inch (2.5 cm) or less. Bend the bottom 6 inches (15 cm) of mesh at a 90-degree angle and bury it 6 inches deep, facing away from the orchard, to keep rabbits from digging under the fence. If you are building a fence to exclude deer and rabbits are also a potential problem, it is a good idea to add rabbitproof fencing along the bottom. Unless you are already building a deer fence, the cost of a rabbit fence may be prohibitive for a large orchard when you only need it for a few years. Tree guards are an alternative.

Tree Guards. You can make tree guards from wire mesh (Figure 73), hardware cloth, plastic, paper, or cardboard. Cylinders made from poultry netting or hardware cloth, secured with stakes or wooden spreaders, offer the best protection against rabbits. Make the cylinders at least 2½ feet (0.75 m) tall to keep jackrabbits from reaching foliage and limbs by standing on their back legs.

Rabbits can kill young trees quickly by chewing the bark off their trunks. This damage is similar to that caused by meadow mice, but appears higher on the tree trunk.

W. P. GORENZEL

Jackrabbits are grayish brown with long ears and large hind legs.

Figure 73. Wire mesh cylinders secured with stakes will prevent rabbit damage to young trees. If mesh is small enough and buried several inches, the cylinders will protect trees from voles as well; if tall enough, they will prevent deer damage.

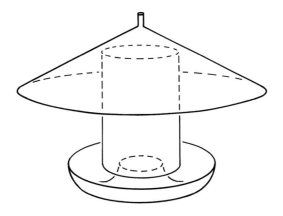

Figure 74. Self-feeding type bait stations designed for rabbits consist of a covered container, which holds and dispenses anticoagulant bait.

If you need protection against voles as well, use smaller-mesh wire and bury the bottom of the cylinder (see the section above on managing voles). The tree guard offers a practical way to prevent damage when you are replanting a few trees in an established orchard.

Baiting. Poison baits may be the most practical means of control for large numbers of jackrabbits or for jackrabbits that are attacking trees over a large area. Baits cannot be used for cottontail or brush rabbits. Multiple-dose baits for jackrabbit control are available from your county agricultural commissioner. These baits are placed in bait stations specifically designed for rabbits (Figure 74). Place bait stations containing 1 to 5 pounds (0.5 to 2 kg) of bait near trails and secure them so they cannot easily be tipped over. Use as many stations as is necessary to ensure that all rabbits have easy access to bait, spacing them 50 to 200 feet (15 to 60 m) apart along the perimeter where rabbits are entering the orchard. Inspect bait stations every morning for the first several days to keep bait supplies replenished; it may take this long before rabbits become accustomed to feeding at the stations. Increase either the amount of bait in the stations or the number of stations if all the bait is consumed in a single night. If no bait is taken after several days, try moving the stations to new locations. Replace bait that becomes wet or moldy. It usually takes 2 to 4 weeks or longer before results are seen with multiple-dose bait. Continue baiting until feeding ceases and you no longer observe rabbits. Be sure to dispose of unused bait properly at the end of the baiting program, and bury or burn the rabbit carcasses on a regular basis. See Table 30 for restrictions related to endangered species.

Other Methods. Shooting, applying repellents, and trapping may provide effective control for small populations of rabbits, or may be used to temporarily reduce damage until other measures such as fencing or tree guards can be put in place.

You can shoot all three types of rabbits if they are causing damage. If small numbers of rabbits are involved, this may be all that is necessary to prevent significant damage while trees are young. For best results, patrol the orchards early in the morning and late in the evening.

Repellents may provide temporary control of rabbit damage. They are sprayed or painted on tree trunks in the dormant season or on foliage and trunks during the growing season. Labels specify the proper application timing. Repeat applications as needed to protect new growth and to replenish repellent that is washed off by rain or irrigation.

Box-type or similar traps can provide effective control for small populations of cottontail or brush rabbits. Trapping is not effective against jackrabbits, since they do not readily enter traps.

Mule Deer
Odocoileus hemionus

Deer can be serious pests of newly planted trees in some foothill and coastal orchards and in Central Valley orchards near riparian habitats. Young trees can be severely stunted, deformed, or killed when deer browse on new shoots. Deer also feed on new growth on older trees, but this seldom causes significant damage. Bucks occasionally break limbs or injure bark when they use trees to rub the velvet off their antlers.

Management Guidelines

Deer feed mostly at night. To confirm their presence, look for tracks and fecal pellets in the vicinity of damaged trees. You may also use spotlights to check for deer at night. If deer are causing significant damage, deerproof fencing provides the most effective and lasting control. It is costly, but if you are planting orchards where deer will present continuing problems, it will pay for itself in the long run.

Fencing. Fencing is most effective at excluding deer when it is put in place before you plant the orchard. Fencing must be at least 7 feet (2.2 m) high to exclude deer. On sloping terrain, an 8-foot (2.5 m) or taller fence may be necessary. Woven wire fences are used most often in California; however, electric fences have gained some popularity in the past decade.

Woven Wire Fences. Fences made of woven wire can effectively exclude deer if they are tall enough. You can use a 6-foot fence of woven wire with several strands of smooth or barbed wire along the top to extend the height to 7 or 8 feet. Be sure the fence is tight to the ground, or deer will crawl under. Check the fence periodically to make sure it is in good repair and that no areas have washed out, allowing deer to crawl under the fence. A smaller mesh installed and properly buried along the bottom of the fence will exclude rabbits as well as deer (see the section above on rabbits).

Wire mesh cylinders around individual trees may be effective where a few new trees are being planted in a location subject to deer damage. Make the cylinders at least 4 feet (1.2 m) tall and of large enough diameter to keep deer from reaching over them to the foliage. Secure the cylinders with wooden stakes so they cannot be tipped over.

Electric Fences. Electric fencing is less expensive to install than woven mesh fencing, but will cost more to maintain. High-tensile wire is the best choice because it is more resilient than other types; it can absorb the impact of deer, falling limbs, and farm equipment without stretching or breaking. Use a high-voltage, low-impedance power source that provides sufficient voltage to repel deer while being less likely to short out when

The pale, distorted regrowth that follows deer damage may be confused with glyphosate injury. The bitten shoot tip shown here is characteristic of deer damage.

vegetation touches the wires. Control vegetation around the base of the fence; in wet weather, contact with wet foliage can drain enough voltage from the fence to render it ineffective.

Other Controls. Habitat management usually is not an option for deer control because the deer travel long distances to reach food sources. Some repellents may offer some protection to tree foliage, at least for a short time; they must be reapplied after rains and as new foliage emerges. Noisemaking devices may be effective for a few days, but deer quickly grow accustomed to them. If only a few deer are involved, having someone patrol newly planted orchards at night with a spotlight to frighten deer away may prove effective. The California Department of Fish and Game will sometimes issue depredation permits to allow you to shoot a few animals when they are causing damage. This may be necessary if a deer gets inside a fenced orchard and is not able to escape. Shooting will not solve a serious deer problem, but may prevent damage long enough to allow you to construct a fence.

Birds

Several bird species may cause substantial damage by feeding on ripening fruit. House finches and crowned sparrows may also invade orchards to feed on fruit buds during the dormant season or shortly before bloom. Bird damage usually is most severe in orchards that are adjacent to wild or brushy areas, where birds find refuge, breeding sites, and other sources of food. Orchards surrounded by other orchards often have fewer problems with birds. Table 31 briefly describes the most common species that cause damage in stone fruits, explains their legal status, and lists available management options.

Monitoring

Regular monitoring will help you determine when damage actually starts so you can start control actions early. Birds are much more difficult to control once they have become used to feeding in a particular orchard. Become familiar with damaging species so you can distinguish them from the many nonpest birds that may frequent orchards. Figures in Table 31 will help you identify pest species, and several bird identification guides are listed in the references at the back of this book.

To monitor the occurrence of bird damage, it is easier to watch for the movement of birds into or within the orchard than to see the damage itself. This is particularly true of bud damage in winter, which is hard to see and may go undetected until bloom. Bud damage usually occurs in the upper parts of trees on the margins of an orchard, next to brushy or wooded habitat from which flocks of house finches or crowned sparrows move into the orchard. Plan to watch for bird activity once a week in locations where you anticipate this type of injury. As fruit begin to ripen, look for damaged fruit or fruit that has been knocked from the tree.

Bird counts can help you decide when to take control actions and whether the controls you have used are having an effect. Where birds are moving into the orchard from adjacent habitat, they can be counted by a stationary observer. Keep records of bird species, counts, and locations for each season; they will help you plan control actions in advance. This way you can have control devices on hand and in working order when they are needed.

A number of bird species may cause substantial damage when they feed on ripening fruit.

The adult white-crowned sparrow (*shown here*) has prominent black and white stripes on the head. The stripes are dark brown and light brown on immature birds. Golden-crowned sparrows have a single yellowish stripe across the top of the head.

Table 31. Common Bird Pests of Stone Fruits, Legal Status, and Management Options.

Bird name and silhouette	Description	Legal status and restrictions	Control options
Crowned sparrow (*Zonotrichia* spp.)	Two species, 6 to 7 in. Typical sparrow coloring of brownish on black with grayish breast. Adult white-crowned sparrow has three white and four black stripes on head. Golden-crowned sparrow has dull gold crown with black border. Small or large flocks feed on dormant flower buds and ripening fruit.	Classified as migratory nongame bird. Can be controlled with depreda-tion permit from the U.S. Fish and Wildlife Service or under the supervision of the county agricultural commissioner.	Frightening, trapping
Crow (*Corvus brachyrhynchos*)	Large, chunky, black bird, 17 to 21 in. Heavy black bill and feet. Groups of a few birds or large flocks feed on ripening fruit.	Classified as migratory nongame bird. Can be killed by landowners, tenants, or persons authorized by landowners or tenants when damaging crops.	Frightening, shooting
European starling (*Sturnus vulgaris*)	7½ to 8½ in. with short tail. Bill is yellow in spring and summer, dark in winter. Plumage iridescent black or purplish, heavily speckled with white. Large flocks feed on ripening fruit.	Classified as nongame bird that may be killed at any time. No federal restrictions.	Frightening, trapping, shooting
House finch (*Carpodacus mexicanus*)	5 to 6 in. Male has rosy red or orangish head, rump, and breast, with brownish back and wings, and brown streaks on sides. Female lacks the red or orange coloration. Small to large flocks feed on dormant flower buds and ripening fruit.	Classified as migratory nongame bird. Can be controlled with depreda-tion permit from the U.S. Fish and Wildlife Service or under the supervision of the county agricultural commissioner.	Frightening,* trapping
Scrub jay (*Aphelocoma coerulescens*)	Aggressive bird 10 to 12 in. Head, wings, and tail are blue, underparts and back are gray, throat white. No crest. Usually solitary birds, sometimes groups, feed on ripening fruit. May feed on opening flowers of early-blooming stone fruits such as apricots, especially in backyard situations.	Classified as migratory nongame bird. May be killed with depre-dation permit from the U.S. Fish and Wildlife Service.	Frightening, shooting
Yellow-billed magpie (*Pica nuttalli*)	Large, noisy bird, 16 to 20 in. Distinct black and white markings on body with very long tail. Small groups feed on ripening fruit.	Classified as migratory nongame bird. No permit required to control birds damaging crops.	Frightening, shooting

* Most methods are not very effective for this species.

The starling has purplish black, iridescent plumage that is speckled with white. The bill is yellow in spring and summer, dark in winter.

House finches are small, grayish brown birds with dark streaks on the breast. Males are colored reddish or orange on head, throat, and rump.

Management Guidelines

Frightening devices—noisemakers and visual repellents—are the primary means of controlling bird damage in stone fruits. To be effective, several different methods should be used in rotation and you should start using them as soon as birds appear. Once birds have become used to feeding in an orchard, they are much harder to frighten away. Trapping can be effective against house finches and starlings. Remove brush piles in or near orchards; they offer refuge and loafing sites for birds and may exacerbate problems.

Frightening. The most effective way to frighten birds from the orchard is to use a combination of noisemakers and visual repellents. For maximum effectiveness, rotate from one type of frightening device to another and do not use one combination of devices for more than a week; otherwise, birds will become used to it. Monitor bird activity while using frightening devices and switch to a different type if birds appear to be getting used to the technique you are using.

Roving patrols that fire shell crackers, bird bombs, or whistler bombs are among the most effective ways to frighten birds from orchards. Stationary noisemakers such as gas cannons (propane exploders) and electronic noisemakers are most effective if you use at least one device for every 5 acres and elevate them above the level of the tree canopy. Move the devices to new locations every 3 to 5 days so the birds will take longer to get used to them.

The most commonly used visual repellents are large "scare-eye" balloons and mylar streamers. Attach these devices to poles so they are above the tree canopy and use them in combination with noisemakers to increase their effectiveness. Use one type of visual repellent with each type of noisemaker, and switch to a different visual repellent when you switch noisemakers.

The most effective bird frightening program makes use of as many different kinds of noisemakers and visual repellents as practical. An example follows:

first week:	Patrol orchard firing cracker shells.
second week:	Propane exploders.
third week:	Propane exploders and patrol orchard firing cracker shells.
fourth week:	Electronic noisemakers with "scare-eye" balloons near trees where damage is most severe.

Shooting. Birds that usually invade orchards in small numbers, such as scrub jays and magpies, often can be controlled by shooting. Check with California Department of Fish and Game officials before shooting any birds. A depredation permit is required if you want to shoot scrub jays. Permits are not presently required for shooting crows, magpies, or starlings that are causing damage, but it is a good idea to check with authorities because regulations may change. Where permissible, occasionally shooting at a few birds will increase the effectiveness of your other noisemaking techniques, because the birds will begin associating loud noises with the real hazards of firearms.

Trapping. Trapping can be an effective way to control house finches and starlings, especially if it is conducted over a relatively large area; for instance, if several adjacent growers conduct a trapping program. The most effective trap for these species is the modified Australian crow trap. Diagrams and details of its use are given in *Vertebrate Pest Control Handbook*, listed in the references. Successful trapping must take into account the behavior patterns of the birds being controlled. Place traps in suitable locations with adequate food and water to keep the trapped birds alive. Trapping is best carried out by someone experienced with the technique. For house finches and crowned sparrows, trapping must be conducted under the supervision of the county agricultural commissioner.

Protective Netting. You can prevent the access of birds to ripening fruit by placing ½- to ¾-inch mesh plastic netting over trees. While not practical for commercial orchards, this can be a very effective way to protect backyard fruit trees. For best protection, attach the netting to a frame that holds it away from the tree. If you place netting directly on the tree, birds will be able to reach fruit on the outer edges of the canopy. Also, netting that is attached to a frame can be moved out of the away to allow easy access for picking. Plastic netting ("bird netting") for the home gardener is available at most garden stores.

The head, wings, and tail of the scrub jay are blue; breast and back are gray.

Pest Damage Table

This table lists pest damage symptoms that may occur on stone fruits, what the likely causes are, and which stone fruits they may affect. Use this table to help identify the cause of a problem you have encountered on a stone fruit crop. Symptoms are listed by the part of the plant affected, and the table refers you to pages in the text where you will find descriptions, illustrations, information on pest biology, and management recommendations.

The symbols indicate which stone fruit is affected:

◗ Apricot ◖ Cherry ◉ Peach/Nectarine ● Plum ◗ Prune ◖ Peach only ◯ Nectarine only

Symptoms on flowers	Possible cause	Comments	Pages
Brown, dead, or dying flower parts	**Brown rot** ◗ ◖ ◉ ● ◗	Fuzzy tufts of spores usually present when conditions are damp.	115–120
	Jacket rot ◗ ◖ ◉ ● ◗	Browning underneath calyx ("jacket") extends into young fruit.	128
	Bacterial blast ◗ ◖ ◉ ● ◗	Associated foliage wilted and dark; tufts of spores never present; look for reddish flecking in phloem of shoot.	140–142
	Frost ◗ ◖ ◉ ● ◗	Follows low temperatures (below about 28°F).	42
Holes chewed in flower parts	**Leafrollers** ◗ ◖ ◉ ● ◗	Webbing usually present.	72–74
	Green fruitworms ◗ ◖ ◉ ● ◗	No webbing present.	75–76
Color breaks on flower petals	**Peach mosaic** ◉ ● ◗	Known to occur only south of Tehachapi Mountains.	152
Flower parts distorted or missing	**Lack of winter chilling** ◖	Check temperature records for chilling hours.	7

LEAVES

Symptoms on leaves	Possible cause	Comments	Pages
Holes in edges of leaves, leaves may appear tattered	**Leafrollers**	Leaves rolled up, tied together, or tied to the surface of fruit with webbing.	72–74
	Green fruitworms	No webbing present; leaves not rolled.	75–76
	Codling moth	No webbing present; leaves not rolled. Occurs on prunes only in a few locations.	77–78
	Western tussock moth	No webbing present; look for colorful caterpillars with long tufts of hair. Coastal orchards.	79
	Cribrate weevil	Scallop-shaped notches in leaf edges; leaves may be tattered or skeletonized; look for weevils in soil around base of tree during the day. Late spring and summer.	101
	Prunus necrotic ringspot virus	Necrotic lesions that fall out of leaves; leaves usually distorted with yellow mottling or discoloration.	157
Small holes in center of leaves	**Shot hole**	Tan spots with reddish margins fall out of leaf, leaving small holes.	125–127
	Noninfectious plum shot hole	Brown spots or patches on older leaves of certain varieties; spots fall out giving a shothole or tattered appearance.	161
	Prunus necrotic ringspot virus	Necrotic lesions that fall out of leaves; accompanied by distortion, yellow mottling.	157
	Leaf spot	Angular, brown spots fall out of leaves, leaving holes; other symptoms of leaf spot present.	133
Leaf surface eaten away, leaving network of veins	**Redhumped caterpillar**	Look for large numbers of colorful caterpillars with red hump on back, or large numbers of cast skins.	78–79
	Cribrate weevil	Some leaves may have scallop-shaped notches in edges or may be completely eaten; look for weevils in soil around base of tree during the day. Late spring and summer.	101
	Cherry slug	Look for small, black, sluglike larvae. Coastal orchards.	103
Leaves eaten away completely, or with midvein and some lateral veins remaining	**Redhumped caterpillar**	Look for large numbers of colorful caterpillars with red hump on back, or large numbers of cast skins.	78–79
	Tent caterpillars	Look for large numbers of colorful caterpillars or clusters of cast skins; tentlike webbing may be present.	80

 Apricot   Cherry    Peach/Nectarine   Plum   Prune   Peach only   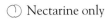 Nectarine only

Symptoms on leaves	Possible cause	Comments	Pages
	Cribrate weevil ① ✿ ⦿ ● ◗	No webbing; some leaves with scallop-shaped holes chewed in margins; look for weevils in soil around base of tree during the day. Late spring and summer.	101
	Deer ① ✿ ⦿ ● ◗	Leaves bitten off; whole tree affected in young orchard, lower branches affected in mature orchard; look for hoofprints and droppings.	215–216
Leaves eaten away completely from the ends of branches, which are covered with dense webbing	**Fall webworm** ● ◗	Large numbers of orange-yellow caterpillars inside webbing.	80
Tan, reddish, or brown spots or patches	**Shot hole** ① ⦿	Tan spots with reddish margins; tiny, dark brown spots develop in tan area.	125–127
	Noninfectious plum shot hole ●	Brown spots or patches on older leaves of certain varieties; spots fall out giving a shothole or tattered appearance.	161
	Nitrogen deficiency ① ✿ ⦿ ● ◗	Red spots on yellow leaves at base of shoots; reddish petioles and midvein; terminal leaves are pale.	163
	Leaf spot ✿	Spots tend to be angular, delimited by leaf veins; undersides turn white following damp weather; spots may fall out of leaves, leaving shot holes.	133
	Plum rusty blotch ●	Red spots inside rusty brown areas; spots fall out, leaving shothole appearance.	162
	Boron toxicity ① ✿ ⦿ ● ◗	Brown, necrotic spots or patches along midvein; twig cankers and misshapen fruit occur; have soil and water analyzed for boron. Orchards on west side of Central Valley most likely to be affected.	166
	Oxyfluorfen injury ① ✿ ⦿ ● ◗	Browning of leaf margins or brown spots on leaves. Occurs if spray drift contacts leaves or if warm weather follows a soil application in late winter.	168
Distorted leaves with yellowing or brown patches or spots	**X-disease** ✿ ⦿	See Table 22 on page 146.	148–151
	Certain viruses ✿ ⦿ ● ◗	See Table 22 on page 146.	
	Eriophyid mites ① ✿ ⦿ ● ◗	Small yellow spots on young leaves; leaf margins curl upward; use hand lens to look for tiny triangular mites.	108–109
	Copper deficiency ① ✿ ⦿ ● ◗	Rosettes of distorted leaves; yellowing and necrotic spots or patches; have leaf tissue analyzed to confirm cause.	165

LEAVES

 Apricot   Cherry   Peach/Nectarine   Plum   Prune    Peach only   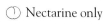 Nectarine only

LEAVES

Symptoms on leaves	Possible cause	Comments	Pages
	Boron deficiency ◖ ⬤ ◗ ● ◗	Distorted, discolored terminals and dieback of shoot tips.	166
Distorted, puckered, curled leaves with blisterlike patches of red or yellow discoloration	Leaf curl ◖	Surface of discolored areas becomes whitish and powdery during damp weather.	129–130
	Plum pockets ●	Surface of discolored areas becomes whitish and powdery during damp weather. Occurs rarely on plums in California.	129–130
Distorted leaves with little or no discoloration	Crinkle leaf ⬤	Leaf margins distorted and deeply indented; leaves usually have pale or light yellow mottling.	159
	Deep suture ⬤	Abnormally long, narrow leaves with deep indentations; no discoloration; fruit develop deeply indented sutures.	159
	Certain viruses ⬤ ◖ ●	Leaflike growths from midvein may be present on underside of leaves. See Table 22 on page 146.	
	Glyphosate injury ◖ ⬤ ◖ ● ◗	Narrow, needlelike leaves; foliage may be pale or reddish; leaves often in compact rosettes at shoot tips. Occurs when spray drift contacted buds the previous fall.	167
Distorted, tightly curled leaves	Aphids ◖ ⬤ ◖ ● ◗	Aphids or cast skins present inside leaves; leaves often shiny and sticky with honeydew. Seldom a problem on apricots.	93–95
Yellow patches, spots, or patterns with no leaf distortion	Rust ◖ ⬤ ◖ ● ◗	Bright yellow angular spots on upper leaf surface with rusty colored patches on lower leaf surface. Occurs rarely on apricots, cherries, nectarines, and plums.	130–132
	X-disease ⬤ ◖	See Table 22 on page 146.	148–151
	Certain viruses ⬤ ◖ ● ◗	See Table 22 on page 146.	
	Scab ◖ ◖ ●	Yellow patches turn grayish; fruit symptoms also present. Occurs rarely on apricots, plums.	132
	Plum rusty blotch ●	Yellow patches that turn rusty brown; red spots may develop and fall out, leaving shothole appearance.	162
	Magnesium deficiency ◖ ⬤ ◖ ● ◗	V-shaped area, widest at the base of the leaf, remains green around lateral veins while rest of leaf turns yellow.	166
	Dichlobenil injury ◖ ⬤ ◖ ● ◗	Yellow halos on leaf margins; more likely on coarse-textured soil low in organic matter.	167
	Norflurazon injury ◖ ⬤ ◖ ● ◗	Veins of mature leaves turn yellow or white; purple discoloration of petioles.	167

◖ Apricot	⬤ Cherry	◖ Peach/Nectarine	● Plum	◗ Prune	◖ Peach only	◖ Nectarine only

Symptoms on leaves	Possible cause	Comments	Pages
	Simazine injury ◖ ◖ ◖ ● ◗	Yellowing or bleaching between veins, starting at leaf margin and spreading toward midvein.	168
Pale yellow stippling or mottling	**Webspinning spider mites** **European red mite** ◖ ◖ ◖ ● ◗	Use hand lens to look for mites on leaves; webbing may be present.	103–108
	Brown mite ◖ ◖ ◖ ● ◗	Leaves may become mottled brown; use hand lens to look for mites on leaves or shoots early in the morning.	108
	Certain viruses ◖ ◖ ● ◗	See Table 22 on page 146.	
Yellowing of entire leaves	**Phytophthora root and crown rot** ◖ ◖ ◖ ● ◗	Entire tree usually affected; reddish brown canker present underneath bark of crown and roots.	134–136
	Armillaria root rot ◖ ◖ ◖ ● ◗	Part or all of tree usually affected; dark canker with white mycelium present underneath bark of lower trunk and crown; affected wood is light, soft, and punky; dark rhizomorphs may be present on roots.	137–139
	Nitrogen deficiency ◖ ◖ ◖ ● ◗	Entire leaves turn yellow, starting at the base of shoots.	163
	Potassium deficiency ◖ ◖ ◖ ● ◗	Leaf margins turn brown and curl; defoliation of branch terminals may occur.	164
	Iron deficiency ◖ ◖ ◖ ● ◗	Leaf veins remain bright green while leaf turns yellow to nearly white; youngest leaves most affected.	164
	Manganese deficiency ◖ ◖ ◖ ● ◗	Leaf veins remain green while leaf turns yellow; oldest leaves most affected.	165
Whitish or grayish patches on leaf surface	**Powdery mildew** ◖ ◖ ◖ ● ◗	Leaves sometimes distorted on apricot, plum, prune; often distorted on nectarine and peach; usually distorted on cherry. Filamentous growth visible with hand lens on leaf surface.	120–125
Silvery or gray discoloration of leaves	**Eriophyid mites** ◖	Use a hand lens to look for tiny triangular-shaped mites.	108–109
	Silver leaf ◖ ◖ ◖ ● ◗	Small, brown or purple, shelflike growths eventually develop on affected branches; heartwood of affected branches brown, dry, and crumbly. Occurs occasionally.	145–146
Stunting and/or rosetting of foliage	**Zinc deficiency** ◖ ◖ ◖ ● ◗	Rosettes of small, pale leaves at shoot tips.	163
	X-disease ◖	Trees on Colt, Mazzard, or Stockton Morello rootstock.	148–151
	Certain viruses ◖ ◖ ● ◗	See Table 22 on page 146.	

LEAVES

◖ Apricot   ◖ Cherry   ◖ Peach/Nectarine   ● Plum   ◗ Prune   ◖ Peach only   ◖ Nectarine only

LEAVES

Symptoms on leaves	Possible cause	Comments	Pages
	Glyphosate injury ◖ ⌇ ◎ ● ◗	Rosettes of very narrow leaves at shoot tips; leaves may be pale or reddish. Occurs when spray drift contacted buds the previous fall.	167
Wilted or dead leaves at shoot tip	**Brown rot** ◖ ⌇ ◎ ● ◗	Associated with blighted blossoms; fuzzy tufts of spores may be present following wet weather; no tunneling or frass.	115–120
	Bacterial canker ◖ ⌇ ◎ ● ◗	Dead leaves usually very dark brown or black; tufts of spores never present; reddish brown flecks in phloem of shoot.	140–142
	Peach twig borer ◖ ⌇ ◎ ● ◗	Usually only a few leaves affected; larval tunnel inside shoot tip, larva may be present. Similar to oriental fruit moth, usually with more frass.	62–67
	Oriental fruit moth ◖ ⌇ ◎ ● ◗	Similar to peach twig borer. Occurs infrequently on apricots, cherries, plums, and prunes.	68–71
	Western flower thrips ◖ ⌇ ◎ ● ◗	One or two very small leaves on young shoot; leaves curled; no tunneling or frass.	91–93
	Lygus bugs, *Calocoris* ◖ ⌇ ◎ ● ◗	Usually a few new leaves on young shoots; no tunneling or frass; look for bugs.	84–85
All foliage on one or a few branches wilted, yellow, or brown	**Bacterial canker** ◖ ⌇ ◎ ● ◗	Gumming usually present on branch; reddish brown canker underneath bark; reddish flecks in phloem at margin of canker. Most common in late winter and spring.	140–142
	X-disease ⌇	On trees high-grafted onto Mahaleb scaffold.	148–151
	Eutypa dieback ◖ ⌇	Gumming usually present on branch, associated with pruning cut; foliage remains attached; dark, roughened area on bark with U-shaped or V-shaped discoloration of wood visible if affected branch cut in cross-section. More common in mid-summer.	142–143
	Verticillium wilt ◖ ⌇ ◎ ● ◗	No gumming on bark surface; dead leaves fall off; dark discoloration of xylem visible when limb cut in cross-section. Occurs more frequently on apricots and cherries, occasionally on nectarines and peaches, rarely on plums and prunes.	139
	Cytospora canker ◖ ⌇ ◎ ● ◗	Small, white dots at the tips of small bumps on surface of dead branch; pink or amber material exudes from the pimplelike bumps during wet weather; limb dieback originates at sunburned area on bark. Occurs on prunes and European plums, occasionally on nectarines and peaches, rarely on apricots and cherries.	144–145

 Apricot   Cherry   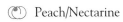 Peach/Nectarine   Plum   Prune   Peach only   ◯ Nectarine only

Symptoms on leaves	Possible cause	Comments	Pages
	Ceratocystis canker 〇 ⸰ 〇 ● ◗	Reddish brown canker underneath bark of trunk, associated with bark injury; gumming usually present on trunk. Occurs on prunes; rarely seen on apricots, cherries, nectarines, peaches, and plums.	143–144
Foliage on entire tree turns pale, yellow, or reddish; tree appears wilted	Phytophthora root and crown rot 〇 ⸰ 〇 ● ◗	Reddish brown canker present underneath bark of crown, roots, lower trunk. Whole tree eventually dies.	134–136
	Bacterial canker 〇 ⸰ 〇 ● ◗	Reddish brown canker underneath bark of trunk; gumming or watersoaking usually present on trunk. Scion eventually dies; regrowth from rootstock.	140–142
	X-disease ⸰	Trees on Mahaleb rootstock; dark band of discolored phloem develops at graft union. Whole tree dies.	148–151
	Armillaria root rot 〇 ⸰ 〇 ● ◗	Dark discoloration of wood of lower trunk, crown; white mycelium underneath bark at crown; affected wood is light, soft, and punky; dark rhizomorphs may be present on roots. Whole tree eventually dies.	137–139
	Tomato ringspot virus ⸰ 〇 ● ◗	Dark band of discolored phloem at graft union, visible by removing bark, or surface of wood is pitted and grooved. Whole tree eventually dies.	153–155
	Root knot nematodes 〇 ⸰ 〇 ● ◗	Examine tree roots for presence of tiny galls on feeder roots.	169–176
	Pocket gophers 〇 ⸰ 〇 ● ◗	Bark chewed off crown and upper roots below the soil line; look for gopher mounds, tunnel next to roots. Whole tree eventually dies.	208–211
	Voles (meadow mice) 〇 ⸰ 〇 ● ◗	Bark chewed off crown and lower trunk; look for tooth marks on wood and signs of vole activity: fresh runways, burrows, and droppings. Whole tree eventually dies.	211–212
Premature fall colors	X-disease ⸰	Look for graft union aberrations on Mahaleb rootstock.	148–151
	Tomato ringspot virus 〇 ● ◗	Look for deep pits and grooves in wood underneath bark of lower trunk. Look for brown line in phloem at graft union of *Prunus domestica* scions on Myrobalan plum or peach rootstocks.	153–155
Shiny material (honeydew), black sooty mold	Aphids 〇 ⸰ 〇 ● ◗	Leaves usually curled and distorted; aphids or cast skins present on leaves; seldom a problem on apricots.	93–95
	European fruit lecanium 〇 ⸰ 〇 ● ◗	Leaves not distorted; look for large scale coverings on twigs.	90

〇 Apricot   ⸰ Cherry   〇 Peach/Nectarine   ● Plum   ◗ Prune   〇 Peach only   〇 Nectarine only

Symptoms on leaves	Possible cause	Comments	Pages
	Black scale 🍒	Leaves not distorted; look for large scale coverings, some with H-shaped ridge on top.	91
Premature defoliation	**Webspinning spider mites** **European red mite** 🍑 🍒 🍑 ● ◐	Large numbers of mites on remaining leaves can be seen with a hand lens; webbing may be present.	103–108
	Rust ●	Leaf symptoms of rust, bright yellow spots on upper leaf surface, present.	130–132
	Potassium deficiency 🍑 🍒 🍑 ● ◐	Terminals die back; leaves turn yellow and brown before falling.	164

LEAVES

Symptoms on fruit	Possible cause	Comments	Pages
Small holes penetrating into fruit with reddish brown, granular frass at the opening	**Peach twig borer**	Damage usually is shallow; larva may be present inside fruit, sometimes around pit near stem end.	62–67
	Oriental fruit moth	Damage usually penetrates to pit; larva may be present, feeding around pit. Occurs infrequently on apricots, cherries, plums, and prunes.	68–71
	Codling moth	Abundant frass on surface and inside fruit; hole usually penetrates to pit; larva may be present. Occurs rarely on peaches, usually near other hosts such as apples, pears, or walnuts. Occurs on prunes only in a few locations.	77–78
Gouges or shallow holes in surface	**Leafrollers**	Often at stem end of fruit; webbing and frass present; leaves may be attached to fruit with webbing; green or ripe fruit affected.	72–74
	Green fruitworms	Gouges tend to be deep; no webbing present; green fruit affected.	75–76
	Western tussock moth	Shallow gouges in green fruit; no webbing present; look for colorful caterpillars with long tufts of hair. Coastal orchards.	79
	Earwigs	Shallow gouges in surface of ripe fruit; tiny dark droppings may be present; earwigs may contaminate fruit at harvest; may be inside apricots around pit.	100
	Cankerworms	Shallow or deep gouges in green fruit; no webbing.	76
	Birds	Small or large gouges in ripe fruit; obvious speck marks in fruit flesh give wound a star-shaped edge.	216–219
Shallow gouges that have healed over with a corky layer	**Green fruitworms**	Damage appears on small, green fruit; may cover much of fruit.	75–76
	Katydids	Damage may appear on green or ripe fruit; small area of fruit surface affected.	102
Corky scarring on surface	**Western flower thrips**	Scars appear as streaks or netlike pattern; not associated with gouges or depressions in surface of fruit.	91–93
	Russet scab	Shiny patches on green fruit turn corky before fruit ripens; often in a circular pattern around the blossom end.	160
	Wind scab	Corky streaks or patches usually longitudinal; affected fruit concentrated on windward side of tree. Occurs primarily on European plums.	160

FRUIT

 Apricot   Cherry    Peach/Nectarine   Plum   Prune   Peach only   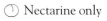 Nectarine only

Symptoms on fruit	Possible cause	Comments	Pages
Soft brown areas, may spread over most of fruit	**Brown rot** ◖ ◖ ◖ ◖ ◖	Fuzzy, tan tufts of spores develop inside brown, decayed area.	115–120
	Green fruit rot ◖ ◖ ◖ ◖ ◖	Brown area develops on small, green fruit; associated with dead flower parts.	128
Reddish spots on surface	**San Jose scale** ◖ ◖ ◖ ◖ ◖	Use hand lens to look for scale in center of spots; check twigs or bark for scale colonies.	86–89
	Shot hole ◖ ◖	Spots (> ½₅ inch, 1 mm) usually have tan centers; leaf symptoms also present.	125–127
	Brown rot ◖	Very small spots (< ½₅ inch, 1 mm) on green fruit develop into rot when fruit ripen.	115–120
	Nectarine pox ◯	Red pimples on certain yellow-skinned nectarine varieties.	161
	Fog spot ◖	Margins of red spots are dark; spots turn scabby; no symptoms on foliage.	132–133
Green or red to purple patches on ripe fruit	**Powdery mildew** ◖ ◖	Filamentous or tufted growth may be visible with a hand lens.	120–125
Orange or tan irregular patches or streaks	**Powdery mildew** ◖	Apple trees with powdery mildew nearby.	120–125
Grayish black spots with green or yellow margins	**Scab** ◖ ◖ ●	Symptoms also may be present on leaves and shoots — yellow blotches that turn gray. Occurs rarely on apricots, plums.	132
Pale or yellow patches, halos, or spots	**Western flower thrips** ●	Pale halo around small depressions or punctures, or yellow spots where eggs laid in surface of fruit.	91–93
	Powdery mildew ●	Yellow patches turn scabby; no powdery mildew symptoms on leaves.	120–125
Small, dark spots on fruit surface	**Stink bugs** **Lygus bugs** ◖	Whitish or brown, corky tissue is present in fruit flesh underneath skin; gumming may be present; young fruit may be severely distorted.	81–85
	Bacterial canker ◖ ◖ ◖ ● ◖	Foliage or shoot symptoms of bacterial canker usually present; no gumming on fruit.	140–142
	Nectarine pox ◯	Small, scabby lesions on certain nectarine varieties.	161
Tiny brown to black flecks	**Brown rot** ◖ ◖ ◖ ● ◖	Dormant or quiescent infections that develop into rot when fruit ripen.	115–120
Sunken spots or patches with dark centers, may have gum deposits	**Stink bugs** ◖	Whitish or brown, corky tissue underneath skin of surface spots; young fruit may be severely distorted.	81–84

 Apricot   Cherry    Peach/Nectarine   Plum   Prune   Peach only   ◯ Nectarine only

Symptoms on fruit	Possible cause	Comments	Pages
	Lygus bugs	Fruit surface may crack; brown, corky tissue underneath skin of surface spots.	84–85
	Rust	Green or yellow halos around margin of sunken spots; no gum; rust colored spore masses underneath skin; leaf symptoms of rust also present.	130–132
Circular, orange-brown spots	**Anthracnose**	Pattern of brown and orange rings in spot	133
Shriveled, dried fruit clinging to shoot	**Brown rot**	May be associated with dead leaves; fuzzy tufts of spores develop during damp weather.	115–120
Whitish or grayish patches	**Powdery mildew**	Patches usually look powdery; filamentous or tufted white growth can be seen with hand lens. As cherry fruit ripen, affected areas become sunken and distorted.	120–125
Wartlike growths or bumps on surface	**Leaf curl**	Reddish, wartlike growths on young fruit; associated with leaf symptoms of leaf curl.	129–130
	Peach wart	Green, wartlike growths on young fruit; usually several, concentrated around blossom end; all fruit on a branch affected.	158–159
	Peach false wart	Green, wartlike growths on young fruit; one or two per fruit, with a few fruit per tree affected.	161
Whitish or silvery discoloration on surface	**Western flower thrips**		91–93
Stunted, distorted, or misshapen fruit	**Stink bugs**	Gumming usually present; sunken areas have shallow patches of corky tissue underneath skin.	81–84
	X-disease	Trees on Colt, Mazzard, or Stockton Morello rootstock.	148–151
	Certain viruses	See Table 22 on page 146.	
	Powdery mildew	Filamentous growth on surface of distorted areas visible with a hand lens.	120–125
	Deep suture	Suture line deeply indented; associated leaves are abnormally long and narrow with deep indentations.	159
	Boron toxicity	Necrotic spots on leaves and twig cankers also present; have soil and water analyzed for boron. Orchards on west side of Central Valley most likely to be affected.	166

FRUIT

 Apricot   Cherry   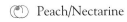 Peach/Nectarine   Plum   Prune   Peach only    Nectarine only

Symptoms on fruit	Possible cause	Comments	Pages
Withered, soft, bladderlike fruit lacking a pit	**Plum pockets** ●	Occurs rarely; associated with leaf curl type symptoms on foliage.	129–130
Premature yellowing and drop	**Lack of pollination** ⋖ ●	Pollenizer not present or bloom did not overlap.	8, 32–33
	Aborted fruit ●	Fruit drop in late spring is normal for many plums ("June drop").	9
Shiny material (honeydew), black sooty mold	**Aphids** ◖ ⋖ ◐ ● ◗	Foliage usually distorted; look for aphids or cast skins on affected leaves; seldom a problem on apricots.	93–95
	European fruit lecanium ◖ ⋖ ◐ ● ◗	Honeydew and sooty mold on leaves; leaves not distorted; look for large scale coverings on twigs or immature scale on leaves.	90
Fruit doubling, spurs (fasciations)	**Abnormal development** ◖ ⋖ ◐ ● ◗	Increased by water stress or heat stress during late summer (midsummer for cherries) of the previous season.	8

FRUIT

◖ Apricot   Cherry   ◐ Peach/Nectarine   ● Plum   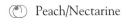 Prune   Peach only   Nectarine only

Symptoms on shoots, twigs	Possible cause	Comments	Pages
Cankers, gumming on twigs, shoots, or spurs	**Brown rot** Ⓐ Ⓒ Ⓟ ● ◗	Associated with blighted blossoms and wilted or dead leaves; fuzzy tufts of spores develop during damp weather.	115–120
	Bacterial canker Ⓐ Ⓒ Ⓟ ● ◗	Associated with wilted leaves that usually are dark brown or black; reddish flecks in phloem; tufts of spores not present.	140–142
	Boron toxicity Ⓐ Ⓒ Ⓟ ● ◗	Necrotic spots on leaves, misshapen fruit; have soil and water analyzed for boron. Orchards on west side of Central Valley most likely to be affected.	166
Dead shoot tips, with wilted or dead leaves	**Brown rot** Ⓐ Ⓒ Ⓟ ● ◗	Associated with blighted blossoms; fuzzy tufts of spores develop during damp weather.	115–120
	Bacterial canker Ⓐ Ⓒ Ⓟ ● ◗	Leaves usually are dark brown or black; reddish flecks in phloem; tufts of spores not present.	140–142
	Peach twig borer Ⓐ Ⓒ Ⓟ ● ◗	Usually only a few leaves affected; larval tunnel inside shoot tip, larva may be present. Similar to oriental fruit moth usually with more frass.	62–67
	Oriental fruit moth Ⓐ Ⓒ Ⓟ ● ◗	Similar to peach twig borer. Occurs infrequently on apricots, cherries, plums, and prunes.	68–71
	Lygus bugs, *Calocoris* Ⓐ Ⓒ Ⓟ ● ◗	Usually a few new leaves on young shoots; no tunneling or frass; look for bugs.	84–85
Wilting and dieback of entire shoot	**Brown rot** Ⓐ Ⓒ Ⓟ ● ◗	Associated with blighted blossoms; fuzzy tufts of spores develop during damp weather.	115–120
	Bacterial canker Ⓐ Ⓒ Ⓟ ● ◗	Leaves usually are dark brown or black; reddish flecks in phloem; tufts of spores not present.	140–142
	Branch and twig borer Ⓐ Ⓒ Ⓟ ● ◗	Small round hole present in axil of shoot.	100
Red spots on green twigs	**San Jose scale** Ⓐ Ⓒ Ⓟ ● ◗	Use hand lens to look for scale in center of spots; may see similar symptoms on fruit.	86–89
Red or yellow, blisterlike patches on young, green shoots	**Leaf curl** Ⓟ	Foliage symptoms also present.	129–130
	Plum pockets ●	Foliage and fruit symptoms also present. Occurs rarely on plums in California.	129–130
Tan spots surrounded by black or purplish areas	**Shot hole** Ⓐ Ⓟ	Dark brown dots in center of tan spots; gummy, dead buds also present. Twig lesions occur rarely on apricots.	125–127
Dead buds	**Bacterial canker** Ⓐ Ⓒ Ⓟ ● ◗	Gumming usually present on twig; reddish flecking may be present in phloem of twig.	140–142
	Shot hole Ⓐ Ⓟ	Usually shiny with gum; twig lesions also present; visible during dormant season but most obvious after healthy buds begin to open.	125–127

Ⓐ Apricot   Ⓒ Cherry   Ⓟ Peach/Nectarine   ● Plum   ◗ Prune   ⓟ Peach only   ⓝ Nectarine only

Symptoms on shoots, twigs	Possible cause	Comments	Pages
Dead buds (continued)	Glyphosate injury ◐ ◄ ◑ ● ◗	Occurs when drift from spring application contacts opening buds.	167
	Lack of winter chilling ◐ ◄ ◑ ● ◗	Dead buds drop off easily; surviving buds open over a prolonged period; check temperature records for chilling hours.	7
	Insufficient water in fall ◐ ◄ ◑ ● ◗	Check irrigation and rainfall records.	37–42
Yellow blotches that turn grayish brown or black	Scab ◐ ◑ ●	Fruit and leaf symptoms usually present. Occurs rarely on apricots, plums.	132
Small cracks on twigs	Rust ◑	Associated with foliage symptoms of the disease; rust-colored spore masses usually visible underneath bark with a hand lens.	130–132
New shoots bitten off	Rabbits ◐ ◄ ◑ ● ◗	New shoots chewed off within a few feet of the ground; look for droppings.	212–214
	Deer ◐ ◄ ◑ ● ◗	New shoots chewed off young trees or the lower part of mature trees; look for hoof prints and droppings.	215–216
Bark chewed off twigs	Cribrate weevil ◐ ◄ ◑ ● ◗	Symptoms of foliage feeding also present; look for weevils in soil around base of tree during the day.	101
New growth fails to leaf out, dies back	Oil injury ◐ ◄ ◑ ● ◗	Follows application of an oil spray.	62

SHOOTS, TWIGS

 Apricot    Cherry   Peach/Nectarine   Plum   Prune   Peach only   Nectarine only

Symptoms on trunk or branches	Possible cause	Comments	Pages
Wilting or dieback of entire branch	**Bacterial canker**	Gumming on bark; reddish brown canker underneath bark; reddish flecks in phloem at margin of canker.	140–142
	San Jose scale	Longitudinal cracking of bark; use hand lens to look for scale on bark surface.	86–89
	Eutypa dieback	Gumming on bark, usually near a pruning wound; U-shaped or V-shaped section of wood is discolored dark brown if affected branch cut in cross-section.	142–143
	Wood borers	Look for gumming, frass, or exit holes.	96–100
	Phytophthora pruning wound canker	Gum deposits on bark associated with a pruning wound; reddish brown canker underneath bark, usually with a zonate margin.	145
	Verticillium wilt	Dark discoloration of xylem visible if affected branch cut in cross-section. Occurs more frequently on apricots and cherries, occasionally on nectarines and peaches, rarely on plums and prunes.	139
	Ceratocystis canker	Reddish brown canker underneath bark of trunk, associated with bark injury; gumming usually present on trunk. Occurs on prunes; rarely seen on apricots, cherries, nectarines, peaches and plums.	143–144
	Cytospora canker	Small, white dots at the tips of small bumps on surface of dead branch; pink or amber material exudes from the pimplelike bumps during wet weather; limb dieback originates at sunburned area on bark. Occurs on prunes and European plums, occasionally on nectarines and peaches, rarely on apricots and cherries.	144–145
Gum deposits on bark surface	**Phytophthora crown rot**	Reddish brown canker underneath bark with no white mycelium present; foliage of tree pale, wilted, or dead.	134–136
	Bacterial canker	Reddish brown canker underneath outer bark; reddish flecking in phloem at margin of canker.	140–142
	Eutypa dieback	Usually associated with pruning wound; entire branch dies back; U-shaped or V-shaped discoloration of wood visible if affected branch cut in cross-section.	142–143
	Phytophthora pruning wound canker	Associated with pruning wound; reddish brown canker underneath bark, usually with zonate margin; dieback of affected branch.	145

TRUNK OR BRANCHES

 Apricot   Cherry 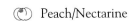 Peach/Nectarine   Plum   Prune   Peach only Nectarine only

TRUNK OR BRANCHES

Symptoms on trunk or branches	Possible cause	Comments	Pages
	Ceratocystis canker	Associated with injury to trunk; reddish brown canker underneath bark; dieback of one or more scaffold limbs. Occurs on prunes; rarely seen on apricots, cherries, nectarines, peaches, and plums.	143–144
	Certain viruses	See Table 22 on page 146.	
Gum deposits and frass on bark surface	Peachtree borer	Gum deposits and frass on crown or lower trunk; large larva may be found by carefully cutting away bark.	98–99
	American plum borer, prune limb borer	Gum and frass occur in crotch or near pruning wound or gall; webbing often present.	99–100
Holes in bark	Flatheaded borer	Elliptical; about ¼ inch long; no gumming; often associated with sunburned area.	97
	Shothole borer	Circular; about ¹⁄₁₆ inch in diameter; many holes found together; gum deposits often present.	98–99
Bark chewed off branches or trunk	Ground squirrels	Look for open burrow systems in or near orchard and presence of squirrels during the day.	205–208
	Voles (meadow mice)	Bark chewed off base of trunk and crown, a few inches above and below ground; small tooth marks in wood; look for small burrows, runways, and droppings.	211–212
	Rabbits	Bark chewed off trunk within a few feet of the ground; tooth marks on wood; look for droppings.	212–214
	Cribrate weevil	On young trees; foliage damage also present; look for weevils in soil around base of tree.	101
Prominent, smooth or rough swellings on trunk, crown, or roots	Crown gall	Surface of swelling is smooth at first, turning rough later.	136–137
Cracking of bark	San Jose scale	Use hand lens to look for scale coverings; may also see symptoms on twigs and fruit.	86–89
	Glyphosate	May occur following spray drift onto mature foliage.	167
Blackened areas of dead bark on branch	Eutypa dieback	Dieback of affected branch; U-shaped or V-shaped discoloration of wood visible if affected branch cut in cross-section.	142–143

Symptoms on trunk or branches	Possible cause	Comments	Pages
White, tan, or brown growths on surface of wood, often with shelflike shape ("conks")	**Wood rot, silver leaf** 🍑 🍒 🍑 ● ◗	Wood of affected branches becomes light, soft, and punky (white rot) or brown, dry, and crumbly (brown rot).	145–146
Dark, scaly area on bark	**Sunburn** 🍑 🍒 🍑 ● ◗	Develops on limb surfaces exposed to the sun, usually that face south or west; bark often cracks.	28, 144

TRUNK OR BRANCHES

 Apricot   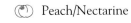 Cherry   Peach/Nectarine   Plum   Prune   Peach only   Nectarine only

References

Sources for UC Publications Listed

UC DANR: Communication Services, University of California Division of Agriculture and Natural Resources, 6701 San Pablo Avenue, Oakland, CA 94608. Free catalog on request. World Wide Web site, http://danrcs.ucdavis.edu

UC IPM: University of California Statewide Integrated Pest Management Project, 2102C Wickson Hall, UC Davis, Davis, CA 95616. World Wide Web site, http://www. ipm.ucdavis.edu/

General

Apricots and Apricot Processing. In: *Encyclopedia of Food Science and Technology.* 1992. Y. H. Hui ed. John Wiley & Sons, New York.

Biological Control in the Western United States. 1995. UC DANR Publication 3361.

California Grape and Tree Fruit League. 1540 East Shaw Ave., Ste. 120, Fresno, CA 93710-8000. (559) 226-6330.

California Sweet Cherry Production Workshop Insects and Diseases. 1992. S. M. Southwick ed. Available from Pomology Dept., UC Davis, Davis, CA 95616.

California Sweet Cherry Production Workshop Proceedings. 1992. S. M. Southwick ed. Available from Pomology Dept., UC Davis, Davis, CA 95616.

California Tree Fruit Agreement. 975 I St., Reedley, CA 93854. (559) 638-8260.

Common-Sense Pest Control. 1991. W. Olkowski, S. Daar, and H. Olkowski. Taunton Press, Newtown, CT.

Covercrops for California Agriculture. 1989. UC DANR Publication 21471.

Natural Enemies Handbook: The Illustrated Guide to Biological Pest Control. 1998. UC DANR Publication 3386.

Peaches, Plums, and Nectarines: Growing and Handling for Fresh Market, 1989. UC DANR Publication 3331.

Postharvest Technology of Horticultural Crops, 2nd ed. 1992. UC DANR Publication 3311.

Prune Orchard Management. 1981. UC DANR Publication 3269.

Pruning Fruit and Nut Trees. 1980. UC DANR Publication 21171.

Soil Solarization: A Nonpesticidal Method for Controlling Diseases, Nematodes, and Weeds. 1997. UC DANR Publication 21377.

Stone Fruit Orchard Pests: Identification, Biology, and Control. 1985. P. L. Sholberg, F. G. Zalkin, and R. F. Hobza. California Department of Food and Agriculture Pest Management Analysis and Planning Program.

Temperate Zone Pomology: Physiology and Culture, 3rd ed. 1993. M. N. Westwood. Timber Press, Portland, OR.

UC Fruit and Nut Information Center. World Wide Web site, http://fruitsandnuts.ucdavis.edu/

Soil, Water, Weather, and Nutrients

CIMIS: California Irrigation Management Information System. Department of Water Resources, P.O. Box 942836, Sacramento, CA 94236-0001. (916) 653-9847. The CIMIS World Wide Web site can be accessed from the California Data Exchange Center, http://cdec.water.ca.gov/

DDU. Degree-Day Utility Version 2.3. 1994. Program and documentation for MS-DOS computers. Available from UC IPM.

Degree-days. Documentation and models for a range of pests available at UC IPM World Wide Web site, http://www. ipm.ucdavis.edu/

Determining Daily Reference Evapotranspiration (ETo). 1992. UC DANR Publication 21426.

Drip Irrigation Management. 1981. UC DANR Publication 21259.

An Easy Way to Calculate Degree-Days. 1986. UC DANR Publication 7174.

Irrigation Scheduling: A Guide for Efficient On-Farm Water Management. 1989. UC DANR Publication 21454.

Managing and Modifying Problem Soils. 1974. UC DANR Publication 2791.

Managing Compacted and Layered Soils. 1976. UC DANR Publication 2635.

Micro-Irrigation of Trees and Vines. 1996. UC DANR Publication 3378.

Organic Soil Amendments and Fertilizers. 1992. UC DANR Publication 21505.

Soil and Plant Tissue Testing in California. 1983. UC DANR Publication 1879.

Soil Temperatures in California. 1983. UC DANR Publication 1908.

Surface Irrigation. 1995. UC DANR Publication 3379.

Water-Holding Characteristics of California Soils. 1989. UC DANR Publication 21463.

Western Fertilizer Handbook: Horticulture Edition. 1990. Interstate Printers and Publishers, P.O. Box 50, Danville, IL 61834.

Pesticide Application and Safety

Apricot Pest Management Guidelines. In *UC IPM Pest Management Guidelines.* Also available from University of California Cooperative Extension offices and at the UC IPM World Wide Web site.

Cherry Pest Management Guidelines. In *UC IPM Pest Management Guidelines.* Also available from University of California Cooperative Extension offices and at the UC IPM World Wide Web site.

The Illustrated Guide to Pesticide Safety, Worker's Edition. 1999 UC DANR Publication 21488.

The Illustrated Guide to Pesticide Safety, Instructor's Edition. 1999. UC DANR Publication 21489.

Managing Insects and Mites with Spray Oils. 1992. UC DANR Publication 3347.

Nectarine Pest Management Guidelines. In *UC IPM Pest Management Guidelines.* Also available from University of California Cooperative Extension offices and at the UC IPM World Wide Web site.

Peach Pest Management Guidelines. In *UC IPM Pest Management Guidelines.* Also available from University of California Cooperative Extension offices and at the UC IPM World Wide Web site.

Plum Pest Management Guidelines. In *UC IPM Pest Management Guidelines.* Also available from University of California Cooperative Extension offices and at the UC IPM World Wide Web site.

Prune Pest Management Guidelines. In *UC IPM Pest Management Guidelines.* Also available from University of California Cooperative Extension offices and at the UC IPM World Wide Web site.

The Safe and Effective Use of Pesticides, 6th ed.1999. UC DANR Publication 3324.

UC IPM Pest Management Guidelines. Revised continuously. UC DANR Publication 3339.

Insects and Mites

Biological Control and Insect Pest Management. 1979. UC DANR Publication 1911.

California Insects. 1979. J. A. Powell and C. L. Hogue, University of California Press, Berkeley.

Destructive and Useful Insects. 4th ed. 1962. C. L. Metcalf, W. P. Flint, and R. L. Metcalf, McGraw-Hill, New York.

Insect Identification Handbook. 1984. UC DANR Publication 4099.

Insect Pests of Farm, Garden, and Orchard, 7th ed. 1979. R. H. Davidson and W. F. Lyon, John Wiley & Sons, New York.

Insects, Mites, and Other Invertebrates and Their Control in California. 1994. UC DANR Publication 4044.

An Introduction to the Study of Insects. 6th ed. 1989. D. J. Borror, C. A. Triplehorn, and N. F. Johnson. Saunders College Publishing, Philadelphia.

Orchard Pest Management: A Resource Guide for the Pacific Northwest. 1993. E. H. Beers, J. F. Brunner, M. J. Willett, and G. M. Warner, eds. Good Fruit Grower, Yakima, WA.

Diseases and Nematodes

Compendium of Stone Fruit Diseases. 1995. J. M. Ogawa et al., eds. American Phytopathological Society, St. Paul.

Diseases of Temperate Zone Tree Fruit and Nut Crops. 1991. UC DANR Publication 3345.

General Recommendations for Nematode Sampling. 1981. UC DANR Publication 21234.

Phytonematology Study Guide. 1985. UC DANR Publication 4045.

Plant Pathology, 4th ed. 1997. G. N. Agrios. Academic Press, San Diego.

Weeds

Applied Weed Science. 1985. M. A. Ross and C. A. Lembi, Burgess, Minneapolis.

The Grower's Weed Identification Handbook. 1998. UC DANR Publication 4030.

Growers Weed Management Guide. 1989. H. M. Kempen, Thomson Publications, Fresno, CA.

How to Identify Plants. 1957. H. D. Harrington and L. W. Durrell, Sage Press, Denver.

Selective Chemical Weed Control. 1986. UC DANR Publication 1919.

Weeds of the West. 1992. T. D. Whitson, ed., Western Society of Weed Science, Newark, CA. Also available as UC DANR Publication 3350.

Weed Science, 3rd ed. 1996. W. P. Anderson. West Publishing, Minneapolis–St. Paul.

Vertebrates

The Audubon Society Field Guide to North American Birds: Western Region. 1977. M. D. F. Udvardy. A. A. Knopf, New York.

Controlling Ground Squirrels around Structures, Gardens, and Small Farms. 1980. UC DANR Publication 21179.

A Field Guide to Western Birds, 3rd ed. 1990. R. T. Peterson. Houghton Mifflin, Boston.

Vertebrate Pest Control Handbook. 1986. J. P. Clark. California Department of Food and Agriculture, Division of Plant Industry.

Home Garden

Designing and Maintaining Your Edible Landscape Naturally. 1986. R. Kourik. Metamorphic Press, Santa Rosa, CA.

Pests of the Garden and Small Farm: A Grower's Guide to Using Less Pesticide, 2nd ed. 1999. UC DANR Publication 3332.

Pests of Landscape Trees and Shrubs. 1994. UC DANR Publication 3359.

Soil and Water Management for Home Gardeners. 1974. UC DANR Publication 2258.

Sweet Cherries for the Home Grounds. 1977. UC DANR Publication 2951.

Wildlife Pest Control around Gardens and Homes. 1984. UC DANR Publication 21385.

Sources of Beneficial Organisms

Directory of Least-Toxic Pest Control Products. Published annually in *The IPM Practitioner.* Biointegral Resource Center, Berkeley, CA.

Suppliers of Beneficial Organisms in North America. 1992. C. D. Hunter. California Department of Pesticide Regulation, Environmental Monitoring and Pest Management, Sacramento, CA. Also available online at: http://www. cdpr.ca.gov/docs/dprdocs/goodbug/organism.htm

A Worldwide Guide to Beneficial Animals Used for Pest Control Purposes. 1992. W. T. Thomson. Thomson Publications, Fresno, CA.

Glossary

abiotic disorder. A disease caused by a factor other than a pathogen.

acaricide. A pesticide that kills mites; miticide.

aestivation (estivation). A state of inactivity during the summer months.

air carrier sprayer. A sprayer that uses a blast of air to distribute a pesticide-water mixture into the canopy of the crop being treated (air blast sprayer).

allowable depletion. The fraction (or percentage) of available water that can be withdrawn before a crop plant may be adversely affected if not irrigated.

annual. A plant that normally completes its life cycle of germination, growth, reproduction, and death in a single year.

anther. The pollen-producing organ of a flower (see Figure 3).

anticoagulant. A substance that prevents blood from clotting, resulting in hemorrhage; may be used as a rodenticide.

apical dominance. Growth of the bud at the apex of a stem or tuber while growth of all other buds on the stem or tuber is inhibited.

apical meristem. Undifferentiated cells at the tip of a stem or root that are able to divide and differentiate into specialized tissues.

apothecium (plural, apothecia). Cup-shaped, spore-forming structures formed by certain types of Ascomycete fungi such as *Monilinia* spp. and *Sclerotinia* spp.

ascospore. A sexually produced spore formed within the ascus of an Ascomycete fungus.

ascus (plural, asci). The saclike cell of a hypha of an Ascomycete fungus within which ascospores are formed following meiosis.

auricles. In grasses, small, earlike projections that grow out from the leaf sheath where it meets the leaf blade.

available moisture. The amount of water held in the soil that can be extracted by plants.

axil. The upper angle between a branch or petiole and the stem from which it grows.

axillary bud. A bud that forms in the axil of a leaf.

basidiocarp. Spore-forming structure of a Basidiomycete fungus in which basidiospores are formed following meiosis.

biennial. A plant that completes its life cycle in two years, usually flowering the second year (see *annual*).

biofix. An identifiable point in the life cycle of the pest when you may begin a degree-day accumulation or take a management action.

biotic disease. A disease caused by a pathogen, such as a bacterium, fungus, phytoplasma, or virus.

blastospore. An asexual spore formed by budding.

broad-spectrum pesticide. A pesticide that kills a large number of unrelated species.

bud conidia. Asexual spores formed by budding; blastospores.

calyx. The sepals of a flower, which enclose the unopened flower bud; often referred to as the "jacket" or "shuck" in stone fruits.

cambium. The thin layer of undifferentiated, actively growing tissue between phloem and xylem.

canker. A dead, discolored, often sunken area (lesion) on a root, trunk, stem, or branch.

caterpillar. The larva of a butterfly, moth, sawfly, or scorpionfly.

catfacing. Disfigurement or malformation of fruit; in the case of stone fruits, sometimes the result of stink bug injury to expanding fruit.

certified planting stock. Stone fruit trees that have received a certification tag from the California Department of Food and Agriculture; production practices must meet standards for freedom from pest problems and plant samples from certified orchards must test free of viruses.

chilling requirement. In stone fruits, generally defined as the accumulated number of hours between 32° and 45°F (0° and 7°C) that fruit buds must receive to complete dormancy and achieve optimum bloom (see Table 2).

chlamydospore. A thick-walled spore formed from the cell of a fungus hypha.

chlorophyll. The green pigment of plants that captures the solar energy necessary for photosynthesis.

chlorosis. Yellowing or bleaching of normally green plant tissue, usually caused by the loss of chlorophyll.

cleistothecium (plural, cleistothecia). The spherical, closed structure of certain Ascomycete fungi such as powdery mildews, within which one or more asci and ascospores are formed.

clonal rootstock. Rootstock that is propagated vegetatively.

cocoon. A sheath, usually of silk, formed by an insect larva as a chamber for pupation.

conidium (plural, conidia). An asexual fungus spore formed by fragmentation or budding at the tip of a specialized hypha.

contact herbicide. An herbicide that causes localized injury to the plant tissue it contacts.

control action guideline. A guideline used to determine if pest control action is needed.

cork cambium. The layer of cambium on the outside of the phloem that gives rise to the outer bark (see Figure 2).

crawler. The active first instar of a scale insect.

cross-pollination. The transfer of pollen from the flowers of one plant to the flowers of another.

cross-resistance. In pest management, resistance of a pest population to a pesticide to which it *has not* been exposed that accompanies the development of resistance to a pesticide to which it *has* been exposed.

crown. The point at or just below the soil surface where the main stem (trunk) and roots join.

cultivar. A variety or strain developed and grown under cultivation.

degree-day. A unit of measurement that is a product of temperature and time, abbreviated °D (see Figures 15 and 16).

delayed-dormant. Refers to the treatment period in fruit tree crops, beginning when buds begin to swell and continuing until the beginning of green tip development.

denitrification. The conversion of nitrates into nitrites or gaseous forms of nitrogen, usually by the action of soil microbes.

developmental threshold. The lowest temperature at which growth occurs in a given species.

dormancy. A physical or physiological state in which a plant is not actively growing.

economic threshold. A level of pest population or damage at which the cost of a control action equals the crop value gained from that control action.

enation. A tissue malformation or overgrowth caused by a virus infection.

endocarp. The inner layer of the fruit wall; the stone or pit of stone fruits (see Figure 4).

estivation. See *aestivation*.

evapotranspiration. The loss of soil moisture due to evaporation from the soil surface and transpiration by plants.

exocarp. The outermost layer of the fruit wall; the skin or peel of stone fruits (see Figure 4).

field capacity. The moisture level in soil after saturation and runoff.

flower bud. A bud that contains flower parts.

fumigation. Treatment with a pesticide active ingredient that is in gaseous form under treatment conditions.

girdling. In stone fruits, the practice of removing a thin strip of bark around the trunk or scaffold limbs to increase fruit size and yield and to accelerate maturity in early-season fresh market peaches and nectarines.

hibernaculum (plural, hibernacula). A shelter occupied during the winter by an insect, notably peach twig borer.

hibernation. Passing the winter in a torpid or dormant state in which the body temperature and metabolic rate drop to very low levels.

honeydew. An excretion from insects, such as aphids, mealybugs, whiteflies, and soft scales, consisting of modified plant sap.

hypha (plural, hyphae). A tubular filament that is the structural unit of a fungus.

inflorescence. A flower cluster.

inoculum. Any part or stage of a pathogen, such as spores or virus particles, that can infect a host.

instar. An insect between successive molts; the first instar is between hatching and the first molt.

internode. The area of a stem between nodes.

invertebrate. An animal having no internal skeleton.

June-drop. A drop of young fruit that occurs usually in April or May on some varieties of stone fruits, especially plums.

juvenile. The immature form of a nematode that hatches from an egg and molts several times before becoming an adult.

larva (plural, larvae). The immature form of an insect that hatches from an egg, feeds, and then enters a pupal stage.

latent period. The time between when a vector acquires a pathogen and when the vector becomes able to transmit the pathogen to a new host; also, the time between the infection of a host plant and the production of inoculum by the infection.

leaching fraction. The proportion of applied irrigation water that is added to meet the crop's leaching requirement.

leaching requirement. The amount of water in excess of a crop's evapotranspiration requirement that is needed to maintain maximum yield by leaching harmful salts from the root zone.

lesion. A localized area of diseased tissue, such as a canker or leaf spot.

ligule. An outgrowth of the upper side of a grass leaf blade where it joins the leaf sheath (see Figure 63).

mandibles. Jaws; the forwardmost pair of mouthparts of an insect.

meristem. The collection of cells at the growing point of a plant that are capable of cell division.

mesocarp. The middle layer of the fruit wall; the edible flesh of stone fruits (see Figure 4).

microsclerotia (singular, microsclerotium). Very small sclerotia such as those produced by the Verticillium wilt fungus.

molt. In insects and other anthropods, the shedding of skin before entering another stage of growth.

mosaic. A foliage symptom of certain virus diseases that consists of a mingling of patches of darker green with light green or yellow.

mummy. An unharvested nut or fruit remaining on the tree, often the dried remains of a fruit decayed by brown rot; the crusty skin of an aphid whose inside has been consumed by a parasite.

mycelium (plural, mycelia). The vegetative body of a fungus consisting of a mass of slender filaments called hyphae.

natural enemies. Predators, parasites, or pathogens that are considered beneficial because they attack and kill organisms that we normally consider to be pests.

necrosis. The death of tissue accompanied by dark brown discoloration, usually occurring in a well-defined part of a plant such as the portion of a leaf between leaf veins or the xylem or phloem in a stem or tuber.

node. The slightly enlarged part of a stem where buds are formed and where leaves, stems, and flowers originate.

nymph. The immature stage of insects such as lygus bugs and aphids that gradually acquires adult form through a series of molts without passing through a pupal stage.

oospore. A type of sexual spore produced after the union of gametes from two morphologically distinct, specialized hyphae; characteristic of the group of fungi to which *Phytophthora* spp. belong.

ovule. A rudimentary seed, which before fertilization contains the female gametophyte, with egg cell.

parasite. An organism that lives in or on the body of another organism (the host), from which it derives its food without killing the host directly; also describes an insect that spends its immature stages in the body of a host, which is killed just before the parasite pupates.

parthenogenesis. Development of the egg without fertilization.

pathogen. A disease-causing organism.

peduncle. The stem of an individual flower or fruit.

perennial. A plant that lives three or more years and flowers at least twice (see *annual*).

pericarp. The fruit wall that develops from the ovary wall (see Figure 4).

perithecia. Globular or flask-shaped structures produced by certain Ascomycete fungi, within which asci and ascospores are formed.

persistent virus. A virus that systemically infects its vector and usually is transmitted for the remainder of the vector's life.

pest resurgence. The increase of a pest population following a pesticide treatment to levels higher than before treatment, as a result of the pesticide having killed natural enemies of the pest.

petiole. The stalk connecting a leaf or leaflets to a stem.

pheromone. A chemical produced by an animal to communicate with other members of its species.

pheromone confusion. Pheromone mating disruption.

pheromone mating disruption. The disruption of the mating of certain lepidopterous (moth) pests by dispensing synthetic chemicals that mimic the pheromones produced by females to attract males.

phloem. The food-conducting tissue of a plant's vascular system (see Figure 2).

phloem-feeding. The characteristic of an organism that withdraws nutrients from the phloem of a host plant.

photosynthate. The products of photosynthesis, used to support growth, respiration, and fruit production.

photosynthesis. The process whereby plants use light energy to form sugars and other compounds needed to support growth and development.

phytotoxicity. The ability of a material such as a pesticide or fertilizer to cause injury to plants.

pistil. The female part of a flower, usually consisting of ovules, ovary, style, and stigma (see Figure 3).

pollenizer. The producer of pollen; in stone fruits, a variety whose pollen can successfully pollinate the flowers of another self-sterile variety of the same species.

pollination. The transfer of pollen from a stamen to a stigma.

pollinator. The agent of pollen transfer, usually an insect such as a honey bee.

postemergence herbicide. An herbicide applied after the emergence of weeds.

predator. An animal that attacks and feeds on other animals (the prey), usually eating most or all of the prey organism and consuming many prey during its lifetime.

preemergence herbicide. An herbicide applied before target weeds emerge.

primary inoculum. The initial source of a pathogen that starts disease development in a given location.

propagule. Any part of a plant from which a new plant can grow, including seeds, bulbs, rootstocks, etc.

protectant fungicide. A fungicide that protects a plant from infection by a pathogen.

pupa (plural, pupae). The nonfeeding, inactive stage between larva and adult in insects with complete metamorphosis.

pycnidium (plural, pycnidia). A small spherical or flask-shaped structure formed by certain types of fungi, inside which asexual spores are produced.

receptacle. The apex of the flower stem that bears the organs of the flower (see Figure 3).

respiration. The process by which nutrients are metabolized to provide the energy needed for cellular activity.

rhizome. An underground, horizontal stem.

rhizomorph. A rootlike structure produced by the fungus *Armillaria mellea*, which can grow from the root of an infected host plant to the root of an uninfected host plant.

rootstock. An underground stem or rhizome; the lower portion of a graft, which develops into the root system.

rugose. A rough appearance of leaves in which veins are sunken and interveinal tissue is raised, caused by certain virus infections.

sanitation. Any activity that reduces the spread of pathogen inoculum, such as removal and destruction of infected plant parts or cleaning of tools and field equipment.

scion. The portion above a graft that becomes the trunk, branch, and tree top; the cultivar or variety used for that part of a graft.

sclerotium (plural, sclerotia). A compact mass of hyphae, sometimes including host tissue, capable of surviving unfavorable environmental conditions.

secondary pest outbreak. The sudden increase in a pest population that is normally at low or nondamaging levels, caused by the destruction of natural enemies by treatment with a nonselective pesticide to control a primary pest.

seed leaf. The leaf formed in a seed and present on a seedling at germination; cotyledon.

seedling rootstock. A rootstock propagated from seed.

selective pesticide. A pesticide that is more toxic to target pests than to natural enemies.

self-fruitful. Able to produce seed and a crop of fruit when self-pollinated.

self-sterile. Unable to produce seed when self-pollinated.

sporangium (plural, sporangia). A microbial structure that contains asexual spores.

sporodochium (plural, sporodochia). A cushion-shaped stroma covered with conidia-forming hyphae.

spur. A short woody shoot that is the primary fruiting structure for most fruit trees.

stamen. A flower structure made up of the pollen-bearing anther and a stalk or filament (see Figure 3).

stele. The central cylinder inside the cortex of the roots and stems of vascular plants; contains the vascular or conducting tissue.

stigma. The receptive portion of the female flower part to which pollen adheres (see Figure 3).

stolon. A stem that grows horizontally along the surface of the ground.

stoma (plural, stomata). A natural opening in a leaf surface that serves for gas exchange and water evaporation and has the ability to open and close in response to environmental conditions.

stroma. A compact, usually spore-producing structure formed from a fungal mycelium on the surface of a host.

systemic fungicide. A fungicide that is capable of being translocated to some extent within a treated plant.

systemic herbicide. An herbicide that is able to move throughout a plant after being applied to leaf surfaces (*translocated herbicide*).

tensiometer. An instrument that measures how tightly water is held by the soil, used for estimating water content of the soil.

translocated herbicide. A systemic herbicide.

transpiration. The evaporation of water from plant tissue, usually through stomata.

treatment threshold. A level of pest population or damage, usually measured by a specified monitoring method, at which a pesticide application is recommended.

trichome. Epidermal hair on a plant; trichomes make up the fuzz on a peach.

tuber. An enlarged, short, fleshy, underground stem.

vascular cambium. A cylinder of meristematic tissue that lies between the wood and the bark (see Figure 2).

vascular tissue. Plant tissue that conducts water and nutrients throughout the plant.

vector. An organism that is able to transport and transmit a pathogen to a host.

vegetative. Of plant parts, such as roots, stems, and leaves, or plant growth not involved in the production of seed.

xylem. The plant tissue that conducts water and nutrients from the roots up through the plant (see Figure 2).

yield threshold depletion. The amount of water corresponding to the allowable depletion.

zoospore. A motile spore.

Appendix I
Bloom Stages
of Stone Fruits

Figure 75. Bloom stages of apricot.

Dormant bud

First swell

Red bud

First white

Popcorn

Full bloom

Petal fall

Jacket stage

Jacket split

Figure 76. Bloom stages of cherry.

Dormant bud

First swell

Green tip

First white

Popcorn

Full bloom

Petal fall

Jacket stage

Jacket split

Figure 77. Bloom stages of nectarine and peach.

Dormant bud

First swell

Green tip

First pink

Popcorn

Full bloom

Petal fall

Jacket stage

Jacket split

Figure 78. Bloom stages of Japanese plum.

Dormant bud

First swell

Green tip

First white

Popcorn

Full bloom ("Snowball bloom")

Petal fall

Jacket stage

Jacket split

Figure 79. Bloom stages of French prune.

Dormant bud

First swell

Green tip

First white

Popcorn

Full bloom

Petal fall

Jacket stage

Jacket split

Appendix II
Degree-Day
Reference Tables

Table 32. Degree-Day Table for Peach Twig Borer and Codling Moth.
To find the degree-days for a day, follow the column and row of the day's
minimum and maximum temperatures to where they intersect. For odd-
numbered temperatures, interpolate between the tabulated values.

METHOD: Single sine - Above   LOWER THRESHOLD: 50°F (10°C)
Horizontal cutoff   UPPER THRESHOLD: 88°F (31°C)

MINIMUM TEMPERATURES (°F)

MAX TEMPS	34	36	38	40	42	44	46	48	50	52	54	56	58	60	62	64	66	68	70	72	74	76	78	80	82	84	86	88
48	0	0	0	0	0	0	0	0																				
50	0	0	0	0	0	0	0	0	0																			
52	0	0	0	0	0	0	1	1	1	2																		
54	1	1	1	1	1	1	1	2	2	3	4																	
56	1	1	2	2	2	2	2	2	3	4	5	6																
58	2	2	2	2	3	3	3	3	4	5	6	7	8															
60	3	3	3	3	3	4	4	4	5	6	7	8	9	10														
62	4	4	4	4	4	5	5	5	6	7	8	9	10	11	12													
64	4	4	5	5	5	5	6	6	7	8	9	10	11	12	13	14												
66	5	5	6	6	6	6	7	7	8	9	10	11	12	13	14	15	16											
68	6	6	6	7	7	7	8	8	9	10	11	12	13	14	15	16	17	18										
70	7	7	7	8	8	8	9	9	10	11	12	13	14	15	16	17	18	19	20									
72	8	8	8	8	9	9	10	10	11	12	13	14	15	16	17	18	19	20	21	22								
74	8	9	9	9	10	10	11	11	12	13	14	15	16	17	18	19	20	21	22	23	24							
76	9	10	10	10	11	11	12	12	13	14	15	16	17	18	19	20	21	22	23	24	25	26						
78	10	11	11	11	12	12	13	13	14	15	16	17	18	19	20	21	22	23	24	25	26	27	28					
80	11	11	12	12	13	13	14	14	15	16	17	18	19	20	21	22	23	24	25	26	27	28	29	30				
82	12	12	13	13	14	14	15	15	16	17	18	19	20	21	22	23	24	25	26	27	28	29	30	31	32			
84	13	13	14	14	15	15	16	16	17	18	19	20	21	22	23	24	25	26	27	28	29	30	31	32	33	34		
86	14	14	15	15	15	16	17	17	18	19	20	21	22	23	24	25	26	27	28	29	30	31	32	33	34	35	36	
88	15	15	16	16	16	17	18	18	19	20	21	22	23	24	25	26	27	28	29	30	31	32	33	34	35	36	37	38
90	16	16	16	17	17	18	18	19	20	21	22	23	24	25	26	27	28	29	30	31	32	33	34	35	36	36	37	38
92	16	17	17	17	18	18	19	20	20	21	22	23	24	25	26	27	28	29	30	31	32	33	34	35	36	37	37	38
94	17	17	18	18	18	19	20	20	21	22	23	24	25	26	27	28	29	30	31	32	33	33	34	35	36	37	38	38
96	17	18	18	19	19	20	20	21	22	23	23	24	25	26	27	28	29	30	31	32	33	34	35	35	36	37	38	38
98	18	18	19	19	19	20	21	21	22	23	24	25	26	27	28	29	30	30	31	32	33	34	35	36	36	37	38	38
100	18	19	19	19	20	20	21	22	22	23	24	25	26	27	28	29	30	31	32	32	33	34	35	36	36	37	38	38
102	19	19	19	20	20	21	21	22	23	24	25	26	27	27	28	29	30	31	32	33	34	34	35	36	37	37	38	38
104	19	19	20	20	21	21	22	22	23	24	25	26	27	28	29	30	30	31	32	33	34	34	35	36	37	37	38	38
106	19	20	20	21	21	22	22	23	24	24	25	26	27	28	29	30	31	31	32	33	34	35	35	36	37	37	38	38
108	20	20	20	21	21	22	22	23	24	25	26	27	27	28	29	30	31	32	32	33	34	35	35	36	37	37	38	38
110	20	20	21	21	22	22	23	23	24	25	26	27	28	28	29	30	31	32	33	33	34	35	36	36	37	37	38	38
112	20	21	21	22	22	22	23	24	24	25	26	27	28	29	30	30	31	32	33	34	34	35	36	36	37	37	38	38
114	21	21	21	22	22	23	23	24	25	26	26	27	28	29	30	31	31	32	33	34	34	35	36	36	37	37	38	38
116	21	21	22	22	23	23	24	24	25	26	27	27	28	29	30	31	31	32	33	34	34	35	36	36	37	37	38	38
118	21	21	22	22	23	23	24	24	25	26	27	28	28	29	30	31	32	32	33	34	35	35	36	36	37	37	38	38

Table 33. Degree-Day Table for Oriental Fruit Moth. To find the degree-days for a day, follow the column and row of the day's minimum and maximum temperatures to where they intersect. For odd-numbered temperatures, interpolate between the tabulated values.

METHOD: Single sine - Above   LOWER THRESHOLD: 45°F (7°C)
Horizontal cutoff   UPPER THRESHOLD: 90°F (32°C)

MINIMUM TEMPERATURES (°F)

MAX TEMPS	34	36	38	40	42	44	46	48	50	52	54	56	58	60	62	64	66	68	70	72	74	76	78	80	82	84	86	88
48	1	1	1	1	1	1	2	3																				
50	1	1	1	2	2	2	3	4	5																			
52	2	2	2	2	3	3	4	5	6	7																		
54	3	3	3	3	4	4	5	6	7	8	9																	
56	4	4	4	4	5	5	6	7	8	9	10	11																
58	4	5	5	5	6	6	7	8	9	10	11	12	13															
60	5	5	6	6	7	7	8	9	10	11	12	13	14	15														
62	6	6	7	7	8	8	9	10	11	12	13	14	15	16	17													
64	7	7	8	8	8	9	10	11	12	13	14	15	16	17	18	19												
66	8	8	9	9	9	10	11	12	13	14	15	16	17	18	19	20	21											
68	9	9	9	10	10	11	12	13	14	15	16	17	18	19	20	21	22	23										
70	10	10	10	11	11	12	13	14	15	16	17	18	19	20	21	22	23	24	25									
72	11	11	11	12	12	13	14	15	16	17	18	19	20	21	22	23	24	25	26	27								
74	12	12	12	13	13	14	15	16	17	18	19	20	21	22	23	24	25	26	27	28	29							
76	12	13	13	14	14	15	16	17	18	19	20	21	22	23	24	25	26	27	28	29	30	31						
78	13	14	14	15	15	16	17	18	19	20	21	22	23	24	25	26	27	28	29	30	31	32	33					
80	14	15	15	16	16	17	18	19	20	21	22	23	24	25	26	27	28	29	30	31	32	33	34	35				
82	15	16	16	17	17	18	19	20	21	22	23	24	25	26	27	28	29	30	31	32	33	34	35	36	37			
84	16	17	17	18	18	19	20	21	22	23	24	25	26	27	28	29	30	31	32	33	34	35	36	37	38	39		
86	17	18	18	19	19	20	21	22	23	24	25	26	27	28	29	30	31	32	33	34	35	36	37	38	39	40	41	
88	18	19	19	20	20	21	22	23	24	25	26	27	28	29	30	31	32	33	34	35	36	37	38	39	40	41	42	43
90	19	20	20	21	21	22	23	24	25	26	27	28	29	30	31	32	33	34	35	36	37	38	39	40	41	42	43	44
92	20	20	21	21	22	23	24	25	26	27	28	29	30	31	32	33	34	35	36	37	38	39	40	41	42	43	43	44
94	21	21	22	22	23	24	25	25	26	27	28	29	30	31	32	33	34	35	36	37	38	39	40	41	42	43	44	44
96	21	22	22	23	23	24	25	26	27	28	29	30	31	32	33	34	35	36	37	38	39	40	40	41	42	43	44	45
98	22	22	23	23	24	25	26	27	28	29	30	30	31	32	33	34	35	36	37	38	39	40	41	42	42	43	44	45
100	22	23	23	24	24	25	26	27	28	29	30	31	32	33	34	35	36	37	37	38	39	40	41	42	43	43	44	45
102	23	23	24	24	25	26	27	28	28	29	30	31	32	33	34	35	36	37	38	39	39	40	41	42	43	43	44	45
104	23	24	24	25	25	26	27	28	29	30	31	32	33	34	34	35	36	37	38	39	40	41	41	42	43	44	44	45
106	24	24	25	25	26	27	27	28	29	30	31	32	33	34	35	36	37	37	38	39	40	41	41	42	43	44	44	45
108	24	24	25	26	26	27	28	29	30	31	31	32	33	34	35	36	37	38	38	39	40	41	42	42	43	44	44	45
110	24	25	25	26	27	27	28	29	30	31	32	33	34	34	35	36	37	38	39	39	40	41	42	42	43	44	44	45
112	25	25	26	26	27	28	28	29	30	31	32	33	34	35	35	36	37	38	39	40	40	41	42	43	43	44	44	45
114	25	25	26	27	27	28	29	30	30	31	32	33	34	35	36	37	37	38	39	40	41	41	42	43	43	44	44	45
116	25	26	26	27	27	28	29	30	31	32	33	33	34	35	36	37	38	38	39	40	41	41	42	43	43	44	44	45
118	26	26	27	27	28	28	29	30	31	32	33	34	34	35	36	37	38	38	39	40	41	41	42	43	43	44	44	45

Table 34. Degree-Day Table for San Jose Scale. To find the degree-days for a day, follow the column and row of the day's minimum and maximum temperatures to where they intersect. For odd-numbered temperatures, interpolate between the tabulated values.

METHOD: Single sine - Above   LOWER THRESHOLD: 51°F (11°C)
Horizontal cutoff   UPPER THRESHOLD: 90°F (32°C)

MINIMUM TEMPERATURES (°F)

MAX TEMPS	34	36	38	40	42	44	46	48	50	52	54	56	58	60	62	64	66	68	70	72	74	76	78	80	82	84	86	88
48	0	0	0	0	0	0	0	0																				
50	0	0	0	0	0	0	0	0	0																			
52	0	0	0	0	0	0	0	0	0	1																		
54	1	1	1	1	1	1	1	1	1	2	3																	
56	1	1	1	1	1	1	2	2	2	3	4	5																
58	2	2	2	2	2	2	2	3	3	4	5	6	7															
60	2	2	3	3	3	3	3	4	4	5	6	7	8	9														
62	3	3	3	4	4	4	4	5	5	6	7	8	9	10	11													
64	4	4	4	4	5	5	5	6	6	7	8	9	10	11	12	13												
66	5	5	5	5	5	6	6	7	7	8	9	10	11	12	13	14	15											
68	5	6	6	6	6	7	7	8	8	9	10	11	12	13	14	15	16	17										
70	6	6	7	7	7	8	8	8	9	10	11	12	13	14	15	16	17	18	19									
72	7	7	8	8	8	9	9	9	10	11	12	13	14	15	16	17	18	19	20	21								
74	8	8	8	9	9	9	10	10	11	12	13	14	15	16	17	18	19	20	21	22	23							
76	9	9	9	10	10	10	11	11	12	13	14	15	16	17	18	19	20	21	22	23	24	25						
78	10	10	10	11	11	11	12	12	13	14	15	16	17	18	19	20	21	22	23	24	25	26	27					
80	11	11	11	12	12	12	13	13	14	15	16	17	18	19	20	21	22	23	24	25	26	27	28	29				
82	11	12	12	12	13	13	14	14	15	16	17	18	19	20	21	22	23	24	25	26	27	28	29	30	31			
84	12	13	13	13	14	14	15	15	16	17	18	19	20	21	22	23	24	25	26	27	28	29	30	31	32	33		
86	13	14	14	14	15	15	16	16	17	18	19	20	21	22	23	24	25	26	27	28	29	30	31	32	33	34	35	
88	14	15	15	15	16	16	17	17	18	19	20	21	22	23	24	25	26	27	28	29	30	31	32	33	34	35	36	37
90	15	15	16	16	17	17	18	18	19	20	21	22	23	24	25	26	27	28	29	30	31	32	33	34	35	36	37	38
92	16	16	17	17	17	18	19	19	20	21	22	23	24	25	26	27	28	29	30	31	32	33	34	35	36	37	37	38
94	17	17	17	18	18	19	19	20	21	21	22	23	24	25	26	27	28	29	30	31	32	33	34	35	36	37	38	38
96	17	17	18	18	19	19	20	20	21	22	23	24	25	26	27	28	29	30	31	32	33	34	34	35	36	37	38	39
98	18	18	18	19	19	20	20	21	22	23	24	24	25	26	27	28	29	30	31	32	33	34	35	36	36	37	38	39
100	18	18	19	19	20	20	21	21	22	23	24	25	26	27	28	29	30	31	31	32	33	34	35	36	37	37	38	39
102	19	19	19	20	20	21	21	22	23	23	24	25	26	27	28	29	30	31	32	33	33	34	35	36	37	37	38	39
104	19	19	20	20	21	21	22	22	23	24	25	26	27	28	28	29	30	31	32	33	34	35	35	36	37	38	38	39
106	19	20	20	21	21	21	22	23	23	24	25	26	27	28	29	30	31	31	32	33	34	35	35	36	37	38	38	39
108	20	20	20	21	21	22	22	23	24	25	25	26	27	28	29	30	31	32	32	33	34	35	36	36	37	38	38	39
110	20	20	21	21	22	22	23	23	24	25	26	27	28	28	29	30	31	32	33	33	34	35	36	36	37	38	38	39
112	20	21	21	22	22	22	23	24	24	25	26	27	28	29	29	30	31	32	33	34	34	35	36	37	37	38	38	39
114	21	21	21	22	22	23	23	24	25	25	26	27	28	29	30	31	31	32	33	34	35	35	36	37	37	38	38	39
116	21	21	22	22	23	23	24	24	25	26	27	27	28	29	30	31	32	32	33	34	35	35	36	37	37	38	38	39
118	21	22	22	22	23	23	24	24	25	26	27	28	28	29	30	31	32	32	33	34	35	35	36	37	37	38	38	39

Index